T0332256

The Newsmongers

N^{THE}ewsmongers

A HISTORY OF
TABLOID JOURNALISM

TERRY KIRBY

REAKTION BOOKS

To Angie and my sons, Leo and Max

Published by
Reaktion Books Ltd
Unit 32, Waterside
44–48 Wharf Road
London N1 7UX, UK
www.reaktionbooks.co.uk

First published 2024
Copyright © Terry Kirby 2024

Printed and bound in Great Britain
by TJ Books Ltd, Padstow, Cornwall

A catalogue record for this book is available from the British Library

ISBN 978 1 78914 941 8

CONTENTS

'I mean to make the *Herald* the great organ of social life, the prime element of civilisation, the channel through which native talent, native genius and native power may bubble up daily . . . I shall mix together commerce and business, pure religion and morals, literature and poetry, the drama and dramatic purity till the *Herald* shall outstrip everything in the conception of man.'

JAMES GORDON BENNETT (1795–1872),
FOUNDER AND EDITOR OF THE *NEW YORK HERALD*

'GOTCHA'

Headline on the first edition of *The Sun* newspaper, published 4 May 1982, after an Argentine warship was sunk by a British submarine during the Falklands conflict. It was replaced in later editions with a more nuanced headline.

1

'STRANGE NEWES'

In 1900 Alfred Harmsworth could do no wrong. The founder of a string of successful and popular magazines, he had earned sufficient riches to launch the *Daily Mail* newspaper four years previously. This paper would eventually define popular journalism in the early twentieth century. In some ways, it still does, in the early decades of the twenty-first.

At the end of that year, Harmsworth, who had drawn many of his ideas from the exuberant populist journalism deployed in the fierce newspaper wars of New York over the previous decade or so, was invited by one of the combatants, Joseph Pulitzer, who would, in his will, establish the benchmark prize for excellence in American journalism, to edit an edition of his *New York World* newspaper, which at that time had the biggest circulation in the city. Harmsworth, the dazzling young newspaper genius from London, still only in his thirties, would be given free rein over the edition published on 1 January 1901, which many credited as being the true first day of the new century.

Charged by Pulitzer to produce 'the newspaper of the future', Harmsworth, never lacking in self-belief, took to his task with relish. He could experiment at will and had little to lose. He cut the size of the broadsheet *World* in half, adapted the typography to suit and, 'dressed in a black tie as Pulitzer had decreed, strode through the newsroom telling reporters not to submit anything longer than 250 words'.[1] He knew that on the front page he had to deliver a clear statement of intent to his New York readers to explain the radically different paper, words that would effectively describe the new style of newspaper he had just created. The word he alighted on was 'tabloid'.

He was not the first person to use the word, but he was the first to apply it to a form of journalism, although the style itself was not new. Sixteen years before, the drugs company Burroughs, Wellcome & Co. had trademarked the word 'tabloid' – a linguistic portmanteau of 'tablet' and 'alkaloid' – to describe certain drugs in tablet form. It had come to mean anything compressed or concentrated for easy assimilation. Although Harmsworth had long advocated for and practised a more concise and focused style of written journalism – a 'small, portable and neatly indexed publication' – neither he nor others had ever publicly given it a label.[2] But now he reached for that very word for the first time to describe this new style of newspaper and its appeal to readers.

So, on the front page that rolled off the presses on New Year's Eve 1900, in a statement beneath the headline 'The Daily Time-Saver', Harmsworth wrote these words:

> The *World* enters to-day upon the Twentieth or Time-Saving Century. I claim that by my system of condensed or tabloid journalism hundreds of working hours can be saved each year. By glancing down the subjoined list of contents and fol-lowing the arrangement of the pages the outline of the day's news can be gathered in sixty seconds.

The paper had sold out by nine o'clock the following morning, and a further 100,000 copies were immediately printed.[3] The birth of a new century had spawned the tabloid era, its ethos set out, as it should be, in just a few words. But its gestation had begun a long, long time before.

Enter the Newsmongers

They were called 'newsmongers': Joseph Pecke, a twice-imprisoned 'bald-headed buzzard' of low intelligence who helped create polit-ical reporting for the masses; John Crouch, lover of claret, peddler of smut, who understood the public's love of gossip and scandal; Nathanial Butter, publisher of Shakespeare and Homer and the first real newspaper proprietor, producer of hundreds of newsletters and pamphlets, who in return for a lifetime of hard work keeping the public informed was lampooned in the theatre and died a pauper;

and the extraordinary figure of Mary de la Riviere 'Delia' Manley, who may have been the first female editor. And another Nathaniel, one Nathaniel Mist, jailed several times for his Jacobite views, who became the first newspaper publisher to deliberately appeal to a huge and largely untapped, working-class audience. In America, decades before Harmsworth put together that front page in December 1900, a combination of the success of Britain's 'penny press' and the harsh realities of poverty in New York's Bowery had inspired an ambitious dental student, Horatio Sheppard, to take the first steps to creating what ultimately became the sleaze-obsessed 'yellow journalism' of late nineteenth-century America when he realized the potential of mass-produced cheap news. From these newsmongers and entrepreneurs, via disparate routes, sprang the great popular journalism of the early twentieth century – and, ultimately, today's tabloid and popular journalism.

We need to define our terms to avoid confusion. What exactly do we mean when we refer to 'tabloid', 'red-top' or 'yellow' journalism? These were and are labels that have become associated, often in a derogatory way, with a certain type of newspaper journalism aimed at a mass-market readership. 'Tabloid' has long lost its original meaning as understood by Harmsworth; today it is seen as referring both to the physical size of newspapers, some of which are not and never have been 'populist', and to a particular journalistic approach. Harmsworth was also using 'tabloid' to describe a style of writing and presentation. It would be many decades before newspapers would be shrunk physically and the description 'tabloid' would not refer simply to the physical size of a newspaper but shape the nature of its content. As Roy Peter Clark of the Poynter Institute for Media Studies in the United States puts it: 'The size of the container influences the form of content and the tone. It required a re-thinking of both news judgement, content, story forms, design and photography.'[4] Harmsworth had clearly recognized this that night in New York.

But the word 'tabloid' has now taken on new meanings and become shorthand for a kind of journalism that prioritizes superficial reporting, scandal and sensation over sober facts; that specializes in gossip and innuendo; that creates and then criticizes the cult of celebrity; that somehow glorifies crime, trivia and sleaze and criminalizes unorthodoxy; that panders to the lowest instincts of a readership that wants to be titillated and entertained in equal measure, rather than informed and enlightened. Its journalists use methods and tactics that might be unorthodox, disreputable, unethical or illegal in pursuit of the stories and the mass readerships their wealthy and cynical owners covet. Such is the public's understanding of 'tabloid' today. It is a long, long way from a nineteenth-century aspirin.

Such a clichéd and stereotypical summary is itself worthy of the very worst type of journalism, whatever the label attached to it. There is a contrasting view: that such journalism should go under another name, 'popular' journalism, which describes an effective means of conveying important information to a wide readership rather than an elite one: an audience that might be less educated but is still anxious to be informed while being entertained. And so a simpler use of language, a more visual appeal and a different style lexicon have evolved to create what we see and read today: a more egalitarian approach to what many want to read, attuned to the realities of everyday life for ordinary people.

The practitioners of this second approach believed they had a mission to explain, that to bring the doings of the world home to an ordinary person was a crucial element of an informed society and a worthy endeavour, as well as a profitable one. At its peak, the *Daily Mirror*, created by Northcliffe, was read by more than 12 million people every day and embodied this creed. No daily newspaper in Britain had matched it in terms of circulation and its influence among both the mass of people and those in positions of authority. Equally, it would be wrong to forget that, whether you call it tabloid or simply popular journalism, it has undoubtedly sometimes been a force for good and, as all great journalism should, told truth to power. It has questioned and criticized the organs of the state and officialdom and stood up for those in society who lack access to power – the less fortunate, or simply ordinary people.

Two other terms must also be considered. First, 'red-top' is a phrase derived from the colour of the masthead or title page of a tabloid newspaper and is often used as a convenient alternative to 'tabloid', but it is a relatively new term; today, not all popular newspapers have red mastheads. 'Yellow journalism' was and is a term used in a similar fashion in the United States, its derivation, as we shall see, related to a now-forgotten cartoon character. In addition, 'tabloid journalism' does not simply describe the physical size of a newspaper: some newspapers have never adopted what might be termed 'tabloid values' but have chosen to go tabloid in size rather than culture.

The bulk of newspaper readership is now online and there may well come a point soon when physical newspapers as we know them will cease to exist. Yet tabloid journalism does not equate simply to newspapers, either in print or online: its many customs and conventions can be found in magazines and broadcast journalism, in entertainment and across popular culture. It is, in short, all around us. Tabloid is a state of mind and a method of practice. Further, its mores and conventions now inhabit the infinite spaces of social media. Indeed, social media has injected new life and new opportunities into tabloid journalism, whereby the custom of both celebrities and the general public sharing their lives online, creating the stories and pictures themselves, means journalists need not even leave their desks to unearth them. Today, we are all newsmongers on Planet Tabloid. But how did we get here?

The First Tablets, of Stone

News and the concept of news, of sharing information, has existed since human beings first began to communicate with each other. Primitive cave paintings were works of art as well as a form of processing knowledge for others: 'Here be tigers, beware.' People needed to know where food could be found, who was friend and who was foe. Ancient civilizations needed to communicate with each other, between settlements, across valleys, over oceans. Merchants, warriors and travellers carried news by word of mouth; official proclamations were announced in marketplaces and then inscribed on stone tablets or on papyrus. Some ancient scrolls carried gossip – which ruler had taken another wife, which merchant was untrustworthy, or, in the case of some Mesopotamian scrolls dating from about 1500 BC, accusations of corruption against a town mayor. In ancient and early modern cultures, up until the invention of printing, travelling players, bards, minstrels and town criers would carry news from one community to the next in the form of poems, ballads and tales. Sometimes myths and legends, sometimes the hard realities of life, these were recounted at firesides in homes and taverns and at fairs. The Greeks used a complicated system of flares and fires to carry news of wars and turmoil from one mountaintop to another; both they and the Romans would enjoy their news through the medium of theatre and their gossip and innuendo through the spoken word but also in frescoes and cartoons. The Romans instigated the *acta diurna*, the 'daily acts', or state gazette, which was carved on stone or metal and posted on a board in public places. It contained official proclamations, summaries of political debates and announcements of births and deaths. The ancient Chinese empire had something similar, the *tipao*, handwritten newsletters sent to provincial administrators. Eventually other, less official postings would detail recent crimes, disasters or divorces among the ruling classes.

Ultimately, high-ranking officials and politicians would develop their own networks of contacts and correspondents to share and circulate news. The great Roman politician and lawyer Cicero circulated copies of his speeches for public consumption – a sort of early press release – and when he departed to become governor of Cilicia, in modern-day Turkey and a long way from the centre of power in Rome, he asked his friend Marcus Caelius Rufus to send him copies of each day's gazette along with his letters. But Cicero, an acute political operator, needed more than just official news. 'Others will write, many will bring me news, much too will reach me even in the way of rumour,' Cicero wrote. He wanted and expected both news and gossip. One response from a friend recorded by Cicero included news of the divorce of a prominent Roman who, after his wife left him for someone else, 'sent back her whole wardrobe' – a detail worthy of any tabloid story today. Cicero later complained that he was receiving too much news from Rome concerning trials and crimes, in which he took less interest than society gossip.

As literacy spread, those who could read and write exchanged letters, which conveyed news and the affairs of state. Ancient tablets of stone were replaced by handwritten manuscripts and newsletters, dictated by kings and emperors to scribes and distributed around their lands to important people to announce their conquests and triumphs; others contained written-down news ballads composed in response to major events. Educated scribes would set down information and oral histories into manuscripts, such as the Anglo-Saxon Chronicles, a chronology of events in Anglo-Saxon England. The Bayeux tapestry, created by skilled French embroiderers, told the story of the Norman invasion of Britain – the first graphic novel. The news this recounted would eventually trickle down to workers, serfs and servants. Today, news travels the world in seconds, sometimes still on tablets, but digital ones. In a few years, newspapers in physical form may cease to exist. But in between has come the era of the printed word.

In 1476, newly returned from Europe, where he had launched his first printing press in Bruges, William Caxton set up shop in Westminster Abbey, soon producing the first printed edition of Geoffrey Chaucer's *The Canterbury Tales*. Around 1500 Caxton's associate, Wynkyn de Worde, established his business near Shoe Lane. So began the tradition of printing in the area around Fleet Street – originally an important medieval trade route – and Ludgate Hill. The area was ideally situated, both strategically and socially: close to important bridges across the Thames and the routes to the north, and convenient for the City, the Inns of Court and Westminster. In the years to come, it would become known too for its taverns and coffee-houses, and, in the twentieth century, for the pubs and other watering holes that became the haunt of journalists before, during and after their work.

The age of the handwritten manuscript was ending and the age of printing had arrived. Across Europe, there was increasing public hunger for information and the official accounts of wars, celebrations of kingly triumphs or news of court appointments were printed in large numbers. Soon they came to be seen as instruments of state power and control. In 1486 the recently crowned Henry VII printed and circulated a papal bull recognizing his right to the throne. In 1493 Christopher Columbus's own handwritten account to the Spanish court of his discovery of 'the Indies' was set into type and printed. Hundreds of copies were made available within just a few weeks of his return, and it was soon being reprinted and circulated throughout Europe.

In England, in Tudor times the state had long regarded any type of printing and the dissemination of information to the wider public as potentially seditious and treasonable, so strict controls were imposed on those who sought to distribute what became known as news pamphlets. In London, these were usually sold at locations such as St Paul's Cathedral, where the nave, 'Paul's walk', had long been a place for news to be exchanged orally. In major towns, they would be hawked at public gatherings. In the fifteenth century printers and stationers often wrote newsletters on the side, while retired army captains were also thought to be good at the job of sending despatches about wars, since they had an understanding of military matters. But they appealed only to those few who could read. The vast majority of the population could not.

In 1538 Henry VIII ordered that all printed matter had to be approved by the Privy Council prior to publication. The news that was officially permitted was limited to one-off 'relations', single printed sheets that covered specific events. Any unofficial reference to political events was strictly off-limits. While Henry allowed pamphlets containing lyrical descriptions of the coronation of Anne Boleyn to be printed in 1533, there is no evidence anything official was circulated after he ordered her execution. Under Elizabeth I, who set up the first intelligence services, state control was even stronger. In 1585 the Star Chamber set the number of approved printers at just twenty, plus the universities of Oxford and Cambridge. Pamphlets such as 'Newe newes, containing a short rehearsal of Stukely's and Morice's Rebellion. 1577' and 'Newes from the North, or a conference between Simon Certain and Pierce Plowman' were produced. Wary of royal disapproval, Shakespeare himself, the greatest of all chroniclers of English history, whose writings shaped public perception of monarchy, would stick to earlier eras for his historical plays or frame his stories in allegorical terms, setting them in far-off Verona or ancient Athens to carefully avoid any suggestion he was writing about contemporary events and therefore risking official censure. He succeeded, with one notable exception: in 1601 the Earl of Essex sponsored an unsuccessful revolt against Elizabeth, shortly after the earl's followers had attended a performance of the Bard's *Richard II*. Elizabeth believed they had derived encouragement from a scene in which Richard is deposed and her censor ordered the scene to be cut from printed editions of the play. Inevitably, there were unofficial channels, and it became commonplace for nobles, merchants and state officials to employ 'news-writers' to send them regular confidential despatches conveying the news of the day – whether it was the intrigues of court, whether the king was seeking another wife or if Elizabeth really was still a virgin. Such knowledge has always appealed.

By the time Nathaniel Butter turned his hand to the news business, he was already a successful publisher, having been responsible for registering the first edition of Shakespeare's *King Lear* with the

Stationers' Company in 1607, although this was not printed until the following year by Nicholas Oakes, as well as the works of other playwrights of the era and translations of Homer's *Iliad* and *Odyssey*. In the early seventeenth century publishing remained a risky business, since anything deemed critical of the Stuart king James I could incur punishment. In 1620 Butter, who had also printed a number of political pamphlets, was briefly imprisoned for publishing one critical of the new Holy Roman Emperor, Ferdinand II. The following year, Butter became part of an alliance of publishers and printers determined to print weekly news sheets, known as 'corantos' in Holland and other parts of northern Europe. These were to be sold for one groat, or four pennies, and were intended largely to satisfy public hunger for news of the conflicts raging in central Europe that would eventually be known as the Thirty Years War. Containing translated items of news from various countries, they are believed to have been first published in the early part of 1621, although no copies appear to have survived. One of the group, a printer called Thomas Archer, was briefly jailed for not having the correct licence. Butter himself was subsequently granted a licence and became the dominant publisher. All the surviving copies of *Corante; or, News from Italy, Germany, Hungarie, Spaine and France*, the earliest of which dates from 24 September 1621, bear his initials. Although it contained no domestic news, this could probably be described as the first British newspaper.

Copies were distributed to selected subscribers and sold on the streets, as well as from Butter's shop in the precincts of St Paul's Cathedral. By this time, this printing shop, said to be 'at the sign of Pied Bull', was becoming a kind of early news agency, where news despatches were sent from abroad and where customers could find the latest pamphlets. Items of news would also be physically brought there by people such as John Pory (a figure closely associated with Butter), a well-travelled diplomat and politician who had returned from the Virginia colony in the United States where he had been elected Speaker of the Assembly. Pory had turned himself into a prototype news correspondent, contributing to Butter's publications but also selling regular news reports based on his regular letters and exchanges with a wide variety of his contacts. By now Butter had also retained Captain Thomas Gainsford, a university-educated professional soldier who was also an author published by Butter, to translate, compile and edit the news books, making him possibly the first journalist who could be described as an editor. In 1624 Butter and another of his group, Nicholas Bourne, who became the financier, began publishing the first so-called 'news books', pamphlets that derived their name from their quarto size, entitled the *Certain News of the Present Week*, or the *Weekly News*. This innovation of Butter's caused an explosion of imitators, most of whose efforts were more sporadic and ephemeral than Butter's. According to the nineteenth-century writer James Grant, 'Nathaniel Butter's *Weekly News* was the first English newspaper which appeared duly numbered like our newspapers of the present day.'[5]

Away from official news, a different picture of everyday life began to emerge. Other pamphlets and news books were clearly designed to appeal to the less well-educated masses, did not offend the state censors with political comment and were aimed at an audience more interested in gossip, scandal and colourful sensationalism. Or, as Mitchell Stephens puts it in *A History of News*,

> Anyone who clings to the notion that the sensationalism practised by Rupert Murdoch or even the most shameless present-day journalist is unprecedented could be set straight by spending a few minutes with any of a number of sixteenth and seventeenth century newsbooks.[6]

Typical headlines included 'Hevy newes of an horrible earthquake' and 'A straunge and terrible wunder wrought in the parish church of Bongay', which contained the immortal paragraph: 'In a great tempest of violente raine, lightning and thunder . . . an horrible shaped thing was sensibly perceived of the people then and there assembled, which in the twinkling of an eye, mortally wrung the necks of several worshippers.' Accounts of horrific crimes were particularly popular. They included the gory *The Bloudy booke, or the Tragicall and desperate end of Sir John Fites (alias) Fitz*, who murdered a married couple 'eager and thirstie of blood, without all compassion'. Butter himself was not averse to publishing more salacious material, which was less likely to attract the attentions of the official censors. One of his publications in 1624 was the graphically illustrated news book *The Crying Murther: Contayning the cruell and most horrible Butchery of Mr Trat*, which in some detail recounted

The Crying Murther . . . , a typical news book from 1624.

the murder and dismemberment of the unfortunate Trat. Its author claimed it was based on 'intelligence which I have received from credible persons, engaged in their trial'. Such stories would often be accompanied by stern moral asides; the murderers of Mr Trat are reported to have been duly hanged and to have died 'obstinate and unrepenting sinners'.

Stories of monsters, supernatural events and horrific punishments meted out to blasphemers and others were highly popular. These included 'Wonderful and Strange Newes out of Suffolke and Essex where it Rayned Wheat the Space of Six or Seven Miles', 'Newes from Scotland, declaring the damnable life of Doctor Fian, a notable sorcerer, who was burned at Edenborough in January last', and 'Strange newes from Lancaster, containing an account of a prodigious monster born in the township of Addlington in Lancashire, with two bodies joyned to one back'. Clearly this was a case of conjoined twins; anything out of the ordinary – the weather or criminal behaviour – was inevitably attributed to supernatural or evil forces. Perhaps public taste has not changed very much: several centuries later, the *Daily Sport* and the *Daily Star* in the UK and the *National Enquirer* in the United States would build their circulations on stories with headlines such as 'Statue of Elvis Found on Mars' and 'Adam and Eve Found in Asia'. In June 2023, as this book was being completed, the *Daily Star* led its front page one day with the headline 'I Was Abducted by Long-Fingered Aliens at RAF Airfield Who Made Me Forget for 30 Years'.

By now Butter was sufficiently well known and well established for playwrights to lampoon him from the stage. The most brutal of these was Ben Jonson, who had already attacked the business of news gathering in his 1621 masque *News from the New World Discovered in the Moon*, which criticized the 'curious uncertainties' of the witchcraft, murders and 'strange newes' of earlier pamphlets and news sheets. His satirical take on the business of newsmongering, *The Staple of News*, was first performed at the Blackfriars Theatre in late 1625. Although much of the play is actually a satire on early ideas of capitalism, some of the action takes place in the office of the publisher of the *Staple of News*, which was clearly based on Butter's premises: the dialogue is liberally sprinkled with puns on his name. Jonson also makes clear his distaste for 'this hungering and thirsting after published pamphlets of news, set out every Saturday, but made at home, and no syllable of truth in them'. One of Jonson's characters addresses what are said to be 'gossip scouts' in the city:

You must get o' this *News*, to store your *Office*,
Who dines and sups i' the town? where, and *with whom?*

'Twill be beneficial: when you are stor'd,
And as we like our fare, we shall reward you.

Here already was a society where it was normal for news of gossip and scandal to be exchanged for money. Soon publications would have a range of different titles: news books were priced at one or two pennies and so were able to achieve a wider circulation. A variety of different names were ascribed to them: they were called *Passages*, then *Mercuries, Intelligencers, Posts, Spies* and *Scouts*. Some related to single events, while others reported on a number of incidents. And crude woodcuts would sometimes appear – the first illustrations.

Undeterred by his critics and the threat of official sanction, Butter, in alliance with Bourne, continued publishing his news books under various titles, although he was banned again by the Privy Council in 1632 for publishing reports about the Thirty Years War. In place of the weekly news books, they began to publish European history (actually thinly disguised news of the ongoing conflict) in the *Swedish Intelligencer* and the *German Intelligencer*. In 1638 Butter was finally granted a patent by Charles I to revive the corantos and publish what was tantamount to news as well as history, but again confined himself to the war. A year later, he was banned again amid the unrest ahead of the English Civil War.

Censorship ended, at least for a while, when the Star Chamber – which had inflicted severe punishment on the authors and publishers of unauthorized written works – was abolished in 1641. Butter was approaching seventy but made one last foray into publishing reports from Parliament, by then a hotbed of opposition to Charles I, and was imprisoned again in 1643 'for committing sedition as an intelligencer'. Shortly afterwards, he appears to have retired from publishing and died in 1664 in relative obscurity and poverty. His obituary described him as 'an old stationer, died very poore'. It is not perhaps the highest accolade for the determined man who had done more than anyone before him to pioneer what would become popular journalism, despite official censorship, imprisonment and public mockery.

The end of the Star Chamber and the continuing battle between Parliament and Charles I provided new opportunities for journalism to satisfy the public hunger for news of the running conflict.

Later that same year, there appeared *A Perfect Diurnall of Some Passages in Parliament*, or, as written on its title page, *The Heads of Severall Proceedings in this Present Parliament from the 22 of November to the 29, 1641*. Written by one Samuel Pecke, a scrivener or clerk in Westminster Hall, and published by William Cooke, a legal publisher from Furnival's Inn, this was not only the first reporting of the doings of Parliament but the first true reporting of English news, although its most direct descendant today is probably Hansard, the official report of parliamentary proceedings, rather than, say, the *Daily Star*. There were soon other *Diurnals*, but Cooke and Pecke led the field and demand was such that they often had to use two printers.

Little is known about Pecke today, although one account describes him as a 'bald-headed buzzard . . . with a Hawks nose, a meagre countenance . . . constant in nothing but wenching, lying and drinking'.[7] Pecke was also twice imprisoned for various infringements of the law, which says something about his endeavours. But one story that he recounted would echo down the centuries: on Tuesday, 30 January 1649, Pecke wrote: 'This day the King was beheaded, over against the Banqueting house, by White-Hall.' The report was a factual description of the event and reported the king's last words and how he prepared himself, ending: 'when the King's head was cut off, the Executioner held it up and showed it to the spectators.' This is the first instance, perhaps, of true, on-the-spot reportage.

Most pamphlets or news books took sides in the conflict between Royalists and Parliamentarians before and during the Civil War, which began in 1642. During the 1640s and '50s hundreds of titles were printed, some several times a week. Many were sold on the streets of London by female hawkers, who became known as 'Mercury Women'. One Mercury Woman makes an appearance in *The Staple of News*, asking for a 'groat's worth of any news' to take to her local vicar. Other news books were sent to subscribers around the country. Here, for the first time, news driven by the political and religious divisions of the country was printed and distributed on a weekly basis, giving the public much-needed information about the tumultuous events taking place around them. Already, as Jonson had shown, journalists were not entirely popular, a fact confirmed by the anonymous author of a one-off 1642 publication, *A Presse full of Pamphlets*, who moaned: 'This kind of new invented profession . . . [with their quest for] new Newes were a menace to ordered society' and complained that they were drunkards, guilty of 'fabulous invention'. In 1648 another publication, *Mercurius Anti Mercurius*, used even stronger language, attacking this 'filthy Avairy, this moth-eating crew of News-mongers . . . every Jack-sprat that hath a pen in his ink-horn is ready to gather up the Excrements of the Kingdom.'

The author might well have been describing John Crouch, who was arguably the first properly scurrilous and politically biased satirist-journalist, and professed a liking for claret and tobacco. A Royalist, Crouch is best known for *The Man in the Moone*, first published in 1649, which took its name from older ballads and folk rhymes ('Our man in the moon drinks clarret,/ With powder-beef, turnep, and carret'). More than fifty weekly issues, each of about eight pages, railed against the Parliamentarians, utilizing crude language and doggerel, rhymes, ballads and, its closest thing to news, items of gossip, all of which were designed to make fun of the Puritans, criticizing their sexual immorality and their oppression of the poor. 'The majority of his news items were based on hearsay or rumour. Very often these reports were wildly inaccurate.'[8] While Crouch may have been more of a political activist than a true journalist, he created a model for modern contemporaries who can be found inhabiting the comment pages of both tabloid and more serious newspapers today. Accusations of inaccuracy and repeating hearsay have not gone away.

There were further parliamentary attempts at restrictions and censorship – prompting John Milton to publish his polemic *Areopagitica*, a defence of freedom of speech, in 1644 – and unofficial news books were banned in 1655 by Oliver Cromwell. After the Restoration they were again banned by Charles II in the Licensing of the Press Act of 1662, which restricted printing to the universities of Oxford and Cambridge and members of the Stationers' Company; the political content of all publications had to be approved, resulting in a series of entirely Royalist-supporting pamphlets. In the end, sequestered in Oxford during the plague, Charles II decided to create the Crown's own publication, first published in 1665 as the *Oxford Gazette* and renamed the *London Gazette* the following year when the court returned to the capital. It was the first truly recognizable newspaper, rather than a news book: a single sheet with columns divided by a rule, and as the official voice of the Crown was nothing Butter, Pecke or Crouch might have been associated with. Published every weekday by the Stationery Office, it continues today as the official record of government business.

The public's hunger for news, whether political and social scandal or the proceedings of the courts, continued to be satisfied with unofficial and handwritten newsletters, which, as well as being sent by post around the country, now found a new outlet in London's burgeoning coffee-houses. These, first opened in 1652 in London and Oxford, became instantly fashionable. They were centres of debate and discussion where gossip and news was circulated and where news books and pamphlets, both official and unofficial, were sold and exchanged. They became the haunts of the putative journalists and gossip scouts of the day. Sometimes dubbed 'penny universities' – a penny being the price of a cup of coffee – there were more than five hundred in London alone by 1759.

By now some licensed newspapers were also beginning to satisfy the public's taste for sex, scandal and 'real life stories', more than 250 years before *The Sun*. One publisher who escaped the censor was Benjamin Harris, an anti-Catholic pamphleteer and Whig publisher who edited one of the first attempts at gathering local news, the *Domestick Intelligence; or, News both from City and Country*. This was published from 1679 to 1681 and demonstrated, alongside earnest political debate, an increasing appetite for sensationalism: one issue reports on a man found hanging 'By the Arms in a Wood . . . with his Head and Hands cut off and his bowels pulled out'. Harris later moved to Boston in the new colonies and established a coffee-house where foreign newspapers and books were sold. In 1690 he published *Publick Occurrences Both Forreign and Domestick*, the first newspaper to be published in America, and perhaps set the tone for what was to follow with a claim that the king of France 'used to lie with his Sons Wife' and a report on the suicide of a man who hanged himself 'in the Cow House'. Harris came up with the novel idea of including, among its four pages, one that was completely blank; purchasers could add their own items of news on to this page to pass it on. It was closed down by the authorities after one issue.

Others satisfied the public appetite for news that was neither political nor foreign. In 1681 the *Loyal Protestant and True Domestick Intelligencer*, a Tory-supporting publication, reported the case of a woman who went 'beast like on all Fours, with her Posteriors Bare and the Dog effectively performing'. This was supposedly her remedy for venereal disease. The following year, perhaps initiating a tradition of stories about religious figures and sex that continues to this day, it told the story of a minister who 'laid with two Wenches ten nights at a Guinny a Night'. And in 1690 the *Athenian Mercury*, published twice weekly by bookseller John Dunton, featured the first advice column, in which a group of experts, the so-called Athenian Society, answered queries from readers on all manner of topics, such as religion, science and politics. Two centuries later, Lord Northcliffe himself would use the idea as a basis for his first magazine, *Answers to Correspondents*. And one of the staples of the *Daily Mirror* newspaper, at the height of its mid-twentieth-century popularity, was a 'Live Letters' page, 'conducted by the Old Codgers' who provided witty asides and comments in response to readers' letters. And so the concept of a club or society within the newspaper was created. Among the members of the Athenian Society was Daniel Defoe, the author of *Robinson Crusoe*, who became one of the most prolific journalists of the era.

The *Mercury* was highly popular, and a female reader's inquiry into whether she was able to submit questions led to a boom in queries about social manners, dress, love and marriage. This prompted a spin-off publication, the *Ladies Mercury*, devoted entirely to questions from women. From these beginnings would grow a whole industry of advice columns in newspapers and in particular those devoted almost entirely to issues of sex and relationships, another essential ingredient of the tabloid formula.

When Parliament accidentally failed to renew the Licensing of the Press Act in 1695, official censorship and licensing ended, if only by default, and the age of newspapers really began. This was despite the constant threat of being thrown into prison on charges of sedition and libel, which would hang over journalists for several decades to come. The *Daily Courant*, first published in 1702 and consisting almost entirely of translations of news from European news sheets in order to stay on the right side of the authorities, was the first daily newspaper in a model we would recognize today. By the end of the first decade of the eighteenth century, there were around eighteen different titles being published in London.

The newsmongers were here to stay, if now also frequently the subject of criticism. In his *History of England*, Thomas Macaulay describes these early hacks:

Godfrey Kneller,
Daniel Defoe,
17th–18th century,
oil on canvas.

The newswriter ambled from coffee room to coffee room, squeezed himself into the sessions house at the Old Bailey . . . perhaps obtained admission to the gallery at Whitehall and noticed how the King and Duke looked. In this way he gathered materials for his weekly epistles designed to enlighten some country town or some bunch of rustic magistrates. Such were the sources from which the inhabitants of the largest provincial cities and the great body of the gentry and clergy, learned almost all they knew of the history of their own tribe.[9]

The poet and satirist Samuel Butler was more acerbic: for him, the newsmonger was 'a retailer of rumour that takes up upon trust and sells as cheap as he buys'.[10]

As the Georgian era began, there was an explosion of titles: morning and evening newspapers suddenly proliferated, alongside tri-weekly papers, the first magazines and weekly journals, some political, some more literary. In a more socially liberal society, there was a growing thirst for news and information about both the public and private lives of the aristocracy: this was the era when the seeds of our modern obsession with the lives of celebrities and other public figures were sown. Many of the new newspapers were serious, aimed at overwhelmingly male, educated and upper-class readers. And many were passed around coffee-houses, read and debated. But as the passion for news spread among the public, even those who could not read would gather in taverns or on the street to hear newspapers and journals being read to them. A single weekly publication might be read or heard by as many as forty people.

Defoe, a businessman, spy, novelist, political pamphleteer and author, was also a prodigious journalist and commentator who was among those who helped lay the foundations of the modern popular press. He can be credited with creating the first real diary or gossip column in his *Review*, which was first published in 1704, lasted until 1713 and was devoted mainly to serious political commentary and essays. He appropriated the idea behind John Dunton's 'Athenian Society' for his own publication and created a column called 'Advice from the Scandalous Club', announcing it as 'a little diversion' at the end of every paper. 'Here he dispensed advice on morals and manners in a style mixing rectitude with ribaldry, ranging through the field of human frailty to cover such vices as duelling, swearing and the lustful escapades of the clergy.' He also pioneered the idea of writing about the indiscretions of the well-known by using aliases, thinly disguised descriptions and allusions to disguise true identities and avoid accusations of libel.[11] A typical entry might begin, 'A Poor Whore made a sad Complaint this Week at the Club and demanded Justice against a Certain Eminent Citizen who had exacted her Performance but cheated her of her Wages.'[12] Here, another founding principle of tabloid journalism was being laid down: to titillate and entertain the reader under the guise of a high moral tone.

Defoe, who also worked for a number of different newspapers, mixed with both politicians and the lowlife of London. He is credited with pioneering that other tabloid staple: crime reporting. He interviewed criminals and, it was claimed, 'stood on the scaffold' to collect the dying words of convicts, which were published by John Applebee in his *Weekly Journal* and in a pamphlet of the last speeches of recently executed criminals, although most believed this was not the work of Defoe. Nevertheless, Defoe was a true pioneer of explaining matters simply for the benefit of the widest possible audience: 'He wrote excellent, clear, uncluttered, reporterly English, full of relatively short sentences of plain description.' And Defoe was a real reporter: 'He believed in going and seeing with his own eyes.'[13]

All publications so far had been aimed very much at an upper-class, almost exclusively male readership, who were literary and politically educated. But at the end of 1709, there appeared the tri-weekly *Female Tatler*, allegedly edited by one Phoebe Crackenthorpe, 'a Lady that Knows Everything' (although this was, of course, a nom de plume). Crackenthorpe dispensed advice to women on issues of the day, providing a model for many future women-centred advice columns. Hers was the first publication aimed directly at women. The identity of the real Mrs Crackenthorpe remains in doubt, although many believe it was the extraordinary and colourful figure of Mary de la Riviere Manley, a Jersey-born writer and playwright and author of two controversial volumes about the 'New Atalantis', an island in the Mediterranean. These recounted serial amorous encounters between young women and men – thinly disguised Whig politicians – set on a mythical island.

Later, the editorship of the *Female Tatler* was handed over to 'A Society of Ladies' (another nod to the club concept) at the very point that she was arrested for seditious libel over the 'Atalantis' publications, spending several days in prison. Manley later concentrated mainly on romantic stories and plays but returned to political journalism as editor of Jonathan Swift's *Examiner* for some months in 1710–11, renewing her attacks on Whig propaganda by using her talent for acquiring and circulating gossip, although her writing at this point was said to lack the clear female perspective she brought to her other work. However, 'She was uncrowned queen of gossip . . . the first woman editor to realise that through print, "private intelligence" could be public political currency' – as every tabloid journalist since has known.[14]

After women, there came a publication aimed directly at the 'common people': the *Weekly Journal*, the work of Nathaniel Mist, which was launched in 1716. A staunch Jacobite who wanted to see the return of the Stuarts to the throne, Mist was arrested several times for sedition, spent time in jail and was pilloried at Charing Cross and the Royal Exchange. He deliberately set out to appeal to a mass audience in order to disseminate his political views more widely, and his paper contained more domestic news than any other before it. Condemned by his rivals for vulgarity, he was clearly a pioneer in establishing an effective news-gathering network. *Read's Weekly Journal* claimed, perhaps enviously, that Mist had 'an agent scraping the Jails in Middlesex and Surrey of their Commitments, another had a warrant for scouring the Ale-houses and Gin-shops for such as dye of excessive Drinking; a person is posted at the Savoy to take up Deserters and another in the Park to watch the Motions of the Guards'.

Some of Mist's stories 'read like the cast list of the *Beggar's Opera*: highwaymen, prostitutes, receivers and thief-takers', a formula that would indeed come to be endlessly repeated.[15] His notoriety led to some of his issues becoming collector's items and in 1741 the *Daily Gazetteer* recollected that 'Mist's treasonable Papers were sold sometimes for Half a Guinea a-piece'. He clearly worried the authorities. In 1717 Charles Delafaye, a senior civil servant and himself a former editor, recruited Defoe to work with Mist to tone down his anti-government writings and to spy on him; Defoe later claimed to have prevented a number of his more inflammatory pieces reaching print under the guise of friendship, although they later fell out in 1724. Although Mist attempted to stay on the right side of the law by couching his critical writing in moral parables from history – rather like Shakespeare – he was forced to flee to France in 1728. He continued to publish in London, but then largely confined himself to Jacobite plotting and his business interests in France until his death in 1737.

Newspapers now became more and more important to the daily lives of all classes, with weekly sales rising from around 45,000 in 1710 to 210,000 by the 1750s. Despite the arrests for sedition, they were comparatively free to publish what they wanted, at least compared with some of their European neighbours. After visiting England in 1730, the French philosopher Montesquieu recorded his surprise at the freedom of the press: 'When you see the devil in the periodicals, you can believe that the people will rebel tomorrow. You merely need to get your mind around the fact that, in England as elsewhere, the people are discontented with their ministers and write in the periodicals what is thought elsewhere.' As a French nobleman keenly aware of the need to keep the sometimes rebellious masses under control, he noted how a roofer will have his newspaper brought up to him while he is working – a metaphorical warning that 'If the rabble can get ideas so high, they might hurl rubble down.' He also commented wryly that although the king might be regularly libelled, the taxes levied allowed him to profit every time it happened.[16]

As the eighteenth century wore on, newspapers began to serve a newly self-confident and outgoing society. In London's taverns, eating houses, theatres, music halls and gambling houses, life throbbed and sexual freedom exerted itself – one in five London women were estimated to be involved in prostitution. The resort of Brighton and the spas of Cheltenham, and Bath, the latter presided over by Beau Nash, became the playgrounds of the Georgian upper classes. This was meat and drink to the newsmongers of the era. The comings and goings of the aristocracy and their fringes – salon hostesses, actors and actresses, courtesans, society beauties and young bucks around town and in the fashionable spas – became of immense interest not just to themselves, but to those who could never achieve entry to those circles, in much the same way that today's stories of Instagram influencers, models and reality TV stars are relayed in the tabloids and greedily devoured by those whose lifestyles are much less glossy. 'A Man of any Distinction cannot steal out of Town for a Day or two, but the Secret is immediately made known to the World,' complained a correspondent to the *Gentleman's Magazine*, while simultaneously calling for even more candour about the affairs of the upper classes, saying that newspapers should report 'when His Grace or his Lordship went to Bed to his Lady – When he broke his custom, and Kept His Word with his Tradesman or Dependents . . . these Articles would be News.'[17] Newspapers and journals came and went: the *Female Spectator* in 1744 followed the model of the *Female Tatler*, but with less gossip and more advice to readers; the *Old Whig* was dominated by stories of horrific crimes and tragic deaths, such as that of the brewery employee who was boiled alive in a vat and the sweep who discovered the 'long-smoked' body of a burglar who had been trapped in a chimney, while the *Morning Post* focused on the doings of the aristocracy. It is said to have blackmailed the then Prince of Wales when it published references to him having married an older Roman Catholic widow.

By now, there was concern about the standards of the press that is mirrored 250 years later: the obsession with celebrity and trivia, and lurid and often graphic reports of crimes, including murders, sodomy, bestiality and the activities of highwaymen, and the trials that followed, as well as reports of the many public punishments, such as mutilations, floggings and hangings. The public's appetite for crime stories was satisfied by the *Dying Confessions* new sheets, similar to John Applebee's *Weekly Journal* which circulated after hangings and purported to carry the last admissions of those being taken to the scaffold, always with a moral message woven into the penitent words. After being informed by his bookseller that his customers were reading only newspapers, the author Henry Fielding wrote, 'There is scarce a syllable of truth in any of them,' adding:

> There is, in reality, nothing in them at all. And this also must be allowed by their readers, if paragraphs which contain neither wit, nor humour, nor sense, nor the least importance, may be properly said to contain nothing. Such are the arrival of my Lord with a great equipage, the marriage of Miss of great beauty and merit, and the death of Mr. Who was never heard of in his life, &c., &c.[18]

A few years later, a correspondent to the *Gentleman's Magazine* railed against the obsessions of the press: 'Pages of unconnected occurrences, consisting of politics, religion, picking of pockets, puffs, casualties, deaths, marriages, bankruptcies, preferments, resignations, executive, lottery tickets, French chicken gloves, auctioneers, quack doctors . . . not a syllable of news.'[19] In 1730 Eustace Budgell, one of *The Spectator*'s founding essayists, who later became an MP, similarly complained about the content of newspapers, which he said comprised:

> Robberies, bloody Murders, Accounts of Draymen's Carts that have run over People, with the adventures of Post-Boys, Tide Waiters and Messengers &c. The Promotions, Deaths and Marriages of the Nobility, Gentry and Clergy and of the Days when some of the Royal Family go to the Play House or take the Air.[20]

Most of these would also form the basis of a tabloid editor's news list today.

The thirst for news, particularly of the more sleazy and scandalous variety, had led to the rise of a new class of journalists far removed from the more literary and politically orientated figures such as Defoe. These were the 'penny-a-liners', the first freelancers, non-aligned, rootless individuals who moved from court to coffee-house in search of stories:

> A horrible murder . . . rejoices the hearts of the Penny-a-Liners. They call it a 'windfall.' To work they set directly, and everything connected with the murdered party and the murderer, is hunted out by them with an alacrity which exceeds all belief. If no romantic materials exist, they call in the aid of their inventive faculties. They consider anything bearing on the romantic or horrible as a sort of mine, which they work with most exemplary industry.

So said James Grant, former editor of the *Morning Chronicle* and the *Morning Advertiser*. 'They are altogether a singular race; they are a class, in a great measure, by themselves; they live by the press, and yet they do not, strictly speaking, belong to the press. They have no regular sum for their labours; sometimes no sum at all.'[21]

Even by the standards of such a freewheeling climate a campaign launched by one paper in 1753 was unprecedented in its vicious antisemitism. By 1750 the tri-weekly, pro-Jacobite, Tory-supporting *London Evening Post* had become one of the most influential papers in the country. Its publisher John Meres and founder Richard Nutt both robustly opposed the Whig government and were often punished by the authorities. Meres was jailed for criticism of a parliamentary trade act while Nutt was fined and pilloried for a libel of the government. In 1753 the newspaper's target was an insignificant piece of legislation, the Jewish Naturalisation Bill, which would grant naturalization rights to a small number of Jewish merchants and financiers.

Brittanicus, the lead commentator of the *Post*, which had often argued the Church of England was in danger, claimed that the Act would allow Jews to buy the land and thereby gain power:

> It is not to be doubted but all the Hebrew Race wheresoever scatter'd, will flock over, and this Nation be enrich'd with all the Tribes of Israel . . . That when they are naturalis'd, they will buy Lands . . . they will therefore . . . choose Members of Parliament, who can doubt, if we reflect on the vast Riches

they are Masters of, and the Manner in which our Boroughs have of late elected?

Antisemitic language and use of historic tropes of 'swamping' began to dominate the *Post*'s increasingly hysterical columns. As well as the words of its own columnists, it reprinted anything critical of the Act by other publications, along with numerous letters denouncing Jews. It repeated ancient tropes of Jews indulging in ritual murder, sacrifice and cannibalism and crucifying Jesus Christ, and mocked circumcision, as well as devising an antisemitic version of the ancient ballad 'The Roast Beef of Old England', which the paper said it 'recommended to be sung by the few Christians that may be remaining in this Country One Hundred Years hence'. Eventually, in face of such opposition, the bill was dropped.

The historian G. A. Cranfield wrote:

> The *Post*'s campaign against the 'Jew Bill' was undoubt-edly one of the most remarkable propaganda campaigns in English history. However exaggerated and ludicrous many of its attacks may seem to be, they had clearly struck a respon-sive chord in the hearts of many of its readers. The *Post*'s amazing mixture of political opportunism, religious fervour, and Rabelaisian humour were largely responsible in forcing the ministry to repeal the Bill.[22]

While the campaign was a political one, it also used a series of standard tabloid tactics to stoke public opinion: faux outrage to inflate public concern, a high moral tone, incendiary language and a disregard for basic facts, marshalled to suit its purpose.

By the early nineteenth century the old independent printers and publishers such as Nash and Mist had been replaced by more com-mercial concerns, with owner-proprietors employing printers for their exclusive use. Newspapers, still largely vociferously politically aligned, were moving on from the model of sole editor-publisher-journalist, such as Mist, to news-gathering, employing specialist writers and penny-a-liners to bring in stories and content. The modern newsroom was being created.

By this time, there were 52 regularly published newspapers in London and more than a hundred elsewhere in the country. As newspapers grew more confident, respectable and recognized, there was also, again, a strong reaction from the political and ruling classes to the criticism contained within them: journalists were jailed for seditious libel if they dared call the government or the Crown to account. This followed the emergence of what became known as the 'radical press', which agitated for parliamentary reform and campaigned against political corruption. Journalists and editors themselves remained subject to bribery and corruption, usually by politicians: Henry White, founder of the *Independent Whig* and then the *Sunday Times* in 1821, admitted: 'Every editor is a ready agent of venality and corruption and every journal has its price.'[23]

At the same time, there was concern among the political and upper classes that there might be a revolutionary upsurge among the lower orders, mirroring the French Revolution which had begun in 1789. The Stamp Act of 1712 had imposed extra costs on newspapers and all publishers. These were increased in 1797 and again, dramatically, in 1815, which put the price of radical publications beyond the reach of the poor. In the wake of the Peterloo Massacre in 1819, there were further restrictions imposed in the Six Acts of the same year, which extended the scope of the Stamp Acts. This was aimed directly at the section of the press serving the working classes, rather than the by-now establishment-focused *Times* and *Telegraph*. The result was that cheaper radical publications aimed at the growing lower and working classes were suddenly put beyond their means: the average price of newspapers reached around sevenpence after 1815, roughly the daily wage of a working man, and would remain so until the middle of the nineteenth century, when the tax was abolished. There was a brief upsurge in cheaper, 'unstamped' papers, which became very popular and railed against the state on behalf of the common man; these were then suppressed when the government changed the tax rules again, to the benefit of papers like *The Times*. The overall tone of the press was much less robust than in the previous century. 'The variety and vitality of the newspaper press in the Grub Street years of the 18th century had given way to a grey uniformity.'[24]

It was in magazines rather than in newspapers that society's appetite for crime, scandal and gossip now most manifested itself. The popularity of cheap 'penny dreadfuls' – weekly serialized fictional stories of horrific crimes and supernatural events, aimed at young working-class men and featuring characters such as Sweeney Todd and Dick Turpin – also increased the public demand for real-life true crime stories. But after the Stamp Acts there was little, if anything, that catered for the new working class – miners and mill workers, labourers building the new roads and railways – whose wages remained low. New radical newspapers reported on social reformers and their causes, such as the fight for the abolition of slavery – the *Manchester Guardian* was founded specifically to promote 'liberal concerns' in the aftermath of the Peterloo Massacre – but the sober language and august tone of such publications remained rooted in the ruling educated classes, largely interested only in politics and public affairs. For those who could read, books – the first half of the nineteenth century saw the emergence and popularity of the literary novel – were mostly too expensive and bore no relationship to everyday concerns. These new working classes, who would form the core of the tabloid readership of the next century, were not yet commuters: most worked close to home in factories, workshops, mills and mines and a six-day working week was the norm. What little leisure time they had was spent in time-honoured fashion at taverns and alehouses, in music halls or at public fetes and fairs, particularly on public holidays. Newspapers were not their priority.

The Society for the Diffusion of Useful Knowledge, founded in London in 1826 by Whig MP and social reformer Henry Brougham, who had been deeply critical of the obsession with crime, scandal and trivia of some of the established press and had been attacked by them, published the *Penny Magazine* in 1832 in alliance with Charles Knight, a publisher and journalist. Priced at one penny, published on a Saturday and aimed at an audience that might include a large number of semi-literate buyers at a time when roughly half the population could not read, it was lavishly illustrated and avoided current news and political content, focusing instead on informative, educational articles. Echoing the drive for self-education among the working classes, it was the first real mass-market publication aimed at them, although its serious, high-minded tone would eventually be its undoing. Knight was concerned to ensure high-quality woodcuts as illustrations: 'He seems to have consciously intended this emphasis upon pictures as a means of bringing printed matter to the attention of a public unaccustomed to reading. Even the illiterate found a good pennyworth of enjoyment in the illustrations each issue of the *Penny Magazine* contained.'[25]

Within a year, it was selling around 200,000 a week, a huge circulation at the time. And a key principle had been established – to reach a mass audience, publications needed to be both cheap and well illustrated. In the UK the *Penny Magazine* was among a number of precursors to a late nineteenth-century raft of publications aimed at enlightening the general public. *Tit-Bits*, a collection of interesting stories and facts aimed at the new market catering to educated young people, was published by George Newnes, who employed two men: Alfred Harmsworth and Arthur Pearson. Between them, they would do more than any others to create popular journalism in Britain.

2

THE RISE OF THE MOGULS

The second half of the nineteenth century and the early part of the twentieth saw the rise of the newspaper moguls: those whose names would go down in history and who would make a fortune out of realizing exactly where public taste lay and how to cater for it among the newly literate masses. This was the era of lords Northcliffe and Beaverbrook, of Joseph Pulitzer and William Randolph Hearst, all names embedded in any history of journalism. There were two others, now largely forgotten, but equally influential: James Gordon Bennett, the destitute Scottish immigrant who single-handedly created the mass-circulation American newspaper, and George Riddell, the golf-mad London solicitor who transformed the *News of the World* into the biggest-selling newspaper in the world. While very different men, they all shared certain qualities: ruthless ambition, a knack for understanding and anticipating public taste and a realization that mass-market newspapers could make them very rich indeed.

A raft of innovations, coupled with increasing literacy among the working classes, would expand the market for newspapers during the mid-nineteenth century and pave the way for the *News of the World* and the modern popular press. The *Illustrated London News*, first published in 1842, became the first properly illustrated newspaper. It was published by Herbert Ingham, a newsagent from Nottingham who had realized that newspaper sales increased when they included illustrations, usually engravings (it is surprising that this had not been fully appreciated before). At sixpence a copy, it was not really aimed at a populist audience but soon spawned a raft of cheaper imitators, such as the *Pictorial Times*, started by engraver Henry Vizetelly, who was later among those who campaigned for the repeal of the Stamp Act to allow them to publish at a cheaper price. He also published the *Illustrated Times Weekly*, priced at twopence, ahead of the abolition of the Act in 1855 and was threatened with fines, but the paper survived and thrived. Its engravers included the renowned French artist Gustave Doré. Vizetelly himself subsequently became the Paris Correspondent of the *Illustrated London News* and had a long career as a writer and publisher. Abolition of paper duty in 1861 allowed even cheaper publications, such as the *Penny Illustrated Paper*, which again had a popular agenda; a raft of imitators followed, including the *Illustrated Police News*, first published in 1864, which took graphic reporting to another level entirely, illustrated with many engravings of horrific crimes and tragedies such as transport accidents, which had been the staple of the Victorian penny dreadfuls.

It was, however, the advent of the Sunday-only papers that truly created the second of the prime building blocks of the popular press of the late nineteenth century. Sunday papers were cheaper because they cost less to produce, usually being mostly printed during off-peak periods over the course of the week. They could cater to a different audience, one that had the leisure time to read, and by adopting a more popular tone they appealed to the working masses, whose Sundays were their only day of respite from their toils in the factories, mills and mines of the new Britain after the Industrial Revolution.

Founded in 1801, the *Weekly Dispatch* became the first Sunday newspaper in 1815 when it was taken over by barrister Robert Bell and renamed *Bell's Sunday Dispatch*. Bell introduced 'the now familiar formula of sex, sport and sensationalism' with headlines such as 'Dreadful Murder and Suicide' and many detailed reports from courts and of crimes. The paper created a template for such reporting that would much later be taken up by one other publication with even greater success.[1]

Among the new Sunday publications was *John Bull* magazine, whose editor and principal author was Theodore Hook. It quickly gained a large circulation among the educated classes for its mixture of serious political comment and trivia. Hook, a prankster, author and socialite friend of the dissolute Prince Regent, kept his role a secret in order to be able to move in fashionable circles, where guessing his identity became something of an obsession. One of his principal scoops was to obtain a list of some of the titled ladies who were guests at the home of Queen Caroline, the estranged wife of George IV, and then append comments such as 'strangely susceptible to the charms of her own sex' and 'mixed up with a disgraceful and criminal affection for a menial servant'. Another was to publish the names and addresses of jurors who had convicted soldiers who killed two rioters on the day of the queen's funeral. Hook was later arrested for fraud, spent time in a debtors' prison and wrote a number of novels as well as continuing with some journalism before his death in 1841. The poet Coleridge compared his genius to that of Dante.[2]

Lloyd's Weekly Newspaper was founded in 1842 by publisher Edward Lloyd, who had made his fortune in penny dreadful magazines and by plagiarizing versions of Dickens's novels. It was originally titled *Lloyd's Penny Illustrated Newspaper*, was sold for a penny and contained only illustrations, to avoid the stamp duty on newspapers. Within a year, however, he was forced to raise the price and change the name. *Lloyd's Weekly Newspaper* was a relatively sober and balanced publication delivering general news coverage, albeit aimed at a largely working-class audience. By the end of the century it had the distinction of becoming the first newspaper to regularly sell a million copies.

So, in 1843, these various models had laid the path for the publication that would eventually dominate the Sunday market and become the biggest-selling paper in the Western world. It created the template for tabloid newspapers over much of the twentieth century, earned its place in social and cultural history and became the foundation of Rupert Murdoch's British empire, leading eventually to the greatest ever scandal to affect British journalism and ultimately its closure – the *News of the World*.

'News for the Millions'

When he launched the *News of the World* in 1843, John Browne Bell was already a veteran of publishing in the Victorian era. No relation to Robert Bell, he was the son of John Bell, who had launched the *Morning Post* and *Bell's Weekly Messenger*, which were among those that had helped create the thriving Sunday market. By the time he was in his thirties, Browne Bell and his father, who had disinherited his son, were publishing rivals, both launching magazines aimed at women. Browne Bell followed with other general-interest and political publications, two fashion magazines, a Monday newspaper aimed at those in the agricultural trade and a Sunday newspaper, *The Planet.* The *News of the World*, printed at premises just off the Strand, was aimed at the *Lloyd's Weekly Newspaper* market, but also at more middle-class and even upper-class readers, with a mixture of general domestic and overseas news, jokes, literary writing and coverage of the more sensational crime stories. Priced at threepence in order to just undercut its rivals, right from the start the *News of the World* exhibited the same self-confident bullishness that would continue right until its demise, announcing itself as 'The Cheapest, Largest and Best Newspaper' which would deliver 'News for the Millions' and would be 'the novelty of Nations and the wonder of the world'.[3] The front page promised that the *News of the World* would give the poorer classes a paper they could afford and the middle and richer classes a paper they could not afford to ignore on account of its large circulation. Crucially, Browne Bell boosted that circulation by bypassing London news vendors – who demanded that the paper be increased in price to preserve their profits – and selling directly to provincial newsagents, thereby ensuring a solid sale in the provinces for decades to come; these provincial readers became the cornerstone of the paper's remarkable twentieth-century rise in circulation. In the end, the London vendors relented and agreed to sell the paper to satisfy public demand. By Browne Bell's death in 1855, the paper had a circulation of 200,000 a week, though sales would later slump because the paper refused to cut its price when newspaper taxes were abolished and competition became more intense.

What was remarkable about the early history of the *News of the World*, given its later reputation for specializing in crime, sleaze and sensation, was its role as an organ of serious news, with a network of correspondents and an extensive news-gathering operation, as well as its reputation for being a liberal and radical publication. In its early years, the coverage was wide-ranging, containing overseas news, fashion, theatre and literary content, as well as news of agriculture and markets. There was public hunger for coverage of the Crimean War and the Indian Mutiny in the 1850s and then the American Civil War in 1861, which helped boost circulation, with the paper often publishing special editions as early as Friday when important events occurred. Much of the credit for its extensive news-gathering operation was due to the first editor, Henry Drake Bruen, who was determined that the paper would live up to its self-important title. But, in what became its defining trademark, there were also whole pages devoted to lurid stories of crime and lengthy court reports, including public executions, until they ended in 1868. These were often reported in considerable depth, detailing the final hours and last words of the condemned, as well as their weight and the length of the 'drop'. While other papers, such as the *Sunday Dispatch*, did not shy away from such stories, the *News of the World* gained a reputation for both the prominence and space it devoted to them and the graphic nature of some of the reporting. The divorce courts, where hearings were then public, was also a rich source of material, while stories of vice – police raids on brothels, arrests of 'immoral' women and the resulting prosecutions – were given huge amounts of coverage, a practice that continued throughout the paper's existence.

The *News of the World* was not the leader here, but entering an expanding market where the readers were greedy for more. The popular weekly the *Illustrated Police News* had capitalized on the public appetite for penny dreadfuls or 'penny bloods'. Although arguably not really a newspaper at all, the *Illustrated Police News* was socially conscious and radical from its inception, declaring support for universal suffrage, fair wages for the police and proper housing for the working classes, who could be assumed to form the bulk of its readership and for which it was full of praise. It took a serious rather than sensational tone and even included an 'answers to correspondents' column, where legal questions were dealt with by a barrister.[4] But its unique selling point was the pages of dramatic images under headlines such as 'The Murder of Mr Gold on the Brighton Railway' and 'Boys Murder Their Mother'. 'The Horrible Discovery At Gloucester' related to the unearthing of the bodies of a number of dead babies and 'Mrs Pearsey's Dream the Night before Her Execution' depicted the sleeping murderer of a love rival reliving her crimes in her dreams ahead of her date with the scaffold, a common theme. Hangings were of particular interest, as they had been for many years. The *Illustrated Police News* added one key element to the tabloid practice: its illustrators were the stars of the show and were relied upon to provide several engravings that would fill a whole page. Although in some cases these illustrators would be allowed close access to crime and accident scenes, most were representational – a 'how-it-might-have-looked' – particularly when portraying actual crimes, arrests or the moment of the fatal tragedy itself.[5] The practice of 'mocking up' an illustration when an actual image was not available would persist in parts of Fleet Street until the present day.

Such reporting reached its pinnacle with the Jack the Ripper murders in London's Whitechapel area in the latter half of 1888, which filled newspaper columns and fuelled circulations for many months. The *News of the World* attempted to outdo the *Illustrated Police News*. 'Another Horrible Murder in Whitechapel and Another Fiendish Murder in the East End' ran the headlines as one atrocity succeeded another, each more diabolical than the one before. No gory details escaped the writer's attention as interest in the crimes mounted. After the discovery of a fourth victim, one reporter wrote: 'The victim is again a woman of the "unfortunate" class but the circumstances are so atrocious and revolting as to render it difficult to state the facts.' Nevertheless, a full account of the injuries and disembowelment she had suffered followed, with some xenophobic slurs thrown in: 'One would have to go to the wilds of Hungary or search the records of French lower peasant life before a more sickening and revolting tragedy could be told.'[6] The *News of the World* was not alone in its reporting of the Ripper horrors: *The Times*, then the serious voice of the upper classes, also gave the murders prominent coverage, publishing six leading articles on the case, with its detailed report of the final killing running to 5,000 words.

But the *Illustrated Police News* was still ahead of the rest. Despite accusations that it was inspiring as well as reporting crimes and being voted 'The Worst Newspaper in England' by readers of the *Pall Mall Gazette*, it continued to thrive, reaching a weekly circulation of 300,000 by the mid-1880s. This put it in the top six of all weekly publications, then headed by *Lloyd's Weekly Newspaper* with 612,000. As the century drew to a close, it added more elements to its content, including sports reports and overseas news. It also began to run images of 'glamorous' women, while its crime sketches and engravings became more explicit, the text racier. Irrespective of the actual facts of the story, the images would feature women with hourglass figures, where possible in their nightclothes or underwear,

Illustrated Police News front page dedicated to Jack the Ripper, 22 September 1888.

their décolletages on display. There were now pictures of women not involved in crime or tragedy, too: chorus girls, bathing beauties and burlesque stars.[7] The paper also began a column of 'Saucy Songs' full of mild sexual innuendo. This was surely a potent mix that would be reflected in the tabloid and popular agenda for many years to come and would not have gone unnoticed at the paper that claimed to be the best in the world. But the *News of the World* was going through a transition.

After Browne Bell's death in 1855, the paper remained in the hands of his family but its circulation began to decline. It ultimately lacked the capital needed to improve printing facilities and could only watch as other publications, like the *Illustrated Police News* and the *Sunday Dispatch*, stole its readers. In 1891 the company was sold to Henry Lascelles Carr, who had turned the Cardiff-based *Western Mail* into a powerful, successful regional newspaper espousing a kind of radical Conservatism that backed mine-owners but supported greater rights for workers and community facilities such as parks and town bands. Carr's nephew William Emsley Carr, who had worked with him on the *Western Mail*, was installed as editor and remained in post for a remarkable fifty years, becoming the longest-serving editor of any national newspaper. Carr was joined by a London solicitor called George Riddell, who had looked after the *Western Mail*'s legal matters in London and was now drafted in to help manage the *News of the World*'s business side. Together, Carr and Riddell would turn the *News of the World* into the biggest-selling English-language Sunday newspaper in the world – but would also sow the seeds of its demise.

As the Victorian era drew to a close, three wholly new newspapers would be created in the space of just over a decade, the *Daily Mail*, the *Daily Express* and the *Daily Mirror*, while one – the *News of the World* – was substantially reinvigorated. Fuelled by fierce competition for readers, these four newspapers between themselves would define popular and tabloid journalism for the next seventy years. Imitators and challengers emerged and either died or remained in their shadows. It was not until the 1970s and the arrival of Rupert Murdoch's *Sun* that a serious competitor emerged to challenge their hegemony. Until then, these newspapers would dominate the landscape, reflect and influence public taste, hold politicians to account and change the public discourse for ever. But across the Atlantic, in New York, the tabloid wars were already under way.

The Birth of Yellow Journalism

Horatio Sheppard, a New York medical student, was neither a printer nor a publisher, but simply out to make his fortune. In the overcrowded and poverty-stricken Bowery district of the city, he saw that traders were selling small items at a penny – one cent – apiece. Calculating that a large number of small-value sales could realize a fortune every bit as large as a small number of high-priced sales, and aware that other newspapers were selling for around six cents, Sheppard hawked his idea for a penny newspaper around many printers for more than a year until eventually linking up with two other men, Francis Story and Horace Greeley, both of whom were printers and aspirant publishers. Greeley, however, insisted that the paper must be marketed at two cents, not one cent. Sheppard was forced to agree but this sealed the fate of the *Morning Post*, which never sold more than a few hundred copies and lasted barely a month after its first publication on 1 January 1833. Sheppard returned to medicine and Greeley went on to become a well-known editor and politician. The *Morning Post* would have faded from history had it not been seen as 'the seed of the Cheap press'.[8]

That seed took root in Benjamin Day, a printer from New England who had come to New York to work. In the depression of 1833 he started the *New York Sun*, priced at one penny, as a way of making money from the fact that poverty-stricken New Yorkers, particularly the growing immigrant community who had come to the New World to seek their fortune, might favour a cheap, daily paper, similar to those that had achieved popularity in England, as well as to penny dreadfuls. At the top of every page was printed the motto, 'The object of this paper is to lay before the public, at a price within the means of every one, all the news of the day, and at the same time offer an advantageous medium for advertisements.' The paper soon became a success in a city growing at a huge pace and riven by poverty, crime and gang wars. Day was blessed with abundant human-interest stories.

Until then, u.s. newspapers had been aimed at political or 'mercantile' readers; they cost at least six cents and, unlike most papers in Britain, were generally bought on subscription – it wasn't normally possible to buy a single copy on the day. Penny papers changed the business model. They were not subsidized by political parties or commercial ventures, depending instead on advertising revenue, which in turn was linked to circulation. Day realized that his paper had to entertain a new mass audience of middle- and working-class readers; the paper was sold in the street by newsboys, homeless urchins who earned thirty cents a day and roamed the pavements shrieking out lurid headlines. The *New York Sun*'s motto was 'It shines for ALL', reflecting its intention to reach a mass market.

It was also the first newspaper in the United States to popularize publishing police and court reports, including descriptions of arrests for drunkenness, theft and violence, which were delivered in brief paragraphs and in a succinct, direct and often vivid style of reporting. It pioneered the hiring of reporters to go out and find stories. The paper's most popular reporter was George Wisner, an Englishman who had been a crime reporter in London, and who would certainly have been aware of the popularity of crime and court stories among working-class readers; he was so successful he later became the paper's co-owner.[9]

The *New York Sun*'s most serious rival arrived in 1835 in the shape of the *New York Herald*, started by John Gordon Bennett, a Scottish immigrant and a teacher-turned-journalist who had became assistant editor of the more sedate *New York Courier* and *Enquirer*; its creation began the first real circulation war among popular newspapers. Frustrated by the sober tone of the majority of newspapers, Bennett, already in debt, borrowed $500, set up shop in a Wall Street basement and wrote, printed and sold the *Herald* on the streets himself. With its pages devoted to murders, robberies and advertisements for patent medicines, abortionists and prostitutes (thinly disguised), the paper quickly gained a reputation for sensationalism: 'Its four-page, five-column tabloid format was considered by many to be as ugly as its content.'[10] At the same time, in contrast to the *New York Sun*, the *Herald* aspired to be credible, serious and distinct from the political partisanship that guided almost all other publications: 'We shall support no party . . . and we care nothing for any election,' Bennett declared in his first issue. Mindful of its readership of white-collar clerks intent on bettering themselves, Bennett included a Wall Street column giving daily updates on stock prices and advice on investments. While Bennett was criticized for the sleazier aspects of the newspaper, he was committed to factual reporting and loved to break news stories, sending his reporters to cover both high and low society, declaring:

> I mean to make the Herald the great organ of social life, the prime element of civilisation, the channel through which native talent, native genius and native power may bubble up daily... I shall mix together commerce and business, pure religion and morals, literature and poetry, the drama and dramatic purity till the Herald shall outstrip everything in the conception of man.[11]

In response to the success of the *Herald*, the *New York Sun* launched a series of hoax stories about life on the moon, which saw its circulation rise exponentially. Only when the *Herald* claimed the articles were false did the *Sun* come clean, although its circulation of around 19,000 barely suffered. The articles were probably written by the paper's editor, Richard Adams Locke, a descendant of the seventeenth-century English philosopher John Locke. 'Locke's moon hoax was the forerunner of all of those extra-terrestrial alien invasion stories that in modern times have become a staple of the sensationalist supermarket tabloids and cable television specials.'[12] The tradition in the early news sheets of reporting 'Strange Newes' – stories that readers only half-believe, but revel in the enjoyment of thinking they might just possibly be true – was used by almost every tabloid newspaper thereafter.

The story for which the *Herald* would become most celebrated was that of the brutal murder of fashionable prostitute Helen Jewett and the subsequent trial and acquittal of the suspect, office clerk Richard P. Robinson. In the spring of 1836 the story and its coverage became a pivotal event in the growth of American tabloid newspapers. While the reporting of sex crimes and violence was nothing new, it was the first such scandal to be given really detailed coverage, with the *Herald* making the story its own by creating a dramatic and detailed narrative of the case. The trial polarized the *Herald* and the *Sun*, the former of which was sympathetic to Robinson while the latter, the paper of the working man, argued that Robinson had been able to use money and influence to ensure his acquittal, following evidence of an alibi. The case also saw the first example of the 'extra' or special edition, which, with the use of new and higher-speed

Constantine von Grimm ('Nemo'), caricature of James Gordon Bennett Jr, *Vanity Fair*, 1884.

presses, could be on the street in a matter of hours. 'We give the additional testimony up to the latest hour,' the paper trumpeted. The *Sun* accused Bennett of being bribed by Robinson; the *Herald* then published a letter supposedly from the 'real' murderer, which, in an angry editorial, the *Sun* described as a 'diabolical forgery by James Gordon Bennett, the unprincipled editor . . . we have long known this man to be more unblushingly unprincipled than any other that pollutes the public press.'[13] Bennett wasn't troubled: by the time of the acquittal, the *Herald*'s circulation had risen from 4,000 to 16,000 and by August 1836 it was able to double its price. Two years after founding it, Bennett claimed his own worth to be near $100,000 and the *Herald* was the city's leading newspaper.

Bennett was not just a sensationalist. He initiated many of the traits of the modern populist newspaper: sports reports, society gossip and an advice column. 'His adroit use of telegraph, pony express, and even offshore ships to intercept European dispatches set high standards for rapid news gathering.'[14] But he was no liberal: the *Herald* often employed racist language and he supported Southern secession, attacked unions, opposed the abolition of slavery and criticized Abraham Lincoln. By 1860 the paper claimed to have the largest circulation in the USA. His name lives on; there are streets named after him in New York and Paris and the expression of incredulity or astonishment 'Gordon Bennett!' derives from his exploits.

Before his death in 1871, Bennett ceded control of the paper to his son, James Gordon Bennett Jr, who spent most of his life in Paris. Although he rarely visited the New York offices, was a reckless drunk and spent wildly on indulgences such as cars and speedboats, he had acute journalistic sensibilities and a more worldly view of events. Despite the geographical distance, he managed to exert a tight hold over the paper for more than four decades. It was Bennett Jr who was responsible for one of the most audacious journalistic stunts of all time when in late 1869 he ordered one of his correspondents, the Welsh-born Henry Stanley, to spare no expense in finding the Scottish explorer and missionary Dr David Livingstone. Livingstone had not contacted the outside world for several years while searching for the source of the Nile in central Africa. Bennett's motive was twofold – to get a good story and make a calculated jibe at the British establishment, who were seemingly uninterested in the fate of Livingstone.

Journalistic licence ran through the story, as it has done in many tabloid 'exclusives' since. Livingstone, well known in missionary circles, was not a household name on either side of the Atlantic and since he was not widely known to be 'lost' there was no public clamour for him to be 'found'. Although ill, he could have attempted to return home and he refused Stanley's entreaties to accompany him back to England. Indeed, he was not particularly happy that the expedition to find him had been funded by the *Herald*, which he termed 'a despicable paper'.[15]

However, the men became firm friends and travelled together for a further five months. Livingstone remained in Africa and died two years later. Stanley's story, published in the 2 May 1872 edition of the *Herald* under the headline 'Livingstone Safe', created an international sensation, partly because the *Herald* declared it to be – again, another tabloid tactic. Although Stanley's account was greeted with some cynicism, since the paper had a reputation for making up stories, he had extensive proofs and returned a celebrity. His life continued in its extraordinary fashion – he took part in more expeditions to Africa, became a colonial administrator for Belgium in the Congo, returned to England to marry the artist Dorothy Tennant, was elected Liberal MP for Lambeth North and was knighted for services to Empire.

The *Herald* certainly embodied many of the qualities of what would later be known as 'yellow journalism', later alternatively labelled tabloid, which was itself the product of a fierce circulation war between the two newspaper proprietors who would define American journalism for decades and would in turn influence the development of newspapers back in Britain.

By the second half of the nineteenth century, technological advances were helping to create a speedier, more hard-nosed style of writing. The invention of the rotary press in 1843 allowed more copies to be printed, while Samuel Morse's electric telegraph the following year allowed swifter means of communication from reporters on the ground. Journalistic practices were further refined by momentous events such as the American Civil War, which provided journalists with a real, dramatic conflict on their own doorstep. War reporting made it necessary to transmit copy rapidly over the still-new telegraph service, where every word cost money and the threat of disrupted lines of communication was ever present. It thereby

Joseph Pulitzer on a composite front cover of his newspapers, *c.* 1904, chromolithograph.

contributed to the advent of a more rapid, concise style of writing. Thus was the inverted pyramid of news writing born: key facts at the top, the rest in descending order of importance. The leisurely, literary-style essays of the Georgian and Victorian eras were being replaced by modern news writing on both sides of the Atlantic.

The new journalism, yellow or not, was being created. And the two men who did more than any others to bring that about were William Randolph Hearst and Joseph Pulitzer. They could not have been more different: Pulitzer, a Jewish immigrant, had a burning social conscience and a desire to provide both information and enter-tainment to the masses; Hearst was the indulged son of a wealthy

Californian politician and businessman, and only wanted to make more money. In their rivalry, they would change journalism for ever.

Born in Hungary in 1847 to a middle-class Jewish family, Joseph Pulitzer wanted to join the military but was rejected by European armies because of his poor health and eyesight. However, he was able to enlist in the Union Army in the Civil War, which brought him to America. After the war he travelled to St Louis, learned English and law and became a reporter on a German-language newspaper serving the local immigrant community. Hard work earned him a controlling interest in the paper, giving him the money to buy the most important paper in the city, the *St Louis Post-Dispatch*, in 1878. Although by now wealthy and part of St Louis's social elite, Pulitzer used his platform to expose municipal corruption and tax dodging among the local rich, in the face of strong opposition. In 1882 in New York, on his way to Europe, Pulitzer noted that the small-circulation *New York World* was struggling and up for sale. He snapped it up cheaply and remade the *World* in line with his vision. 'He turned the World into an advocate for the common worker, both immigrant and native born, and shone a spotlight on the corrupt practices of local businessmen and corrupt officials. He also included plenty of reports about street crime and lurid scandal.'[16] Pulitzer promised readers:

> We will always fight for progress and reform, never tolerate injustice or corruption, always fight demagogues of all parties, always oppose privileged classes and public plunderers, never lack sympathy with the poor, always remain devoted to the public welfare, never be satisfied with merely printing news, always be drastically independent, never be afraid to attack wrong, whether by predatory plutocracy or predatory poverty.[17]

All of this was portrayed with vigour and large, dramatic headlines: one story about the tragic deaths of hundreds of babies in a heatwave was headlined 'HOW BABIES ARE BAKED'. While he drove his reporters hard and understood the journalistic tactic of highlighting juicy details and employing dramatic language, Pulitzer was a stickler for accuracy and proper research, a sign in the newsroom reading 'Accuracy, Accuracy, Accuracy! Who? What? Where? When? How? The Facts – The Colour – The Facts!'

Pulitzer's style of investigative reporting eventually became known in New York, perhaps inappropriately, as 'muckraking'. As Harold Evans, former editor of the *Sunday Times*, pointed out in its defence:

> Crooks in City Hall. Opium in children's cough syrup. Rats in the meat packing factory. Cruelty to child workers . . . Scandal followed scandal in the early 1900s as a new breed of writers investigated the evils of laissez-faire America . . . The muckrakers were the heart of Progressivism, that shifting coalition of sentiment striving to make the American dream come true in the machine age. Their articles, with facts borne out by subsequent commissions, were read passionately in new national mass-circulation magazines by millions of the fast-growing aspiring white-collar middle class.[18]

And 'muckraking' drove sales. The circulation of the *World* went from 15,700 in May 1883 to 250,000 by 1887, easily overtaking the

William Randolph Hearst, early 20th century.

Herald and soon doubling that figure, making it the biggest newspaper in the country.

Among those Pulitzer employed in the *World*'s first few years was the wealthy Harvard dropout William Randolph Hearst. Hearst needed to learn the trade of journalism to prepare to take over the *San Francisco Examiner*, the loss-making newspaper his businessman father, Senator George Hearst, had bought to further his own political career. Hearst Jr had become interested in newspapers, at least the money to be made from them, after his success as the co-business manager of the college humour magazine the *Harvard Lampoon*. But he clearly had an instinctive understanding of popular journalism. Writing to his father in 1885, the young Hearst demonstrated a remarkable 'depth of understanding about newspapers as well as an extraordinary insight concerning journalism of the future'.[19] Hearst told his father:

> it would be well to make the paper as far as possible original, to clip only when absolutely necessary and to imitate only some such leading journal as the *New York World* which is undoubtedly the best paper of that class to which the *Examiner* belongs – that class which appeals to the people and which depends for its success upon enterprise, energy and a certain startling originality and not upon the wisdom of its political opinions or the lofty style of its editorials.[20]

Hearst had understood that in this new journalism,

> the *World* catered to the immigrant, the workingman, the semiliterate, who had swelled the population of New York City to almost 3 million. Headlines were therefore of utmost importance for an urban newspaper; they must be concise, direct, informative – and definitely 'bold' and large in type. As one immigrant put it, the headlines 'are easy to understand, and you know all the news.' Sketches, both profuse and descriptive, were a necessary companion to any story, which must be told in a simple, direct way; in other words, the sentence structure must be 'uncomplicated' and the vocabulary 'simple'. Equally important, reporters must focus on stories of interest: the ageless success formula of love and sex,

Nellie Bly, *c*. 1890.

tragedy and pathos, crime and violence. But above all else, Hearst realised that the *World* was entertaining, with stories having to do with sensationalism as well as local concerns.[21]

In March 1887 Hearst took control of the *Examiner* and transformed it editorially, with massively increased advertising and shameless self-promotion. The paper was bold and aggressive in its appeal: 'One-half-inch black headlines, usually three or four in eight columns (instead of nine), appeared where previously one-fourth-inch headlines had been the standard. By March 8 these attention-getters increased to every column and were up and down the page instead of only at the top.' Hearst set about recruiting a stellar staff: 'a remarkably talented but highly eccentric group of men and women, to whom he paid generous salaries and treated with great patience'. They included columnist Ambrose Bierce, 'an evil-tempered man who habitually carried a loaded pistol to ward off readers . . . infuriated by his columns'.[22] Bierce worked on and off for Hearst for two decades.

Both Hearst and Pulitzer employed star women reporters, then something of a rarity. Pulitzer hired Nellie Bly, who had pioneered investigative reporting – mainly of employment conditions for women – in her native Pittsburgh, after she talked her way into his office and agreed to feign mental illness to gain admission to a notoriously brutal asylum for women in New York. Her reports caused a sensation, ushering in the era of 'stunt girl' journalism. Her stunt was to replicate, largely on her own, the journey in Jules Verne's book *Around the World in Eighty Days*, completing the trip herself with eight days to spare, helped by Pulitzer hiring a train to take her from San Francisco to New York. Bly's biographer, Brooke Kroeger, wrote:

> The employment of 'stunt girls' has often been dismissed as a circulation-boosting gimmick of the sensationalist press. However, the genre also provided women with their first collective opportunity to demonstrate that, as a class, they had the skills necessary for the highest level of general reporting. The stunt girls, with Bly as their prototype, were the first women to enter the journalistic mainstream in the twentieth century.[23]

Bly continued to write about poverty and labour conditions for women for the *World* and, much later, reported on the First World War.

Hearst, not to be outdone, hired former chorus girl Winifred Sweet, who, under the pen name Annie Laurie, became the first of Hearst's 'sob sisters', a kind of parallel track to stunt girls, purveyors of human-interest stories guaranteed to bring tears to the eyes of readers. But she was also a stunt girl, once faking collapse in the street so she could be taken to hospital and witness the appalling conditions suffered by the poor in San Francisco's emergency wards. Some of the *Examiner*'s human interest stories were exaggerated. In one case, a reporter made up a story about three orphan boys, prompting an outpouring of donations from readers and forcing the paper to photograph some ragged street children, dress them in new clothes and photograph them again for the next edition.

The *Examiner*'s mix of sensationalist stories, proper investigative reporting, star writers, extensive use of pictures, sob-story campaigns and increased advertising made it hugely successful. By the mid-1890s Hearst had set his eyes on New York and in 1895 bought the ailing *Morning Journal*, where he repeated his successful formula: a vigorous layout, banner headlines and the recruitment of talented staff, including Bierce and humorist Mark Twain. Hearst poached Pulitzer's most valued editors, artists and reporters by offering massively inflated salaries. He increased its size to twelve pages and reduced its cost to a penny, assailing the *World*, which cost two cents, with a masthead slogan: 'You can't get more than all the news. You can't pay less than one cent.' Hearst was 'losing money on every copy he sold, and the more copies he sold the more money he lost, but he didn't care. He wanted circulation.'[24] Pulitzer, by now 48 years old, blind, ill, tyrannical and of such a nervous disposition that the sound of rustling paper could send him into a whirlwind of rage, attempted to ignore his first and only serious competitor. But losing staff forced him to fight back.

Among those whom Hearst stole from the *World* was cartoonist Richard. F. Outcault, who drew a regular colour cartoon strip called *Hogan's Alley*. This documented characters from the poverty-stricken areas of New York and prominently featured a young boy called Mickey Dugan. Dugan became known as 'the Yellow Kid': he was shaven-headed – the implication being that it was because of lice – and wore an oversized yellow nightshirt. The 'Yellow Kid' strip was immensely popular. Hearst wanted the cartoon for himself and poached Outcault, whose cartoon became more violent and vulgar but retained its popularity. But because Outcault had not been able to copyright the image of the character, Pulitzer employed another artist to create a similar cartoon, with the result that for about a year the same character appeared in both papers. The term 'yellow journalism' appears to have originated from comments about the style of their journalism made by Ervin Wardman, publisher of the *New York Press*, and by Charles A. Dana, now the proprietor and editor of the *New York Sun*, when they called for a boycott of both papers because of their aggressive sensationalism; they were supported by some libraries and public institutions. There may well have been a good deal of self-interest in the move by Wardman and Dana. There is also evidence the phrase had been used informally by journalists in the city for a while.

The battle between the two led to accusations of sensationalism and, in some cases, falsification. 'Sensationalism, through it had always existed to some extent, was taken to new extremes.'[25] Pulitzer, despite his ethical intentions, was sucked into the battle. Corners were cut and he was 'not above "punching up" . . . by exaggerating the importance of juicy details or employing creative language'.[26] At the *Morning Journal*, Hearst was more laissez-faire about controlling his staff: 'There, as had happened at the *San Francisco Examiner*, stories were padded or outright fabricated, often by exhausted broke employees.'[27] Hearst expected big, loud headlines and striking images: 'One thing Hearst demanded from his papers was excitement. He would read every one of them carefully every day. If the issue did not contain an adequate number of shocks he would grumble, "this is like reading the telephone directory."'[28]

Backed by extensive promotional campaigns, the *Journal* attempted to undercut the power base of the *World*: its support for Democratic politicians and the city's poor was more vociferous and more active, it launched campaigns for public parks and an eight-hour working day and it opposed big business. It exposed police corruption and actively investigated crimes ahead of the police, claiming to have once solved a particularly grisly murder. Employee numbers rose and staff were sent around the country and the world. The size of headlines and number of pages increased and by 1897 its Sunday edition was printed in colour, more than eighty years before colour images were commonplace in the UK. Its circulation matched the *World*'s, at around 600,000 daily sales each. Competition between the two men and their papers was intense. Both outsold their other rivals in the packed New York daily newspaper market and Dana and Warman's campaign was a failure – readers were unmoved.

The *Journal* and the *World* were far and away the most popular papers in the city . . . A moral crusade by their competitors
was doomed to fail. The yellow journals were undeniably
more entertaining and possessed more energy than any other
paper in New York. No one was going to stop reading them
in favour of their more boring counterparts.[29]

The yellow journalism wars reached their height in the coverage
of a real war: the now largely forgotten four-month-long Spanish–
American War of 1898, which followed a dispute between the two
countries over Cuba. Both Hearst and Pulitzer took an overheated,
nationalistic approach in agitating for the war, which neither country really wanted. Many believe that Hearst actually conjured up
public support for the war – that in order to satisfy his gargantuan
hunger for circulation he needed not only to report the news but
to make it. In his biography of Hearst, W. A. Swanberg wrote: 'It
was an unnecessary war. It was the newspaper's war. Above all it
was Hearst's war.' In meetings Hearst habitually referred to it as
'our war', according to Swanberg.[30] This is reinforced by the possibly apocryphal story of Hearst saying to a photographer unable
to find any evidence of fighting: 'You furnish the pictures, I'll furnish the war.' (This approach may have been the inspiration for
the speech by Lord Copper, proprietor of the fictional *Daily Beast*,
in Evelyn Waugh's great satire of the early twentieth-century journalism, *Scoop*, when he sends a reporter to cover a war in Africa:
'A few sharp victories, some conspicuous acts of personal bravery . . . and a colourful entry to the capital. That is the *Beast* policy
for the war.' However, many others suggested the model was
Lord Beaverbrook.) At the height of the conflict, both papers had
amassed around 1.5 million daily readers.

When the war ended, so too did the conflict between the newspapers. Hearst began to expand his interests into other newspapers
and magazines, as well as launching his political career, which never
took off in the same way as his journalism. Pulitzer, embarrassed
at the excesses, shrank back from sensationalism and reinstated
his commitment to investigating corruption in public life as well as
reinforcing journalistic standards. The *World* retained its circulation lead over the *Sun* and, in a generous gesture to the rising star
from over the pond, invited Alfred Harmsworth to edit the edition

Alfred Harmsworth,
c. 1910-15.

of 1 January 1901, ushering in the twentieth century. Harmsworth, in using the word 'tabloid', changed all the reference points for journalism, although few noticed at the time.

Pulitzer donated $2 million to fund the Columbia School of Journalism and, perhaps to assuage his guilt, established the Pulitzer Prize to recognize excellence in journalism; it is still known as a benchmark of quality in journalism today. So yellow journalism, in fact, eventually helped support quality in journalistic work. Although Pulitzer's name lives on in the award, as a person he is far less well known. Hearst much more so as the thinly disguised model for *Citizen Kane*, the title character of the remarkable 1941 film by Orson Welles, now widely considered to be one of the greatest movies ever made. By the 1930s Hearst presided over a huge empire, which included, as well as a large stable of newspapers with around 20 million readers, radio, newsreels, film magazines and news agencies. His voice and influence were strong and ubiquitous. Although at the point *Citizen Kane* was made, his corporation had been weakened by the Great Depression, it was still a powerful entity and as such all mention of the film and any advertising for it were banned in all his publications. His journalists attacked Welles at every opportunity and he used his influence in Hollywood to try to undermine the film's impact. While *Kane* was critically lauded and nominated

Front cover of *Tit-Bits*, 24 June 1882.

for nine Academy Awards, it received only one, for Best Original Screenplay, and was not at that time a commercial success.

Hearst lived until 1951, but it was the journalism of his early decades that had the most profound influence. He set the benchmark for interventionist, strident journalism, unafraid to cover the seamier side of life or to fight back against its critics. Dozens of copy-cat newspapers sprang up around the United States, some sleazier than others. He set new benchmarks for popular, and what would become tabloid, journalism. In Britain, too, the influence of yellow journalism was felt during the 1890s. No more so than at the *News of the World*, undergoing a transformation by a man very different in personality to Hearst but equally adept at understanding public taste. And then came Alfred Harmsworth, who was busy inventing popular journalism for the new middle classes.

'The Chief'

The man who first used the word 'tabloid' to describe his new type of condensed and concentrated journalism, who built the first great British newspaper empire and became known as 'the Chief' to all who worked for him, died at the age of only 57, his brain addled by disease. The influence and obsessions of Alfred Harmsworth, later Lord Northcliffe, continue to shape the newspapers that many of us read every day both as physical copies and online, which are still controlled by his brother's family.

Born to a middle-class Anglo-Irish family in Dublin in 1865, Harmsworth was one of the sixteen children born to Alfred Harmsworth Sr, a teacher-turned-barrister and alcoholic, and his Irish wife, Geraldine. It was she who kept the family together and, after they moved to London in search of work, kicked the teen-age Alfred Jr out of their Hampstead home when he impregnated a chambermaid. Homeless, he was forced to find a way to earn a living and so sought out journalism – a venture he did with astonishing success. He would also spend the rest of his life trying to please his mother.

Harmsworth had already shown an aptitude for the trade he would use to make his fortune. He was a voracious reader and a good writer. When Harmsworth was in his teens, George Jealous, founder and editor of the *Hampstead and Highgate Express*, who had given Alfred a toy printing set when he was a child, asked him to write short articles for the paper during the summer holidays. Before he was sixteen, he had persuaded J. V. Milne, father of the writer A. A. Milne and headmaster of Harmsworth's school, Henley House School in Kilburn, to let him launch a school magazine, the first of many launches. With characteristic self-confidence, he declared in the first issue that the *Henley House School Magazine* would become 'a marked success'; in the second, he congratulated himself on the accuracy of his prediction.[31] He would adhere to this policy of overwhelming self-confidence all his life.

Harmsworth, all his biographers agree, was by his mid-teens hardworking and excellent at sport, impressively tall, blond, blessed with striking good looks and full of a precocious confidence. He was gregarious and outgoing, and had drawn up a career masterplan, which he called his 'Schemo Magnifico'. After being thrown out of home and abandoning any idea of university, his innate self-belief enabled him to work for a number of newspapers and make several good contacts. One of these was George Newnes, editor of *Tit-Bits*,

Harold Harmsworth, later Viscount Rothermere, *c.* 1910–15.

a magazine devoted to odd and interesting facts and stories rather than everyday news. Harmsworth wrote two books for Newnes, one on ways to earn money and the other on railways. Ill health led him to move to Coventry, out of London's polluted air, where he worked on publications including *Bicycling News*, and for the Iliffe family, later owners of the *Birmingham Post* and *Evening Mail*. By the age of 21 he had been offered a partnership in the company. He turned it down, because his ambitions extended beyond the world of provincial newspapers. He had enough experience and, above all, confidence in his own abilities to be able to borrow money to launch his own series of magazines, beginning with the weekly *Answers to Correspondents*, in 1888. Printed on A4-sized paper, it expanded on the *Tit-Bits* model of interesting oddities and facts and continued the tradition of Dunston's *Athenian Mercury* and Defoe's 'Advice from the Scandalous Club'. It was assembled by Harmsworth and his new wife, Mary, at their rented home in West Hampstead, where they were desperately short of money. The first edition to be sold contained the blatantly made-up line 'praised by the Clergy, the Press and the Public' and was actually numbered as issue three in a neat bit of promotional sleight-of-hand. Its subjects would typically be 'How Madmen Write', 'How Divers Dress' and 'A Year Only Eighty-Seven Days Long', and it was supported by various promotional stunts, giveaway prizes and puzzle competitions.

By now Alfred had been joined by his younger brother, Harold, who provided the financial acumen the mercurial and driven Alfred sorely lacked, leaving him free to concentrate on journalism. *Answers* was followed by *Comic Cuts*, a joke-packed pictorial magazine for adults with the slogan 'Amusing Without Being Vulgar'. Both magazines were a huge success. They were followed by many others, some intended for a distinctly female and middle-class market, with titles such as *Home Sweet Home* and *Home Chat*. Others were aimed at the teenage boy market that had been created by 'penny dreadfuls', with titles like *Boys' Home Journal*. By the fifth birthday of *Answers*, the firm's combined weekly sales figure was around 1.5 million, the largest of any magazine company in the world. Harmsworth was still in his twenties.

The two brothers, who had become rich and successful within such a short time, had ambitions to break into newspapers. In 1894 they were approached by two experienced Fleet Street journalists,

Louis Tracy and Kennedy Jones, with the idea that they should purchase the almost bankrupt *London Evening News*. London's nine evening papers were all fighting for survival and the *Evening News* struggled the most. They saw an opportunity to acquire a paper at a relatively low price, which would enable them to test their plans for launching a new national newspaper. Alfred's populist presentation – short, eye-catching stories, illustrations to break up the text (an innovation from the U.S. newspapers he was keenly studying) and a women's page – combined with Harold's business flair confounded the cynics in the rest of Fleet Street. The streetwise Glaswegian Kennedy Jones was put into the editor's chair. Possibly the first hard-bitten, instinctively populist editor in the yellow journalism mould that Fleet Street had seen, he stayed with Harmsworth for many years. Jones's mantra was 'Don't forget you are writing for the meanest intelligence,' in direct contrast to the more lofty image that the editors and owners of *The Times* and *The Telegraph* had of their readers. Within a year, circulation of the *London Evening News* had grown to 160,000; it became the biggest-selling evening newspaper in the world. By 1896 its profits enabled Harmsworth to launch his

First edition of the *Daily Mail*, 4 May 1896.

first newspaper from scratch – the *Daily Mail*. This was the paper that would transform popular journalism.

Harmsworth knew what was happening in America, with the successes of Hearst and Pulitzer, and was influenced by what was now, in the mid-1890s, being termed 'new journalism', although 'yellow journalism' was also often used as an alternative. The term was coined to distinguish a more populist approach than the formal reporting of the serious-minded papers, with their emphasis on politics and foreign affairs, but distinct from gossip-, scandal- and crime-orientated publications like the *News of the World*. The Victorian age was ending; there was increased literacy and a new, educated middle class whose tastes fell between the more scandalous gossip sheets and the highbrow, masculine-centred journalism of *The Times* and *The Telegraph*, aimed at a readership among the cultural, business and political elites. (The term 'new journalism' returned to popular use in the late 1960s and early '70s in a different way, describing a style of usually highly subjective, colourful journalism, often written in first-person reportage.)

Journalists now started to develop a more acute social conscience, reflecting the ideas of the radical press of the nineteenth century. One of the drivers of this was W. T. Stead, editor of the *Pall Mall Gazette*, who deplored the seamy stories of the *News of the World* and campaigned over moral issues such as child prostitution, which led to him being jailed for publishing an interview with a sixteen-year-old girl who offered to sell him her virginity. But Stead's headlines themselves were, to some eyes, titillating: 'The Confessions of a Brothel Keeper', 'Strapping Girls Down' and 'I Order Five Virgins', to take a few. Stead was denounced by MPs and other newspapers for 'offensive' and 'lascivious curiosity'.[32]

Another crusader was T. P. O'Connor, the Irish-born politician who, inspired by the success of Hearst and Pulitzer in America, launched *The Star* in 1888, a four-times-a-week evening newspaper, one of whose writers was George Bernard Shaw, which aimed to champion the underprivileged and campaign for social justice. Like other popular practitioners, it also aimed to be 'animated, readable and stirring' and to 'do away with the hackneyed style of obsolete journalism and verbose and prolix articles'.[33] It used colourful and direct language, put news on the front page and was the first newspaper to carry a political cartoon; despite its serious-minded and radical approach, it became known for its lurid, teasing headlines, never more so than in its extensive coverage of the Jack the Ripper case. Its success was at the expense of other papers, such as the *Evening News*, setting the scene for its purchase by the Harmsworths. By the mid-1890s both papers competed for the highest circulation in London.

The 'new journalism' would revive a staple of all popular journalism: the personal details of public figures, which, after the excesses of Georgian times, had taken a back seat during the prudish Victorian era. O'Connor praised 'new journalism', citing its similarity to historical writing in its desire to describe 'the habits, the clothes or the home and social life of any person'. He added: 'I hold that the desire for personal details with regard to public men is healthy, rational and should be yielded to.'[34] Harmsworth was no social reformer, but he embraced the O'Connor definition in its determination to put personality at the forefront of its reporting.

After 65 days of dummy runs, on the night of 3 May 1896 the first copies of the *Daily Mail* came off the presses. Harmsworth, not having slept for two nights, signed the first copy for his mother, Geraldine. The style of the front page drew on the best elements of all the other daily newspapers, but right from the start the *Mail* knew its audience (as it still does today). On either side of the masthead two boxes defined its appeal: 'THE BUSY MAN'S DAILY JOURNAL', said one, while the other proclaimed: 'A PENNY NEWSPAPER FOR ONE HALFPENNY'. The *Mail* was aimed at the new commuting classes, City workers trundling in from the suburbs on the new Underground lines and trams, the aspirant lower middle classes and the upper working classes. Stories were short, headlines were sharp and focused and there was a blend of hard news and softer features aimed at women, who were given their first 'women's page', together with literary serials, also largely aimed at women.

The formula for the *Mail* drew on a variety of sources – nothing, apart from a designated women's page, was absolutely new – but what Harmsworth, assisted by the tough and experienced Kennedy Jones as second-in-command, did brilliantly was to synthesize the best of the elements he wanted from elsewhere: the direct style of writing of papers like *The Star*, the colourful, personalized reporting so popular in America, together with the menu of crime and court stories, sport and entertainment news that had made the Sunday papers so successful.

The paper was – and would always be – concisely edited: sub-editors skilled at knocking poorly written copy into shape, spotting errors, trimming the excess fat and writing eye-catching headlines would take a greater role than ever before in reinforcing the paper's open and accessible writing style. 'Explain, simplify, clarify' was the instruction Harmsworth gave his journalists. 'All the news in the smallest space,' the paper boasted. What was also important was what was missing from 'all the news': the closely printed paragraphs of political speeches, routine parliamentary debates, legal judgements, City news and columns of foreign correspondence that characterized a paper like *The Times*, which had an overwhelmingly male, monied, usually entitled, politically aware readership with the leisure time to absorb these long dry, impersonal screeds, were largely absent.

> The main difference between the *Daily Mail* style new journalism and the old journalism was that the new papers were more thoroughly edited. Instead of printing huge slabs of undigested verbatim reports, news was rewritten to suit the perceived tastes and interests of its readers, shortened so that more stories could be included and still leave room for advertisments that grew more profitable as circulation expanded. Unlike the old papers, which assumed that their readers had sufficient leisure to wade through the unedited report of a two-hour speech and sufficient education to decide for themselves which were the most significant passages, the new journalism increased the possibility of slanting the news by emphasis or omission to suit the political views of the proprietor.[35]

There was even discussion about dropping the leader columns – the editorials in which newspapers give their own view on the world – but they were retained, in more limited form than elsewhere, on the first day, offering views on trams, crime and 'motor car travel'.

Although the shortened stories created more room, there were also fewer advertisements than in other papers – although, as in all newspapers, they still dominated the front page – because Harmsworth decided they 'spoilt the paper'. This caused some friction with his more cost-conscious brother. Harmsworth spent his money on other innovations that would give the *Mail* a head-start over its competitors: new linotype machines and a modern printing room where the paper was cut and folded at high speed. And Harmsworth's obsession with new technologies led him to install a device that would help to revolutionize the speed at which newspapers could receive information – the telephone. This would soon connect London with the *Mail*'s new offices in Paris and New York and to Harmsworth's own homes.

Harmsworth's *Mail* would create the template for modern popular journalism; he told his staff: 'Every day there is an event which ought to be the outstanding feature of the news column. The clever news editor puts his finger on that, the other man misses it altogether.' And: 'It is hard news that catches readers, features that hold them. Always have a woman's story at the top of all the main news pages in your paper.'[36]

The paper's biggest editorial innovation was on page seven, billed as 'The Daily Magazine No 1 – an Entirely New Idea in Morning Journalism', with an accompanying editorial saying its object was to 'amuse, interest and instruct during the leisure moments of the day'. Harmsworth said the magazine was designed to appeal to both sexes:

> Movements in women's world – that is to say changes in dress, toilet matters, cookery and home matters generally – are as much entitled to receive attention as nine out of ten of the matters which are treated on in the ordinary daily paper. Therefore two columns are set aside for ladies. The man who has not time for this class of reading can leave it severely alone and lose nothing; he gets his Money Market and all the latest news on the other pages.[37]

The page included recipes, pictures of a homemade school dress, a piece about courtship among the Boers of South Africa and a serialized fiction story. The model for the *Daily Mail* and what would become the Femail pages was up and running and would change remarkably little over the succeeding years.

Despite being condemned by the then prime minister Lord Salisbury as 'a newspaper produced by office boys for office boys', it was a success.[38] The first edition sold an extraordinary 397,215 copies and within a couple of years it was up to 500,000. One of its early writers and news editors, Tom Clark, summed up in his diaries how the *Mail* owed its success to 'its play on the snobbishness of all of us – all of us except the very rich and the very poor, to whom snobbishness is not important; for the rich have nothing to gain by it, and the poor have nothing to lose'.[39]

That appeal to the middle classes would come to define the *Mail*. It would also form part of what would become the tabloid mindset: interest in the lives of others, the ordinary, humble person as well as the rich and famous. The newspaper conveyed 'a world fit for the middle classes to live in'.[40] 'Its jingoism, imperialism, nationalism and patriotism – as well as the emotional tone of the copy – captured the feeling of the Edwardian middle classes during a period of relative political and social stability.'[41] But the paper also displayed little care for wider humanity:

> Looking back, what it [the *Daily Mail*] lacked most noticeably was a social conscience ... Alfred [Harmsworth] had no desire to start looking for social evils, and no need. What he had to keep in mind were the tastes of a new public that was becoming better educated and more prosperous, that wanted its rosebushes and tobacco and silk corsets and tasty dishes, that liked to wave a flag for the Queen and see foreigners slip on a banana skin.[42]

While setting out to appeal to women, the *Mail* also reflected Harmsworth's somewhat fixed approach to them, saying in one of his notes to staff:

> Nine women out of ten would rather read about an evening dress costing a great deal of money – the sort of dress they will never in their lives have a chance of wearing, than about a simple frock such as they could afford. A recipe for a dish requiring a pint of cream, a dozen eggs, and the breasts of three chickens pleases them better than being told how to make Irish stew.[43]

By the end of the decade and the century, aided by public interest in the Boer War, circulation was around a million. And while Harmsworth's vision and eye for detail shaped the paper on a daily basis, he was never known as 'the editor' – a title held by several underlings in succession. Harmsworth was known simply as 'The

Chief'. On that New Year's Eve of 1900, when he coined the word 'tabloid' for his particular and now well-honed style of journalism, he was welcoming a new century during which the word would take on new meanings, not all of them good ones.

Enter the Beaver

George Newnes, the publisher of *Tit-Bits*, who was so influential in Harmsworth's career, can also claim to have played a part in the newspaper that, for many years, would be the main rival to the *Daily Mail* – the *Daily Express*. Newnes had employed Somerset-born aspirant journalist Arthur Pearson straight from Winchester School. Under Newnes, whose principal assistant he quickly became, Pearson learnt his trade and how to create popular publications for a broad audience. After six years he left and, like Harmsworth, set up his own publishing business, which was an immediate success, his *Pearson's Weekly* – whose aim was to 'Elevate, Interest and Amuse' – rapidly selling a quarter of a million copies. A number of other magazines followed, such as the penny magazine *Home Notes* and the more literary and political *Pearson's Magazine*, and two early comics. Like Harmsworth, he became rich very quickly, and in 1900, aware of how the *Mail* had created an entirely new market, launched the *Daily Express*, priced at just a halfpenny and aimed at a similar readership with a similar blend of news and features directed at a female audience. Its biggest innovation was to put news stories on the front page, rather than advertisements, but this affected its revenue. Competing with the *Mail* for readers, it struggled to make money for several years. Like James Gordon Bennett and Stanley, Pearson hired an explorer in search of sensational stories, paying the extraordinary figure of Hesketh Vernon Hesketh-Prichard, an author, adventurer, big game hunter and cricketer who had already written for *Pearson's Weekly*, to go first to unexplored Haiti and then Patagonia in search of the giant ground sloth. Hesketh-Prichard's accounts of his travels were said to have enthralled readers of the *Express*. Pearson also expanded into provincial newspapers, briefly owned the *Evening Standard*, launched more magazines and went into book publishing, but failing eyesight led him to step back and he was forced eventually to merge his company with that of his mentor, Newnes, an arrangement that was completed after Pearson's death in 1921, long after he had sold off the *Express*. That company would eventually become part of the International Publishing Corporation, which, many decades later, would own the *Mirror* newspapers.

In 1902 Pearson had also recruited, firstly as foreign editor and then as editor, the American journalist R. D. Blumenfeld. Blumenfeld was well versed in the yellow journalism wars, seeing British newspapers as full of 'great, heavy sided blanket sheets full of dull advertisements and duller news announcements'.[44] Blumenfeld would keep the *Express* afloat for many years until it attracted the interest of Canadian-born Max Aitken, a Conservative MP and businessman anxious to secure the paper's support for his party. In 1912 he began funding the *Express* and in 1916 bought it completely from Pearson. As Lord Beaverbrook, he would turn it into the biggest-selling British newspaper.

3

'SEE THAT YOU SECURE A COPY FOR MADAM'

Five people were key to the success of the *Daily Mirror* in its first two decades, not one of whom was its founder, Alfred Harmsworth. They included two rumbustious drunks who would be counted among the most celebrated journalists of the era, both possessing in abundance what, many decades later, the great reporter Nicholas Tomalin described as the 'rat-like cunning' necessary to succeed in the trade; a Hungarian photographic technician who changed the way we see images in newspapers; an eighteen-year-old girl from Stockton-on-Tees who would go on to found a showbusiness dynasty; and a French actress-turned-journalist, known to walk the streets of *fin de siècle* Paris with her pet lion, named, of course, 'Tiger', on a lead.

The last was Marguerite Durand, an early feminist who campaigned for universal suffrage and to establish trade unions for working women. In 1897, backed by the Rothschild banking family, she set up and ran *La Fronde* (literally 'The Slingshot', named after the 1648 anti-monarchist rebellion), the first daily newspaper staffed entirely by women, aside from the building's caretaker. At its peak, it commanded a circulation of around 50,000. It campaigned on feminist issues, social reform and political activism and covered traditionally male subjects such as sport. Without it, the *Daily Mirror* might never have existed.

In 1903, seeing what *La Fronde* had achieved and aware of the success of upmarket women's magazines such as *The Lady*, Alfred Harmsworth, serial launcher of publications and creator of the massively successful *Daily Mail*, decided he had to create a new national paper entirely for women. Having made a point of catering to female

The reporters' room and the composing room of *La Fronde*, images from *The Sketch*, 2 February 1898.

readers in the *Mail* and having witnessed the success of several of the magazines he published aimed at women, it must have seemed the logical thing to do. At a time when women were generally still much marginalized in society, Harmsworth's *Mail* had a section aimed purely at women, albeit covering conventionally female subjects such as cookery, clothes, hairstyles and sewing patterns. It had employed the first woman war correspondent, Lady Sarah Wilson, who had earned widespread fame for her reporting during the Boer War. Harmsworth himself was surrounded and influenced by strong women. His wife, Molly, had helped him put together his first magazine, *Answers to Correspondents*, and his mother, Geraldine, was an important influence throughout his life: he had witnessed her holding her large family together while his father struggled with alcoholism. In 1903 Harmsworth, not yet forty, was becoming richer every day on the back of the *Mail*'s success; his power and confidence was ever-increasing. With his brother Harold he had just bought the ailing *Weekly Dispatch* from George Newnes, his former employer, and was determined to turn around its fortunes, which in time he did. 'The Chief' must have felt anything he touched would turn to gold.

Paradoxically, Harmsworth would never subscribe to Durand's agenda of suffrage, politics and social issues. He was strongly opposed to votes for women and his interest in social reform was zero. His newspaper would not appeal to the 'naughty New Woman who smoked cigarettes and had unthinkable notions about the vote'. Instead, it 'would attract bright, home-loving ladies, who in turn would attract advertisers of clothes, jewellery, and furniture'.[1] The *Daily Mirror*, as it would be named, would also be produced almost entirely by women, although in the production and printing process men would still be in charge. It would be half the size of a broadsheet, the first tabloid daily newspaper, although still some years away from what we would today call a tabloid in its culture and approach. Harmsworth appointed Mary Howarth, a pioneering woman journalist and at the time features editor of the *Mail*, as the first woman editor of a national daily newspaper, for the salary of £50 a month – a fraction of what her male equivalents were earning. She was not the first female editor of a national newspaper: that honour had already gone to Rachel Beer, who had been editor of the *Sunday Observer*, which was owned by the family of her husband, since 1891.

Harmsworth was in no doubt as to whom the paper was aimed at: 'See that you secure a copy for madam,' urged a front-page promotion in the *Daily Mail* on launch day, 2 November 1903. And the first edition – twenty tabloid pages for a penny – included a signed editorial by Harmsworth promising a broad range of coverage, from 'flowers on the dinner table to the disposition of forces in the Far East'. It went on:

> The *Daily Mirror* is new, because it represents in journalism a development that is entirely new and modern in the world; it is unlike any other newspaper because it attempts what no other newspaper has ever attempted. It is no mere bulletin

of fashion, but a reflection of women's interests, women's thoughts, women's work. The sane and healthy occupation of domestic life.

The front page of a paper clearly aimed at 'gentlewomen' was entirely comprised of advertisements for clothes, jewellery and perfume, while the main story inside was that the king was going to drive a motor car between Buckingham Palace and Windsor Castle. Another story was about how crowded Claridge's was at lunchtime. The rest of the content was equally light and frothy; columns included 'Where Notable People Spent the Weekend' and 'Fashionable Announcements', while the recipe of the day included 'sole à la Savoy and filets de perdreau'. The tone appeared upmarket and aspirational – there was a weather forecast for Biarritz but not Birmingham – and well out of kilter with the more mundane suburban appeal of the other Harmsworth newspapers, particularly the *Mail*.

Unfortunately for Harmsworth and Howarth, it was a disaster, despite a massive promotional campaign. The initial print run of 270,000 was wildly optimistic; the female audience never materialized and within a few weeks it was selling just 25,000 copies. Some saw it simply as another Harmsworth stunt and claimed that it was never his long-term intention to run the paper with an all-women staff. Others said it was only designed to please his mother, although she later urged him to get rid of it. Whether the staff were poorly selected – they were largely drawn from fashion and literary magazines – or simply lacked the right experience was never clear, but with little time to prepare for the launch (unlike in the case of the *Mail*), many of the women buckled under the pressure on the first day, collapsing in panic and tears. Harmsworth sent champagne to revive them. Kennedy Jones, who had been assigned to supervise, later wrote of being astounded 'at the gulf that is fixed between the male and female mind'. He was forced to rename the column headlined 'Our French Letter' as 'Yesterday in Paris' and had to ask male sub-editors to remove some other unintentional sexual references open to dubious interpretation.[2] Harmsworth, never one to tolerate failure for long, acted swiftly and brutally. He asked Henry Hamilton Fyfe, a tough Scotsman who was then editor of the *Morning Advertiser*, the newspaper for the licensing trade, to replace

The Daily Mirror.

No. 1.   MONDAY, NOVEMBER 2, 1903.   One Penny.

READ PAGE THREE FIRST.

First edition of the *Daily Mirror*, 2 November 1903.

Howarth and sort out the mess. Fyfe wrote later that this failure, the first real one Harmsworth had known, hurt him considerably. 'It won't do as a paper for women,' Harmsworth told Fyfe. 'It's taught me two things – that women can't write and don't want to read. But we've got to do something with it.'[3] Howarth could at least return to her berth at the *Mail*, but the rest of the women, who had endured a torrid few weeks, were summarily sacked. Fyfe later recalled that the women tearfully begged him to be allowed to stay and left presents on his desk. 'It was a horrid experience . . . like drowning kittens.'[4]

Harmsworth planned to relaunch the *Mirror* in January. He was aided by an innovation that would revolutionize all journalism: the use of news pictures in daily newspapers. Until this point, photographs could not be used in newspapers unless they were printed very slowly – too slowly for mass-circulation publications – and illustrations had been confined to woodcuts, drawings and cartoons. Arkas Sapt, a Hungarian who edited Harmsworth's *Home Sweet Home* magazine, developed a solution using half-tone blocks, making it possible to print photographs at high speed. He demonstrated that the *Mirror* could print 24,000 copies an hour with pictures on four pages – more than double that of the *Daily Graphic*, the existing 'illustrated' newspaper, which carried woodcut images. After a test run of pictures showing Japanese soldiers in the Far East, the *Mirror* was relaunched on 25 January 1904 as the *Daily Illustrated Mirror* and reduced in price to a halfpenny, the same price as the *Mail* and the *Daily Express*. The key selling point was made obvious across the top of the front page: 'News in Photographs – See Pages 8 and 9' was repeated three times. Underneath, occupying the whole of the front page, was a picture of a popular actress, Miss Marie Studholme, with the caption 'The talented young actress who is playing one of the principal parts in the "The Orchid" at the Gaiety Theatre'. Images of young women would become one of the key selling points of all tabloid journalism. The effect was dramatic – it was a completely different kind of newspaper, where up-to-date images shared space and prominence with text. Within a month, circulation had reached 140,000 and was still rising. Harmsworth then allowed himself an extraordinary mea culpa on the front page of 27 February: 'How I Lost £100,000 on the *Daily Mirror*'. It was, he said, a 'flat, rank and unmitigated failure'. He added: 'It was another instance of the failures made by a mere man in diagnosing women's needs. Some people say that a woman never really knows what she wants. It is certain she knew what she didn't want. She didn't want the *Daily Mirror*.' But with that seemingly invincible self-confidence of his he concluded: 'The *Daily Illustrated Mirror* which has replaced it is certainly one of the simplest journalistic successes with which I have been associated.'

He was right of course. Many of both sexes did want the new *Mirror*: the rise in circulation seemed unstoppable. There were the usual *Daily Mail*-style promotional wheezes and competitions and, for the first time, the *Mirror* displayed the social conscience that would become its hallmark, with stories about child poverty in London and an editorial by Ffye denouncing the country for tolerating malnutrition in 'the Imperial capital'. Fyfe made it clear that the newspaper supported the recently formed Labour Party and declared that socialism was 'the creed of the future' – which, of course, greatly displeased Harmsworth.

Writing many years later, Fyfe set down what was possibly the textbook definition of the serious-minded but popular tabloid newspaper, one that still holds true today:

> The shape and content of the *Daily Mirror* recommended it strongly to those who needed something to help them through their half-hour's journey to work in the morning. Packed in tram, train, or omnibus, standing up perhaps and holding on to a strap with one hand, they required in the other, not a journal to stir thought or supply serious information, but one to entertain them, occupy their minds pleasantly, prevent them from thinking. It was easier to look at pictures than to read print. The news was displayed and worded in a manner that made assimilation simple. Everything in the *Daily Mirror* was calculated to be easy of absorption by the most ordinary intelligence.[5]

Fyfe had recruited the remarkable figure of Hannen Swaffer, then editor of *Harmsworth's Weekly Despatch*, to manage the art department, which organized the photographic coverage. A grammar-school boy from Kent who had learnt his trade in local newspapers, Swaffer was a chain-smoking, scruffy drunkard with strong left-wing views. His straggly long hair topped by a felt hat, he was dubbed 'the

Poet' by Northcliffe on account of his bohemian appearance. He
was assisted by the equally raffish Harry Guy 'Bart' Bartholomew,
a poorly educated former office boy whom Northcliffe had funded
to go to the Slade School of Art; there was unfounded speculation
that he was Northcliffe's illegitimate son. Both men were argumentative and heavy drinkers: Swaffer was stick-thin, mercurial,
quick-thinking, a cigarette always dangling from his lips, while
Bartholomew was stocky and combative. He had become an artist
and illustrator. Although he was later described by Northcliffe's
nephew Cecil Harmsworth King as 'a drunk illiterate', he became
a legendary picture editor and developed technical innovations that
advanced newspaper photography in leaps and bounds. He introduced the simple idea of a 'bold cut' to focus the dramatic content
of images. Swaffer later wrote: 'I had the ideas and Bart was the
master technician.'[6] Together, they transformed the *Mirror* and
helped create the genre of photojournalism. All journalism would
forever be in their debt.

The paper was swamped by thousands of photographs sent in
by amateurs as well as those from the growing number of picture
agencies, for all of which Swaffer was happy to pay large sums.

> The pace was furious. Thousands of amateur snaps were sent
> to the paper; piles of mail bags were emptied all over the
> floor, acid from the engraving rooms . . . rotted the sewers in
> Fleet Street resulting in a huge bill for repairs. Swaffer and
> Bartholomew's experiments in speeding up the block-making
> process – frequently carried out when they were both the
> worse for wear from booze – caused fuse boxes to explode
> with unnerving frequency, leaving Swaffer, Bart and others
> working by candle-light.[7]

Both men worked long hours. Swaffer would often sleep in a
made-up bed in a large cupboard in his office. They worked to make
bulky cameras more portable and to reduce exposure time, and they
encouraged photographers to take risky shots. Fyfe wrote later:

> A paper that could reproduce photographs directly would be
> a novelty with an immediate and compelling appeal. I formed
> the opinion that this man [Arkas Sapt] was certainly not mad,

though perhaps eccentric, and that what he had discovered might, if it satisfied our tests, make the fortune of the *Daily Mirror*. I was right. It did.[8]

There were photographs from Vesuvius, from hot air balloons and Zeppelin airships; of British troops abroad, sporting heroes, cute animals and the funeral of the emperor of Japan. But two types of image would introduce the public to subjects that only a proportion might have seen at first hand but which would eventually become the bedrock of the tabloid newspaper in the UK: young women in theatre, showbusiness and society, and the royal family. One of the first editions of the new *Daily Illustrated Mirror* contained pictures of King Edward VII and his wife and children; circulation trebled overnight.

In 1907 Fyfe was replaced by Alexander Kenealy, like Swaffer and Bartholomew an argumentative heavy drinker, who had earned his tabloid spurs working for Hearst's newspapers. Drawing on that experience, he specialized in stunts to get the paper talked about, once putting a beehive on the *Mirror* building's roof to prove it was possible to make honey in central London, then coating thousands of bees in white flour and offering prizes to anyone who found one. When he died in 1915 he was described as 'the Man Who Saved the *Mirror*', although the work of Swaffer and Bartholomew had arguably given Kenealy the key ingredients for success.

There was one image that would particularly resonate: in 1908 the *Mirror* launched the grandly titled 'World's Most Beautiful Woman' contest – a stunt to fill the paper with pictures of attractive young women – and invited readers to submit photographs. The finalists would have their portraits taken by society photographer Stuart Neame in his Bond Street studio. The winner, eighteen-year-old Ivy Close from Stockton-on-Tees, was, as part of her prize, painted by artist Arthur Hacker for an exhibition at the Royal Academy, then featured on the front of the *Mirror*. The tabloid love affair with pictures of pretty young women began to accelerate: *The Sun*'s Page 3 and the media careers of a number of its stars would be the culmination. This was not just a random picture – like that of Miss Marie Studholme or of a woman who might have done something noteworthy. No, this was the beginning of the symbiotic narrative relationship: the newspaper would create the personality and then follow their story.

# The Daily Mirror

THE MORNING JOURNAL WITH THE SECOND LARGEST NET SALE

No. 2,044. | Registered at the G. P. O. as a Newspaper. | MONDAY, MAY 16, 1910 | One Halfpenny.

EDWARD THE PEACEMAKER AT PEACE: THE LATE KING PHOTOGRAPHED ON HIS DEATH-BED AT BUCKINGHAM PALACE.

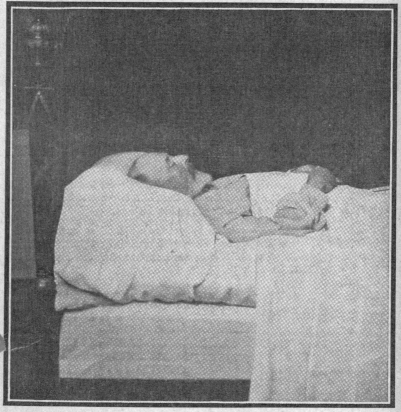

"He looked splendid—I use the word in its regal significance—and as he lay dead his features seemed to reveal the majesty of kingship more than at any moment I remember." These are the words of Sir Luke Fildes, the eminent painter, and were spoken by him after he had left the death-chamber at Buckingham Palace, whither he had been summoned to make a sketch of King Edward the Peacemaker lying on his deathbed. The photograph, which was taken by command of Queen Alexandra by Messrs. W. and D. Downey, of 57, Ebury-street, S.W., May 7, 1910, shows his Majesty after death.

King Edward VII on his deathbed, *Daily Mirror*, 16 May 1910.

The *Mirror* could do this because Ivy Close's leap to fame was not over as quickly as it began. As well as a pretty face, she proved to have genuine talent, leading to a long career as a silent film star in Britain and America. She also married Neame – their wedding was another *Mirror* front page – and their son, Ronald Neame, became a successful film producer (of David Lean's *Brief Encounter*) and director (*The Prime of Miss Jean Brodie*). In 2016 his grandson Gareth Neame, by then one of Britain's leading television producers, responsible for popular television dramas *Spooks* and *Downton Abbey*, alongside others, tracked down the Hacker painting of his great-grandmother Ivy to the Ferens Art Gallery in Hull, where it was in storage because it had deteriorated. He paid for its restoration and rehanging and, in a further tribute, inserted a reference to one of Close's films into an episode of *Downton Abbey*.

Throughout Kenealy's reign, despite frequent violent arguments with Swaffer, the photographs they published would serve to document history: in May 1910 the front page carried the extraordinary image – impossible today – of Edward VII's dead body, taken by the court photographer and bought from him by Swaffer, who had heard about the pictures while in a pub. Some feared retribution from the Palace over such an intrusion, but Queen Alexandra made it known she had approved the exclusive sale to the *Mirror* because, she said, it was her favourite newspaper. When the photograph was reprinted after the funeral, the paper sold around 2 million copies. In 1912, in the wake of the sinking of the *Titanic*, it carried more pictures of the ill-fated liner than any other newspaper. They had been bought up by Swaffer from an Edgware Road photography shop within hours of his having heard of the disaster, although Northcliffe rejected Swaffer's demands that they should also go on the back page. There were disputes between the Bartholomew/Swaffer axis and Northcliffe over whether the *Mail*, which went to press earlier, should have first use: Bartholomew once reputedly cut himself smashing a photographic plate to prevent its being used by the *Mail*.[9] In 1913 the *Mirror* published a photograph of the cairn covering the recently discovered bodies of Antarctic explorer Captain Robert Scott and two of his colleagues and, shortly afterwards, a series of photographs of Emily Davison, the suffragette who died after being trampled by the king's horse at Epsom. By now, the *Mirror*, started on a whim and almost strangled at birth, had overtaken the

Mail's circulation of 800,000 and was the biggest-selling newspaper in Britain.

Harmsworth, knighted in 1904 and ennobled the following year as Lord Northcliffe, was, at the age of forty, said to be the youngest ever peer. Sitting in the Lords for the Conservative Party, he sought power as he had always done, both political and professional. Despite its growing success, Northcliffe was never quite happy with the *Mirror*, which he viewed as 'the bastard offspring' of his family of newspapers and lacking the prestige the *Mail* enjoyed. And opinion of the paper in high society and among his professional peers was low: it was a halfpenny picture paper and the newspaper photographer was seen by other journalists as 'an animal beneath contempt', as Swaffer later recalled.[10]

Northcliffe's mother, whose opinion was sacrosanct, kept saying how much the paper appalled her and urged him to get rid of it. He had accused all the staff under Fyfe of being socialists and said the paper under Kenealy was a 'ghastly mess'.[11] He disliked the stunts, the crowding of sometimes poor pictures on the front page and the light-heartedness of the writing. He did, however, like the way in which the circulation kept rising. But by early 1914 he was increasingly preoccupied with his political aspirations and the rest of his now extensive newspaper empire: the *Evening News*, the more right-wing *Daily Mail* and the influential *Times*, which he had bought in 1908 and which gave him a trusted voice in the ear of the establishment. He had a foot in the more popular end of the Sunday market with the *Dispatch*. He sold his *Mirror* shares to his brother, Harold, who shortly after became Lord Rothermere, for £100,000, the size of his original investment. He was convinced his brother would ruin it. Its daily sales at that point were more than 1 million.

The *Mirror* had a good First World War. Rothermere, a natural accountant and manager, the restraining hand on his brother's shoulder, who had helped turn their innovations and energy into a newspaper empire, had embarked on a regime of cost-cutting that had brought the *Mirror* into good financial order. He was not distracted by his wartime role as minister for aircraft, allowing Ed Flynn, the editor who succeeded Kenealy and Swaffer, largely to run the paper, aided by Bartholomew. Rothermere's major intervention during the war came when he heard that a rival lookalike Sunday picture paper was being planned by the Hulton newspaper group,

ALLIES' DRASTIC ARMISTICE TERMS TO HUNS

The Daily Mirror

CERTIFIED CIRCULATION LARGER THAN THAT OF ANY OTHER DAILY PICTURE PAPER

No. 4,696. Registered at the G.P.O. as a Newspaper. TUESDAY, NOVEMBER 12, 1918 One Penny.

HOW LONDON HAILED THE END OF WAR

The King and Queen appeared on the balcony at Buckingham Palace to acknowledge the cheers of the crowd that gathered to congratulate their Majesties on the victory.

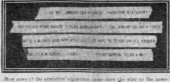
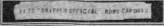

How news of the armistice signature came over the wire to the newspaper offices. A facsimile of it is automatically printed on the tape machine. The cheers which greeted it were the first to be raised.

Home on short leave, but now safe for always from the dangers of Hun bullet and steel.

An historic message as it came over the wire. It is dramatic that the last British war communiqué should proclaim our forces at Mons.

"Now entitled to rejoice" and doing it. Daddy has beaten the Huns and is coming home.

Nothing gave greater satisfaction to all of us than the news that the cessation of hostilities found the British armies once more in possession of Mons, where the immortal

"Contemptibles" first taught the Huns what British valour and steadfastness could do. They left the town as defenders of a forlorn hope; they re-entered it conquerors indeed.

the Manchester-based owners of the *Daily Sketch*, a middle-market tabloid founded in 1909, and the *Sporting Chronicle*: in response, he established the *Sunday Pictorial* in just over a week, which repeated much of the *Daily Mirror* formula and was an immediate success, selling almost 2 million copies within a few weeks of its launch in 1915. Such were the power and resources of the Harmsworth empire.

Flynn decreed that the *Mirror* would become the forces' paper and sent thousands of copies to the trenches carrying news from home. The soldiers themselves came largely from the same working-class communities that the *Mirror* was by then serving and, because news photographers and reporters were not initially allowed near the front line, it encouraged soldiers to send in their pictures, giving the paper a major scoop by publishing the first ever images of a tank in action. Rejected by the Royal Flying Corps because of his poor eyesight, Bartholomew decided to become a war photographer and joined the Canadian Army, taking pictures that would be published in the *Mirror* and later exhibited at the Imperial War Museum; three from the Battle of Ypres in 1918 are still in the museum's archive. The *Mirror* ran images of battles and conflicts around the world, including the first daylight German air raid over London, and by the end of the war its sales had risen to more than 1 million, bringing it into direct competition with the *Mail* for the top spot.

After the war, Swaffer left to write a gossip column for the *Daily Sketch*; he would have a long and illustrious career working for several newspapers, eventually becoming a renowned drama critic known as 'the Pope of Fleet Street'. He would also forsake alcohol for spiritualism. Bartholomew remained at the *Mirror* and would later rise to the very top. Ever inventive, he was responsible for a new method of photographic transmission which became known as the Bartlane Process, developed by him and a production executive at the *New York Daily News*. This enabled images to be transmitted across the Atlantic from New York to London in fewer than three hours using submarine cable lines. Now, images from Broadway and Wall Street could appear in the *Mirror* the following day. The world was beginning to shrink, thanks to journalism. But Northcliffe, the man who had done so much to bring this about, was nearing the end.

The Golf-Mad Magnate

In the early years of the twentieth century Northcliffe's name would be first on the lips of most people asked to name a British newspaper baron – long before the arrival of Rupert Murdoch or Robert Maxwell. Others would cite Lord Beaverbrook, who turned the *Daily Express* into the world's biggest-selling daily paper. Indeed, the name William Randolph Hearst might also be mentioned.

The name of George Riddell, later Baron Riddell, is far less well known. But Riddell helped create the remarkably stable company that would run the *News of the World* for nearly eighty years, as well as cementing the paper's early reputation as a serious organ among the great and the good, not just one interested in crime and scandal. This would be a factor in building its remarkable Sunday circulation to one that would outshine any daily paper. While Northcliffe aspired to political power and needed to demonstrate his influence, Riddell worked quietly behind the scenes, becoming much more of an intimate of key political figures of the era, particularly David Lloyd George and Winston Churchill. While Riddell was just as ferociously ambitious and determined to make money as Northcliffe, he was more clubbable and used his obsession with golf as a means of influence and his wealth to extend social favours. Northcliffe, full of ego and self-promotion, never seemed quite that subtle.

By the time Riddell, born in Brixton, became involved in the *News of the World*, he had already taken control of the London solicitor's firm to which he had originally been articled. He had invested in property and bought shares in the *Western Mail*. For helping the Western Mail company with the *News of the World* purchase in 1891, he received shares in lieu of fees. He became company secretary of the *News of the World* within a couple of years and gradually increased his stake and involvement until, by 1903, aged 38, he had become the managing director. Over the next few years, he bought a range of other publications, including the literary magazine *John O' London's Weekly* and *Country Life*.

His greatest acquisition was the friendship of the young Welsh Liberal politician David Lloyd George, whom he met through his *Western Mail* connections. The two men, both ambitious and of a similar age, became close friends for many years and benefited each other in ways that would today be frowned upon because of

Baron (George)
Riddell, *c.* 1920–25.

the potential for corruption. (The relationship between Murdoch executives such as Rebekah Wade and Andy Coulson, both editors of the *News of the World*, and prime ministers Tony Blair and David Cameron examined during the Leveson Inquiry was arguably much less close than that between Riddell and Lloyd George.)

Remarkably, there was never any whiff of public disapprobation or controversy. The pair met frequently, usually over breakfast, lunch or dinner. In 1909 Lloyd George, by then Chancellor of the Exchequer, helped to persuade prime minister Herbert Asquith to give Riddell a knighthood because of the support the *News of the World* could give to the Liberal Party, while Riddell, who had become extremely wealthy, would provide the politician with a car, a house,

use of some country properties and media advice. In return, the politician gave Riddell access to government secrets once, after lunch, opening his red box to give him a preview of his Budget speech. 'We discussed the effect of a general rise in wages of five shillings per week,' Riddell noted in his diary.[12] This would be unthinkable today.

Riddell became a major power broker. At the golf course he bought, Walton Heath, Churchill, Lloyd George and the Prince of Wales were visitors, alongside William Carr and other journalists. He built a house nearby for Lloyd George, although it was later destroyed in an arson attack by suffragettes. Lloyd George relied upon Riddell for other things: he helped draft the settlement to a miners' strike in 1912, and was asked to sound out Conservative views on the Marconi scandal of 1913 – members of the Liberal Government were accused of profiting from advanced knowledge of a government contract – and to publicly quell speculation about politicians being customers of a certain Piccadilly brothel. During the First World War, by which time Riddell was chair of the Newspaper Proprietors Association, he acted as a bridge between the press and the coalition government, of which Lloyd George was prime minister from 1916. Riddell became a frequent, casual visitor to 11 and then 10 Downing Street. In the aftermath of the First World War he became the official press link between the peace conferences and the British media, although he is said to have pressed the prime minister to provide more authentic information to the media. A peerage was his reward, but only after Lloyd George and other newspaper heads persuaded George V to overcome his reservations about appointing a divorced person to the House of Lords. The new Baron Riddell, the first ever divorcee to enter the Lords, told Lloyd George: 'Our friendship has been one of the joys of my life.'[13] In later years, their relationship cooled over political differences, although Lloyd George suspected that it was because once he left office, he was of less use to the newspaper, of which Riddell had become chairman in 1923.

Riddell, assisted by Carr, had also set about remodelling the *News of the World* both as a newspaper and a business. He worked hard to improve the paper's regional distribution, recruiting direct selling agents around the country and improving and expanding the means of transporting papers. By 1933 Ralph Blumenfeld, the former editor of the *Daily Express*, noted: 'The paper is uncommonly well managed with as perfect an organisation as can be made.'[14]

Riddell was an enthusiastic publicist for the *News of the World*, always carrying a pocketful of handbills advertising the paper, which he scattered wherever he went, but also clearly felt a little embarrassed about some of the content. He told former *Mirror* editor Fyfe that if, when he reached the gates of heaven, St Peter frowned upon his association with the *News of the World*, 'I will urge in extenuation my connection with *John O'London's Weekly* and *Country Life*.'[15] Riddell was always out to serve his own ends: 'He was encouraging extensive coverage in the paper of Britain's music halls at a time when he was buying and selling music hall sites and he organised advertising stunts with the use of a gramophone produced by the company of which he was a director.' Harry Aldridge, who became chairman of the company after Riddell's death, said that Riddell would never do anything unless it had been calculated to benefit him financially, quoting Riddell as saying: 'Every man has a price.'[16]

But Riddell was not just a good marketing manager. Although not trained as a journalist, he clearly had all the right instincts: 'He was a strong advocate of opening out the paper, brightening up its presentation of news with larger headlines and illustrations – particularly drawings of court cases – in place of the tightly packed pages of old. The public, he said, no longer had the time to sit back and read columns of close print.'[17] Then there were promotional wheezes: 'hunt the sovereign' and 'popular barmaids' competitions, again setting down what would become part of the tabloid template. Carr and Riddell had been aware of the success of the *Illustrated Police News* as well as the 'new journalism' of the largely New York-based popular newspapers and saw how their paper needed to keep on top of public taste.

The *News of the World* earned a reputation for speedy and detailed news coverage, bringing out special editions for big stories that broke from the second half of the week onwards. Its small staff doubled their roles to cover sport and courts and politics. It reported in serious fashion on politics and foreign affairs. But its mainstay was its continued tradition of 'solid, careful, objective presentation of police court reports of rape, seduction, violence and marital infidelity'.[18] The paper believed that by reporting the punishment, particularly any words of admonishment from the bench, in as much detail as the offence, it was acting as a moral arbiter to prevent crime, although to some, the details, particularly in sex crime cases, appeared salacious. Riddell once told a brewery owner, who had remarked on the number of crime stories, that his paper was only reporting what the breweries' beer had caused. Its crime stories accrued extra details as a result of the bottle of Scotch delivered to the duty inspector at Scotland Yard every Saturday – a tradition of paying police for stories that would continue right up until the paper's demise in 2011 and as its executives would acknowledge in front of MPs. The paper also revived the tradition of repentant criminals confessing their misdeeds to journalists – the kind of scaffold confessions that had been so popular among readers in the seventeenth century. In 1935 Dr Buck Ruxton arranged for his confession to a double murder to be conveyed to the paper's crime reporter, Norman Rae, so that it could be made public after his execution.

It was this largely unvarying formula that lay behind the rise in circulation of the paper from around 40,000 a week when the two men took over to around 4 million at the time of Carr's death in 1941. It had become the biggest-selling newspaper in the world and a fixture in the British home. Much of that was due to Riddell, who died in 1934, his ashes scattered on the eighth hole of his golf course. Despite their latterly strained relations he still left Lloyd George £1,000 in his will, and he bequeathed the same amount to Winston Churchill. The Newspaper Press Fund and the Royal Free Hospital in Hampstead each received £250,000. He was, as his entry in the *Oxford Dictionary of National Biography* noted, a man of 'strange contradictions':

> He was masterful yet extraordinarily considerate; sure of his own judgement yet always open to persuasion. Few rich men had so few wants. He was keenly interested in making money, but not in spending it upon himself. His clothes were shabby, he drank little, was indifferent to food, but smoked incessantly. A man of amazing industry, he had an insatiable curiosity, made manifest by cross-examining everyone with whom he came into contact.[19]

And he helped create a newspaper that had a fixed and fond place in British culture. George Orwell would sum up perfectly the place of the *News of the World* in society when he wrote:

It is Sunday afternoon, preferably before the war. The wife is already asleep in the armchair, and the children have been sent out for a nice long walk. You put your feet up on the sofa, settle your spectacles on your nose, and open the *News of the World*. Roast beef and Yorkshire, or roast pork and apple sauce, followed up by suet pudding and driven home, as it were, by a cup of mahogany-brown tea, have put you in just the right mood. Your pipe is drawing sweetly, the sofa cushions are soft underneath you, the fire is well alight, the air is warm and stagnant. In these blissful circumstances, what is it that you want to read about? Naturally, about a murder.[20]

The paper would quote the passage with pride when it finally closed in 2011 as a result of allegations that it hacked the voicemail of a murder victim. It made no mention of George Riddell.

'They say I am mad, send your best man to cover the story'

Having largely lost interest in the *Daily Mirror*, Northcliffe had become increasingly involved in politics, while at the same time pursuing his own idiosyncratic causes in the *Daily Mail*. One was a campaign for 'standard' – that is, wholemeal – bread, which he pursued with vigour, instructing the editor, Thomas Marlowe, to print a story about its virtues every day of the year, one of which included a list of aristocratic wholemeal-bread eaters. He also had a long-running obsession with sweet pea flowers, and offered £1,000 for the best example. The nascent motor car and motor omnibus also elicited great support in the *Mail*, as did aviation, with a £10,000 prize awarded to the first person to fly from London to Manchester.

Northcliffe used the *Mail* and his other newspapers to campaign for increased spending on defence and air as a result of his long-standing concern about the growing threat of an increasingly militarized Germany. He referred to that country as Britain's 'secret and insidious enemy' and warned about the possibility of an 'Armageddon'. He had once told an interviewer: 'Yes, we detest the Germans, we detest them cordially and they make themselves detested by all of Europe.'[21]

His newspapers campaigned vociferously for conscription, more ammunition and other resources and said anyone who voted Liberal was helping Germany. When war broke out in 1914, the editor of *The Star*, in an echo of the competition between Hearst and Pulitzer over the Spanish–American war, claimed: 'Next to the Kaiser, Lord Northcliffe has done more than any living man to bring about the war.' It was a *Daily Mail* reporter, Lovat Fraser, who first used the word 'Huns' to describe German troops. Thus 'at a stroke was created the image of a terrifying, ape-like savage that threatened to rape and plunder all of Europe, and beyond.'[22] The headline above the leader column read: 'The paper that persistently forewarned the public about the war.' Northcliffe's newspapers boosted his long-standing obsession with Germany by carrying inflammatory stories about German atrocities. In August 1914 the *Mail* reported that German soldiers had murdered five civilians, and shortly afterwards Maxwell Fyfe, by now back working for the *Mail* as a reporter, claimed that Germans had cut off the hands of Red Cross workers and had used women and children as shields in battle. There was never any support for the account.

As with the *Mirror*, Northcliffe was anxious for the troops in the trenches to regard the *Mail*, now selling considerably more than 1.3 million a day, as their official newspaper and thousands of copies were delivered daily to the front line. And, like the *Mirror*, the *Mail* offered payment for letters home from soldiers. Northcliffe was angry with the military for banning reporters from the front line and threatening them with arrest for being there. The *Mail* subsequently attacked Lord Kitchener for sending troops into battle with 'the wrong kind of shell', an attack on a national hero that resulted in a remarkable 1 million drop in circulation overnight. Northcliffe responded to widespread criticism with typically robust self-confidence: 'I don't know what you men think and I don't care. And the day will come when you will all know that I am right.'[23]

Northcliffe was now an enormously strong and influential voice, if not one that was welcomed by everyone. According to Tom Clarke, who became a *Mail* news editor:

It seemed to us at this time that Northcliffe had attained a position of extraordinary power in the land. Although one never heard him boasting, his bearing suggested that he believed he had saved England from the follies of incompetent government . . . His campaigns up to date had certainly met with remarkable success. He had scored his first hit by getting Kitchener at the War Office. He had said racing must be stopped, and it was. He had said the shell scandal must be put right by the formation of a Ministry, and the Munitions Ministry was formed under Lloyd George . . . He had said single men must go first, and it was so. He had demanded a smaller Cabinet to get on with the war, and a special War Council of the Cabinet had been set up.

As the war progressed, Northcliffe became as much a politician as he was a journalist and publisher, using the *Mail* to campaign in support of Riddell's friend Lloyd George, then war secretary, and to remove the prime minister Herbert Asquith and others from the War Cabinet because of their perceived failures. Although Clarke later wrote that Northcliffe was dissuaded from calling Asquith 'a national danger in print', he instructed Clarke to use pictures of Lloyd George and Asquith side by side: 'Get a smiling picture of Lloyd George and get the worst possible picture of Asquith.' Clarke felt this was unkind, but Northcliffe replied: 'Rough methods are needed if we are not to lose the war . . . it's the only way.'[24] When the government fell, the *Mail*'s front page, at Northcliffe's insistence, was comprised entirely of pictures of the outgoing ministers, including Asquith and Winston Churchill, under the banner heading 'The Passing of the Failures'. This was newspaper power exerted in its rawest, most naked fashion.

The following year, Northcliffe was appointed chairman of the new Civil Aerial Transport Committee and later agreed to go to the United States as head of the British war mission. His power was summed up by the *New York Sun*: 'Maker and unmaker of ministries; furious critic of slovenliness and incapacity and certainly regarded at home as the most powerful figure in British public life outside a responsible Ministry . . . he is a man of extraordinary energy and executive capacity.'[25] Northcliffe spent only a few months in America before returning to Britain and resigning from the government, in order, he said, to preserve his independence. But Lloyd George needed his support and made him a viscount, perhaps to compensate for his distancing from Riddell. Northcliffe returned to government service again in 1918 at the request of Lord Beaverbrook, then minister for propaganda, to work as director of propaganda, which mainly involved the dropping of leaflets behind enemy lines. One of his critics wrote: 'The democracy, whose bulwark is Parliament, has been unseated, and mobocracy, whose dictator is Lord Northcliffe, is in power.'[26] Northcliffe also became concerned about the implications of the Russian Revolution and was persuaded that it was important to support the Labour Party as a bulwark against Communism; so much so that he donated space to the party during the 1918 general election.

Even after the Armistice, the *Mail* kept up its campaign against Germany – its slogan during much of 1919 was 'They Will Cheat You Yet, Those Junkers'. The word 'Huns' still appeared regularly in headlines. Lloyd George would later attack Northcliffe in Parliament: he denounced Northcliffe's 'diseased vanity', accusing him of trying to sow dissent between the Allies, and asserting that 'not even that kind of disease is a justification for so black a crime against humanity.'[27] The implication was that Northcliffe was suffering from mental illness, and Lloyd George tapped his head as he spoke to make the point clear.

As peace descended on Europe, and in the wake of Lloyd George's attack, the political influence of Northcliffe and the *Mail* declined. So it was back to campaigns: one to promote the Sandringham Hat – a sort of truncated top hat – fell flat, despite the endorsement of Winston Churchill, but another sponsoring Dame Nellie Melba, the renowned opera singer, to perform the first wireless concert in history, broadcast from Marconi's studios in Essex to both Britain and the United States, was a massive success. In the summer of 1920 the *Mail* encouraged children to arrange the words 'DAILY MAIL WORLD RECORD NET SALE 1,121,790' out of sand, stones, flowers and so on in a place visible to the public – one Scout group created the figure on the summit of Snowdon. The paper also sent a prudish local councillor from Kent – who had campaigned for bathing skirts for men – on a tour of seaside resorts, where he was, of course, suitably horrified. Also, perhaps seeing how the *Mirror*'s pictures of 'bathing beauties' were going down well with male and *Mail* readers, Northcliffe ordered an increase in the number of pictures of 'attractive young ladies', telling Clarke: 'I have no use for a man who cannot appreciate a pretty ankle.'[28]

Northcliffe remained attached to the conventional view of a woman's role in society, as mother and keeper of the household. The

Mail developed something of an obsession with so-called flappers, or modern young women, and how they were wearing shockingly short skirts, smoking and driving. These were all steps on the road to what became the tabloid preoccupation with and objectification of the female form. By the 2000s the *Mail* and in particular the *MailOnline* would regularly attract criticism for its almost obsessive approach to women's bodies – and indeed their wider roles in society – and whether they did or did not fit a particular orthodoxy of which it was the sole arbiter.

In his later years, Northcliffe made one last significant personal and professional friendship, the reverberations of which are still felt today. Keith Murdoch was a young Australian reporter who had exposed Australian and British incompetence over the Gallipoli landings in 1915 which had resulted in devastating losses. Murdoch's investigation – never published because of British government interference – influenced Northcliffe to mount an angry campaign in the *Mail* to get to the truth of what had happened at Gallipoli. Northcliffe continued to give Murdoch advice and help – including a role reporting for *The Times* on a tour of Australia by the Prince of Wales – which enabled him eventually to create his own newspaper empire.

The relationship was almost that of father and son. Murdoch would write to Northcliffe in 1920: 'You have been the biggest influence and biggest force over me . . . largely from the example I have steadily seen in you and the standard that you have set me.' When Murdoch became editor of the *Melbourne Herald* in January 1921, Northcliffe sent him advice, which included the following, a prescription for popular journalism:

> The first editorial should be the second thing read every day, the first being the main news . . . smiling pictures make people smile . . . people like to read about profiteering. Most of them would like to be profiteers themselves and would if they had the chance. The church notes are good. People who drink, smoke and swear have no idea of the interest in church matters. Sport can be overdone, even in Australia . . . Every woman in the world would read about artificial pearls. I still notice in the *Herald* an absence of 'items'. Columns of items a day give the reader a great feeling of satisfaction with

his three-pennyworth. My young men say you don't have enough stockings in the paper. I am afraid I am no longer a judge of that.[29]

Later that year, Murdoch asked Northcliffe for £5,000 to help him to purchase the *Sydney Herald*. Northcliffe swiftly sent the money with the casual instruction to 'lose it if you like.' The closeness of the relationship earned Murdoch the nickname 'Lord Southcliffe', and he was accused by Catholic newspapers and other commentators of being a yellow journalist and bringing '*Daily Mail* journalism' to Australia. Murdoch wrote to Northcliffe: 'I wish I had.'[30]

In the middle of 1921 Northcliffe had embarked on a world tour, which attracted sarcastic responses from papers such as the *Morning Star* and *Punch*. 'For while "the Chief" goes round the world, how will the world go round?' asked *The Star*. Northcliffe's orders to his staff, usually delivered over one of his many telephones, always insistent and demanding, had now taken on an air of eccentricity. He told Clarke ahead of a trip to the United States: 'Express delight at everything. You will be told that America has won the war. To that you must demur. Don't wear spats.'[31] And to his foreign correspondent F. W. Wile: 'Clean your typewriter; take your winkle pin and clean out the d's, a's, o's and other letters.'[32]

The end, when it came, was – for a man used to such political and professional power, who had cajoled and berated both his staff and government and always forced them to bend to his will, who had inspired fear and undying loyalty in equal measure and who had done so much to create modern, popular, tabloid journalism – unutterably sad. While he was still a force within his newspapers, his political power had begun to drain away. He began to verbally and physically abuse his staff and coldly rejected an urgent request from Murdoch – of whom he had been so fond – to loan him a printing engineer. He appointed the commissionaire on reception in the *Mail* building to be 'chief censor of advertising' because he had developed a dislike of 'coarse . . . and offensive' adverts. He was convinced German or Bolshevik agents were trying to poison or shoot him and accused his private secretary of being among their number. Northcliffe summoned Henry Wickham Steed, then editor of *The Times*, to Paris where he told Steed he had been threatened by a man with a Perrier bottle but that he had saved himself by putting out the man's eye with a walking stick. He asked Steed to hold his hand, as he was afraid of falling out of bed.

When Northcliffe returned to the UK, his family were forced to dispel rumours that he had a mental illness; he hardly helped matters by going around asking people, 'Am I mad?' He had suffered dramatic weight loss and his robust physicality diminished: 'His vitality had gone, his face was puffy. His chin was sunk and his mouth had lost its firmness . . . he was a different man,' wrote Swaffer later, visiting him. 'The fires that burned within him had burned too fiercely all those years. People who heard him knew it was the end.'[33] His brothers had all the telephones in his house disconnected but one. He found it and is said to have immediately telephoned the night editor of the *Daily Mail*. Various versions circulated later as to what he said: Clarke wrote in his diary:

> Despite efforts to keep him at bay, he had succeeded again in telephoning one or two people. He speaks in a whisper. He says he hears that people say he is mad. 'They are watching me.' And he wants the best reporter sent down to see him, as he thinks that's a good story, and a good reporter ought to get the full story.[34]

Northcliffe spent his final weeks sealed in a specially built hut on the roof of the Duke of Devonshire's house in Carlton Gardens in St James's. For much of the time he was raving and uncontrollable, although he had moments of normality: as he neared the end, his only two comprehensible messages were: 'Tell mother she was the only one!' and a second which bears the hallmark of a true journalist:

> I wish to be laid as near Mother as possible at North Finchley and I do not wish anything erect from the ground or any words except my name and the year I was born and this year upon the stone. In the *Times*, I should like a page reviewing my life-work by someone who really knows and a leading article by the best man on the night.[35]

Northcliffe died on 14 August 1922, aged 57. Although there were strong rumours he had been suffering from syphilis, much later his death was officially recorded as being from *Streptococcus*, a blood infection that can cause massive organ damage and, as had become apparent, affect the brain. In his will, he left three months' salary to each of his 6,000 employees.

Online, you can still find the British Pathé newsreel footage of the funeral three days later: the massed thousands outside Westminster Abbey, some clinging to buttresses and railings for a better view, the lines of black-clad dignitaries entering the Abbey and, later, the long procession of hearses to North Finchley cemetery in the suburbs. Many more lined the route to the cemetery, where there were yet bigger crowds, packed densely among the bushes and overhanging trees, scrambling to see the final internment of the Chief, the man who had transformed British newspapers. Clarke wrote in his diary: 'Today we have buried the Chief. A vast crowd in and outside Westminster Abbey . . . Hannen Swaffer opposite me. I saw he was weeping.'[36]

The historian of *The Times*, who remained anonymous, later described Northcliffe succinctly:

> The creator of *Answers* (1888), *Comic Cuts* (1890), *Sunday Companion* (1894), *Home Chat* (1895), the *Daily Mail* (1896), and the *Daily Mirror* (1903), the restorer of the *Evening News*, and the saviour of *The Times*, was unquestionably the greatest popular journalist of his time. To begin with, his technical capacities ranged widely. He had performed all the work of the editorial, advertising or layout man, and knew the uses and costs of copy, type, ink, paper and binding. Northcliffe was not an illiterate proprietor. He began as a writer, always liked writing, and was writing within six weeks of his death. Alfred Harmsworth was a journalist at the age of sixteen, a proprietor at twenty-two, a baronet at thirty-eight, a baron at forty, and a viscount at fifty. The supreme popular journalist was a failure in everything else.[37]

And dead seven years later, a burnt-out, diseased and incoherent shell.

Northcliffe's legacy was both immediate and far-reaching. He was the first great media mogul to preside over a powerful communications empire in the United Kingdom. Although Hearst and Pulitzer had preceded him, the size of the United States and the concentration of readers on the East and West coasts created a different, more diverse landscape in which there was no real national newspaper. In Britain, whatever Northcliffe wanted to say was being read by millions of people right across the country the following morning. He had created two newspapers from scratch, the *Mail* and the *Mirror*; he had rescued the *Evening News* and *The Times* and at one point owned 39 per cent of morning newspapers. He also owned, at various points, *The Observer*, the *Sunday Pictorial* and the *Sunday Dispatch*. Had he lived long enough, the emerging medium of radio – the first BBC broadcasts were not until late 1922 – would doubtless have attracted his attention. And television? What would Northcliffe, with his fascination for the new and technological advancement, have made of the potential of broadcasting media? He had helped in the massive expansion of newspaper circulation, which would educate, inform and entertain the new massed working and lower-middle classes of the growing industrial cities in the first decades of the twentieth century. At the time of Northcliffe's death, the *Daily Mail*, with a circulation of 1.75 million, was the biggest-selling newspaper in the country, with around half the total daily circulation of newspapers. Improved technology allowed faster printing processes and many newspapers opened northern printing sites, usually in Manchester, to cut down further on distribution costs and timings.

A growing, urbanized, more literate society was buying more newspapers. Many people now lived in areas newspapers could reach every morning through an extensive railway network, which was largely in place by 1900, and, after 1918, with rapidly improved journey times through new technology. Between 1890 and 1930 the population of Britain's seven largest cities grew by 150 per cent. At the same time, the population was becoming used to seeing images to tell stories – the first cinemas and, shortly afterwards, the first newsreels appeared in Britain in the 1900s. The photographs in the *Mirror* and then the *Mail* were but a logical consequence. The dense grey columns of *The Times* and the *Daily Telegraph*, appealing to a largely masculine sensibility rooted in Victorian political and social structures, seemed dull by comparison. And newspapers had become big businesses. The population was better informed about the wider world than ever before. A new breed, the newspaper barons, was being created. Now, they went to war.

The Moguls at War

Control of Northcliffe's empire passed to Harold Harmsworth, Lord Rothermere, his duller but more business-minded brother. Rothermere would move the papers into a public company and enter a ferocious battle with the *Express*, which he would lose. His opponent was Max Aitken, later Lord Beaverbrook, who would turn the *Daily Express* into the world's biggest-circulation newspaper. Unlike Northcliffe, either of the Murdochs, Hearst or Pulitzer, Aitken, apart from a brief period in his Canadian youth as a local correspondent of the *Montreal Star*, was not a journalist by upbringing, trade or inclination. He was a businessman-turned-politician and newspapers became his way of imposing his views on the world. Whatever else may have been said about Northcliffe, newspapers were his lifeblood right to the very end – 'send your best man to cover the story' – but for Beaverbrook, like many of the earliest newsmongers, they were simply a means to air his political biases. In 1947 he told the Royal Commission on the Press they were run purely for propaganda purposes and he would never allow editors to oppose policies dear to his heart. Cecil Harmsworth King, Northcliffe's nephew, who soon revitalized the *Mirror*, later described him as 'the first evil man to figure in British public life for a very long time'.[38] But he was perhaps a more complex figure than that. Despite his newspapers' attacks on the Labour Party, he enjoyed the company of Labour politicians such as Michael Foot and Nye Bevan and the author H. G. Wells, and gave money to the left-wing newspaper *Tribune*.

After dabbling in insurance and journalism, the young Aitken had begun dealing on the Canadian stock market and used the money he made to buy up cement companies. In 1909, at the age of only thirty and with a near monopoly of the Canadian cement industry, he was forced to pay back large sums to shareholders after being accused of manipulating share prices. He left for London soon after, perhaps with the intention of a clean start. In Britain, he rose rapidly to power: after befriending Conservatives and becoming a party donor, he was elected Conservative MP for Ashton-under-Lyne, in Staffordshire, in 1910. The following year, he was among a group of Conservative supporters who bought *The Globe*, the oldest of London's seven evening newspapers, and began to invest in the *Daily Express*, still very much in the shadow of the *Daily Mail*. In

1916 he obtained a controlling interest from its original owner, Arthur Pearson, but kept the fact hidden to avoid compromising the *Express*'s attacks on prime minister Herbert Asquith over the way the war was being pursued. Although not in office, he was close to senior figures and was ennobled as Lord Beaverbrook later that year by the new prime minister, Lloyd George, another example of the Liberal politician, friend of Riddell and Northcliffe, favouring press barons. As the war neared its end, he became minister of propaganda, employing Northcliffe as director of propaganda. So, how did he achieve this extraordinary rise? 'Northcliffe was a journalistic visionary, it is not clear Beaverbrook had any vision at all.' But although Beaverbrook was principally a manipulator of journalists with no profound knowledge of how newspapers were produced, he had an instinct for the public taste that never faltered and 'crucially he was unencumbered by the constant concern for accuracy and ethical conduct that was the rock of all the Northcliffe papers.'[39]

After 1918 he became embroiled in a different kind of war – the *Express*, the *Mail*, the *Mirror* and the *Daily Herald* were locked in battle for much of the 1920s and '30s. In 1919 the *Express*'s circulation was under 400,000, but by 1930 it was 1,693,000, slowly eroding that of the *Mail*. In 1918 he launched a Sunday edition of the *Express* and in 1929 purchased the *Evening Standard*, another of London's evening newspapers.

In 1930 the *Express* initiated a feature that would soon become a staple of all popular newspapers – the astrology column. The birth of Princess Margaret, younger sister to Queen Elizabeth, in August 1930 was a great human-interest story. The editor, John Gordon, had the idea of running a horoscope predicting the new royal's future. Gordon approached the most famous astrologer of the day, known as Cheiro, who claimed to have read the palms and told the fortunes of many famous people. Cheiro was not available and the job was given to his assistant, Richard Harold Naylor. With perhaps some certainty when it came to a young royal but, it transpired, with accuracy, Naylor predicted her life would be 'eventful'. The column was popular and Naylor was asked to write a second article shortly afterwards, on the horoscopes of those born in September. In another, published the following month, he predicted: 'A British aircraft will be in danger between October 8 and 15.' On 5 October the passenger airship R101 was wrecked in a storm near Paris; 48 people died. That was good enough for the *Express* and Naylor was given a weekly column, 'What the Stars Foretell', which became one of the paper's most popular features, lasting until the early 1940s. By 1937 he was also giving weekly predictions for each of the twelve star signs in a column called 'Your Stars'. Soon, every national newspaper was running its own horoscope column, although Naylor was the undisputed king, receiving up to 28,000 letters a week. Arthur Christiansen, who made his name on the *Sunday Express* before going on to become a legendary editor of the *Daily Express*, later observed: 'Naylor and his horoscopes became a power in the land. If he said that Monday was a bad day for buying, then the buyers of more than one West End store waited for the stars to become more propitious. His column was a huge success.'[40] Today, every popular daily newspaper has an astrology column. The *Express* newspapers would also popularize the use of cartoons, first the political cartoons of David Low and, from 1943 onwards, the much-loved characters of Giles, which continued until 1991. The *Sunday Express* was also the first British newspaper to carry a crossword puzzle, again the beginning of a trend that continues to this day.

David George Boyce, author of several books on the era of the press barons, believed that the *Express* succeeded not just because of its aggressively populist stance, 'but also [because of] its optimism, enthusiasm, and claim to speak for those who were, like Beaverbrook himself, determined to stand up for themselves and take control of their own lives'.[41] This was a departure from the Northcliffe tone, which tended to have a streak of carping criticism and pessimism, something which many would argue still inhabits the *Daily Mail* psyche. As Martin Conboy noted, it was the 'unbounded enthusiasm and confidence' that marked its difference from the more individualistic approach of the *Mail*.[42] In his opening manifesto in the *Express* in March 1919, Beaverbrook had emphasized this upbeat, individualistic tone: 'It [the *Express*] will uphold the right of people to advance their own interests and shape their own lives and will oppose all attempts to interfere with the simple and healthy pleasures of the nation.'[43] An editorial in May 1920, under the headline 'The World Is Becoming Better', claimed: 'The universal mind is abroad with its hatred of injustice and tyranny and with its love of fairness and good will to men . . . humanity moves on.' In a speech in 1922 he made his view even plainer: 'It is the duty of newspapers to advocate a policy of optimism in the broadest sense and to declare almost daily their belief in the future of England.' This when he was no longer minister of propaganda. The historian A.J.P. Taylor put the *Express*'s success down to the fact that its owner was indifferent to the British class system, holding that 'there was no difference between rich and poor except that the rich had more money.'[44] Beaverbrook was delighted when Taylor favourably reviewed a book he had written and it led to a close friendship between the two, with Taylor, a Labour Party member, acknowledging Beaverbrook's charm and his ability to 'steal the hearts of men'.[45] Taylor would eventually write a biography of Beaverbrook.

The *Express* may not have been quite as explicit in its reporting of court stories as the *News of the World*, but it certainly included its share of crime and court stories, divorces and scandal, tales of heroism and human-interest stories, whether they concerned the emerging stars and starlets of Hollywood, 'society' figures or the era's sports stars. 'Blumenfeld produced a paper which drew heavily on the *Daily Mail* with news, a women's section, money matters and sports figured prominently. Leisure pages with stories such as "Popular Phrases: What do they mean?" were clearly inspired by the *Daily Mail*.'[46]

This reflected the fact that at this point, popular newspapers focused more on these stories than on coverage of politics and public policy – in an era that witnessed the General Strike, the Great Depression, the first Labour government and the rise of fascism in Britain and across Europe. As for the trend towards shorter, snappily written stories, always accompanied by images, many put this down to the growth of cinema. As former *Times* editor Henry Wickham Steed noted in 1938, the shortening of stories and articles was due to people becoming accustomed to 'impressions that could be received through the eye without mental effort'. He also attributed the rise in importance of pictures to women readers, who he believed preferred them. Steed acknowledged the new reality for many journalists: 'However easy it maybe to put pen to paper and to spin out phrases, it is far less easy to put into three hundred words what used to be said in one thousand or more.'[47] There was in addition a widespread belief that in a society more engaged and complex than before, particularly for commuters, readers were too busy for longer articles and lacked the time for the leisurely reading and reflection of the pre-war era. Not for nothing did the *Daily Mail* style itself 'The Busy Man's Newspaper'.

Into this mix had come a new challenge to all the popular papers. The *Daily Herald* was an odd beast in the popular newspaper jungle, more celebrated for its unusual birth, its involvement in the circulation wars and its reincarnation in the 1960s as something called *The Sun* than what it actually achieved during its period as a newspaper in its own right. While the *Mirror, Mail* and *Express* were all the progeny of rich proprietors desiring money and power, the *Herald* was founded in 1912 by a group of trade union activists aware that the *Mirror*, while appealing to a mass readership, was never going to actually support anything connected with socialism or the Labour Party, formed just twelve years previously. The *Herald* was funded by Labour Party backers and the trade unions, supported the suffragette cause and the anti-colonial movement and had a left-wing intellectual appeal. Always struggling financially, it was forced to switch to weekly publication during the First World War, but retained its radical stance by opposing conscription and supporting the Russian Revolution in 1917. It resumed daily publication in 1919 – the war poet Siegfried Sassoon was its literary editor for a short period – but struggled until it was taken over by the Trades Union Congress in 1922 and became the official voice of the Labour movement throughout the 1920s. In 1929 the publishers Odhams, who owned the popular Sunday paper *The People*, which itself was modelled on the early *Daily Mirror*, took over commercial management of the paper, with guarantees of future support for the Labour movement. A relaunch in 1930 saw the content transformed to the new orthodoxy: human-interest stories, more and bigger photographs and an appeal to women readers: 'The re-invention of the *Herald* was the clearest sign yet of the triumph of the Northcliffe revolution. It was no longer possible to sustain the nineteenth-century model of popular political journalism amidst the cut-throat competition of the twentieth century.'[48]

4

THE PREROGATIVE OF THE HARLOT

On 17 March 1931 Stanley Baldwin, Conservative Party leader and former prime minister, decided it was time to hit back. Baldwin had been under relentless criticism from the newspapers controlled by the two pre-eminent press barons – lords Rothermere and Beaverbrook – who had accused him of running an 'insolent plutocracy' and of being unable to improve the country's economy. To retain his grip on the party, he needed his supporter Duff Cooper to win a by-election due in three days' time and defeat the preferred candidate of the two lords. In the days running up to the by-election, the *Mail* had run attacks on both Baldwin and Cooper.

Despite the circulation war between the two papers, Rothermere and Beaverbrook were in political alignment, not just in support of the Conservatives but on the subject of who should lead the party. They had both taken against Baldwin, who had lost out to Ramsay MacDonald in the 1929 general election, believing him too soft and socialist in his principles. As a result the two lords had formed the United Empire Party, with the aim of deposing Baldwin and promoting Beaverbrook's campaign for Empire Free Trade, which was supported in all the newspapers of their two groups. Rothermere's papers also lobbied for Beaverbrook, already a Tory MP, to become leader of the party. 'There is no man living in this country today with more likelihood of succeeding to the Premiership of Great Britain than Lord Beaverbrook,' claimed the *Sunday Dispatch*, which had been renamed by Rothermere from the *Weekly Dispatch*.[1]

But on that March day, giving a speech in support of Cooper at a by-election rally, Baldwin delivered a ringing condemnation of the power of newspaper owners, which would echo down the decades; many believe its central tenet remains true both pre- and post-Leveson:

> The papers conducted by Lord Rothermere and Lord Beaverbrook are not newspapers in the ordinary acceptance of the term. They are engines of propaganda for the constantly changing policies, desires, personal wishes, personal likes and dislikes of two men. Their methods are direct falsehoods, misrepresentation, half-truths, the alteration of the speaker's meaning by publishing a sentence apart from the context . . . What the proprietorship of these papers is aiming at is power, and power without responsibility – the prerogative of the harlot throughout the ages.[2]

The powerful last line had come, with permission, from Baldwin's cousin the writer Rudyard Kipling. Ironically, Kipling had coined it during a conversation with Beaverbrook, with whom he had become friends. Beaverbrook had told him: 'What I want is power. Kiss 'em one day and kick 'em the next.'

Whether or not the speech had an immediate impact, the attacks on Baldwin backfired. Cooper won the seat with a sizeable majority and Baldwin would enter the national government as Lord President of the Council alongside MacDonald and eventually serve a third term as prime minister in 1935–7. The United Empire was disbanded, but neither Rothermere or Beaverbrook would shy away from political intervention in the future, and neither would Rothermere end his fascination with fascists.

Gift Wars and Fascism

The 1930s would see the greatest ever expansion in newspaper readership, with daily sales rising from 4.7 million in 1926 to 10.6 million in 1939. At the start of the 1930s, the *Express* was selling around 1.6 million daily and challenging the *Daily Mail*, which had dropped from around 2 million to 1.85 million. Their readership was different to that of the newly relaunched *Herald*, which was targeting the rising numbers of working-class, Labour-supporting readers; it swiftly amassed sales, soon reaching a daily average of 1 million, and increasing to 2 million by 1933. It sucked away sales from the *Daily Mail*, which dropped to 1.58 million in 1937 while the *Mirror* dropped from 1 million in 1920 to 700,000 in 1934.

In the early years of the decade, Odhams, the new owners of the *Herald*, had generated new sales by a relentless campaign of free gifts and offers: pens, tea sets, glassware, clothes and shoes, dictionaries and complete bound sets of the works of Dickens were offered to those who took out subscriptions. It paid Labour Party members to recruit new readers and by the mid-1930s employed more than 50,000 people as door-to-door salesmen. The *Mail*, the *Express* and eventually the *Mirror* were forced to follow the *Herald*'s example, recruiting salesmen and offering even more free gifts in return for subscriptions. At a meeting of newspaper owners at the Savoy in 1933 designed to broker an agreement to end what Beaverbrook had dubbed 'madness', Odhams refused to drop the latest Dickens promotion and was greeted with a declaration from the *Express* owner that 'This is war.' As a result, its readers, and those of the *Mail*, were soon able to enjoy their own Dickens offers. Each paper tried

Lord Beaverbrook
during the Second
World War.

desperately to top the others, the *Express* once giving away 10,000 pairs of silk stockings. Readers soon realized that, if they kept swapping subscriptions after the usual minimum contract period of two or three months, they would be able to keep themselves in clothes and household goods for a relatively small outlay. But buying of readers could not last; there was a mutual climbdown. Both the *Mirror* and the *Express* reinvented their brands, with the latter spending money instead on improving its editorial appeal and the *Mirror* experiencing what was effectively an internal coup.

The ending of the circulation-boosting gift wars in 1933 was a pivotal moment, coinciding with the elevation to key roles of a group of men who would shape the two newspapers that would dominate the mass-circulation popular market for most of the next three decades. At the *Daily Mirror*, Harry Guy Bartholomew became editorial director and, alongside Cecil Harmsworth King and the young Welsh genius Hugh Cudlipp, would wrench the paper away from the grim grip of Rothermere's fascination with elements of fascism and reinvent it for the new working classes. At the *Express*, Arthur Christiansen became editor, holding power there until 1957 and delivering his own version of a popular newspaper. The tabloid wars had entered the modern era.

Rothermere remained enthused by fascism and right-wing causes, becoming, according to one historian, 'perhaps the most influential single propagandist for fascism between the wars'.[3] In October 1922, the *Mail* backed Benito Mussolini to run Italy and in May of the following year Rothermere published a leader, 'What Europe Owes Mussolini', expressing his 'profound admiration' for the Italian leader for stopping Bolshevism.[4] In October 1924, just four days before the general election, the *Mail* published the notorious Zinoviev letter under the headline 'Civil War Plot by Socialist Masters'. The letter, alleging that British Communists were being ordered by Moscow to foment armed insurrection in working-class areas of the UK, caused a sensation. Ramsay MacDonald's Labour government lost the election by a huge margin. It was only much later that it emerged that the letter was a forgery, concocted by rogue MI5 agents and leaked by them to the *Mail*. But it helped boost the *Mail*'s circulation, which by 1926 was 2 million a day, helping to make Rothermere the third richest man in the country, with a personal wealth of £25 million.

Lord Rothermere with Adolf Hitler, 1937.

In 1928, in a leader again written by Rothermere, the *Mail* once again praised Mussolini as 'the great figure of the age. Mussolini will probably dominate the history of the twentieth century as Napoleon dominated the early nineteenth century.'[5] After the failure of his attempt to unseat Baldwin and following his obsession with Mussolini, Rothermere became a strong supporter of Adolf Hitler, visiting and writing to him several times. He also supported the British Union of Fascists, led by Oswald Mosley. After visiting Hitler in the wake of the Nazis' securing seats in the German parliament, Rothermere wrote favourably of the movement in the *Daily Mail* and said he hoped Hitler, who he said was changing the world for the better, would become chancellor: 'We can do nothing to check this movement [the Nazis], and I believe it would be a blunder for the British people to take up an attitude of hostility towards it.'[6] Shortly afterwards he wrote in the *Mail* denying that he was antisemitic.

His support for Mosley led to probably the most infamous headline ever published in the *Mail*, on 8 January 1934: 'Hurrah for the Blackshirts!' it read, over an article endorsing Mosley, saying that

Italy and Germany had become the best-governed nations in Europe and that Britain's survival as a great power was dependent on the existence of a 'well organised party of the right' willing to show the same 'directness of purpose'. For decades, right up until the twenty-first century, the headline would regularly be used against the *Daily Mail* by its critics. A few days later, an article in the *Mirror* by Rothermere was headlined, 'Give the Blackshirts a Helping Hand', in which he said Mosley was misunderstood and urged readers to join the movement. 'As a purely British organisation, the Blackshirts will respect those principles of tolerance which are traditional in British politics.' In the *Sunday Pictorial*, an extensive picture feature showed Mosley's Blackshirts in their 'Black House' headquarters. All the papers enthusiastically covered Mosley's speeches and activities – a 1934 Union Flag-bedecked rally at Olympia was advertised and promoted in the *Mail* and *Mirror* – although perhaps the nadir was the *Mirror*'s photography contest to find Britain's best-looking female fascist, which Mosley himself objected to. Rothermere's extraordinary flirtation with Mosley ended when the two fell out over a business deal involving supplying cigarettes to shops, and when British Jewish companies began to withdraw their advertising from Rothermere's papers because of Mosley's antisemitic views.[7]

Rothermere made several more visits to meet the Führer, as well as other leading Nazis like Göring. In 1937 he stayed with Hitler and Goebbels in the Bavarian Alps. It emerged much later that in the summer of 1939, as war loomed, he wrote to 'My Dear Führer' praising his 'superhuman work in regenerating his country' and saying there was no problem between the two countries

'Give the Blackshirts a Helping Hand', headline, *Daily Mirror*, 22 January 1934.

that could not be solved by consultation and negotiation; he also wrote to both von Ribbentrop and Rudolf Hess urging cooperation.[8] However, it later emerged that he was additionally reporting back to British government ministers on Hitler, urging them to prepare for war, which leaves his true intent more ambiguous, or perhaps just naive: it seems possible that he was simply keeping in with both sides. When war broke out, the *Mail* publicly supported Britain – it had no other choice given its readership and the public mood – but Rothermere's views had not gone down well amid the patriotic fervour of war being declared.

Under what many would later see as the dead hand of Lord Rothermere, the *Daily Mirror* had languished during most of the 1920s and early '30s, its circulation and distinctive identity slowly slipping away in the face of competition from rivals like the *Express* and, more damagingly, the *Daily Herald*. Rothermere had used profits from the *Mirror* and the *Sunday Pictorial* to fund the *Mail* and other ventures as well as the free-gift wars. And the *Mirror* was losing its appeal to the working class, which had been its early mainstay. In the General Strike of 1926, the paper had backed the government rather than the workers, and in the 1930s Rothermere told *Mirror* editors to aim the paper at the new suburban middle classes who holidayed in France and had tea at the tennis club; the paper's pictures, once so revolutionary, were now of society figures and middle-class country girls and debutantes, or 'girls in pearls', as they were often known. Bill Hagerty, a senior executive on the paper during the 1970s and '80s, later wrote: 'Rothermere was a sad and unfulfilled man whose 17-year stewardship of the paper . . . transformed him from a groundbreaking, vital young buck of communication and entertainment to a prematurely middle-aged, middle-class dullard.'[9]

By the mid-1930s Rothermere had followed his brother in largely losing interest in the *Mirror*, progressively selling off his personal stake, although he controlled the board by proxies. The result was a vacuum in executive leadership and editorial direction. Into this gap stepped the robust figure of Harry Guy Bartholomew. In the years since his partnership with Hannen Swaffer had saved the nascent *Mirror* from oblivion, the man described as both a 'drunken illiterate' and 'the godfather of the British tabloids' had steadily worked his way up the ranks to join the board as a director. In 1933, the circulation having dropped over the previous two decades from a peak of 1 million in 1914 to around 800,000, he acted. Persuading the board to make him editorial director, Bartholomew was given daily editorial control of both the *Mirror* and the *Sunday Pictorial*. Crucially, he was backed by the newest member of the Harmsworth family to achieve power in newspapers: Cecil Harmsworth King, the 33-year-old advertising director of the *Mirror* and the son of Geraldine Harmsworth – sister of Northcliffe and Rothermere – and her husband, Sir Louis King, a professor of oriental languages at Trinity College, Dublin. King had joined the family newspaper business after Oxford but had never worked as a journalist and was desperate to prove himself a worthy successor to his uncles; he would ultimately have a bigger influence on the *Mirror* than either of them. Like Northcliffe – and, to a degree, Rothermere – King would shine brilliantly as a newspaper executive and proprietor before, in his later years, descending into a strange obsession that would ultimately tarnish his record.

Bartholomew and King – the former shortish, rotund, 'an inventive energetic showman' with little education; the latter, a patrician, slightly aloof public school- and Oxbridge-educated Harmsworth family member – were then joined by a young Welsh prodigy, Hugh Cudlipp, who would become what many later described as the greatest tabloid editor of them all. These three very different men, who were often at odds with each other, would preside over an era in which the *Mirror* rose again to overtake the *Express*, became the biggest national daily newspaper in the country and emerged as the authentic voice of millions of ordinary working-class people. The building blocks laid down by Hearst and Pulitzer, Northcliffe and Christiansen formed the template, their best ideas improved upon, the worst discarded, in order to create the modern tabloid newspaper. In 1933 Bartholomew and King felt they needed to reconnect the *Mirror* with its roots and its original intentions and cease to be the rather genteel nonentity that it had become, not to mention its fascist cheerleading. They looked to the tabloid papers of New York for inspiration. There, large, sometimes graphic images dominated front pages and the inside pages contained as much sleaze, crime and showbiz as they could cram in.

Crime, Grime and Cheesecake

The leader of what had become the yellow journalism pack in New York was the *Illustrated New York Daily News*, first published in 1919 by Robert McCormick and Joseph Patterson and the first U.S. daily to be printed in tabloid format. Their model in turn had been the *Daily Mirror*, which Patterson had admired while in London during Army service in the First World War, when he had also met Northcliffe. Circulation soared when Patterson dropped 'Illustrated' from the name and put out the *New York Daily News* newsstands serving new immigrants, whose grasp of English was poor, but who liked the prominent use of images. These largely low-income readers, Patterson also discovered, liked comic strips, crime and sports stories.[10] Big, graphic pictures of crime scenes, together with images of celebrities of the age – baseball player Babe Ruth, pioneering aviator Charles Lindbergh and silent screen stars like Rudolph Valentino, whose death in 1926 was treated to six pages of text and photos – were crucial to its appeal. So were pictures of attractive young women, just as in the *Daily Mirror*: one of the *Daily News*'s first stunts was to sponsor a beauty contest and, of course, print pictures of all the contestants. Hollywood stars figured in abundance, from posed studio shots to snatched pictures outside restaurants and nightclubs, as technology developed lighter, more portable, cameras. Probably the *Daily News*'s most infamous photograph appeared in January 1928: the illicitly taken shot by a *News* photographer of the execution in the electric chair of murderer Ruth Snyder, whose trial for killing her husband had already attracted enormous publicity. It appeared underneath the huge headline 'DEAD!' The edition sold out immediately, adding 300,000 extra sales, briefly giving the paper the largest sale per head of population in the world. It was the first time that the execution of a woman had been photographed in the United States. Now just called the *Daily News*, it still publishes today, styling itself 'New York's Hometown Newspaper'.

So began the second era of popular newspaper wars in New York, with its own *New York Daily Mirror* – started by Hearst as competition to the *News* – and another rival, the short-lived *Evening Graphic*, launched by the publisher of 'cheesecake' magazines and similarly full of pictures of glamorous and semi-naked young women. The *Graphic* was often referred to as 'The Porno-graphic' because of its titillating photographs. It was said to possess something called the composograph, a device used for manipulating images and therefore faking photographs. The *Graphic* closed in 1934, but not before it kick-started the careers of gossip columnist Walter Winchell and Ed Sullivan, later to become a massively popular television presenter.

New York in the Roaring Twenties was a raucous, exciting place. The city was expanding rapidly following the influx of immigrants from the Old World and this hub of activity was throbbing with life: Broadway was in full swing, while on the streets of the Bronx and of Brooklyn crime gangs and the Mafia fought violent wars. Prohibition was flouted in nightclubs and speakeasys. And as Matthew Engel noted in his book *Tickle the Public*: 'Amid a million flashes of magnesium sulphate and shouts of "hold-the-front-page" by green-eyeshaded editors, New York journalism ran amok.'[11] By the early 1930s the *New York Daily News* was selling more than 1.3 million copies daily, and rising.

'Make the News Palatable by Lavish Presentation'

In 1929 Blumenfeld had left the *Express*, weary of being marginalized by Beaverbrook; he was replaced by Arthur Beverley Baxter, who saw circulation rise to 2 million. In 1933 he handed over to another editor, who was to have a profound influence on the paper and lead it to its peak of power and influence: Arthur Christiansen, who had begun on local newspapers in his teens and was in Fleet Street by his early twenties, rising up the ranks of the *Sunday Express* to become assistant editor before moving to the *Daily*.

Christiansen was a different creature from most of his peers, less interested in politics, less clubbable, and the first popular editor to truly focus on the technical side of newspaper production. 'The politics were Lord Beaverbrook's, the presentation was mine,' he said.[12] His intent was to 'make the news palatable by lavish presentation', even when it was dull.[13]

Long before they actually shrank to tabloid size, both the *Express* and the *Mail* had begun to change in design to a look dominated by shorter stories, bigger headlines, more emphatic straplines and sub-headings, and more pictures, pretty women, sex and scandal, court cases, campaigning and promotional gimmicks. During the 1930s new ingredients were added that became established parts of the daily menu, still present today: the agony aunt, the horoscope and the crossword. The attention-seeking montage that would soon become the norm for popular newspaper pages – particularly the front page – created a new breed in newspaper newsrooms: the sub-editor, who would become a vital part of the newsroom process. In the past, their job had been to correct any errors in copy and lay out endless columns of grey type, interspersed here and there with headlines and crossheads, plus the odd cartoon or woodcut illustration. But now a whole new power lay in their hands – to mix images and words using what later became known as 'furniture': underlined straps and crossheads, dropped-in quotes, 'white on black' headings. Pages now became individually, slickly designed creations aimed at attracting and keeping the reader. And the front would not just be a page of advertisements or the best half-dozen stories of the day, but a means of selling the rest of the paper as well, urging readers to 'look inside' with teasers and what the advertising industry would dub 'calls to action'. 'Reader, this is where we want to you go next' was the message. Page design became a crucial part of the package.

Christiansen's sub-editing team was the biggest in Fleet Street and it was with them that the practice of sub-editors rewriting much of what was submitted by their own reporters was established in popular newspapers. This was sometimes to enliven a dull news story, cut down a lengthy one or, quite often, combine it with other material to which the out-of-office reporter might not have access, in the days before mobile phones, such as copy on the same subject from stringers, freelancers and news agencies. Of course, on occasion, the resulting hybrid might bear little relation to the words originally submitted and bear the imprint and intentions of an editor always on the lookout for the bigger and better story. To this day, the belief among many reporters that 'the subs write the paper' remains common in Fleet Street. This was less likely – but not unheard of – in the case of specialist correspondents or columnists, whose work tended to be treated with more respect. This editing process represented a fundamental break with the past: reporters, even quite experienced ones, would now sometimes feel distanced from the words on the page – less likely to have a sense of ownership of them and therefore could be less wedded to their accuracy – while sub-editors grew in power but were distanced in another way from the fact-gathering that lies at the root of any reporting. In the gap between, prompted by demanding proprietors and editors, a culture flourished whereby the creed set down in 1921 by C. P. Scott, the legendary editor of the *Manchester Guardian*, that 'comment is free, but facts are sacred,' would be routinely flouted in a climate wherein cynical journalism and the hunger for circulation came to dominate.

But that was for later. What Christiansen did was to try to understand, as did Northcliffe, the mindset of the reader to whom they were appealing. Christiansen thought harder about the practicalities of journalism than Beaverbrook, and wanted his newspaper to appeal to the 'common man', as represented by two imaginary archetypes: the Man on the Rhyl Promenade and the Man on the Back Street in Derby, at whom a slick, dynamic newspaper that communicated the news simply and clearly was aimed.[14] To that end, he enlarged the font for text and headlines and introduced banner headlines across pages and more headlines in the bottom half of the page, to make the pages more appealing and attractive. Headlines would be shorter and more dramatic in tone, and they would no longer end with full stops. The days of the grey column were at an end: the eyes of these new visually literate readers would scan across a page, rather than up and down, and the whole page was designed to attract the reader with its aesthetic appeal.

In addition to snappy, forceful presentation, Christiansen made clear what kind of stories he wanted: stories about people. During the Victorian and Edwardian eras – in contrast to the earlier Regency years and the yellow journalism of the United States – British popular newspapers had been dominated by politicians and the political process, with the private lives of politicians usually deemed off-limits or of insufficient interest. Yes, there was intense interest in personalities – society figures, members of the royal family and the burgeoning number of film stars and sports figures, as well as criminals or heroes of some kind such as Scott of the Antarctic or the early aviation pioneers – but what Christiansen was signalling here was the importance of ordinary people who didn't fall into any of these categories, but whose personal experiences and stories would be used to illustrate the bigger picture. If the government was raising or lowering taxes, what did the Man (or Woman) on the Rhyl Promenade think? A new law to restrict betting? What did the Man (or Woman) on the Back Street in Derby say? It worked, and under Christiansen the *Express* became the dominant force in Fleet

Street over the next two decades. During his editorship, sales overtook those of the *Mail* and *Mirror* and peaked at 2 million in 1936, more than 3 million in 1944 and 4 million in 1949, by which time it was styling itself the 'world's greatest newspaper'. Its masthead was typically upfront and nationalistic, bearing a crusader figure holding a sword and a cross of St George. Since 1932, the *Express* had been housed in its purpose-built, gleaming new art deco building on Fleet Street, later nicknamed the 'Black Lubyanka' by *Private Eye* magazine. Literally and metaphorically, it dominated Fleet Street.

'The Mirror Re-Invented: Sex, Heroism, Drama and Pet-Worship'

When Bartholomew took over the *Mirror*, he immediately ordered that the main picture on the front page be of a man being hanged in California; the impact of the Ruth Snyder image had not been lost on 'Bart'. This was the template they showed to Hugh Cudlipp when he arrived as deputy features editor at the age of just 22 in August 1935. From a lower-middle-class Cardiff family, Cudlipp, both of whose brothers also went into journalism, had already earned a reputation as a reporter in gaudy, slightly sleazy Blackpool, the Las Vegas of Lancashire. Energetic, outgoing and garrulous, Cudlipp was a natural popular journalist, full of ideas, inventive and confident with both the spoken and the written word. In 1933, helped by his older brother, Percy, by then editor of the *Evening Standard*, he joined the *Sunday Chronicle* in London.

The *Mirror* features editor, former advertising executive Basil Nicholson, was disliked by Bartholomew – he had criticized the Bartlane method – and knew he would not last long. This was because Bartholomew had placed an advertisement for a deputy features editor 'ready to take charge' from the current features editor.[15] While Nicholson was a brilliant newspaperman who had already made his mark, he told Cudlipp at his interview for the post: 'We are going to turn the *Daily Mirror* into a real, lively, thrusting tabloid newspaper,' adding, 'Can you start today? Otherwise, I might be fired before you get here.'[16] The model for the *Mirror*, Nicholson told Cudlipp, was now the *New York Daily News*, and the concerns of the paper would be those of ordinary working people: 'Was a pregnant woman, whose husband could not possibly afford a fourth child, interested in a parliamentary debate on foreign affairs which would obviously result in nothing at all? What was the point of publishing pompous articles by avaricious big-wigs when figures proved that nobody would read them?'[17]

By this time, Bartholomew was producing graphic *New York Daily News*-style poster front pages featuring lynching, murder and disasters. 'The *Mirror* was still seen by most of Fleet Street as the absolute pits, a cast off and embarrassment, thrown away first by Northcliffe and then by Rothermere, filled with horror pictures and Yank cartoon strips organised by Bart.'[18] The *Mirror*'s new target were young, probably Labour-voting, working-class men and women who worked in the factories, shops and offices of the new expanding urban areas. Bartholomew was more direct: 'His formula was, roughly, sex, sincerity and sensation,' one of his new recruits, show-business writer Donald Zec, later wrote.[19] King decreed the end of the flirtation with right-wing dictators of the Rothermere era – although there was a Rothermere-inspired relapse in February 1936 with an 'exclusive' interview with Hitler, which carried the headline 'Hitler's "Let's Be Friends" Plea to World', and the following month an appeal for Hitler's 'peace plan' to succeed.

Initially, the changes were wrought almost by stealth. The raunchy elements were delayed until after the first edition, when John Cowley, the company chairman and Rothermere's appointee, had gone home. The daily cycle of news – sleaze, gossip, human interest, crime, court stories and scandal – would largely take care of itself and was now supplemented by cheesecake pictures of show-girls and cartoons, the huge black headlines ramped up to new heights of *Daily News*-style drama: 'REVELLER VANISHES FOR DAYS – COMES BACK AS POP EYED DRAGON SHOUTING WHOOPEE! WHAT A NIGHT!' Nicholson received such headlines with 'maniacal glee', wrote Cudlipp.[20] Nicholson lasted until Christmas, when Cudlipp took over.

One crucial story was held back until the last edition to avoid Cowley and to be too late to be copied by the other papers. At Bartholomew's insistence, the *Mirror* broke with the consensus among other papers of avoiding open discussion of the row between the king, Edward VIII, and the Church of England and the government over his wish to marry American divorcee Wallis Simpson, which had been widely reported in the United States. The *Mirror*'s headline for 3 December 1936, 'The King Wants to Marry

Mrs Simpson. Cabinet Advises "No,"' accompanied by the first ever photograph of Simpson, brought the full story out into the open for the first time in the UK. It caused a sensation, fractured the relationship between newspapers, the government and the monarchy, and was the first time the *Mirror* gave over its entire front page to a comment article. The paper was strongly on the side of the king as the crisis continued, with Cassandra's column headlined 'I Accuse' attacking the establishment for denying the king his wishes.

Once in charge, Cudlipp had begun reinventing the features pages with ingredients that still shape British tabloids to this day. In doing so he was replicating elements first introduced centuries previously. The tradition of the 'agony aunt' – the advice column for women first created by John Dunton's *Athenian Mercury* in 1690 – had begun to blossom in the United States towards the end of the more prudish Victorian era, principally at the hands of two pioneering woman journalists of the 1890s, both reporters, authors and campaigning suffragettes. In 1889 Marie Manning, a reporter on Hearst's *New York Evening Journal*, had initiated one of the first women's pages, the 'Hen Coop', responding to readers' letters seeking personal advice. Published under the pen name Beatrice Fairfax, and subtitled 'She will advise you on the troubles of your HEART', the column became so popular that at one point the New York postal office refused to deliver the vast amount of letters she received.

Its rival was written by Dorothy Dix, the pen name of Elizabeth Meriweather Gilmer, who had begun writing a homely advice column in her local newspaper in New Orleans. In 1901 Hearst recruited her as a crime reporter for the *Evening Journal* and as one of the 'sob sisters' – female journalists who reported on crime and court cases using a highly coloured and personal approach. It was said that no great murder trial was complete until Dix took her place at the press table. In 1917 she left Hearst and returned to advice column writing full time. By the mid-1920s 'Dorothy Dix Talks' was being read in two hundred publications around the world and she was the world's highest-paid woman writer. It was only common sense for Cudlipp to publish Dix's columns in the *Mirror*.

Cudlipp had other ideas for attracting women readers. A series called the 'Charm School' on how to be 'beautiful, charming and popular' led to 60,000 letters over six weeks. A questionnaire to women readers asking for details of their first date, their first kiss and so on received 50,000 replies and the paper was able to proclaim that, on average, the first kiss came five months after the first 'hello' and was received at the age of fifteen and a quarter, usually between 6 p.m. and midnight. Women and girls appeared in the paper in many different ways – as bathing beauties in their swimsuits, as glamorous Hollywood stars and in columns and features.

A new columnist was engaged, the extraordinary figure of actor and writer Godfrey Winn, who wrote a daily full-page piece called 'Personality Parade'. This described both his daily suburban life with his mother, garden and dog in Esher and his glamorous friends, such as Ivor Novello, Noël Coward and W. Somerset Maugham, all written in a slightly wide-eyed, friendly fashion. The fact that Winn was, like Novello and Coward, openly gay could not be mentioned in print, but it added a frisson to his writings, which became incredibly popular and eventually led to him being recruited by the *Express*. Winn later worked as a war correspondent and was the first journalist to cross the Maginot Line; he also became a seaman in the Royal Navy, serving on an Arctic convoy. Another defining figure in the new *Mirror* was William Connor, who wrote as Cassandra. Connor, a former executive for advertising agency J. Walter Thompson, joined at the same time as Cudlipp, who described him as someone who wrote 'without fear' and could make his column 'purr or bark, nuzzle or bite, canter or gallop'. Cudlipp added: 'In a rare gift, his words appeal alike to men and women, young and old, intellectuals and ignoramuses, priest and atheists, judges and old lags, heterosexuals, homosexuals and hermaphrodites.'[21] In turn, Connor recruited Philip Zec, another former advertising colleague, to create political cartoons, one of which regularly accompanied his column and for which he frequently wrote the captions. Zec was followed by his brother, Donald (their father was a Jewish tailor who had fled oppression in Russia), who later became the *Mirror*'s royal reporter and then a celebrated showbusiness writer. All three were crucial to the *Mirror*'s dominance of the tabloid market.

Donald Zec later recalled his first assignment as a reporter – a fire in Soho. His story began: 'Firemen were called to extinguish a blaze . . .'. This met with a 'look of utter contempt and then pity' on the face of his news editor, who declared, 'This is shit,' before handing it to a more experienced reporter who rewrote it as: 'Clad only in her scanties, a blonde, 22-year-old nightclub hostess climbed along a 30ft parapet in a Soho fire last night to rescue her pet cat Timothy.' Zec added: 'Here, in a single sentence of slick hyperbole, were all the elements of popular journalism – sex, heroism, drama and pet-worship.'[22]

Another innovation was 'Live Letter Box', 'conducted by the Old Codgers', a move to brighten up the letters page with a straight lift of the 'Answers to Correspondents' idea. Bartholomew told Cudlipp that every single letter needed to have a reply, regardless of whether or not it was published – that was how you held onto readers. Under Cudlipp, the feature pages became, in his own words, 'stimulating and aggressive, crammed with excitement and surprises . . . articles became brief and punchy. Gossip, barbed and bright . . . And the headlines! For a public nurtured on shock free newspapers, the effect was startling.'[23] Overseen by the 'cantankerous and cunning' Bartholomew, with the calm figure of Cecil Thomas as editor and Cudlipp the adventurous and ambitious features editor, the *Mirror* underwent a renaissance. Within five years, it was challenging the *Express* for dominance of the market. Then came the war.

By this time, Cudlipp had been rewarded for his efforts and, at just 25, in early 1938, was appointed editor of the ailing *Sunday Pictorial* by King, who had been made its editorial director by the *Mirror* board, a role Bartholomew had turned down. Bartholomew was furious that Cudlipp took the job, and refused to give either any help, the start of a rift that would last for nearly two decades. The *Pictorial*, facing strong competition from the resurgent *News of the World*, had seen its circulation drop from 2.4 million in 1925 to around 1.4 million by the time Cudlipp took over. Dubbing the current paper 'a conspiracy to make the English Sabbath duller', Cudlipp set about his task with zeal, introducing the *Mirror*'s formula of shorter, sharper stories, bigger, bolder headlines and a focus on crime and sleaze, human interest and sentimentality, as a result of which sales soared. Three decades before Page 3 in *The Sun*, Cudlipp published the first topless image in a British newspaper. He had commissioned a photograph of a topless girl in an orchard in full springtime blossom. But King told him that he needed to get approval from Cowley, the company chairman, to publish. Cudlipp knew Cowley was a Kent farmer with his own orchard, and the chairman was allegedly so entranced by the blossom on display and the similarity to that on his own trees that he happily and absent-mindedly gave the go-ahead.

Cudlipp, writing a column under the pseudonym Charles Wilberforce, also took the paper in a stronger political direction, warning about Hitler and attacking appeasement and the September 1938 Munich agreement with ferocity. Cudlipp also landed a major scoop with a report of the resignation of the foreign secretary, Anthony Eden, which Cudlipp confirmed by calling Eden at home at midnight. King and Cudlipp launched a campaign for Winston Churchill to join the Cabinet and enrolled him as a columnist, although that did not insulate him from criticism.

After the outbreak of war, Cudlipp was determined to volunteer but his call-up was deferred and he was eventually assigned to the Royal Corps of Signals in December 1940. He spent much of his time in the Army on journalistic duties, producing a magazine at Sandhurst, newsletters for the servicemen on a troopship sailing to Suez and then, at the instigation of Churchill, a regular newsletter for Montgomery's Eighth Army in North Africa.

'The Price of Petrol Has Been Increased by One Penny – Official'

All newspapers continued to publish during the Second World War, although circulations and size were artificially restricted by newsprint rationing, introduced in late 1942. But it was the British government, not Hitler's bombers, that almost closed the *Mirror* down. In the run-up to the war in 1938 and 1939, the *Mirror* and the *Pictorial*, unlike most of the rest of Fleet Street, had attacked Hitler and warned against appeasement, provoking the Führer himself to complain to the British foreign secretary that the paper was damaging relations between the two countries.[24] The day after the outbreak of war, its Cassandra-conceived front page was a 'wanted' poster for Hitler and the paper campaigned relentlessly for Churchill to take over from Chamberlain as prime minister.

Meanwhile, Rothermere, still in control of the *Mail* and *The Times*, who had been so keen to praise Mosley and then Hitler, volunteered his services to his old ally Beaverbrook, who had been appointed minister for aircraft production by Churchill. Beaverbrook, although aware that Rothermere was by now elderly and in poor health, asked him to go to North America to help in the purchase of aluminium. It might have been seen as a lowly role, but Rothermere took it.

Once in New York he fell ill, but then sailed to Bermuda, where he died two weeks later, at the end of November 1940. His last words were said to have been, 'There is nothing more I can do to help my country now.'[25] In contrast to the elaborate 1922 funeral of his brother, Rothermere's burial in Bermuda was attended by a handful of people, the only family member being his granddaughter, the seventeen-year-old Esme Harmsworth. Today, his family still control the company he founded and the *Daily Mail*, the *Mail on Sunday* and *MailOnline*, launched in 1982 and 2003 respectively, which set the template for modern online popular journalism.

Bartholomew had decided the *Mirror* would once again become the paper of the troops and so, despite Churchill's ascendancy, continued to criticize the conduct of the war from the point of view of the humble soldier, complaining about excessive drills and boot polishing, the lack of the right equipment and the follies of the Army top brass. A 'Live Letters'-style column for soldiers' grievances was also started, and the seaside-postcard-style cartoon strip *Jane*, in which a young girl about town often appeared in states of semi-undress, became noticeably more risqué.

> He [Bartholomew] understood the instinctive practical tribal working class patriotism of the troops, the feeling they were being led by upper class idiot officers . . . the yearning the troops had shown for news from home and huge demand from families left at home for pictorial news of what was happening on the front line.[26]

Both papers began to attract official disapproval, with generals complaining to the War Office that it was undermining morale.[27] After two particularly critical Cassandra columns, Churchill wrote to King saying the paper had a spirit of 'hatred and malice against the Government'.[28] An exchange of letters and meetings between King and Churchill followed, after which King assured the prime minister there would be a 'marked change of tone'. It did not last. In November 1941 the *Pictorial* ran a leader suggesting the House of Commons go permanently into recess because it was full of 'second-raters', causing Home Secretary Herbert Morrison to suggest the paper might be officially suppressed because of its 'subversive articles'.

Philip Zec's cartoons, with captions written by Cassandra using the advertising man's turn of phrase, were crucial to the *Mirror*'s coverage. In March 1942, as the climax to a series of cartoons attacking black marketeers, Zec had drawn a stark image of a sailor clinging to a wooden raft on a storm-wracked sea. The meaning of the caption – 'The price of petrol has been increased by one penny – Official' – was perhaps deliberately double-edged as both a rebuke to street profiteers and those who wasted fuel and a bleak portrayal of the reality of how servicemen were suffering in order to keep basic supplies running; everyone had a price to pay, was the message. The cartoon caused an uproar: Churchill now finally wanted the *Mirror* closed down, but Morrison, backed by Beaverbrook, was allowed to give the papers a final warning, telling the Commons that the cartoon was 'evil' and the *Mirror* guilty of 'scurrilous misrepresentations' against the national interest, and summoning Bartholomew and Thomas to tell them the government could close the paper down for spreading defeatism, as it had already done in the case of the communist newspaper the *Daily Worker*. Zec's cartoons did not diminish after Cassandra volunteered for national service. 'His cartoons continued to dominate the slim issues of a *Mirror* that had become the People's Paper and, most importantly, the paper of the serving soldier, sailor and airman.'[29]

Shortly afterwards, following the rationing of newsprint and the loss of staff to the war, Bartholomew and King agreed to take it all down a notch. King noted in his later book: 'We . . . feel that criticism is now futile and merely boring. The war no longer arouses interest and therefore the only possible line . . . is great preoccupation on the young, both in services and factories.'[30] For the remainder of the war, everything was put on hold. Bartholomew and some other *Mirror* staff would eventually help the war effort by working on a highly secret newsletter for submarine crews; Cassandra was eventually seconded to help Cudlipp's forces newspaper *Union Jack*.

Much later, it became known that the German high command had ordered that, when Britain was invaded, the senior executives of the *Mirror* company – Bartholomew, King and Cudlipp as well as Cassandra – would be immediately tracked down and arrested.[31]

'Forward with the People'

The end of the war saw the *Mirror* rise to become the biggest-selling daily newspaper in the country by the end of the decade. Normal service resumed when Cassandra returned to print with his first post-war column, opening with the words: 'As I was saying before I was rudely interrupted . . .' The company chairman, Cowley, seen as something of a restraining force, had passed away towards the war's end and was replaced by Bartholomew, who installed Philip Zec and *Mirror* editor Thomas on the board; King, meanwhile, added the key role of finance director. Despite the country's deep debt to and affection for Churchill, both papers would nail their colours very firmly to the mast of Clement Attlee's Labour Party, determined to capture the national mood of post-war reconstruction and revival and the need to build a different type of society for the returning troops; and circulations would rise as a result. The support was never explicit but its editorials in the run-up to the 1945 election were aimed at the wives and mothers who held proxy votes for the soldiers still abroad, suggesting that there was a need for change, that Churchill's Conservatives were worn out and that Labour would deliver the new deal the country needed. On VE Day, 8 May, another powerful Zec cartoon appeared, depicting a wounded soldier holding out a laurel crown with the words 'Victory and Peace in Europe' and the caption 'Here you are, don't lose it again,' which would rival his earlier oil drawing for power and impact. Shortly afterwards, the motto 'Forward with the People' appeared on the paper's masthead. Labour swept to power in the July election and since the rest of Fleet Street had sided with Churchill, the *Mirror* papers were given considerable credit for Labour's victory, cementing their long-standing 'critical friend' relationship; the symbiosis between them closer than ever. Christiansen and Beaverbrook's *Express*, with its pre-war support for appeasement and its warning that voting for Labour would herald a 'Socialist Gestapo', was the loser, although its circulation would continue to hold firm for some years.

Delayed by Army duties, Cudlipp rejected overtures from the *Daily Mail* and the *Daily Express* and instead returned to his old job at the *Pictorial* in 1946. King longed to see Cudlipp at the helm of the *Mirror* but Bartholomew, who viewed him as a rival and wanted him out, stood in the way. Cudlipp enjoyed several more good years at the *Pictorial* and together with the *Mirror* saw steady rises in circulation, riding on the back of the new welfare state created by the Labour government and the loyalty of its readers, who had been won over by its support for the returning soldiers and their families.

When newsprint restrictions were relaxed in September 1946, the *Mirror*'s circulation leapt to more than 3.2 million; eighteen months later, it was outstripping the *Daily Express*, with sales of 4.1 million compared with the *Express*'s 3.9 million, despite the latter's claim to be the world's greatest newspaper. In 1948 the *Mirror* had a new editor and Bartholomew appointee, Sylvester Bolam, who the following year became the first editor in many years to be jailed for contempt of court, in this case for three months, after publishing details about the 'Acid Bath Murderer', John Haigh, before his trial.

In the late 1940s the post-war resurgence of the print press, coupled with a renewed sense of power among the unions, and in particular the National Union of Journalists, led to calls for an inquiry into the conduct and ownership of newspapers, which resulted in the Royal Commission on the Press of 1947–9. At this point, the Rothermere family owned *The Times*, the *Daily Mail*, the *Sunday Dispatch* and the *Evening News* and still, to a degree, through King, had a powerful influence over the Mirror Group, which had the *Mirror* and the *Sunday Pictorial*. The *Daily Express*, the *Sunday Express* and the *Evening Standard* were owned by Beaverbrook, and were still all staunchly supporting the Conservatives. The *News of the World*, which now had little serious political content, the *Manchester Guardian* and *The Observer* stood alone, relatively speaking. The once-powerful *Daily Herald*, which was constitutionally allied to the Labour Party, had been overshadowed and squeezed by the rise of the *Mirror* and *Express*, which together had a circulation of around 8 million.

The Commission's report concluded, damningly, with an acute observation that is probably even more true today:

> In the popular papers, consideration of news value acts as a distorting medium even apart from any political considerations: it attaches, as we have shown, supreme importance to the new, the exceptional, and the 'human', and it emphasises these elements in the news to the detriment or even the

exclusion of the normal and the continuing. Consequently, the picture is always out of focus. The combination day after day of distortion due to these factors with the distortion aris- ing from political partisanship has a cumulative effect upon the reader. It results, where it is carried farthest, not only in a debasement of standards of taste, but also in a further weak- ening of the foundations of intelligent judgement in public affairs. Political partisanship alone, as we have indicated, deprives the citizen of the evidence on which conclusions should be based: political partisanship in conjunction with a high degree of distortion for news value may lead him to forget that conclusions are, or should be, grounded on evidence.[32]

Despite these words, the commission shied away from making any recommendations for state control or oversight of newspapers and was therefore broadly welcomed by the bulk of the popular publishers, which chose to ignore the criticisms. The commission's work did lead to the establishment of the Press Council, which was designed as an independent body to respond to public complaints about newspapers, but mostly comprised of members of the very same papers it was meant to hold to account: a case of newspapers marking their own homework. It was widely perceived to be in- effectual and lacking teeth and was eventually succeeded by the Press Complaints Commission, but not until 1991.

In the *Mirror*, after Bolam took over as editor in 1948 during the middle of the commission's deliberations, there appeared a front- page editorial by Bolam but widely believed to have been dictated by Bartholomew in partial response to the more restrained approach of Cudlipp and King.[33] The manifesto attacked such 'critics' and delivered an impassioned defence of tabloid 'sensationalism' for its role in serving the public interest: the *Mirror* was a sensational newspaper, he said, and he would make no apology for its presenta- tion of news and views, believing it was a 'valuable public service'. Crucially, he added:

The Mirror is a sensational newspaper. Sensationalism does not mean distorting the truth. It means the vivid and dra- matic presentation of events so as to give them a forceful impact on the mind of the reader. It means big headlines, vigorous writing, simplification into everyday language, and the wide use of illustration and cartoon.[34]

This divide, between those who believe that sensationalism and distortion go hand in hand and those who counter that sensationalism, in Bolam's sense of the word, is what makes some tabloid journalism great, still runs like a fault line through our understanding of – and response to – the tabloid media.

The End of Bart

Bartholomew was by now, in Cudlipp's words, 'increasingly irascible, grotesquely unjust and was hitting the bottle. He was occasionally incoherent and frequently unreliable.'[35] Bartholomew's chance to get rid of Cudlipp came in late 1949, when the *Sunday Pictorial* editor decided not to publish a piece written by King – then on an African tour of company investments – about rioting miners in Nigeria. Cudlipp reasoned that, on a busy news day, it was going to be of little interest to normal readers of a popular Sunday newspaper. King was not a trained journalist or a particularly good writer, which may also have counted against him, and the story was about a distant country of little concern. But some newspapers ran a story on the riot on the Monday morning and Bartholomew used this as a fairly thin excuse for a coup against Cudlipp, who, only slightly annoyed, immediately went off to work for Beaverbrook – who had been courting him for years – and a generous salary at the *Sunday Express*. His two-year interlude there as managing editor enabled him to understand how Beaverbrook exerted control: 'The editors of the *Daily Express*, the *Sunday Express*, the London *Evening Standard* and the Glasgow Citizen enjoyed absolute freedom to agree wholeheartedly with their master's voice.'[36]

King, still in Africa, was unable to intercede and there were some suggestions that he was also piqued with Cudlipp for spiking his story.[37] But Bartholomew himself did not last much longer. In an atmosphere now reminiscent of ancient Rome, in 1951 King, having waited for his moment, engineered a boardroom coup against Bartholomew. Now seventy, Bartholomew was told, bluntly, that he was too old and too drunk and stood in the way of progress.

Bartholomew rejected the board's letter asking him to leave the building and a power struggle ensued in which he attempted to get Zec and Bolam, both now on the board, to support him. Part of Bartholomew's resistance was that he had no other source of income – he had never had a *Mirror* pension or shares – and that he had few other interests in his life. But a pay-off was eventually organized and Bartholomew left the *Mirror*, the paper he had served all his life, rising from office boy to chairman, with a cheque for £20,000, a sizeable amount at that time.[38] King, triumphant, became chairman of what was now a company with global interests, as well as the biggest-selling newspaper in the world. He wrote to Cudlipp: 'Let's get together and make a dent in the history of our times.'[39] The Welshman returned from the *Express* as editorial director of both the *Mirror* and the *Sunday Pictorial*. Shortly afterwards, at a press conference to announce the executive changes, King was asked if it was correct that Bartholomew was 'an illiterate drunkard'. Cudlipp responded that it was an inaccurate characterization: 'He was semi-literate and he wasn't drunk all the time.'[40]

Drunk or not, Bartholomew's influence on the *Mirror* over almost half a century had been profound. The *Mirror* had gone from a stuttering, almost failed experiment, which he had twice helped to reinvent – once after its launch and again in the mid-1930s – to the biggest-selling daily paper in the country. In his later memoir, Donald Zec argued that Bartholomew was the father of British tabloids, although greater perspective might suggest he was not the only one. In 1965, three years after Bartholomew's death, the historian A.J.P. Taylor wrote that in those years, the *Mirror* had for the first time allowed the mass of the English public to find their voice. 'The *Mirror* had no proprietor,' he wrote, clearly referring to Northcliffe and Beaverbrook but perhaps forgetting the Rothermere influence over the board. Taylor went on:

> It was created by the ordinary people on its staff and particularly Harry Guy Bartholomew, the man who worked his way up from office boy to editorial director. The *Daily Mirror* gave an indication as never before what ordinary people in the ordinary sense were thinking. The English people at last found their voice.[41]

A sad postscript to Bartholomew's career came just a year after Taylor's book. A King-commissioned official biography of the *Mirror* by Labour MP and journalist Maurice Edelman included the Taylor quote, but cut out the reference to Bartholomew, replacing it with an ellipsis.[42] Whether it was at King's insistence or simply an unfortunate error was never established. But it was clear that the heirs to Northcliffe were still in control.

Cudlipp's return and King's boardroom coup heralded a decade of unprecedented success for the *Mirror*, with the *Sunday Pictorial* keeping its foot in the Sunday market, although always trailing the *News of the World*. At the same time, the *Express*, still under Beaverbrook's rigid control and pitched at readers who were more aspirational and middle-class than those who chose the *Mirror*, held its own, just under the *Mirror* circulation, although it would eventually suffer from a steadily ageing readership. The *Mirror*, by then under a Cudlipp appointee, the hard-nosed, sweary editor Jack Nener, averaged around 4.4 to 4.8 million throughout the 1950s, the *Express*, with Beaverbrook and Christiansen, always trailing slightly behind, but never dropping below 4 million. A total circulation of around 9 million equated to around 30 million readers – on the basis that newspapers were shared among fellow workers and families – or almost 60 per cent of the population in the mid-1950s.

This was a relatively stable decade, as the economy soared amid the post-war boom and the emerging consumer society. Both papers enjoyed generous staffing levels and astute middle and senior management, both aware of where they stood in the tabloid market; competition from their rivals, such as the *Daily Sketch* and the *Daily Herald*, both ailing, was easily seen off. The *Daily Mail* enjoyed a loyal readership, but it now lacked the stridency and optimism of the *Express*, delivered with brio by Christiansen. On Sundays, the *News of the World* continued in its own, Orwell-defined fashion, while a battle raged in the middle market between the *Sunday Dispatch* and the *Sunday Express*. In 1950 there was a series of stories about flying saucers, which may well have sparked the genre of tabloid 'exclusive' about extra-terrestial life, which continues today with the *Daily Star* in the UK and the *National Enquirer* in the United States. (Almost without anyone noticing, the *Dispatch* became the biggest-selling Sunday paper during the late 1950s, reaching a circulation of

1.5 million. In 1960, it was sold by Rothermere's heirs to the *Express* and the name disappeared.)

At the *Mirror*, the paper's coverage acknowledged its working-class, wartime readership – Nener's version of the paper 'loved charladies, patted doggies, cooed at babies, drank beer with coalminers, stuck two fingers up at the toffs and stood for no nonsense from uppity foreigners' – but did not neglect images of attractive young women, particularly film stars.[43] Also, Cudlipp realized it needed to cater for the new post-war generation, the baby boomers who would soon discover pop music and fashion – the consumer generation to come. For the older generation, there was a new cartoon, 'Andy Capp', featuring a cloth-capped archetypical northern working-class character, cigarette and pint of beer in hand, while Cassandra continued with his acerbic political columns, which became lauded for their range, wit and insight. There was now more glamour and showbusiness too: Donald Zec soon became *the* showbiz writer of Fleet Street, getting close to the stars of the era such as Elizabeth Taylor, Marilyn Monroe and Diana Dors; film reviews became a staple and Zec was welcomed all over Hollywood, becoming a drinking partner of Humphrey Bogart.

The remarkable Marjorie Proops, initially recruited as a fashion artist by Cudlipp before the war, had defected to the *Daily Herald* (lured by Cudlipp's older brother Percy), where she reinvented herself as a columnist before returning to the *Mirror* in 1955 as the voice of 'The Sparkling New Column for Women'. Proops continued to write for the *Mirror* for another four decades, both as a columnist and an agony aunt, reinforcing the paper's reputation among women readers. Alongside Cassandra, Proops and Zec, other writers and reporters almost became household names: Keith Waterhouse, who would go on to be a columnist and novelist (enjoying great success with his book *Billy Liar*), joined as a feature writer, and Peter Wilson became the star sports reporter of the age; Donald Wise was a legendary foreign reporter while Vicky became a renowned cartoonist. Cudlipp was a dominant figure, frequently elbowing aside Nener and others to take charge at key times – the general elections, the death of the George VI and the coronation of the young Queen Elizabeth (an issue which sold 7 million copies) and the Suez Crisis, designing dramatic front pages, inside and centre-page spreads, fizzing with ideas while chomping on a large cigar.

During this period of unmatched success, the *Mirror* building was swimming in alcohol. The whole of Fleet Street was by now a place of regular heavy drinking. The pubs and drinking clubs in the area, often closely associated with individual titles, were places where journalists gathered to relax, argue and gossip, before, during and after what were often very long, hard days – many senior editorial executives would start work at around nine or ten in the morning and would rarely leave until the first edition went to bed around twelve hours later. Long liquid lunches to break up the day became part of this routine for almost all ranks, followed by an evening refresher before going home. This was also drinking with a purpose: editors, executives, reporters and columnists would regularly meet and entertain contacts of all kinds and these encounters almost without exception involved alcohol, funded by generous expenses accounts. 'Boardroom lunches' became a tradition, where people in public life would be invited to meet editors and key writers on an off-the-record basis and where, usually, much drink would be taken, as journalists sought indiscretion and gossip from their guests.

The *Mirror* building was no exception:

> Visit Cudlipp before 11 am and you would be offered a beer (unless it was to be a day of celebration when there would be a champagne conference at 10.30); after 11 he would open a bottle of white wine. While King, Cudlipp and senior journalists like the Political Editor Sydney Jacobson would tend to go to separate lunches with influential people (aperitif, wine, brandy) most feature writers would drift at lunchtime to the Falcon . . . *Mirror* and Pictorial reporters went to Barney Finnegans further up the street, for there was a strict demarcation in Fleet Street's pubs.

In the early evening, Cudlipp would often be seen at El Vino, where 'he could usually be found having a glass of champagne before looking in at the paper, perhaps disappearing to dine (aperitif, wine, brandy) and then returning to see it go to bed.'[44] Unsurprisingly, perhaps, both King and Cudlipp were eventually told by doctors to reduce their drinking.

While many outsiders might have wondered how on earth such a professional paper came to be produced every day to tight deadlines in such circumstances, there are two main reasons. First, most journalists of the era and later prided themselves on their ability to get the job done, whether they were drunk or not (the same thinking applied to foreign correspondents filing from war zones – get it written despite the shells that are landing around you), even if individuals occasionally had to be quietly sent home because they had overdone it. Second, until well into the 2000s generous staffing levels on all the tabloids ensured that there were always enough people to cover for others and get the paper out.

As the 1960s dawned, the *Mirror* moved into modern new buildings in Holborn Circus and King began to expand the business, buying paper producers Reed International and publishers Paul Hamlyn. He eventually took over Odhams Press, too, owners of the by then struggling *Daily Herald*, with guarantees that the two papers would never merge. The *Herald* would never be quite the same paper again, a dullard living in the shadow of the glamorous *Mirror*. The renamed International Publishing Corporation (IPC), chaired by King, became the biggest publishing company in the world. Cudlipp was named *Herald* chairman, though his main focus remained the *Mirror*, where his dramatic 'Shock Issues' devoted large sections of a single paper to social concerns such as housing and race in an effort to educate and inform the readership. These became benchmarks for serious but popular journalism. The *Mirror* also became an early campaigner for membership of the Common Market and, despite the Tories having been in government since the early 1950s, remained a Labour-supporting paper, with King, Cudlipp and senior editors and writers close to leading Labour figures. The party was now led by the modernizing Harold Wilson, for whom Cudlipp supplied the ringing phrase 'the white heat of the technological revolution', delivered in a famous speech in 1963.

By June 1964 the paper was selling more than 5 million copies a day and being read by more than 15 million people daily; what's more, it had no serious competition. It celebrated with a celebrity-packed and champagne-drenched party at the Albert Hall. The *Sunday Pictorial* was now renamed the *Sunday Mirror* to capitalize on the *Mirror* name and it gained a strong foothold in the Sunday market, while never quite challenging the *News of the World*, which sailed on with its own menu of randy vicars, wife-swapping parties and lurid crime and court stories. The *Express*, still under the ageing Beaverbrook until his death in 1964, maintained a nostalgic, Conservative and Empire-era vision for Britain, one that failed to attract the new younger readers flocking to the *Mirror*, and so its circulation declined. After Wilson won a narrow majority at the October 1964 election, the *Mirror* could truly be seen to be voicing the spirit of the nation.

As the 1960s rolled on, the era was reflected in the *Mirror*'s pages – the Beatles and pop music, the mini-skirt and Carnaby Street, the debates over abortion and homosexuality and England's triumph in the 1966 World Cup. Although the papers were shocked by the relatively early death of William 'Cassandra' Connor, aged 57, in April 1967, who had been knighted the previous year, Cudlipp had recruited other star writers, such as women's editor Felicity Green, legendary foreign correspondent James Cameron and a young Australian, John Pilger, who went on to win awards for his investigative foreign reporting. The *Mirror* also introduced a new weekly four-page pull-out section called 'Mirrorscope', which covered big stories with greater detail and analysis. The paper now dominated the British popular newspaper market as part of the largest publishing group in the world. And then King lost the plot. Or rather, he started one.

'Enough Is Enough'

On 10 May 1968 the Daily *Mirror* front page carried the huge headline 'Enough Is Enough' over an opinion piece penned by King and accompanied by his picture, in case there was any doubt as to who was responsible. Also carried in the *Herald* and the *Mirror*'s sister paper in Scotland, the *Daily Record*, the article called for the Labour Party to ditch Harold Wilson because the government was lacking the 'foresight, ability and integrity' to deal with a raft of crises, mainly to do with the country's poor economic performance. The piece claimed the UK was facing the greatest financial crisis in its history, and that there had been 'lies about our reserves'. King had been a director of the Bank of England for several years, so those words carried weight, even if readers were not told he had resigned the previous evening, a move which freed him from any obligation to keep silent for fear of spooking the markets. Next to the article was a news story about the 'disaster' of Labour losing heavily in the local government elections the previous day. The front page was initially shrugged off by Labour, but caused a run on the pound and markets slumped. The rest of the IPC board were angry at both King's breach with Labour and the leak of confidential information from his role with the Bank, for which he was widely condemned, not least by the rest of the media. By the end of the month, King had been sacked, a sad end to a lifetime of involvement in the *Mirror* that had brought it to a pinnacle of success. But how did this spectacular self-immolation come about?

One theory is that, like both his uncles, King became ever more eccentric with age and lost some of his grip on reality. He had lost interest (another Harmsworth trait) in IPC, which had been spread too thinly with too many acquisitions. It was affected by the country's difficult economic situation and burdened by a bloated management structure; losses were mounting. King, imbued with characteristic Harmsworth self-belief, now saw himself as someone who could influence the course of the nation's history. Disappointed by previous Labour leaders, his initial enthusiasm for Wilson had lessened due to the economic situation and increasing trade union militancy. He believed the country was heading for collapse and Wilson doomed to fail. He was also angry Wilson had offered him an ordinary life peerage, rather than the hereditary one he craved. King's wife, Ruth, fuelled a growing megalomania in her husband's mind, writing in her diary: 'For years no political leader. We must have LEADERS. The world has never gone through such a difficult time. Europe could be again 72 years old – standing man to man to White House, Moscow and China, but the one man is C.H.K.'[45]

Before that front page, King had begun to share his views with Cudlipp, other executives and Labour ministers, as well as business leaders, who all remained unconvinced. He put pressure on Cudlipp to use the *Mirror* to attack Wilson but Cudlipp kept stalling him. Richard Crossman, the labour minister, described King's onslaught as 'character assassination' in the tradition of Northcliffe and Rothermere, 'two megalomanic press lords who tried to dictate to Prime Ministers'.[46] Not a single public figure came to his support. Senior figures in both the Labour Party and the Mirror Group felt the relationship between then was about to collapse, to no one's benefit. Cudlipp, so long a professional ally of King, if not

A confrontation between Cecil King (left) and Hugh Cudlipp during the annual meeting of the International Publishing Corporation in London, 7 July 1968.

his personal friend, realized the time had come and joined the IPC directors for a secret meeting of the board in the *Mirror* building on 29 May, held discreetly and away from where King and his wife were dining in his private suite. *The Times* later reported: 'Every director expressed the view that Mr King should go. They made their point . . . with dignity, reluctance and a genuine feeling of sorrow for the man who had given so much of his life in the service of the group.'[47] It was Cudlipp's signature on the letter that told King he should now retire and that he, Cudlipp, would succeed him as chairman. The letter said: 'Your increasing pre-occupation and intervention in national affairs in a personal sense rather than in the objective publishing sense has created a situation . . . detrimental to the present and future conduct of the business of IPC.'[48] There was a brief power struggle when King refused to resign, conceding that he might go in a few months. The board rejected the offer and King was effectively sacked. King later told the *Sunday Express*, 'I have been stabbed in the back for my views.'[49] At the next AGM of IPC, where he had been given permission to speak, he said that he had been ousted 'in a conspiracy of a particularly squalid kind . . . I had been a member of staff for 42 years, a member of the board for 42 years, chairman for 17 years and I was given three hours to clear out.'[50]

Arguments continued for many years over King's motives and the broader background to his actions. Suggestions that somehow MI5 were involved, stoked later by Wilson himself in briefings to journalists and then in the book *Spycatcher*, published in 1987, in which disgruntled former MI5 officer Peter Wright claimed King had been a long-time MI5 agent, were eventually rubbished, although it was true that King's son, Michael, who had worked for the *Daily Mirror* as foreign editor, did have links with the security service. It also emerged later that King had tried to enlist the help of, first, right-wing Conservative MP Enoch Powell, who became *persona non grata* after his 'Rivers of Blood' speech, the now exiled-in-Paris Sir Oswald Mosley and then Earl Mountbatten, the queen's much-respected cousin, to join in some kind of government of national unity to save the country from socialism and decline.

After leaving IPC, King did not back down and continued to travel around the UK and Europe attacking the government and Wilson and still advocating the formation of a national government. Through Peter Stephens, the *Mirror*'s Paris correspondent, he also arranged to meet Mosley for dinner at his home near the city in April 1969. Stephens reported back to Cudlipp that King had told him: 'He [Mosley] is an extremely brilliant man and could still make a useful contribution.' Stephens asked King if he was thinking of including him in his replacement government. King replied: 'Why not? People have forgotten about his past.' Stephens, clearly alarmed, turned down an invitation to the dinner, aware that any involvement with Mosley was still toxic to many and would be an embarrassment to his employers, as well as a reminder of a past that the modern-day *Mirror* might prefer to be brushed over.[51]

King had a number of further meetings with Mosley, recording them favourably in his diaries. Cudlipp later wrote that King's interest in Mosley was 'incomprehensible'.[52] It is perhaps also worth noting, as indicative of the mindset of King and his wife Ruth, that she said to others that King had been forced from the IPC board because 'Jewish bankers had paid out £2,500,000 in bribes to get rid of him.'[53] Writing later, Cudlipp, who did not name Ruth King as the source, said this was a 'monstrous fabrication', not least because 'no one I ever met was more pro-Semitic than Cecil.'[54] Despite King's obsession with a national government and his regular contacts with leading politicians and others, he no longer had a serious public platform and never really gathered substantial support. Relations between Cudlipp and King remained cordial for many years, but King never returned to newspapers or serious public life. He died in retirement in Ireland in 1987. Cudlipp was not invited to the funeral.

Relations with Labour now repaired, Cudlipp reigned supreme at IPC. Widely regarded as the best tabloid editor ever, he presided over a huge publishing empire with newspapers read by many millions of people. But he was, essentially, a brilliant journalist rather than a businessman. And he was about to make the biggest mistake of his career, which would end the *Mirror*'s dominance of the tabloid press. Cudlipp's move would also lead to a complete transformation of the domestic newspaper market, both popular and serious, by giving a foothold to a certain Rupert Murdoch.

5

THE SUN RISES

'**W**e've got nothing to worry about,' Hugh Cudlipp told *Daily Mirror* editor Lee Howard that November night in 1969 when they inspected the first error-strewn, smudged, poorly designed and hastily thrown together edition of the new tabloid-sized *Sun* that was brought to their offices in High Holborn.[1] Just a few weeks previously, Cudlipp and IPC had sold the former *Daily Herald* newspaper to Rupert Murdoch, then a relatively unknown Australian tycoon, still in his thirties, who had recently bought the *News of the World*. Even Larry Lamb, the newly appointed editor of *The Sun*, whose baby it was, would write that it was 'visually crude, sloppily presented and virtually uncorrected'. But he also wrote: 'I had a gut feeling that there could be merit in its very crudeness; there could be lurking in its forty-eight amateurish tabloid pages the kind of rawness, the kind of life and vigour which had for so long been lacking in the complacent, deep piled corridors of Fleet Street.'[2] Lamb was right and Cudlipp, now chairman of IPC, one of the greatest newspaper figures of the era, could not have been more wrong. The reactivated *Sun* would give Murdoch the tabloid success he craved, granting him an influence over British public life and culture that is still a fundamental part of the media landscape of the country five decades later – and still causing controversy.

Murdoch had arrived in Britain from Australia just over a year before, in late October 1968, in a determined frame of mind: he was intent on buying the *News of the World*, the bastion of Sunday popular journalism since 1843, which had been owned by the Carr family since the late nineteenth century. It was the start of a long and sometimes uneasy relationship with the United Kingdom. Although the circulation of the *News of the World* was still an extraordinary 6 million and it had no serious rivals, it had dropped from its peak of 8 million in the 1950s and profits and the share price were faltering. The company, which the former Baron Riddell had created, had grown stale under the hands of the Carr family and failed to expand and diversify; it was ripe for takeover. Murdoch, by then 37 and the owner of a growing media empire in Australia, had long wanted to invest in the UK, which he considered his second home; it was where he had been to university and began his journalism career. He had been steadily and discreetly buying shares in Cudlipp's IPC, which he had long coveted as the epitome of popular tabloid journalism and on which he modelled his own *Mirror* newspaper in Sydney. When Murdoch heard that Robert Maxwell, the Labour MP for whom the phrase 'larger than life' might have been invented and the owner of Pergamon Press, which published scientific and trade journals, was about to buy a whole chunk of shares which could lead to his effective control of the *News of the World*, Murdoch dropped his *Mirror* ambitions and flew to London immediately. The stage was set for an epic confrontation between these two men, both hungry for those 6 million readers and their own power bases in the British tabloid media.

Two Tycoons

So who were they, these two very different men, Murdoch and Maxwell, who would by the second half of the 1980s between them control two huge British newspaper groups with a total readership of around 10 million and exert a dominance over the media that rivalled that of their predecessors? They were uncannily comparable to Hearst and Pulitzer: one the scion of a wealthy Caucasian newspaper dynasty, the other from a humble central European Jewish background and with superficially socialist principles. One was angular, strategic and controlled, he wasted little in terms of words or deeds, the ultimate poker player ready to make the killer move. The other was fleshy, overweight, generous in disposition and size, a charismatic, sometime melodramatic figure of emotion and instinct, optimistic in promises and evasive in actions. The former discreetly entered and left domains of presidents, prime ministers and potentates, content his words would be acted upon; his opponent smiled

First edition of *The Sun*, 17 November 1969.

for the cameras, with a ready handshake for the holder of power, blithely confident of his impact, even when it never happened. Their rivalry would be a recurring subplot in the story of British popular newspapers for more than two decades, but realistically there would only ever be one winner: Murdoch.

In the early 1950s Murdoch's father, Sir Keith Murdoch, a former friend of Northcliffe and head of a regional media empire based around Adelaide, was concerned his son didn't quite have it in him to take over control of the business when he retired or died. He was too quiet, too self-effacing. Those who met him after he arrived in London in 1968 didn't disagree: Harry Evans, appointed as editor of *The Times* in 1981 and fired by Murdoch within a year, described him as 'crippled by shyness'. 'He shuffled, smiled and left sentences in mid-air. He seemed too diffident to be a tycoon and too inarticulate to be a journalist.'[3] When Lady Carr, wife of Sir William Carr, then chairman of the *News of the World*, took Murdoch for lunch at a smart Mayfair restaurant, she found him 'lacking in small talk and a sense of humour'. He also annoyed her by lighting up a cigar before the first course.[4] Almost forty years after Evans's observations, Murdoch admitted to his biographer Michael Wolff to being a workaholic with no friends, who was not interested in culture, sport or social aspirations. Wolff described him thus: 'He's not good at explaining himself . . . he rarely has patience or interest in talking about the past.' And: 'He's, aloof, contained, pre-occupied . . . without flamboyance or personal exaggeration; he's rather buttoned down, in fact.' He also observed that while Murdoch could be animated and entertaining on the subject of the lapses of other people, he was not otherwise a great conversationalist, but a good listener.[5] Countless Murdoch employees would later testify to his lengthy and cruel silences, on the phone or in person, into which they would often stumble and fall.

Sir Keith was wrong in his estimation of his son's ability to run the business. After working on his school newspaper and journal at Geelong and part-time at the *Melbourne Herald*, he went to Oxford to study politics, philosophy and economics at Worcester College. There he was known as 'Red Rupert' for keeping a bust of Lenin in his rooms and being a member of the university Labour Party branch, facts hardly likely to have pleased the much more conservatively inclined Sir Keith. He also worked as manager of the company that published the student newspaper *Cherwell*, gaining formative experience of publishing. Sir Keith died in 1952, just as his son completed his degree at Oxford. Although Rupert could have expected to take over the reins immediately, he stood back and left his mother, Elizabeth, in day-to-day control, while he returned to Britain to work as a junior sub-editor on the *Daily Express*, still under the control of Beaverbrook. Murdoch was given what today would be called 'work experience' in an arrangement set up by Sir Keith before his death. Young Murdoch was duly placed at the lowest rung of the subs' table, out of harm's way, for several months, under the careful eye of Edward Pickering, the managing editor. But each night, unlike the other junior employees, he went back to a room at the Savoy Hotel.[6]

He returned to Australia, aged just 22, to run his father's much-diminished empire. Over the next two decades, this slightly hesitant young man expanded the business to own both tabloid and broadsheet newspapers, as well as radio stations across the subcontinent and a national, serious broadsheet title, *The Australian*. This, then, was the ambitious newspaper baron, still youngish, hardened in both corporate wars as well as newspaper production, who arrived in London ready to do battle again, this time for the *News of the World*. Murdoch was still relatively unknown in the UK; his opponent, Robert Maxwell, was not. Murdoch had been born with a silver spoon in his mouth, gained control of the levers of power in his early twenties and used them to expand his empire. Maxwell's origins and his route to success could not have been more different.

He was born Jan Ludvick Hoch in June 1923, one of five children of a Jewish peasant family living in the poor, remote, rural area of Carpo-Ruthenia, recently absorbed into the new Czechoslovakian state although historically Hungarian. His early years were spent in grinding poverty and strict observance of Orthodox Jewish religious customs. In 1938, as the Nazi shadow fell across Europe, sixteen-year-old Jan Hoch was sent to Budapest to find work. It was only after the Second World War that he learned that his parents and most of the rest of his family had died in the Holocaust. What happened in Budapest remains unclear; Maxwell gave often slightly conflicting explanations. What is confirmed is that, after fighting with Czech forces in Europe, he arrived in England in mid-1940 and joined the British Army's Pioneer Corps. Those who met him at this time described the young soldier as 'scarcely literate' and 'a wild young man from the mountains, quite unruly, like a young bull'.[7] He metamorphosed from peasant soldier to British Army officer, learning English rapidly, undergoing training and eventually joining the British North Staffs Regiment. By now he was a corporal known as Leslie du Maurier, after the then well-known cigarette brand. He took part in the Normandy landings in June 1944, fought his way across France, was involved in the liberation of Paris and, promoted to lieutenant, awarded the Military Cross for his bravery under fire in Germany, the citation praising his 'dash and determination' and lack of regard for his own safety. On the advice of senior officers, he had changed his name again, to Robert Maxwell.[8] It was a remarkable transformation.

After the war ended, he worked for British intelligence interrogating ex-Nazis in Berlin and then in the Foreign Office, helping to create and regulate the nascent post-war German media. Taking British citizenship in 1946, he used the contacts he had built up across Europe and in the post-war émigré world in London to launch himself into the publishing business, mostly of scientific books and journals. By the early 1960s he had built up Pergamon Press as a thriving business, often employing émigrés and refugees from the central European Jewish diaspora who had found themselves in London. 'We all adored him, he was a wonderful employer who gave us opportunities after the war for which we are all very grateful. A great man and a great character,' said one Austrian Jewish refugee who worked for him as a bookkeeper. Now a wealthy and successful businessman, he drove a Rolls-Royce and lived in an Oxfordshire mansion with his wife and growing brood of children. His large stature, black bushy eyebrows and booming voice gave him a sense of authority and power, which he used to great effect. He remained a confirmed socialist and was determined to become a Labour MP. In October 1964 he was elected MP for Buckingham, overturning a Tory majority and giving new prime minister Harold Wilson one of his four-strong majority. He remained a backbencher for several years, never quite being chosen for any elevation.

Some of this may have been due to his background, which for the British media establishment in the 1960s was alarmingly exotic. When Maxwell launched his bid for the *News of the World* in October 1968 by offering to buy shares from one member of the extended Carr family, Stafford Somerfield, long-serving editor of the *News of the World* and close to Sir William Carr, chairman and son of the former editor Elmsley Carr, delivered a verdict on Maxwell which today would be seen as xenophobic and racist. In an editorial, he wrote: 'Why do I think it would not be a good thing for Mr Maxwell, formerly Jan Ludwig Hoch, to gain control of this newspaper, which, I know, has your respect, loyalty and affection – a newspaper which I know is as British as roast beef and Yorkshire pudding?' Somerfield went on to question Maxwell's guarantees of editorial independence and promise to stand down as an MP if he gained control: 'Is it possible for him to support the Socialists one day and be impartial the next? . . . I believe Mr Maxwell is interested in power and money. There is nothing wrong with that, but it is not everything.' He ended with: 'This is a British newspaper, run by British people. Let's keep it that way.'[9] Somerfield's words were, in the context of what followed, almost laughably wrong. The paper was sold to an Australian who didn't live in the UK, who was quite definitely interested in power and money and whose idea of editorial independence was always somewhat fluid. Many felt the attack on Maxwell unjustified, seeing him – at least at that point – as a successful businessman, proudly British, a war hero and an MP.

Murdoch offered the Carrs a deal: he would buy into the company, becoming joint managing director with Sir William, who would also remain as chairman; both Murdoch and Carr began buying *News of the World* shares, but sales were suspended for two months when Maxwell complained to City of London regulators. Allegations of bad faith and dirty tricks on both sides followed. Murdoch then began merging some of his Australian interests into the *News of the World*, giving him a 40 per cent stake, a move many felt broke City rules. His papers also launched an investigation into one of Maxwell's Australian companies; in turn Maxwell floated a bid for some of Murdoch's interests in conjunction with Lord Thompson, then owner of *The Times*, and unsuccessfully tried to use members of the *News of the World* pension fund to stop the takeover with an injunction. In January 1969 a shareholders' meeting finally decided, despite passionate interjections from Maxwell, to back Murdoch, who repeated undertakings to keep Sir William Carr on as chairman. 'The law of the jungle has prevailed,' said Maxwell.[10] Within a few weeks, Murdoch went back on his promise not to buy more shares, which would eventually give him a majority stake. By June he had forced Sir William, who was in poor health, to resign from the company completely. Murdoch had total control of the biggest-circulation British newspaper. It was his first big overseas kill, and would not be his last.

The Sun Rises

They met for the first time in the bar of Rules restaurant in Covent Garden on an autumn Saturday evening in 1969. There was no trouble recognizing each other. Rupert Murdoch drank a whisky and soda and Larry Lamb a dry Martini. Three bottles of Pouilly-Fumé followed, with which they ate two lobsters. After four hours, they left and strolled across Aldwych and along Fleet Street to the *News of the World* offices in Bouverie Street, where the presses were already rolling for that night's edition. They examined the first copies with the professional acumen of two men long steeped in print, which would have smudged their hands. For both, printers' ink ran like blood in their veins. They had a couple of whiskies in Murdoch's office and Lamb was dropped off at his hotel at about 2 a.m.[11] The meeting was to sound out whether Lamb was to be editor of Murdoch's next planned acquisition, or perhaps his gamble: *The Sun* newspaper. At Holborn Circus, Cudlipp and IPC had finally decided to relieve themselves of this burden, which was losing £2 million a year and down to a circulation of 1.75 million. Closing the paper was not a serious option since the unions would have reacted to the plan by shutting down all of IPC's operations – an intolerable prospect. Murdoch had offered a paltry £800,000. Cudlipp trusted Murdoch because, although he did not know him personally, in 1952 he had met and liked Sir Keith, who, Cudlipp would later write, had confessed his worries about his son's Marxist tendencies.[12] Cudlipp now saw Murdoch less as a socialist and more the inheritor of his father's strong commercial traditions. He felt no qualms about the sale or dropping the condition, inherited when IPC bought the *Herald*, that it would continue to support the Labour Party.

In his room, Lamb called his wife at home in Cheshire, where they were living because of his job as northern editor of the *Daily Mail*. The discussions had gone well, he said, but the Australian tycoon told him he needed to speak to 'seven or eight' others on the shortlist and would be in touch in a week or so. Lamb put the phone down, thoughts of sleep and going home in the morning on his mind. The phone rang immediately. It was Murdoch, curt as ever: 'Rupert here. Bugger the shortlist.'[13] And so began probably the most important and far-reaching relationship in tabloid newspapers and popular journalism since Northcliffe, Rothermere and the Bartholomew/Cudlipp/King axis. Its influence on journalism in the UK would be fundamental; some would argue that it led to the tabloidization of popular culture. These were, of course, true newsmongers.

Lamb, forty years old, Yorkshire pit-village-born and grammar-school educated, his family readers of the old *Daily Herald*, had been an ardent socialist and trade union official in his younger days. He had been a sub-editor for the *Daily Mail* and then the *Daily Mirror*, gradually climbing the editorial production ladder to chief sub-editor. By the late 1960s he was seen as future editor material, but moved to Manchester as northern editor of the *Mail* because he believed Cudlipp was blocking his progress. Lamb's name was given to Murdoch when he asked for suggestions for an editor for his new paper. It became clear that night in Rules that they shared a common understanding of what a modern tabloid would look like: resolutely appealing to a less affluent and largely working-class audience, cheeky and irreverent, with a high level of sport and celebrity/ showbiz content, reflecting the growing popularity of TV soaps and pop music, alongside crime and human interest stories. It would be politically aware, never shy of its opinions, but would not preach to readers or bore them with overly serious content – both men felt the *Mirror*'s attempts to 'look serious' with its 'Mirrorscope' and 'Shock Issues' were misjudged. The *Mirror*, they felt, was losing touch with its core readership. And Lamb had a point to prove against Cudlipp. Their new newspaper, while distinct from the *Mirror*, would have to appeal to a similar and broader audience, but a younger and more permissive one, to gain sufficient readers to make it viable. As Roy Greenslade, later briefly editor of the *Daily Mirror* before becoming a media analyst and then a young sub-editor brought to *The Sun* by Lamb, would later write: 'Their vision of the *Sun* was to mould a 1950s-style *Mirror* – irreverent, iconoclastic, instinctive – with a 1970s agenda, pushing at the barriers of taste and convention.' Greenslade also thought Lamb 'brilliant . . . clever, calculating and convinced of his own abilities'.[14]

For Murdoch, here was a golden opportunity to create a tabloid in his own image. The *News of the World*, although he approved of its basic style, was not of his own making: it was, at that point, a broadsheet, something outside his range of experience except at his own *The Australian*; it had a mostly settled staff and in Stafford Somerfield a strong editor who had his own way of doing things. Murdoch would remove him the following year. What Murdoch also had at the *News of the World* were printing presses that were idle for six nights a week: not, in his view, an economic proposition. *The Sun* he bought was simply a name attached to a diminishing circulation. After IPC changed its name from the *Daily Herald* in 1964, the circulation dropped steadily from 1.5 million to about 850,000 in mid-1969, when Cudlipp decided to sell the title, or put it out of its misery. It had never been quite sure of its audience, but it did have a loyal staff, among them some notable journalists, including Clement Freud, later a Liberal MP, who wrote on food and sport, and Nancy Banks-Smith, later a legendary TV critic for *The Guardian*.

When it was put up for sale, the first person to show interest was, of course, Robert Maxwell, still smarting from his recent defeat over the *News of the World*. Maxwell's vision of a smaller-staffed, smaller-circulation paper never really got off the ground and he could not find an editor to work for him. He pulled out. Murdoch, waiting in the wings, already having secured agreement on staffing levels with one of the key print unions, NATSOPA, swooped.

To Lamb's astonishment, Murdoch said he wanted to relaunch *The Sun,* to be printed in Bouverie Street as a tabloid, on Monday, 17 November, just two days after IPC's legal ownership ended and in less than a month's time. Lamb, assembling his top team, was horrified; he had hoped for a longer lead time. Murdoch knew that launching anything late in November, as the nation looked to Christmas, was perilous, but *The Sun*'s accounts showed the money was running out and no advertising was booked. By launching then, they would at least attract some pre-Christmas advertising. What followed was the kind of seat-of-the-pants, last-minute scramble that had characterized some of Murdoch's business ventures before and would again in the future. Lamb would need to recruit enough journalists and support staff to run a six-days-a-week production cycle and they would have to conceive, plan, design and produce a tabloid newspaper to meet their vision. An entirely new newspaper – apart from the title.

The rank and file would come initially from the former staff at *The Sun,* who reapplied for their own jobs. As a top team, Lamb gathered a number of individuals crucial to shaping the character of *The Sun* – and thus tabloid journalism over the next two decades. Bernard Shrimsley was Lamb's deputy; he would later himself edit *The Sun* for two years in the mid-1970s and then go on to edit the *News of the World* for five years. His brother, Anthony Shrimsley, would be *The Sun*'s influential political editor for several years and later became director of communications for the Conservative Party. Both had come from the *Daily Mirror*. Nick Lloyd, recruited from the *Sunday Times* as news editor, would later edit both the *News of the World* and the *Daily Express*. A key priority was women's issues, and as women's editor they recruited Joyce Hopkirk, who sent them two hundred ideas by way of introduction; she would later edit *Cosmopolitan*. One of the cartoonists they employed was Posy Simmonds, drawing the randy *Bear* strip, who went on to further renown, working for many years at *The Guardian*. There were also, as Lamb later noted, 'a handful of Fleet Street's chronic unemployed, some of whose drinking habits had made them almost unemployable. We needed them as much as they needed us.'[15] The final tally of editorial staff was about a hundred. In this era, the *Mirror* and most other popular newspapers had four times as many.

It was hard to believe, Lamb would later write, that the newspaper which would define and dominate the popular market for the next two decades grew out of the chaos at Bouverie Street.[16] The building was then, in his words, something of a backwater, its administrative and support staff geared to producing a paper once a week. Many of them were hostile to the demanding arrivistes from *The Sun*. The canteen and the switchboard only ran a skeleton service on Sundays and there were no cashiers to pay casual staff or provide expenses advances to reporters on stories. 'It took months, with much shouting and desk banging, to convince the *News of the World* management that on a daily newspaper, Sunday was a normal working day.'[17] And just a few days before launch, there were no seats or desks for the new staff; one hundred had to be bought at short notice.

A whole set of new type was ordered, but arrived with only 48 hours to spare. Even then, there were only three letter E's in the largest font size, so a page one headline could not have more than three E's. The printers demanded bonuses for the entire workforce to manufacture more. They also refused to countenance the idea that the broadsheet presses could be converted to tabloid form.

> 'Nonsense,' Murdoch replied, 'All you need is the crushers (the bars which fold the papers to the required size). Asking someone to hold his jacket, Murdoch vaulted on top of one of the presses and prised open a grubby wooden box. Inside, still in their oiled wrappings, were the vital pieces of equipment.[18]

Such were the actions of someone with newspapers in their blood. There was so little time to prepare and no dummy issues or rehearsals. Many of the new raft of journalists were used to writing at length for broadsheets but not with brevity and concision for tabloids, so their work had to be vigorously edited and configured onto pages by sub-editing and production staff, many of whom also had no experience of working on tabloids, where their role is all-important.

So the first edition of *The Sun* produced on the night of 16 November 1969 was hardly a model issue. Printing began late, with the presses started by Murdoch's wife Anna, but only after she had been made an honorary member of NATSOPA. At first, they failed to work. Her membership was not actually an honour, but a necessary requirement. Printers took this kind of thing very seriously – the unions then held such power that journalists or anyone else not a member would not normally be allowed to touch certain machines or carry out tasks considered the sole prerogative of printers. It was a grip on power that Murdoch would later break. Many parts of northern England and Scotland did not get the paper – unlike all other national newspapers, *The Sun* did not then print in Manchester – but those who did obtain a copy saw a paper that, as Lamb recognized, was flawed and hastily thrown together, yet contained the seeds of something that would eventually grow to dominate Fleet Street and influence the tabloid market for decades to come.

That night, Cudlipp and IPC had thrown a party designed as an ironic farewell to their *Sun*, with tables at the Café Royal decorated with dead sunflowers, to distract some key advertisers away from *The Sun*'s own launch party. This dismissal of the new *Sun* was misjudged. Although it would take nearly eight years to finally top the *Mirror*'s circulation – three years longer than Murdoch had hoped and two years ahead of Lamb's private expectation – within a hundred days, by March 1970, the circulation of *The Sun* was around 1.5 million a day. Even assuming it had retained most of the estimated 650,000 IPC-*Sun*-era readers – unlikely, since the nature of the paper was so different – it was a remarkable achievement. Within a year, circulation had reached 2 million and continued to grow steadily, topping the 3.3 million sale of the *Daily Express* – then dominating the middle market but in steady decline – before overtaking the *Mirror*, which had fallen from more than 5 million in early 1969 to 3.8 million in March 1978. By that summer, it regularly sold more than 4 million copies.

That incoherent first issue replicated many of the visual devices employed by the *Mirror* and the American tabloids – screaming headlines, photomontages, variable column widths, underlined headlines and straplines, white-on-black headlines – delivered with vim and vigour and in a formula that would change very little over

Rupert Murdoch holding a copy of the first issue of *The Sun*, 17 November 1969.

the next four decades. The slogan 'Forward with the People' was on the masthead, if hardly original. Much of the features content was a deliberate copy of staples of the *Mirror* menu: the working-class cartoon character Andy Capp was now a younger, likely lad from Liverpool called 'Wack' – with no cloth cap – and the 'Live Letters' column became the 'Liveliest Letters'. The lead story, about doping and horse racing, while not the strongest of scoops, was a neat combination of two things likely to interest its target audience – crime and betting. There was the traditional political exclusive for a new paper – an interview with prime minister Harold Wilson, who would have seen the *Sun*'s residual *Daily Herald* audience as faithful readers. Oddly, there was also a photograph of the daughter of the Duke of Westminster, the country's richest man, and a story speculating on her engagement – hardly likely to appeal to the target audience. But the overall tone was upbeat and positive, with an obvious attempt to appeal to a younger, liberated audience. 'We want you to join this young new virile campaigning newspaper,' said the first day's editorial.

And, in what would become *The Sun*'s trademark, there was much sex and titillation, although a modern-day reader might find the language and presentation used in these years either embarrassingly quaint, sexist, misogynistic or plain offensive. That first edition was liberally sprinkled with pictures of attractive and sometimes partially clothed young girls, although the bare breasts of Page 3 were still a year away. There was a part-serialization of a raunchy Jacqueline Susann book, *The Love Machine*, while the fashion pages carried a feature called 'Undies for Undressing'. Ever since the *Illustrated Police News* had begun using images of women in their underwear, popular newspapers had long been aware that sex and sexuality sold papers – both advertisements and features carrying images of women in various glamorous or partially dressed poses and pictures of pretty girls, actresses and models adorned the pages of the *Mirror* and sometimes the *Mail*, and the *News of the World*. Into this mix, the latter had added the sleazy court stories and 'I made my excuses and left' first-hand accounts by its reporters about suburban brothels, adulterous vicars and wife-swapping parties that became its trademark. But most of the people the *News of the World* wrote about were not in the public eye, although it would later focus only on celebrity-led sex and sleaze stories, and the language used until now had been usually coy and carefully phrased. *The Sun* would aim differently: it would document the sex lives of ordinary people as well as the pop stars and the actors of the emerging celebrity culture and, crucially, use less ambiguous language that spoke clearly to readers. The approach was brash and cheeky, naughty but nice, more akin to the seaside postcards of Donald McGill than the peeking-through-the-net-curtains attitude of the *News of the World* and, sometimes, the *Mirror*. 'Make it breezy not sleazy' was an internal maxim and there was a rule that the words 'win', 'free' and 'sex' should appear on the front page every day.

As Lamb would later stress, '*The Sun* did not invent the bosom, any more than it invented the permissive society' but reflected society back to itself.[19] He wrote: '*The Sun* was in many ways fortunate enough to be born in an age of permissiveness. Society needed a newspaper which recognised it and was part of it – without ever being ahead of it.'[20]

There was a predictable reaction: Lord Longford, then an arbiter of public taste in his role as a social and penal reformer, declared it 'antipodean erotica', while the Press Council said it was a mixture of 'sex and punchy radicalism'.[21] *The Times*, not yet owned by Murdoch, declared: 'Mr Murdoch has not invented sex, but he does show a remarkable enthusiasm for its benefits to circulation, such as a tired old Fleet Street has not seen in recent years; while the *Morning Star* wrote that it was "more like a paraffin lamp in a brothel than a sun".'[22] The feminist academic and author Germaine Greer accused *The Sun* of 'subverting the morals and quality of the working class in a most cynical fashion'.[23] The rest of the industry was divided, but the following year *The Sun* won Newspaper of the Year in the prestigious Granada Television's What the Papers Say Awards – although Lamb was less than impressed by the grudging speech by presenter Brian Inglis, who made it clear he was not happy with the winner.[24]

The women's section – a convention not ditched for many years – carried the strapline 'The women's pages men like to read'. While it had its fair share of titillation and sex-based content, Lamb later stressed: 'We wrote frankly about things like masturbation, menstruation and premenstrual tension, cancer of the breast and cervix and other medical problems simply not talked about at the time. We readily gave advice on complex sexual problems – but we made sure it was written by experts.' But he conceded there was one eye on the main selling point: 'At the same time as we pursued these deadly earnest subjects with deadly earnestness, we strove to maintain an air of bubbling eroticism. Even the problem page was fun in *The Sun*.'[25] Indeed it was, and the paper's agony aunt for many years was the widely respected Claire Rayner, who had a serious reputation as a writer on social and sexual issues.

The Sun's relentless rise over the subsequent decade would always be intertwined with television, which hitherto had often been slightly sniffed at by newspapers, which considered it a rival rather than a complementary medium. Lamb and Murdoch had agreed they would devote more space to television than their rival, and maximized coverage on Saturdays. A pull-out section designed to attract readers unable to afford the *Radio Times* or *TV Times* contained previews and stories about the weekend's television. It would convert the weakest sales day of the week to the strongest. The news pages carried many stories about television and television personalities, mainly soaps – the already long-running *Coronation Street* and then *Crossroads*. Both of these had millions of viewers who precisely fitted the profile *The Sun* was targeting: working-class people, particularly women, were their core viewers.

The Sun would ruthlessly exploit this symbiotic relationship in its television advertising, which itself broke new ground. Its advertisements became intertwined with the content of the paper itself, representing the feverish ingenuity of the staff, driven by Lamb amid the cramped and chaotic conditions of Bouverie Street: 'There was never a week when we didn't have the material to make a commercial. There was never a week when we didn't have an imaginative special offer, a new contest, a new series.' Traditional indifference by journalists to promotional efforts was cast aside: 'There was no such atmosphere on *The Sun*. We bought books, commissioned series, dreamed up offers, all with an eye on their suitability for television promotion. Often we packed ten or twelve different items into a single commercial.'[26] Much of it had an overtone of sex and titillation: 'It's Knickers Week in the Soaraway *Sun*' would be a typical promotional line, featuring giveways, offers and pictures of girls in their underwear; a typical features series might be 'The Huntresses – women who don't wait to be asked'. There was 'Bath Week' – pictures of girls in the bath, special offers and giveaways on bath towels and toiletries; and Romance Week – more underwear offers and prizes for readers' letters on the theme. The commercials themselves would become staples of the advertising breaks of peak-time television viewing – usually on a Sunday and Monday night to sell the paper for the week ahead – and were hard-hitting, fast-paced and noisy montages, always including images of scantily clad young women and delivered at breakneck speed with a rapid-fire voiceover by the young, little-known actor Christopher Timothy, later to find fame in a number of popular television roles. If viewers could be induced to buy the paper for a week, they would probably be hooked into being permanent readers. All of these promotions would involve free-to-enter competitions to win attractive prizes – a year's worth of nappies or groceries, for instance. Not since the great 1930s Dickens giveaways had so much been invested in recruiting readers through promotions and competitions.

The Sun's staff would always stress that when it came to straightforward news – politics and social policy, natural disasters, terrorism and so on – its achievements were overlooked. The hyperactive, driven newsroom would clear pages 1 to 7 if the occasion demanded. And the tradition of stealing ideas from elsewhere would become part of *The Sun*'s modus operandi, taking the old Fleet Street idea of a 'spoiler' – something which aped, conflicted with or simply confused readers over a rival's story – to new heights. 'If any idea had worked well anywhere else we stole it. If it hadn't been tried, we tried it. If the *Mail* or the *Express* or the *Mirror* dared to carry a blurb on Friday for a series scheduled for the following week, we would launch a sizzling spoiling operation on Saturday,' said Lamb. The pace was frenetic: 'feature ideas raised at morning conference were frequently in print by the evening.'[27] All of this inventiveness, restless energy and promotion took place with Murdoch's approval, often from afar. By now a global businessman, Murdoch was often on a plane or in another country, although, when in London, he would frequently attend the morning conference or Lamb's post-first-edition drinks, throwing out ideas right, left and centre. He regularly criticized Lamb for going over the top on stories or for exceeding the boundaries when it came to sex-driven content and showed a minute understanding of the technicalities of newspapers – whether it was advertising revenue, printing techniques or head-line size. But he would always stress, publicly, 'Its not my paper, it's Larry's.' It was a useful distancing device.

Just a year after its launch, the one thing that became more associated with *The Sun*'s success than anything else was the knowledge among readers that, on opening the paper, they would see the naked breasts of a young woman on Page 3. The single pin-up-style picture, with no news value, as opposed to a picture used with a new point – such as an actress in a new film or models used to illustrate stories – was not exactly new to domestic readers. The *Daily Mirror* had regularly featured such images in the previous few years. In the post-1960s climate, American glamour magazines such as *Playboy*, featuring full nudity, occupied the top shelves of newsagents, with slightly tamer British versions alongside them, so newspapers were following a trend rather than leading. But no-one had gone what was termed 'full nipple'.

It was not until the first birthday of *The Sun*, in November 1970, that the first topless photograph appeared on Page 3, a relatively tasteful sideways view of naked model Stephanie Rahn, headlined,

'Birthday Suit!'. In the same issue, two female nudes, shot from the rear, were used to illustrate a feature on 'How to Pick a Mate'. The floodgates opened. Page 3 became a household name, as did some of the women who appeared on the page in later years. The term was a synonym for a particular type of young, buxom, big-haired, wholesome, topless model, regardless of whether or not she ever actually appeared in that slot. The styles of shot tended to be repeated, the captions carefully and coyly written to avoid accusations of crudity, and there was never a glimpse of pubic hair, a small or drooping breast or a less-than-perfect nipple. Body piercings and tattoos were also out. 'We had a firm rule,' said Lamb, 'they had to be nice girls.'[28] That is, suburban, usually working-class, young girls, rather than more knowing showgirls, or those who might frequent Soho nightclubs. They also rejected those more experienced and professional women who had been seen in glamour magazines, although a number would graduate in that direction. Sleazy pictures would not pass, mainly because women's editor Hopkirk and her colleagues had absolute veto. Many would be used as part of *The Sun*'s relentless promotional machine or feature in other parts of the paper. Inevitably, there would be the occasional centre-page poster or pull-out – 'Vote for your Favourite Page 3 Girl!!', and there were, among other promotional wheezes, Page 3 playing cards and a Page 3 calendar. It became a crucial part of *The Sun*'s brand. Writing nearly two decades later, Lamb admitted, as many critics argued, there was 'sexploitation involved'. Lamb was not ashamed, he said, to have created Page 3, but neither was he particularly proud. 'In many ways, I now wish that I hadn't.' How much of the circulation rise over the next few years was attributable to Page 3 cannot be determined. 'I don't think the girls were nearly as significant as was generally supposed,' said Lamb. 'If we left out the Watford dog results, the telephone lines ran hot with complaints. To leave out the Page 3 girl, which we did from time to time, caused scarcely a ripple.'[29]

Many of those featured, otherwise destined for obscurity, became minor celebrities, making pop records and starring in provincial pantomimes, or made a new name in business, all enjoying lucrative careers. And hundreds of parents, usually mothers, would send in pictures of their own bare-breasted daughters, some of whom were underage, urging the paper to put them into print. The loudest criticism came from feminists, churches and those liberals who might have supported the sexual revolution but found Page 3 exploitative and tacky. Some local authorities attempted to remove *The Sun* from libraries; many people would never be seen with it, although Lamb would later claim that it had more affluent readers than *The Guardian* and *The Telegraph* combined. *The Sun* became brilliant at using such criticism for its own ends – Longford's 'antipodean erotica' prompted an upside-down Page 3 picture and a competition in which the prize was an 'antipodean erotica kit'. The councillors who banned *The Sun* from the public library in Sowerby Bridge in Yorkshire were dubbed 'The Silly Burghers of Sowerby Bridge' and the paper offered a prize to readers who could say in no more than a hundred words why this was wrong – the first prize was 'A Weekend in Sowerby Bridge' while the second was, predictably, 'A Week in Sowerby Bridge'. It would be nearly two decades before there was any serious organized attempt to stop the tradition.

There was one other woman who would go on to feature heavily on its pages during that decade. In the 1970 general election, *The Sun* supported Labour: Murdoch, as in his later support for Tony Blair, was always a pragmatist, supporting the politicians that would serve him best. But prime minister Harold Wilson was defeated and Edward Heath became prime minister. At the next election in 1974, called amid an economic and industrial crisis, Lamb, Shrimsley and Murdoch, all firmly anti-union largely because of their experiences at the hands of Fleet Street print unions, backed Heath, who lost his majority. Wilson returned to power. In the second election that year, they hedged their bets and urged readers to vote for the best man or woman, regardless of party. Defeated, Heath resigned and was replaced by Margaret Thatcher, and a whole new era of relations between the government and *The Sun* began.

Thatcher had famously been dubbed 'Maggie Thatcher, Milk Snatcher' and 'The Most Unpopular Woman in Britain' by *The Sun* when in 1970, as secretary of state for education in the Heath Government, she had proposed ending the free school milk allowance. Thatcher needed to get *The Sun* onside and the Tories embarked on a process of wooing the paper, ensuring that its leaders would reflect well on them. 'All was sweetness and light as she and her "boys", as key advisers like Geoffrey Howe and Nicholas Ridley were known to the *Sun*, began to drop in on Lamb's alcohol-smoothed "chewing the fat sessions" after the first edition had gone to press in the early evening.'[30] Thatcher would now flatter Lamb, back in the editor's chair after a brief period as editorial director when Shrimsley, who had occupied his seat, was moved to edit the *News of the World*. The tone of the paper changed, Lamb was drawn into Thatcher's circle and there was an influx of more Tory-minded writers onto the paper, including political editor Walter Terry.

By mid-1978 *The Sun* had reached its circulation peak of more than 4 million – or, on the basis that every edition was read by an average of three people, around 12 million readers – and an election loomed as the Labour government grappled with militant unions and a juddering economy. The subsequent public sector strikes of what *The Sun* – borrowing from Shakespeare's *Richard III* – called 'The Winter of Discontent' of 1978–9 led to prime minister James Callaghan calling a general election in May 1979. Lamb was consulted on the Tory manifesto, became a frequent visitor to Thatcher's home in Chelsea and gave advice to her team on image presentation. On the day of the election, *The Sun* was emphatic: 'A message to Labour supporters: Vote Tory This Time' was the massive front-page headline, alongside an editorial headlined 'The first day of the rest of our lives'. The leader, which continued inside, the longest ever written in *The Sun*, said, 'The Conservatives would give freedom to "run your life as YOU want it",' freedom to work with or without a union card and freedom to spend or save without giving your money to the taxman. The Labour Party, it said, 'has left us'. It continued: 'The special relationship it claims with the trade unions has shown to be a sham. The party has become a refuge of militants, Marxist bullies and class war warriors.' Lamb, previously an abstainer, voted Conservative; Thatcher won by a landslide. She sent Lamb a letter of thanks; he was knighted the following year. Not since the days when David Lloyd George consulted with George Riddell and Northcliffe had there been such closeness between individual politicians and the press.

Of course, *The Sun* was not the only popular paper to fall in love with Thatcher. She and the new breed of Conservatism she heralded – strongly anti-trade union, pro-free market, vigorously against state ownership and intervention, sceptical about what was then still called the Common Market – had also found favour with the *Express* titles and the *Daily Mail*. John Junor, editor of the *Sunday Express*, was knighted alongside Lamb. David English, editor of the

Mail, achieved his knighthood a couple of years later. But their readers – middle- and lower-middle-class people from suburbs and small towns – would be seen to be natural Tories anyway. And, compared to *The Sun*'s readership of around 12 million potential voters, they were statistically less important in terms of achieving the swing the Tories needed. Lamb later reflected the view of many, rejecting the idea that the popular newspapers were 'tools' of the Tories:

> The exact reverse is the truth. The fact is that there were a great many patriotic Britons, including many life-long socialists and not a few influential newspapermen, who recognised that Britain had gone a long, long way down a wrong, wrong road and were desperate for change. To that extent, Mrs Thatcher was their tool.[31]

The Planet Turns Tabloid

The impact of *The Sun* was profound, both in terms of the structure of the popular half of Fleet Street and the way in which newspapers changed their tone: sex and stridency had taken over. Michael Christiansen, son of Arthur and then editor of the *Sunday Mirror*, said in a speech that in terms of journalistic standards, Murdoch's arrival in Fleet Street had put back the clock by ten to fifteen years: 'It now seems that what has happened on my paper is that one's major consideration every week is whether you should have a picture that shows pubic hair.'[32] This annoyed Lamb intensely, because *The Sun* had been scrupulous in avoiding pubic hair. According to Tom Baistow, media commentator for the *New Statesman*, writing some years later, it represented 'the metamorphosis of relatively healthy popular journalism into the junk food of the mass mind market'.[33] The tone of tabloid newspapers would change forever – Page 3 had broken the nipple ban, issues surrounding sex and sexuality had been pushed to the fore and personality ruled, whether celebrities or politicians.

But the impact of *The Sun* was also profound on how newspapers looked. All visual restraint was thrown away and the physical tabloid size became invincible. It also led to the closure of one tabloid, two other newspapers becoming tabloids and the creation of a fifth. The tabloid *Daily Sketch*, which had been owned by the *Daily Mail* since the late 1950s and had a populist but conservative tone, was aimed at a lower-middle-class audience. But throughout the 1960s it had struggled to establish itself in the shadow of the *Mirror, Mail* and *Express* and suffered even more once *The Sun* was launched, dropping from 870,000 readers to 764,000 in the first year of its operation. In 1971 the then Lord Rothermere – Vere Rothermere, son of Harold and now running the company – concluded the losses were too high and decided to close the title. Murdoch toyed with the idea of buying the *Sketch*, but was dissuaded by Lamb and others. It was eventually merged with the *Daily Mail*, which also now converted to a tabloid size. More than four hundred jobs were lost in the process. Rothermere had hoped that significant numbers of the *Sketch*'s readers would be attracted to the *Daily Mail*, but in the end, the *Mail*'s circulation dropped to 1.75 million, lower than before it went tabloid, while *The Sun*'s circulation continued its steady rise. However, the merger and conversion did lead to the *Mail*, under talented editor David English, taking a distinctly more populist tone than it had done previously. Nevertheless, English eventually kept the *Mail* on a steady course, with a determinedly middle-class, middle-brow appeal to a clearly defined market, with a high percentage of women readers. The *Mail* preferred to call their new design 'a compact', to distinguish it from the more downmarket idea of a tabloid, as they would have seen it. Of course, that was simply goading *The Sun*, which adopted a typically teasing tone ahead of its launch: 'Next week in your fun-packed, fact-packed, jam-packed IMPACT compact . . .' and launched a new series of promotions and competitions. Readers unaware of the *Mail*'s plans might have been forgiven for being a little bemused. Another victim was the *Daily Express*, which under Beaverbrook had been selling more than 4 million but which had been in steady decline since Beaverbrook's death in 1964. It eventually dropped to below 3 million average daily sales in 1975, caught between the revitalized *Daily Mail* at one end of its readership and *The Sun* at the other. It was eventually forced to go tabloid in 1977. The *News of the World*, which continued in its own way for many years with its diet of crime, court cases and sleazy exposés, would remain in what had become a comfortable broadsheet format and not turn physically tabloid until 1984.

The biggest target for *The Sun* and the paper with most to lose in terms of its bulk readership was the *Mirror*. As *The Sun* geared up for its launch in 1969, Cudlipp planned to reinvent the *Mirror* as 'Britain's first quality tabloid', with beefed-up content, a style revamp, a more prominent 'Mirrorscope' section to analyse the news of the day and the introduction, a few weeks before *The Sun*'s launch, of a free glossy magazine, to be called *Mirror Magazine*, a version of the colour supplements of the Sunday broadsheet newspapers. It failed spectacularly, losing money. Once *The Sun* sorted its teething problems, it began to look sharper than the *Mirror,* which failed to respond in any significant way. Cudlipp was determined not to go down the sex and titillation route of *The Sun* and adopted a higher tone. But attempts at serious journalism – such as reporter John Pilger's exposé of Cambodia, 'The Killing Fields' – while critically praised, failed to make inroads into *The Sun*'s growing readership.

In those early months, only *Mirror* northern editor Derek Jameson was able to respond: he adopted a more purely tabloid approach for the pages under his control, running more 'sex' stories, promotions and competitions as well as the odd Page 3-style picture. *The Sun* printed early to get copies to the north because it did not print in Manchester, which allowed Jameson, alerted by the London news desk who saw the first editions, a couple of hours to run spoilers on *Sun* stories for the later northern editions. Jameson's more *Sun*-like approach stopped when Tony Miles took over as *Mirror* editor in 1971. With both titles benefiting from the steady decline in *Express* readers, Miles managed to hold the *Mirror* together and maintain the readership at around 4.5 million.

But the winds of change were blowing through Holborn Circus. Cudlipp announced that at the age of nearly sixty, having been an editor or editorial executive since he was 24, it was time to move on, and that at his age it would be an 'unpardonable vanity' to presume to know the tastes and interests of the younger generation to which the paper was striving to appeal.[34] He left early in 1974 to enjoy a long retirement, largely untroubled by suggestions that his complacency in the sale of *The Sun* and the *Mirror*'s response to it had allowed Murdoch to gain a tabloid foothold he would never surrender. Later that year, Miles moved upstairs to become editorial director of the group and Michael Christiansen, son of Arthur and the anointed successor, became editor. Within a few months he had to resign after suffering a severe stroke. His deputy, Mike Molloy, a graphic designer who reinvented himself as a *Mirror* executive, succeeded him.

Molloy was the thirteenth and, at 34, youngest editor of the *Mirror,* still the biggest-selling national newspaper, and would remain in the editor's chair for a remarkable fifteen years, fighting off *The Sun*'s challenge on a daily basis while maintaining the *Mirror*'s own identity. The fact that Molloy had not been a working journalist raised eyebrows – an art school graduate and former messenger on the *Sunday Pictorial,* he had worked as a cartoonist, illustrator and page designer before becoming a features writer and executive. What helped Molloy was that he was likeable, highly sociable and knew the *Mirror* inside out, including where the bodies were buried. He was also lucky in taking over when a number of *Mirror* staff were at their peaks as journalists – Donald Zec, the showbusiness writer; Joyce Hopkirk, who moved from *The Sun* to become women's editor; John Pilger as chief foreign correspondent; Terence Lancaster as political editor; and Geoffrey Goodman as industrial editor. Marjorie Proops, the doyenne of agony aunts, continued alongside the legendary Keith Waterhouse, widely considered to be one of the best columnists in Fleet Street. In 1979 Molloy would also recruit former *Daily Herald* investigative journalist and columnist Paul Foot – stalwart of the Socialist Workers Party and nephew of Labour politician and later party leader Michael Foot – who was given a regular, high-profile column. Molloy had inherited an all-star cast of people who helped him to retain a good proportion of the *Mirror*'s prestige and circulation, but also:

> a motoring correspondent who was disqualified from driving; a gardening correspondent with no garden; a slimming editor who was a stone overweight; a travel editor who was banned from flying on British Airways; and at least one feature writer who hadn't written anything except his expenses in five years.[35]

Such was the character of the *Mirror.*

A major hurdle facing Molloy was Page 3. Molloy tried to replicate it, using one of *The Sun*'s regular models, but the anger from staff, particularly Proops, was such it was not repeated. He improved the look of the paper, introduced book serializations and generally kept a steady hand on the tiller while also enjoying the more social and glamorous side of being editor of a a major newspaper. At the same time, he battled a lack of interest from IPC's latest owners, paper group Reed International, and constant unrest from print unions; there was also a lengthy strike by journalists in 1977 when they discovered that even the cleaning and casual labouring staff earned more than many of them. The strike took the paper off the streets and led to a drop in circulation of almost a million when it returned. It recovered, but in March the following year *The Sun* finally overtook the *Mirror*, when it reached average daily sales of 3.8 million. It was a significant moment.

By now, the planet was turning tabloid. In Germany, *Bild*, published by the giant Axel Springer group since 1952, was on its way to becoming the biggest-selling newspaper in Germany and Europe, reaching a circulation of around 5 million in the early 1980s. Originally modelled on the *Daily Mirror*, the paper was a broadsheet, but picture-led, with a mixture of news, gossip, showbiz and crime stories. It had a stridently conservative tone, supporting right-wing dictatorships and South African apartheid during the 1970s, although it became more celebrity-focused in later decades. Like the *Mirror* and then *The Sun*, the masthead was red and the headlines became progressively shorter, sharper and shoutier. In the 1980s it introduced topless girls on the front page, below the fold, which continued until 2012. Launched in Dublin in 1973, the *Sunday World* was Ireland's first tabloid newspaper, a *Sun/News of the World* lookalike, with a red masthead and a heavily populist agenda of crime and showbiz – and, for Catholic, conservative Ireland, a high level of sex-related content. Irish editions of *The Sun* carried Page 3 pictures from the start.

In the United States, in contrast to the serious-minded and some would say self-important, politics-obsessed broadsheet heavyweights such as the *New York Times* and the *Washington Post*, tabloid newspapers had become increasingly focused on crime and sleaze, putting aside any pretence at news coverage. Leading the field by the 1970s was the *National Enquirer*, which has been founded as a broadsheet in 1926 by a protégé of William Randolph Hearst, but was by now owned by Italian American Generoso Pope. During the late 1950s and '60s it became renowned for its gory headlines, such as 'I Cut Out Her Heart and Stomped on It' in September 1963. Pope pioneered the practice of selling the *Enquirer* at supermarket checkouts, which became standard practice for a raft of similar publications, but the agenda changed to focus more on showbusiness, celebrity and the latest versions of 'Strange Newes' – sightings of UFOs and alien abductions – or human interest stories. Celebrity news, particularly involving marital strife, diets and weight, began to dominate and circulation soared. In one memo to staff in 1973, Pope articulated precisely what had become the tabloid/popular way of reporting quotes: 'Prod, push and probe the main characters in the story, help them frame their answers . . . Don't have the person ask for things, get them to tell the reader their dreams and their hopes.'[36] The man whom Pope chose to run the *Enquirer* from 1974 onward was a British journalist, Iain Calder, a veteran of a bitter 1960s Scottish newspaper circulation war between the *Daily Record* – the *Mirror*'s breezier Scottish cousin – and the *Scottish Daily Express* that at one point had led to both editors being threatened with prison by a judge after sixty journalists converged on a court to try to buy an exclusive with a local thug.

Calder was hired to run the London office of the *Enquirer* and moved to the United States in 1967. He would be the editorial director of the *Enquirer* for twenty years and employed a team of largely British tabloid journalists to help him. As a profile in 1997 would note:

> You get the feeling he wasn't overly scared when Charles Manson issued a death threat against him when he was editing the *Enquirer*. Mr Calder was responsible for bringing British tabloid talents to the dowdy world of American journalism and helped to turn the *National Enquirer* into the monster that it is today. Its diet of celebrity gossip, scandal and freak human interest stories sells three million copies a week, read by around 18 million people.[37]

Under Calder the *Enquirer* would enjoy its greatest period of success. And it did run scoops: one story in 1975 was devoted to the contents of the garbage bins of then U.S. Secretary of State Henry Kissinger – some of which contained some sensitive and private documents – obtained by a reporter who was questioned by police. This sparked a debate about whether the rubbish was personal or private property. Circulation rose to regularly top 4 million, and it had a huge staff and resources. In 1977 an edition with a picture of

Elvis Presley in his coffin sold 6.7 million. In 1982 it ran pictures of the car crash that killed Princess Grace of Monaco.

Its success sparked a range of celebrity gossip magazines sold at U.S. supermarket checkouts. Murdoch himself had seen the success of the *Enquirer* and in 1974 launched *The Star* in direct competition, although it never quite managed to challenge its target and it was sold to the *Enquirer* in 1990. In 1979 Pope himself began the *Weekly World News* to use the black-and-white printing presses that were idle after the *Enquirer* went colour. Some of its stories were human interest features – about survivors of car crashes or accidents – while others about bizarre creatures or the occult never made any pretence at being grounded in reality. *The Sun*, founded in 1983, took a similar path and from 1992 carried a message on its masthead: 'suspend belief for the sake of enjoyment.' More soft-focus weekly magazines, concentrating on a mix of Hollywood celebrities, human interest and a lot of stories about the British royals, would follow in the United States and across Europe. Everyone would soon be living on Planet Tabloid. And that planet would soon be even more crowded.

A Star Is Born

After eight years of steady progress that had changed the nature of tabloid newspapers in Britain, Lamb and Murdoch thought they had triumphed over the *Mirror*. But suddenly a serious challenge came from an unexpected quarter: a brash and shameless lookalike aimed to take *The Sun* on at its own game: the sex business. The *Daily Star* was launched in 1978 by Express Newspapers, which had been in state of decline for some years after Beaverbrook's death in 1964. It was sold by the Beaverbrook family in 1977 to Trafalgar House, a property investment and publishing conglomerate headed by businessman Victor Matthews. His plan was a deliberate replication of *The Sun* as well as using spare printing capacity at its Manchester print site. Tabloid veteran and former *Mirror* northern editor Derek Jameson, then managing editor of the *Mirror*, became editorial director. An unashamedly working-class boy from the East End who had risen up the ranks from Fleet Street messenger at sixteen, Jameson, dubbed 'Sid Yobbo' by *Private Eye*, was frank about the aspirations of the newpaper. He was reported as telling an interviewer it would be all about 'tits, bums, QPR and roll your own fags'. Later, under oath at a libel trial (he had sued the BBC over a radio comedy programme that had made jokes about him; he lost), he denied the phrase, saying it had been misreported by the *Observer* diary (he had pointed out that it was unlikely a northern-based editor promoting a largely northern-based paper would cite a London football club, Queens Park Rangers), but there is no doubt that this was the aim.[38] And, despite the denial, the quote would still be cited whenever the origins of the *Star* or Jameson's journalism was discussed.

He was certainly on record as having told told staff: 'No newspaper in history lost sales by projecting beautiful birds. Sex sells . . . that goes for words and pictures. The *Star* will have its daily quota. Bigger and better than anyone else.'[39] True to his promise, it had sex – somehow the breasts of its 'Starbirds' were bigger and would be the first printed in full colour, the poses less coy and the pictures cropped tightly to make the image more prominent on the page. Even more raunchy pictures of young women were dotted around the paper at the slightest excuse. There was even less interest in routine news stories and political and social issues. There were no pretensions to the more aspirational attitude of *The Sun*, which, echoing Thatcherism, always liked to suggest that its readers lived in a nice new-build house, rather than a grimy tower block on a neglected estate. A brash Australian, Lloyd Turner, a production journalist at the *Express*, was recruited as editor. *The Star* was launched first on a regional basis in Manchester because of *The Sun*'s focus on printing in London, seeking to capitalize on the fact that as a result, *Mirror* sales had held up in the north of England, with its more traditional working-class base. The *Star* was also backed by an extensive promotional campaign, funded by the *Express*, and, crucially, would undercut *The Sun*'s 7p cover price by a penny.

And the *Star* had something new and cheaper than television advertising, which for a time would dominate tabloid newspaper promotional campaigns: bingo. Every day, the *Star* would print a series of numbers which readers would tick off against specially distributed cards, with large cash prizes for the weekly winners. As the *Star*'s London editor, Brian Hitchen, said at the time: 'If you run a £500,000 advertising campaign on TV, you are very lucky if 2 per cent of readers stick with you. With bingo, we are getting a sticking rate of 37 per cent.'[40] Jameson said bingo was 'the biggest and best circulation builder in history, far outstripping anything a newspaper could do editorially'.[41] Every popular title followed suit – *The Sun* and the *Mirror* with a straightforward bingo-style game, the *Mail* with their 'Casino' and the *Express* with the 'Millionaires Club' – with jackpot prizes steadily rising.

The *Star* formula worked – the first edition in November 1978 sold out its 1.4 million print run – and there was clearly a market for a sub-*Sun* lookalike. And, as Murdoch himself would come to realize, even a small price cut can make a difference. The *Star*, conscious of its northern, working-class, largely Labour-voting readership, much less stridently anti-Labour Party and anti-union than *The Sun*, steadily nibbled away at the readerships of both the *Mirror* and *The Sun*, causing the first decline in the latter's readership since its launch. The *Star* would reach a peak of 1.7 million circulation in 1984, although by that time it had switched allegiance to the Conservatives. A *Sun* price rise in 1980 backfired and the *Mirror* began to regain ground. *The Sun*'s rise had been the biggest event in post-war journalism; its influence was enormous and it was a money-making machine. The idea it might diminish in circulation was unthinkable. It was time for Murdoch to take back control.

6

GOTCHA

In early 1981, after a decade of unstoppable success, *The Sun* had stopped rising. Its formula of relentless promotional cam-paigns, naked female breasts on Page 3, sex, showbusiness and sport suddenly seemed just a little tired. Circulation had slipped to 3.6 million from its 4 million peak. The *Daily Star* had gained ground quickly and was a news-stand reminder that *The Sun* did not have complete ownership of the red-top formula, while the *Mirror*'s blend of restrained, slightly serious tabloid and a strong cast of respected writers slowed any further drift of readers, particularly in the north of England, to either of its two rivals. Murdoch had been content to let Lamb – now Sir Larry – run *The Sun* in the same rumbustious way he had done for years. He had been preoccupied with his Australian titles and his first serious foray into American journalism, buying the tabloid evening daily the *New York Post* in 1976, and would also use the huge profits generated by *The Sun* to buy *The Times* and the *Sunday Times*, giving him a dominant pos-ition in the British newspaper market, both tabloid and broadsheet, that still persists today. He now owned the biggest-selling daily newspaper, the two biggest-selling Sunday titles and the newspaper dubbed the 'paper of record' that held a unique role in the life of the British establishment and was once owned by Northcliffe. Murdoch now had a bigger empire than Northcliffe had ever aspired to, with interests in newspapers and television around the globe.

Now he refocused on *The Sun*. Against Lamb's wishes, Murdoch cut the cover price by two pence to match that of the *Star*, backed by a massive promotional campaign. Murdoch also picked up the mood that Lamb was no longer quite as involved as before, his office door closed, the post-deadline drinks less frequent. Despite Lamb's crucial role in creating *The Sun*, Murdoch suggested Lamb was tired and overworked and might like to take a sabbatical for six months. Lamb took the hint and resigned. Murdoch, of course, had someone else in mind to take over, who would, even more than Lamb, come to embody the spirit and ethos of *The Sun* and build on the success of the previous years.

Whatever else might have been said about Kelvin MacKenzie – including the many claims that under him the newspaper was guilty of racism, sexism, homophobia, bullying and story fabrication – no one could deny he had tabloid journalism in his blood, that he was a true newsmonger. Only MacKenzie could take *The Sun* and make it even more *Sun*-like. Only MacKenzie would write a headline that would alienate an entire city and see a drop in local circulation from which it never recovered. And only MacKenzie, many years later, would have his column in *The Sun* suspended because of alleged racial slurs against a footballer. He would make *The Sun* a cheerleader for Margaret Thatcher, who would embody and exploit the aspirational working class with which MacKenzie and *The Sun* identified, although his own background was more middle-class. And

Kelvin MacKenzie, 1989.

his influence played a crucial role in the wider 'tabloidization' of popular culture and the media. This is a man who would go on to bring topless darts to the nation's TV sets.

His parents were both journalists on the weekly *South London Observer*, boosting their income by selling crime and court stories to national newspapers. Both were determinedly aspirational and eventually moved from rough and ready Camberwell to more middle-class, leafy Dulwich, where young Kelvin went to Alleyn's School, a direct grant grammar school. He left with only one O Level – in English literature – to work at seventeen on the weekly *South East London Mercury*. He had other qualifications more relevant to his chosen career: a brash, outgoing nature, a ready wit, a mercurial mind and a breezy, Northcliffe-like utter confidence in his own abilities. As he said to a fellow reporter: 'Apart from you and a couple of others, everyone else here is a wanker.'[1]

MacKenzie's parents were among the modern-day 'penny a liners', for whom news was a commodity to be traded to make money; giving the public information was secondary, a by-product. Among the most successful traders was the Ferrari News Agency, based in southeast London, which thrived on providing stories to the national press, both as routine reporting and one-off commissions to work on exclusive stories – doorstepping, following people, digging out background on crime and court stories. Ferrari's was run by Dan Ferrari, whose son, Nick Ferrari, would later work on the *Sunday Mirror* and eventually at *The Sun* alongside MacKenzie; he became a popular radio presenter on LBC, known for his trenchant right-of-centre views. The agency provided both a training ground and a bridge to Fleet Street for many young journalists; it was a tough, competitive environment and when MacKenzie joined them he was in his element.

Such a job would normally have been a path to becoming a reporter on one of the popular newspapers such as the *Mail*, *Express* or *Mirror*, the last then still the only tabloid red-top. Unexpectedly, MacKenzie took himself off to the Midlands to work on the *Birmingham Post* as a sub-editor. It may have had something to do with the fact that, despite his self-confidence, he was not that good at reporting and writing. Or perhaps, as a newly married man, he preferred the regular shifts. MacKenzie may also have recognized that, in newspapers, it was often sub-editors and production journalists who reached the higher executive levels. Great reporters tend be lone wolves, temperamentally not suited to being office-bound and to the rigorous and demanding cycle of daily production, with its iron-clad meeting times and deadlines. And the *Birmingham Post* could not have been more different to the world of south London crime reporting. Conservative in style and political stance, it was a serious, well-produced morning broadsheet newspaper aimed at a professional readership, with a big emphasis on the industrial and business scene of the Midlands region. The *Post* was the kind of environment where you learned how to edit copy perfectly, write serious headlines and lay out sober pages. It was where young MacKenzie would have been told by senior subs: 'We don't call a house fire a blaze, Kelvin. Blazes, as you should know, are the white stripe that runs down the front of the head of horses.' 'And, by the way, Kelvin, it's the Union Flag, never, ever, the Union Jack.' But he was good at the job. He returned to London to take a sub-editing job on the *Express* before joining *The Sun*'s subbing table in 1973, then nearing its peak, with circulation rising steadily and the *Mirror* in its sights. He rose up the production rankings under Lamb over the next few years and in 1978 Murdoch, liking what he saw, packed him off to New York to be night managing editor of the *New York Post*, which he had acquired two years previously. MacKenzie was one of a number of British tabloid journalists who would further their careers by introducing or reintroducing a more racy style of coverage into American newspapers at the end of the 1970s and early '80s.

The long-established *New York Post* was a mass-market evening tabloid with a target audience of blue-collar Big Apple workers. It was liberal in its outlook, supporting trade unions and state welfare. That, under Murdoch, would soon go. He imported journalists from tabloids in both the United Kingdom and Australia, taking the *New York Post* downmarket, with bigger, bolder headlines and a more sensational approach to news stories. At one stage, the list of senior editors printed daily in the paper did not contain a single American name, while the entire back bench of the *New York Post* was staffed by *Sun*-trained journalists, MacKenzie among them – Murdoch just preferred to work with those whom he knew best. The *New York Post*'s circulation rose to more than 600,000 within three years, the largest evening sale in the United States. Its headlines would include 'How I Became a Mass Murderer' (about letters from a serial killer to his son), '24 Hours of Terror' (a power blackout), 'Behead Threat' (a siege) and so on. It was probably to MacKenzie's lasting regret that he had moved on when the *Post* came up with the headline for which it is still fondly remembered: 'Headless Body in Topless Bar'.

Murdoch was not exactly welcomed by other journalists in the United States: A. M. Rosenthal, the executive editor of the *New York Times*, said that he practised 'mean, ugly, violent journalism'.[2] In an excoriating analysis in 1980, the *Columbia Journalism Review* declared in an unsigned comment piece that Murdoch's 'skin, scandal and sensationalism' approach might appeal to the 'insular reader' with interests only in his 'pocket book'. It noted that news was filtered through the prism of sensationalism: 'And all too often what follows is meant to turn white against black, the comfortable against the poor, the first world against the third.' It went on to say that other newspapers now felt obliged to follow suit (something Murdoch applauded): 'Whether they like it or not, reporters, editors and news directors . . . are already working in a climate Murdoch has helped create.' The second consequence, said the *Review*, was 'civic', arguing, as many did later, that Murdoch's publications had a coarsening effect on culture and discourse, that their headlines inflamed public emotions and social passions, but also that it was wrong to judge them simply as a problem of yellow journalism and that the implications for wider society were much broader. Pointing out that criticism by the rest of the media had been 'powerless to prevent Murdoch's depredations', it concluded: "The matter ought not to be allowed to rest after the press critics have pronounced their anathemas. For *The New York Post* is no longer merely a journalistic problem. It is a social problem – a force for evil.'[3] It was a complaint about Murdoch that would be repeated many times in subsequent years and on both sides of the Atlantic – that he had been responsible for the coarsening of public discourse. But did Murdoch care? By that time the *New York Post* circulation had risen to more than 600,000, becoming the best-selling evening daily in the United States.

MacKenzie returned to *The Sun* as deputy night editor but annoyed Murdoch when, after a few months, he was enticed to the *Daily Express* – at that point sorely in need of revival – with the bigger role of night editor. But it didn't last long: by April 1981, with *The Sun* waning and Lamb out, Murdoch forgave and forgot and offered

MacKenzie the job he had now coveted for many years and pretty much considered his destiny: editor. He was just 35.

Taking over in June 1981, the workaholic, sweary and loud-mouthed MacKenzie re-energized *The Sun* in the same way that the equally boisterous and abusive Bartholomew had revived the *Mirror* in the 1930s. MacKenzie revelled in the persona of a full-on south (or '*sarf*', as he would say) London street fighter.

> It was not just the energy MacKenzie showed in putting in fre-quent twelve-, fourteen- and sixteen-hour days that amazed everyone – it was what he did during them. In another direct contrast to Lamb, he was a total 'hands-on' editor, always out on the floor, flying around, cajoling, wheedling, wise-cracking, browbeating, exhorting. He was one of those people who moved 20 per cent faster and talked 20 per cent louder than anyone else, constantly on the move, poking his stubby fingers into every aspect of the paper and rapping out a series of instant decisions. And administering bollockings.[4]

Bollockings became part of the MacKenzie newsroom persona, administered to all and sundry, high and low. His angry rants at cowering staff brought fear and terror into an already intense envir-onment. Television presenter Matthew Wright, who worked on *The Sun* as a young journalist, said many years later: 'If he humiliated you but you came back smiling, you knew you were one of his gang and he would look after you.'[5]

His attention to detail in every word, every headline, every pic-ture and every bit of furniture became legendary, ripping up pages and starting again if it suited him, anxious for stories, ideas, scams and anything to raise the profile of the paper again. 'Shock and amaze me on every page' was his message to staff. And he hated both the *Mirror* and, for good measure, *The Guardian*.

While MacKenzie would never have characterized himself as par-ticularly serious or lacking fun with the 'Current Bun', as he dubbed the paper, his excessive work ethic shocked many around him and surpassed what he would have seen as the more dilettante approach of the rest of Fleet Street. He held all the broadsheets in contempt. And that infected his staff – the culture of presentism now reigned and would soon dominate Fleet Street as it became locked into the

1980s circulation wars. MacKenzie understood and characterized *The Sun*'s readership in a way Lamb had never quite been able to do. The typical *Sun* reader, MacKenzie would later say, was 'The bloke you see in the pub – a right old fascist, wants to send the wogs back, buy his poxy council house, he's afraid of the unions, afraid of the Russians, hates the queers and weirdoes and drug dealers. He doesn't want to hear about that stuff.'[6] The bulk of *The Sun*'s readership was definitely not the flat-capped working classes of old, secure in the embrace of a job in the factory, the mine or the shipyard and the protection of the unions: this was a new working class made up of socially conservative Thatcher voters, aware that the power of the unions was weakening as the old industries declined. Many were skilled workers, with working-class roots, but more aspirational than their parents; they may have worked in a factory or in the growing service industries and lived in a council flat but dreamed of being able to afford to buy it or even move on to a nice house on a new estate in the suburbs. This was also largely an urban English readership – the self-employed tradesman or car factory worker in the big cities of the Midlands, the east London taxi driver, the delivery driver from Swindon or Southend. The more traditional working-class readers of old were fewer and more wedded to the *Mirror* and, in the north, to the *Star*.

Circulation began to shoot up again, largely due to what would become two universal tabloid staples over the next few years. Shortly after Mackenzie's arrival, Murdoch gave the go-ahead for *The Sun*'s own version of bingo – bigger and better, they claimed, than the *Star*, with prizes of up to £50,000. It was the 1930s all over again, only instead of copies of Dickens, cold, hard cash was bribing readers. MacKenzie began gleefully introducing himself as the 'bingo editor' saying: 'If sales go down they'll blame me. If sales shoot up, I'll never know if it was me or bingo.' Within three months, *The Sun* had added 500,000 new – or returning – readers.

By spring 1982, buoyed by the royal wedding of the previous year and subsequent idolatry of the Princess of Wales, as well as by intensive promotional campaigns and bingo, *The Sun* was back to selling more than 4 million copies daily, an increase of about 600,000 in twelve months; the *Mirror*, meanwhile, had lost another 200,000 readers. Murdoch is reported to have said to MacKenzie: 'How do you feel about that, Kelvin? Six hundred thousand on the circulation and it had fuck all to do with you.'[7] Throughout the rest of the decade, the image of Diana would feature in *The Sun* and all tabloid newspapers on an almost daily basis; MacKenzie's reputation for risk was embellished early in 1982 when the paper published snatched pictures of the pregnant Princess of Wales in a bikini on a Caribbean beach. Buckingham Palace complained bitterly, but MacKenzie shrugged it off. He republished them the next day, using the row as a pretext with what would become a classic *Sun* apology – the paper was 'deeply sorry' to have caused offence, but claimed the images had brought a 'breath of summer into the lives of millions of readers'.[8]

Then Argentina invaded the Falkland Islands. Like *The Sun*, the prime ministership of Margaret Thatcher had, since the initial euphoria of accession, languished a little. While *The Sun* had begun to recover, Thatcher, so enthusiastically backed by Lamb, appeared to be heading for defeat at the next election: the economy was in poor shape, unemployment was rising and there had been riots in the inner cities of London, Liverpool and Birmingham. While many saw the Argentine invasion in April 1982 as a sign of Britain's impotence, the mobilization of the task force would revive, both literally and metaphorically, a Union Flag-waving, jingoistic, nationalistic fervour among a population that had only recently experienced it during the celebrations for the queen's Silver Jubilee in 1977, and then at the royal wedding the previous year. This shared cultural knowledge went further back to the Second World War and the so-called Spirit of the Blitz, the climate MacKenzie was brought up in, a generation on from those who experienced the war at first hand. Thatcher and *The Sun* would ride this tide of public support. *The Sun* became both creator and chronicler of this phenomenon.

The *Daily Mirror* remained true to its Labour affiliations and instincts and opposed the war. The rest of the tabloids had no such qualms and unhesitating support was the order of the day, picking up on the mood of the country: 'Most people would have been pig sick if there hadn't been a fight. They want to get down there and beat the hell out of someone,' said Brian Hitchins, the *Daily Star* editor.[9] This was pretty much the view of *The Sun*. Castigating the *Mirror* as a 'paper warrior; for giving in to force', an editorial stated bluntly: 'Our whole experience with dictators has taught us that if you appease them, in the end you have to pay a far greater price.' For many readers, no further explanation was needed.

The Sun and others were only reflecting the overwhelming public mood – although they were also culpable in shaping it, in an era when newspapers were taken in 80 per cent of British households. Opinion polls showed that one in three people wanted to bomb the Argentine mainland, while one in five thought British troops should invade Argentina itself. *The Sun*'s newsroom went on a war footing, the news editor donned a military tin helmet and there was a huge map of the South Atlantic pinned up in the office. Headlines became increasingly partisan and hysterical, with a front-page slogan, 'The Paper That Supports Our Boys'. 'Stick It Up Your Junta' was the response to the peace talks in New York; this slogan was later put on a T-shirt and sold for £2. The Argentines were 'Argies' or 'Gauchos' while British troops were 'Our Boys'; there was a campaign to boycott Argentine corned beef, an appeal for jokes about 'Argies' and promotional campaigns featuring patriotic women's underwear and garters, modelled, obviously, by Page 3 girls, the headlines saying, 'The Sun Says Knickers to Argentina' and 'Garters to the Tartars'. The paper promoted a video game in which the player acted as a British submarine commander firing a missile at Argentine war ships. Then *The Sun* 'sponsored' a missile, which it claimed would be the first to be fired from the task force, emblazoned with the words 'Up Yours Galtieri', written by *The Sun*'s reporter on board HMS *Invincible*. On the task-force ship *Canberra*, other journalists were angered by this approach and wrote to *The Sun* to protest. *The Sun* appeared anxious for the conflict to begin: 'Navy Storms South Georgia', said the headline, several days before the actual taking of the outlying island; 'In We Go', said the headline above a story saying 'crack troops' were about to invade, three weeks before it actually happened. It was in this febrile atmosphere that MacKenzie would come to write one of his most notorious headlines.

In the early evening of 3 May, the *Sun* newsroom was depleted by a journalists' strike, which was mainly about money and staffing, but also reflected discontent among some staff at the papers's gung-ho coverage. *The Sun* was being produced by a handful of senior executives. When the news wires reported from Buenos Aires that Argentine warship the *General Belgrano* had been hit by British torpedoes, the first reaction was elation, and Wendy Henry, then features editor, exclaimed aloud, 'Gotcha, Argies.' MacKenzie is said to have shouted 'Wendy. You're a bloody genius!' and proceeded to

THE Sun

Tuesday, May 4, 1982　　14p　　TODAY'S TV: PAGE 12

GOTCHA

Our lads sink gunboat and hole cruiser

SUNK *AN Argie patrol boat like this one was sunk by missiles from Royal Navy helicopters after first opening fire on our lads*

From TONY SNOW aboard HMS Invincible

THE NAVY had the Argies on their knees last night after a devastating double punch.

WALLOP: They torpedoed the 14,000-ton Argentina cruiser General Belgrano and left it a useless wreck.

WALLOP: Task Force helicopters sank one Argentine patrol boat and severely damaged another.

BATTLE FOR THE ISLANDS

CRIPPLED *THE Argie cruiser General Belgrano . . . put out of action by Tigerfish torpedoes from our super nuclear sub Conqueror*

UNION BOYCOTTS WAR

A UNION chief is telling seamen on two ships taken over by the Government: "Don't go to war—the union can't protect you."

The astonishing advice comes from George Cartwright the Communist leader of the National Union of Seamen at Felixstowe Port in Suffolk.

The Government has just requisitioned the Townsend Thoresen roll-on, roll-off vessels Baltic Ferry and Nordic Ferry.

'Folly'

The ferries will carry troops and battle equipment in support of the QE2.

Mr Cartwright told the 150 seamen: "Our advice is that it would be folly to go off on a dangerous adventure.

"I'm old enough to remember that one in three merchant seamen were killed in the last war.

"It is not a case of being unpatriotic. We are not at war and our advice is based on union practicalities.

"What we are saying is that if seamen put themselves under military command, they will no longer have our protection.

Question

"There is no question of politics being behind the recommendation. We were asked for our view

and gave our best advice.

"He believes the majority of crew members will decide not to sail to the South Atlantic.

So far I have heard from three seamen who want to go, the rest are non-committal or against joining the task force," Mr Cartwright said.

The Belgrano, which survived the Pearl Harbour attack when it belonged to the U.S. Navy, had been asking for trouble all day.

The cruiser, second largest in the Argy fleet, had been skirting the 200-mile war zone that Britain has set up around the Falkland Islands.

MAJOR

With its 15 six-inch guns our Navy high command were certain that it would have played a major part in any battle to retain the Falklands.

But the Belgrano and

its 1,000 crew needn't worry about the war for some time now.

For the nuclear submarine Conqueror, captained by Commander Richard Wraith, let fly with two torpedoes.

The ship was not sunk and it is not clear how many casualties there were.

HMS Conqueror was built at Cammell Laird's shipyard in Birkenhead for £30million. She was launched in 1969 and Continued on Page Two

'GOTCHA', *The Sun*, 4 May 1982.

use it as the splash headline on the front page he began to frantically put together.[10]

It is axiomatic that the bigger and longer the print run, the earlier the deadlines, and early editions are despatched to the furthest parts of the nation. So, by around 9 p.m., the paper began printing with MacKenzie's front page: a large stock picture of the *Belgrano*, with underneath, in massive type, the headline 'GOTCHA'; a subhead read: 'Our lads sink gunboat and hole cruiser'. The story, largely based on wire copy, hedged its bets on casualties among the 1,200 crew and the actual fate of the ship. Around 1.5 million copies were printed and sent to the north of England, Scotland, Northern Ireland and overseas. The headline was simply a logical culmination of *The Sun*'s coverage: 'It was the equivalent of ZAP! Or POW! Or a headline which *The Sun* used later in the war, WALLOP! They were comic-book exclamations used by the *Sun* to describe a fantasy war which bore no resemblance to reality.'[11]

Elsewhere in Bouverie Street, Rupert Murdoch was closeted with Peter Stephens, the editorial director, when the first edition arrived. Stephens told Murdoch he believed the headline was wrong: 'I rather like it,' Murdoch responded. As more details emerged, MacKenzie had begun to regret his actions, went to apologize to Murdoch and sent a new front page to the printers: a more restrained headline was substituted: 'DID 1,200 ARGIES DROWN?', with a more nuanced story. Murdoch arrived on the editorial floor and told him: 'I wouldn't have pulled it if I were you . . . seemed like a bloody good headline to me.'[12] The final death toll was said to be 323 Argentines and the sinking was denounced by many as a war crime. The next day, the headline was 'ALIVE', and the article detailed how hundreds of personnel had been rescued after the sinking. But it was 'GOTCHA' that would go down in tabloid history

There was now outright conflict between *The Sun* and other parts of Fleet Street. Within days, the Argentinians sank the British warship HMS *Sheffield*, killing twenty Navy personnel. The sinking led the *Mirror* (alongside the left-of-centre *Guardian*) to call again for renewed efforts at peace negotiations. This in turn prompted *The Sun* to run an editorial at the end of the week accusing those expressing caution about the war of treason. 'Dare Call It Treason' was the headline: 'There are traitors in our midst,' it declared, adding: 'A British citizen is either on his country's side – or he is its enemy' and then accusing *The Guardian* and the *Mirror* – a 'timorous, whining publication' – of treason.[13]

The editorial was condemned by Labour MPs, the National Union of Journalists, Peter Preston, the editor of *The Guardian*, and Mike Molloy, editor of the *Mirror*. Molloy considered an action for libel, but instead responded with an editorial of his own, accusing *The Sun* of being 'The Harlot of Fleet Street' and calling it a 'coarse and demented newspaper . . . [which had] fallen from the gutter to the sewer'. None of this deterred MacKenzie and *The Sun* from continuing in the same vein for the rest of the conflict: 'The Paper That Supports Our Boys' would continue with the comic-book headlines 'Argies Blown out of the Sky' and 'Hero Bayonet Troops Kill Fifty'.

Ironically, there was minimal effect on circulation. While overall newspaper readership rose slightly during the conflict, *The Sun* actually lost around 40,000 readers while the *Mirror* added 95,000. Some of these may have been due to the fact that newspapers had by then achieved almost saturation coverage, some to the fact that TV news was seen as a more reliable and up-to-date source. 'GOTCHA' would become one of tabloid journalism's emblematic headlines, forever used by commentators to attack Murdoch, MacKenzie and *The Sun*.

The Sun's belief that it somehow owned the narrative over the Falklands War led to another disastrous error. In autumn 1982 MacKenzie was furious the *Mirror* had obtained an exclusive interview with Marica McKay, the widow of Colonel 'H' Jones, who had been awarded the Victoria Cross for bravery. MacKenzie ordered a spoiler, a Fleet Street tactic designed to take the shine off a rival's exclusive – perhaps piecing together something similar from alternative sources or finding an angle that debunks the exclusive, but always delivered with prominence and verve to attract the reader away from a rival. In this case, the story purported to be an interview with McKay but was culled from already published sources with some words from a scrambled interview with the colonel's mother. It went too far in being labelled 'World Exclusive' and suggested that McKay had indeed spoken directly to *The Sun* herself 'last night'. The *Mirror*, closeted with McKay at the time, could prove otherwise, of course, and, eventually, the Press Council upheld a complaint against *The Sun*, saying it had created a 'deplorable insensitive deception on the public'. 'Lies, Damn Lies' was the headline in the *Mirror*. The furore did not prevent something similar happening two years later when Wendy Henry's features department put together a spoiler interview with Simon Weston, a Falklands veteran disfigured by severe burns during the conflict; he had been the subject of a BBC documentary but had turned down a *Sun* interview request. The piece lingered in great detail on the severity of his injuries. Weston complained, the *Mirror* piled in on *The Sun* again and Henry was suspended from work for a month, on full pay. On both occasions, Murdoch was, at least publicly, unhappy and reprimanded MacKenzie, who just got on with the job.

Victory in the Falklands emboldened both Margaret Thatcher and her most enthusiastic supporter, who backed her strongly when she was re-elected in 1983. MacKenzie would now go to war on Thatcher's behalf wherever necessary: striking miners, once the 'salt of the earth', were now labelled 'Scum of the Earth' in a headline over a report on clashes between police and pickets, while the resurgent left wing of the Labour Party were branded 'loony Lefties', led by 'Bogeyman [Tony] Benn'. The paper employed a New York psychiatrist to put 'Benn on the Couch – a Psychiatrist's View of Britain's Leading Leftie'. Ken Livingstone, then leader of the Greater London Council, was 'Red Ken' and 'The most odious man in Britain'. Europe was, at that point, much less of an issue for government and the country than it later became, but Murdoch was wary of its ambitions, particularly over media ownership, workers' rights and what he saw as instincts that would shackle free trade. Thatcher had an uneasy relationship with the EU and MacKenzie was always ready to mock or criticize Britain's European neighbours: 'Hop Off You Frogs' was the headline – subsequently made into a badge – when the French decided to briefly ban English lamb. Any chance for an insult or a stunt was eagerly taken: 'Ooh Ha! Ha! Readers Share their Froggie Jokes'. A survey that suggested the French use less soap than other European countries led to a cargo of toothbrushes and soap being taken to the French embassy by a Page 3 model and the headline 'Zee French Are Feel-thy – Official'.

Under MacKenzie, who had an eye on a more youthful audience, pop music, celebrity and showbiz stories had a much bigger presence in *The Sun* than with Lamb. There were glamorous new American soaps like *Dynasty* and *Dallas* to write about, capitalizing on their huge television audiences. Then there were the popular domestic ones, particularly *EastEnders*, whose cast of working-class

East London stereotypes engaging in domestic rows, marital cheating, wheeling and dealing and sometimes a little light illegality were perfect tabloid fodder, with papers treating the reporting of fictional storylines as real life and in turn perhaps reflecting something of the lifestyles of their readers.

In the early 1980s the emergence of HIV/AIDS, which devastated gay communities across the world, prompted little sympathy from the tabloids, which, reflecting society at large, had always sneered at and mocked homosexuality. The 1956 attack by Cassandra in the *Mirror* on pianist Liberace as a 'sniggering, chromium-plated, scent-impregnated, luminous . . . fruit flavoured mincing ice covered heap of mother love' was the view of an otherwise liberal, socially concerned columnist and was common; it earned the *Mirror* an £8,000 fine and £27,000 costs. In 1963 the *Sunday Mirror*, then under Michael Christiansen, with Cudlipp as editor-in-chief, had published a guide on 'How to Spot a Possible Homo', warning readers to be wary of any middle-aged man with an 'unnaturally strong affection for his mother' or who was 'a fussy dresser' or 'dyes their hair'.

Although homosexuality had long been legal, being openly gay in public life remained rare. When gay rights campaigner Peter Tatchell ran for Labour in the 1983 Bermondsey by-election, his sexuality dominated coverage, the *Sunday Mirror* reporting that 'his pouting lower lip hardens if anyone disagrees with him.'[14] The terms 'poofs' and 'gay plague' were dotted around *The Sun*'s coverage, which included a picture of emaciated film star Rock Hudson on his deathbed and editorial support for former chief constable of Greater Manchester James Anderton, who had spoken of homosexuals as 'perverts'. When *EastEnders* broadcast the first gay kiss in a soap, the paper published a front-page story titled 'EASTBENDERS'. That was written by one Piers Morgan, a young reporter on *The Sun*, who would also write a regular column, 'The Poofs of Pop', where he speculated on whether various male pop stars were gay or not; Morgan later revealed that he and another reporter would spend their time trying to persuade showbusiness agents to confess their clients' sexuality.[15] There were numerous complaints to the Press Council over these stories, which MacKenzie rejected. Murdoch seemed unconcerned.

Besides, by the mid-1980s Murdoch had other things on his mind. He was moving the goalposts; he was going to change Fleet

Street forever. And while Murdoch was trying to find ways to get ahead of the game, an old adversary had returned and another tabloid had entered the market.

Enter the *Mail on Sunday*

The *Mail on Sunday*, launched during the Falklands War in spring 1982, was created by Vere Harmsworth, now Lord Rothermere following the death of his father in 1978, with the aim of building on the *Daily Mail*'s growing reputation. Right from the start, the two papers would have an uneasy relationship with one another – one which persisted until very recently. Plans to expand in the United States had come to nothing – in part because he was thwarted by Murdoch – so he focused on the home front. Oddly, despite his closeness with David English, the *Mail* editor was kept largely out of the loop in the planning for the new paper. He is said only to have learnt that Rothermere's choice for *Mail on Sunday* editor was Bernard Shrimsley, who had left the editor's chair of the *News of the World* in 1980 amid declining circulation, when Lady 'Bubbles' Rothermere asked him to check out a telephone number she had found in her husband's suit pocket, believing him to be having an affair. English was able to reassure Lady Rothermere and would say later: 'No, he was being unfaithful to me.'[16]

In 1980, reversing the position of his father, Rothermere finalized a deal to merge the *Evening News* with Express Newspapers' *Evening Standard*, ending a period of costly circulation wars and ensuring that, under the deal, the *Standard* would eventually fall completely into the Mail group's hands if the *Express* was sold (as happened in 1985). In early 1982 he lost the battle with Murdoch for control of *The Times* and the *Sunday Times*. English would, however, reject Murdoch's offer to edit the *Sunday Times*. Shrimsley and Rothermere were aiming to produce a Sunday paper very much in the *Mail* mode – aimed at a middle-class market, albeit a slightly younger one than the traditional *Mail* reader – but shied away from the idea of a seven-day operation, as this had proved unsuccessful elsewhere. They also believed that readers wanted a slightly different product on a Sunday. But Shrimsley was also aware that the vigorous *Sunday Express*, in the hands of veteran Thatcherite the determinedly socially conservative Sir John Junor, also dominated that section of the market. Shrimsley also faced two other problems – the *Mail* board had vetoed the creation of a glossy magazine supplement on cost grounds, and English dissuaded his established star writers, such as Ann Leslie and gossip columnist Peter McKay, from contributing.[17] He was also advised by English not to poach staff from the *Express* group in case it provoked a counter-recruitment attempt at the *Mail*, or to recruit from the red-top tabloids, as that might not work out.[18]

He ended up with a slew of largely second-choice journalists, or those from broadsheets with no middle-market tabloid experience. Shrimsley would later write that he was his own worst enemy: 'I only recruited people I liked and that was a problem. So I didn't have the right person in every job.'[19] English's antipathy was clear, but his motive was not. Some, including Rothermere himself, believed he was deliberately setting up Shrimsley to fail, despite his enthusiastic endorsement of the new creation in the advance publicity in his own paper. And fail he did. The first edition of the paper was, by common consent, a disaster: the design was clumsy, the typeface too small, the pictures likewise. The front-page splash, a source of much agonizing for every new paper, was a bonus – an RAF bombing mission in the Falklands – but there were no live images and the back page was about a roller-skating competition in the Netherlands rather than a more established sport like football or the start of the cricket season. And because of antiquated presses, not enough copies were printed; even Shrimsley could not get a copy the next morning.

Within a few weeks, the anticipated 1.25 million circulation had shrunk to around 700,000 and Shrimsley was brutally sacked. Rothermere, of course, turned to English, who, assisted by some of his top lieutenants, including one Paul Dacre, then an assistant news editor, took over. Working long hours and sometimes sleeping in a camp bed in his office for the next three months, he first of all redesigned the whole look of the paper, then allowed *Mail* writers to work for it and expanded the product, adding part-work serializations, a comic supplement and, eventually, a glossy, upmarket, carefully designed and produced colour supplement with a strong appeal to women called *You Magazine*, which eventually, under editor John Leese, would be a major reason for many to buy the paper. By the end of the year, English remained editor-in-chief of both papers but had handed over control of the *Mail on Sunday* to a new editor, former *Daily Mail* executive Stewart Steven. The circulation was over 1 million. By now the *Mail* was selling just under 2 million and rising and its influence now overshadowed the *Express*, now shrinking in circulation and ambition. Cecil King may have departed the stage, but the middle market for tabloids was firmly back in the grip of the heirs of the Northcliffe and Rothermere dynasty.

7

THE *DAILY MAXWELL*

Amid all the razzamatazz, there was always a feeling it was never going to end well. Few would have predicted that the end would be a floating corpse in the Atlantic. But someone almost certainly did note that the date of Robert Maxwell's arrival at the *Daily Mirror*'s offices in Holborn Circus early on Friday, 13 July 1984 – taking possession of the chairman's office as well as his drinks cabinet, in return for his £90 million – was not exactly propitious. Mike Molloy, editor of the *Mirror* for nearly ten years, wearied by a decade of cut-throat competition with *The Sun* and anxious for a change, happily assumed he would be sacked in a clear-out of the top brass. He would stay on for another six years, mostly as editorial director, mostly at Maxwell's beck and call. It would be, he later recalled, 'the most bizarre chapter in [his] life'.[1]

Maxwell's failure to buy first the *News of the World* and then *The Sun* had been followed by two more blows. In October 1969 he was expelled from the board of Pergamon following the collapse of a reverse takeover deal with an American data company. In 1971 a report on the affair by the Department of Trade concluded: 'Notwithstanding Mr Maxwell's acknowledged abilities and energy, he is not in our opinion a person who can be relied upon to exercise proper stewardship of a publicly quoted company.'[2] Maxwell had inflated the share price of Pergamon during the negotiations. These words would frequently be thrown back at him over succeeding decades. Maxwell's financial deals earned him the nickname 'the bouncing Czech' from *Private Eye* magazine and would be seen in a new light after his death. In the same year, his political career ended when he lost his Buckingham seat; he failed to regain it at both general elections in 1974. Faced with these setbacks, many might have stayed out of the limelight for a while. But that was never Maxwell's style.

Maxwell bought back Pergamon in 1974; he would claim he had rebuilt it from scratch but many in the City believed its resurgence was due to the management team installed by banks after the collapse. He remained on the lookout for a national newspaper. In 1975 he was involved in a failed attempt to relaunch the Scottish *Daily Express* after its employees were sacked by the company, who transferred production to Manchester. In 1980 he wanted to buy *The Times* when the Thompson family put it up for sale, but was brushed aside as being unsuitable for that august publication; Murdoch again emerged triumphant. In 1981 Maxwell bought the British Printing Corporation, a large printing and publishing company teetering on the brink of bankruptcy, and made it profitable by slimming down staff, cutting waste and using the company's assets to gamble on the currency and stock markets. In spring 1984 he began discussions with *Observer* owner Tiny Rowland, who was in a dispute with editor Donald Trelford; Maxwell was used as an unsubtle attempt to persuade *The Observer*'s independent directors of what might await the paper if Rowland could not get his own way. In the end, Rowland backed down and Maxwell was again rejected. But by then, he had already turned his sights on the *Daily Mirror*.

Under MacKenzie, *The Sun* appeared, rightly or wrongly, to have its finger on the pulse of the nation, relating more to council-house-owning, aspirant Tory voters than the cloth-capped factory workers of *Mirror* mythology. The *Mirror*, the *Sunday Mirror* and *The People* were now part of the massive Reed International company and felt distinctly unloved within it. But the *Mirror* remained a formidable enterprise, although some argued it was urgently in need of a revamp. Amid its roster of star writers who were practically household names, such as Zec, Pilger, Waterhouse and Proops, together with a large and experienced staff of reporters and editors, new blood was rare. Old hands hung on, enjoying the benefits of generous salaries and expenses. The *Mirror* remained close to the Labour Party, and Molloy and senior staff would be consulted by Jim Callaghan when he was prime minister. It was less enthusiastic about his successor, Michael Foot, and relations became strained for a while, but it was more supportive of the next leader, the more youthful modernizer Neil Kinnock, who became friends with Molloy. As the power of the tabloids grew during the 1970s and '80s, the relationship between the party and the *Mirror* became ever more crucial as Labour sought a counterpoint to the Thatcher-supporting *Sun*.

The *Mirror* as a company was bloated. While its circulation continued to just about hold up, it remained prey to crippling overheads. There were generous staffing levels – individual workloads tended to be light for both celebrated writers and the toilers of the newsroom. 'Some reporters would go for weeks or even months without their byline appearing; while some would be worried about this, others simply enjoyed their pay packets,' one long-time staffer said later.[3] Cash was doled out to reporters heading out on urgent stories with very little accounting for actual need. Expenses for everyday assignments remained generous. There were suggestions of what amounted to actual fraud: 'A lot of people would rack up very high expenses claims, some would get loads of blank receipts for restaurants and taxis and then make up various activities to justify the claims,' recalled one *Mirror* hand.[4] This was an old Fleet Street trick – if you caught a cab, you would ask the driver for a receipt and offer him a generous tip for a few blanks, which would then be filled in, whenever needed, for journeys claimed but never made. The same principle was often applied to receipts for restaurants, hotels, pubs and so on.

Molloy was by now fully immersed in the tabloid/showbiz/politics culture, content to leave the day-to-day running of the paper to his underlings. He loved the access a national newspaper editor was granted and the routine invitations to an endless round of lunches, dinners and parties, whether it was with pop stars or politicians, Wimbledon or the Chelsea Flower Show. His biography, *The Happy Hack*, recounts it all: hobnobbing in Number 10, 'fact-finding visits' to correspondents around the world, hanging out with pop stars like Paul McCartney and Rod Stewart, lunch at Buckingham Palace or with the Prince and Princess of Wales, or jollies to the Cannes Film Festival or the Oscars.[5] It was all a long way from the life of ordinary archetypical working-class *Mirror* readers, whom it presumed was its audience long after they faded into history.

When it came to the printers, another set of rules applied: in the heat of the battle with *The Sun*, the print unions had wrestled concession after concession from the *Mirror* management as they struggled to compete, making them among the best-paid workers in Fleet Street. But here were the infamous Spanish practices: fictitious 'ghost workers' on the payroll, whose pay packets would be shared around; extra payments negotiated for duties long absorbed into the normal working day; extravagant overtime claims happily signed off by foremen and middle managers. Some workers claimed wages under two names, others spent their shifts gambling or drinking. Others clocked in under one name, but then left for another shift elsewhere, under another. 'It was not unknown at the end of a shift for wages packets to remain unclaimed because the printers were too drunk to recall which phony names they had registered under on arrival.' Any threat to this cosy existence was met with resistance in the forms of walkouts and work-to-rule. 'Anxious to keep their papers on the street, the *Mirror*'s management paid their printers' demands and suffered in as much silence as their self-interest determined.'[6] As far back as May 1974, the paper's new Reed-installed advertising director had told an internal conference that because of union and labour costs, the *Mirror* paid £514 to produce a column of advertising, which the paper then sold for £475. By the early 1980s the *Mirror* was still making a loss on every page of advertising it sold.[7]

Reed, weary of, and lacking empathy with, its bloated and corrupted child, decided the Mirror Group should be sold. So in spring 1984 the solid and respectable figure of Clive Thornton, the low-profile but highly successful head of the Abbey National Building Society, was appointed chairman to sort out the company and prepare it for a sale to institutional investors. Key to that were the conditions of editorial independence and support for the Labour Party, immediately putting Thornton on a collision course with both journalists and the unions. The former's expense accounts shocked the teetotal, ascetic Thornton, who drew up a report for the board showing that expenses claims came to £5 million a year, with £1.3 million spent on entertaining alone. Some journalists claimed £8,000 a year in expenses, an inevitable consequence of the drinking and lunching culture that pervaded.[8] Thornton began assuming a more high-profile role, clearly envisaging himself running the company post-flotation and talking up the idea of financial investment by the Labour Party and the unions, who would be granted worker participation. Maxwell was now sniffing around, telling the Labour Party and unions he should take over. Much depended on the actual value of the company: once the accountants had access to the books ahead of the flotation price – and realized some of the scams that had taken place – the value dropped from £100 million to £60 million, with predictions it could fall lower. Maxwell, flush with money from the rise in shares in what he had now renamed the British Printing and Communications Corporation, said he would bid up to £100 million, and announced: 'I regard myself as the saviour of the group against the heavy commercial advantages of its rivals,' promising that 'power will once again truly return to the ninth floor of Holborn Circus.'[9] Maxwell upped the pressure; Reed refused to negotiate. Key Labour figures were uneasy, some arguing it was better to have Maxwell onside than not, aware the wider party and the unions were deeply concerned about losing their one solid reliable voice in the national media. Elsewhere, the *Daily Herald* was no more and the *Morning Star* preached to the converted and the hard left, while the centrist and soft left-leaning readerships of *The Guardian* and *The Observer* were, relatively speaking, too small to count. Thornton

Robert Maxwell holding a copy of the *Daily Mirror* at a press conference to announce his acquisition of Mirror Group, 1984.

ultimately failed to get a no-strike deal from the unions, Reed caved in to Maxwell and after intense negotiations, the deal was done. As Maxwell's biographer Tom Bower noted, the creation of Northcliffe had been sold to the son of a Ruthenian peasant.

So it was that at just after midnight on 13 July 1984, despite promising Reed not to go to the building that night, Maxwell arrived at Holborn Circus and headed straight to the executives' offices. Maxwell believed he was fulfilling his long-desired destiny: 'He would become a great newspaper tycoon, leading from the front, inspiring great feats of reportage. The *Mirror* would once again become a great newspaper with unbridled influence.' He would become a modern colossus, 'bestriding Fleet Street, Westminster and the City', his opinions sought by the great and good, who would in turn seek his help, as they did with Northcliffe and Beaverbrook, in the service of the nation. 'All would seek his advice and help and eagerly await his judicious opinions on solving Britain's major problems.'[10] The reality could not have been more different.

As Maxwell helped himself to the drinks cabinet of the then chief executive, Douglas Long, Molloy, who would describe Maxwell's smile as 'that of Richard III', expected to be sacked. Maxwell, he said, was in Long's chair, 'squatting like some gigantic cuckoo settling itself into a new nest'.[11] Molloy, demob happy, told Maxwell he had asked the Labour Party to stop the takeover. He expected Maxwell would then order his dismissal. Instead, the new owner said he wanted the 'brilliant' Molloy to continue; of course, both were Labour supporters. Maxwell then invited the senior *Mirror* editorial staff to lunch at the Ritz. When Thornton arrived at 7.30 a.m., Maxwell sacked him on the spot. As Thornton left, he was asked by reporters if he had seen Maxwell: 'I could hardly miss him. He was sitting at my desk.'[12] Later that day, after a hostile meeting with unions, Maxwell presided over a typically bombastic press conference: he repeated promises of editorial independence and announced his intention to return the *Mirror* 'to its rightful place as Britain's biggest circulation popular newspaper without sacrificing any of its influence or tone'. He pledged to retain 'a broadly sympathetic approach to the Labour movement' and that the paper would have a 'Britain first' policy: 'I want them to inform Britain, entertain Britain and boost Britain.'[13]

The *Mirror* staff, Molloy included, belted themselves in for the ride, reasoning, in entirely cynical journalistic fashion, that first, it might be fun, and second, they were still getting paid. Maxwell gained crucial support by persuading columnists Joe Haines – legendary former press secretary to Harold Wilson, who had strongly opposed Maxwell's involvement – and Socialist Workers Party supporter Paul Foot, nephew of Michael, as well as the key figure of industrial editor Geoffrey Goodman, to stay on, with a mixture of bribes, flattery and guarantees their work would be free of interference. Maxwell even engaged the now seventy-year-old, retired and enobled Lord Hugh Cudlipp as consultant. Asked to name his price, Cudlipp said he wanted to be the lowest-paid employee, so he would be able tell the truth and walk away if needed. Cudlipp began by telling Maxwell not to put too many photographs of himself into the paper. For the next two years he delivered a weekly report to Maxwell; all his comments and suggestions were ignored.

It became known as the *Daily Maxwell*. Promises of editorial independence were forgotten in the heady joy of his new possession, his new toy. The next day the front page was dominated by a huge picture of a black-browed and beaming Maxwell under the banner headline 'Forward with Britain'. Underneath, Maxwell repeated the paper's support for the Labour Party. In true egalitarian, workers' solidarity style, he would later convert the top of Strand House, a neighbouring block owned by the *Mirror*, into his own personal heliport and penthouse apartment, with numerous staff and a 24-hour kitchen serving the finest foods and wines. He turned Cecil King's former office into what some described as a cross between a sultan's palace and an airport hotel; the corporate logo – a gigantic 'M' superimposed on an image of Planet Earth – was everywhere. Having banned, to mixed responses from staff, both nipples and chequebook journalism but reinstated the slightly tacky wartime comic strip *Jane* – which usually featured the heroine in various modes of undress, and which the *Mirror* had deemed out of date many years previously – one of Maxwell's first ambitions was to tackle *The Sun* at their other own game: bingo. The *Mirror* launched its own 'honest' version, with the winning numbers drawn by celebrities. This was not enough for Maxwell, who then decided the paper was going to give away a million pounds in cash to one lucky winner. Naturally, this was accompanied by television advertising featuring Maxwell declaring his intention to give away a million pounds and also by a massive image on the front page of the *Mirror*: Maxwell with a trolley loaded with wads of money.

Maxwell, echoing the self-importance of Northcliffe, assured staff it was important to feature him as much as possible, since he was a celebrity and would bring in readers. A *Mirror* photographer was assigned to cover all his meetings with the great and the good, from Mother Teresa and the Princess of Wales to his business trips to various Iron Curtain countries, when pictures of him greeting unelected presidents and dictators would dominate page after page. When he met Soviet leader Mikhail Gorbachev, then probably the most important politician in the world because of his reforms, the story was about Maxwell, not about the man who would bring an end to the Warsaw Pact. He intervened – unsuccessfully – in an attempt to solve the long-running miners' strike in 1984–5 and organized a flight full of donated food to Ethiopia as part of the 1985 Bob Geldof-inspired Live Aid famine relief effort. Maxwell kept the plane, donated by British Airways, waiting for four hours because he was watching a football match involving another acquisition, Oxford United. The coverage was about Maxwell, not starving children: 'The personal attendants, the battery of telephones, the huge consumption of food and the sheer need to place himself, rather than the victims, at the centre of attention contrasted strangely with the images of famine.'[14] Not only did he want his charitable, political and business interests reflected, but there was pressure to cover the football clubs he owned, like Oxford and Derby County, and those he was considering investing in, such as Manchester United, despite his lack of knowledge of the game. He launched a campaign against the then highly popular England manager Bobby Robson because of some small perceived error: not a good move to attract readers. Most journalists would shrug their shoulders at some self-promotion by their proprietor, which was usually accepted as the price to pay for keeping the business afloat. As long as editorial independence was maintained – or at least a pretence of it – then all was fine. After all, the journalists working for Northcliffe, Beaverbrook and Murdoch knew, and mostly cynically accepted, what was needed to keep their proprietors happy. But this was another level of self-promotion, to the point of embarrassment at Maxwell's sheer lack of self-awareness.

Then there was the editorial interference. Beaverbrook and Northcliffe would send instructions and notes while Murdoch, famously, would make his views known in a few choice, succinct words. He would never do anything so crude as to grab copy and start rewriting it, at least in public. This is what Maxwell did with one of Goodman's early columns under his reign, although he apologized profusely for the interference the next day, after it was published. Some columnists and leader writers would be told to submit copy for Maxwell's approval, waiting outside his office with the secretaries, PAs and constant queues of people, many from other business interests, all wanting some of Maxwell's time. David Seymour, Haines's deputy as leader writer, would complain: 'The whole [miners'] strike became a blur for me because I was being battered by Maxwell who was jumping up and down on my head telling me what was happening, which I knew was wrong. He just didn't seem to care that we were wrong.'[15]

Maxwell could speak several languages fluently, but, observed Molloy, his understanding of written English remained poor, largely because he rarely read anything. And, despite owning a major newspaper group, unlike Murdoch he really didn't understand newspapers:

> Maxwell had no idea whether an edition of a paper was good or bad because he had no ability to judge how well the work had been done. Whatever the quality, it looked like another newspaper to him. This meant there were no post mortems on poorly executed editions, but also no special days when the boss opened the champagne to celebrate a winner.[16]

Haines would convert completely to the Maxwell cause and eventually become part of his inner circle and the director of some of his companies. Foot and Pilger clung on, despite the damage to their credibility; they were more or less untouchable, even for Maxwell.

The chaos around Maxwell didn't help. He was dashing about buying companies, adding them to his portfolio, taking them apart, launching new ventures and schemes and profiting from some of their assets before moving on, leaving one of his underlings or his two adult sons, Ian and Kevin, to tidy up the mess. They were never able to really run the companies, since he refused to delegate even small matters. There was always a queue of decisions to be made. His attention span was that of a butterfly: he was easily distracted, didn't like to be pressed on details, could not be bothered to read anything more than a few sentences long and would often simply lose or forget vital paperwork. Maxwell would never pay his bills until it was absolutely necessary; he became angry with managers who settled bills without haggling and before they absolutely needed to. Once, after taking a group of *Mirror* executives to Claridge's for lunch, he swept out, airily brushing aside the manager's request for payment and instructing him to send the bill to his office. The manager replied: 'But . . . you always say that Mr Maxwell, sir. And you never pay.' On that occasion, Maxwell did get out his wallet.[17]

His personal style was gross and chaotic. Spending most of the time in his penthouse on the top of Strand House – leaving his wife Betty to run the family home at Headington Hall in Oxfordshire and with most of their children married or living away from home – Maxwell, now massively obese, gorged himself on fine food and drink, often rising in the middle of the night to raid the fridge and urinate over the wall from his heliport. His personal dietary, sexual and toilet habits were the subject of widespread gossip and a source of despair for the maids who had to clean up after him.[18] In public, he was sometimes no better: at formal dinners, his servants would always serve him the first and largest portions; he would sometimes attack the food on the plates of neighbouring diners, if he spied a morsel he particularly fancied. When he finished one of his favoured Cuban cigars, he would plonk the end into the nearest brandy glass, whether it was his own or that of someone else.[19]

The 'Daily Maxwell' attracted widespread derision within the industry and among the wider readership. Some days, there were photographs of him on almost every page in the paper. According to the trade magazine UK *Press Gazette*, during one three-day period the name Maxwell appeared 231 times; loyal and long-serving readers, many baffled by this dominance, complained bitterly. Circulation, which had been holding up against the peak-MacKenzie *Sun* at around 3.4 million in June 1984, plummeted. Within a year, despite spending £5 million on sales and the bingo promotions, the *Mirror* lost 350,000 readers; within a further six months circulation had dropped to 2.9 million. Maxwell's promise to reach 4 million and overtake *The Sun* was in shreds. *Marketing Week* famously commented: 'It takes something close to genius to lose so much circulation so quickly.'[20] Profits, already small, were forecast to become massive losses. This prompted Maxwell to tackle the unions, aware the printing costs of the *Mirror* were around three times higher than those of *The Sun*, which was yet to move to Wapping. Warning the unions that the papers would close if costs were not reduced, by a process of bluff and bullying he eventually agreed settlements at the end of 1985, which involved hundreds of redundancies and an end to many of the notorious overmanning agreements; he would save around £40 million a year.

In 1985 Molloy, weary of dealing with Maxwell on a daily basis, was happy to be shifted upstairs as editorial director of the whole group – a relative sinecure. As he later said, he would occasionally be turned out to parade in front of visitors to explain parts of the business that Maxwell himself didn't understand, and accompany him on trips around the world.[21] He was also able to write three books and lasted until 1990 before happily accepting a decent pay-off. Molloy was replaced by his former deputy Richard Stott, another long-serving and highly experienced *Mirror* man who switched over from being editor of the *Sunday Mirror*. Stott told Maxwell he would accept the job only if Maxwell restrained his interventionist instincts. 'One person can be in charge of the paper's editorial content, either publisher or editor, but not both,' he said in a memo to Maxwell; there should be no confusion over roles. 'I considered myself to be working for the *Mirror*, not for Maxwell; I believed in what the *Mirror* stood for – social justice, decent and honest standards in public life and the right for people with small voices to be heard loud and clear.'[22] Stott, a more natural newsroom creature than Molloy, took back a little control, Maxwell's image appeared far less often and there was a new aggressiveness in the approach to *The Sun*. Although the *Mirror* would never again challenge *The Sun*'s circulation lead, the gap between them narrowed partially because *The Sun* ended its bingo promotions. Under Stott, the *Mirror*'s journalism and particularly its use of colour – which *The Sun* lacked – on big stories regained professional respect. It did see the departure of two of its biggest names: Keith Waterhouse, who became disenchanted with Maxwell and decamped to the *Daily Mail*, and John Pilger, sacked by Stott on the orders of Maxwell, who had decided one of the paper's longest-serving and best-known reporters was overrated.

Fortress Wapping

The significance of Maxwell's deal with the unions – which would reduce costs at the biggest rival to *The Sun* – was clear to Murdoch, as well as the fact that events outside his control were both shaping the future of Fleet Street and threatening his dominance. Typically, he had bigger plans.

By the mid-1980s Fleet Street, as both an institution and a geographical entity, had hit breaking point. A combination of high overheads, cramped, sometimes crumbling and outdated buildings and the restrictive practices of the unions, which had both increased overheads and prevented the introduction of important new technologies that were now being introduced in the provincial media, was putting intolerable pressure on all the major newspaper groups. Worst of all, and the major barrier to dealing with the first two problems, were the print unions, which operated closed shops, exerted considerable power and control over editors and proprietors and were deeply resistant to the introduction of new technologies, fearing for their jobs. Most journalists felt caught in between, but were often angry at the printers, who rarely supported industrial action by the National Union of Journalists – a 1984 strike was a particularly sore point – but were happy to down tools for the slightest reason, leading to lost stories, lost sales and lost readers. Any possibilities of innovation, expansion and modernization were stymied. Proprietors also knew they were sitting on sizeable profits from the cramped and congested buildings they owned in and around Fleet Street, which were rocketing in value as the expansion of the City pushed up property prices.

At the same time, Fleet Street looked on enviously as provincial newspaper groups, some more able to negotiate new agreements with realistic unions such as MacKenzie's old employers the *Birmingham Post and Mail*, switched to offset litho production and away from the traditional hot metal method. In this brave new world, computers were introduced to replace typewriters and words would be input by journalists directly into machines that would produce plates to go onto printing presses, cutting out swathes of printers' jobs in the process. The print unions had watched uneasily as Margaret Thatcher's government introduced laws to restrict union power, eagerly egged on by the leader columns of *The Sun* and the *Mail*.

New industrial relations legislation limited secondary picketing and imposed fines and sequestration of assets for breaking these new laws, as the National Union of Mineworkers had discovered during the bitter strike of 1984–5. If the all-powerful miners could be defeated, the Fleet Street barons could see that print unions would surely suffer the same fate. But the unions knew they still had power over the presses and the ability to inflict serious economic damage; they also had the jobs of thousands to defend. Both sides were squaring up for a defining confrontation.

In mid-1985 in Warrington, Cheshire, Eddy Shah, bullish owner of a string of local free newspapers who had fought and won a long angry battle with the local unions over new working agreements, had shocked Fleet Street when he announced plans for a new daily, full-colour, broadsheet national newspaper to be called *Today*, produced in a non-union plant using the latest computer technology. Although there was cynicism about Shah's ability and doubts he had the experience to make it work, as well as a recognition that provincial printing unions were an entirely different beast from those in London, many also saw that he was showing the way forward. Murdoch would never contemplate *Today* as a serious rival to *The Sun*, but he could well see how the new technology and Shah's approach offered one way forward – why bother negotiating with the unions, when you can just sidestep them altogether?

Talks between Murdoch's holding company for all his British newspaper interests, News International, and unions over the introduction of new technologies – which would lead to considerable redundancies among typesetters and others – were dragging on. Murdoch realized he might have to go down the Shah route, or something like it, and a backup plan had been in preparation for some time. News International had, a few years previously, bought a large site at Wapping in east London, between Docklands and the City and close to main roads out of London. It was, the unions were told, destined to be the home of a putative new London evening newspaper, the *London Post*. What Murdoch really wanted to do was to move all his papers, then scattered around Fleet Street, with *The Sun* and the *News of the World* in Bouverie Street and *The Times* and *Sunday Times* further away in Gray's Inn Road, to the Wapping site and start afresh. In secret, Murdoch began purchasing vast amounts of equipment and large presses and negotiating with the electricians' union, which, lacking the traditions and cus-toms of the printers, was happy to deal with Murdoch. In case railway unions backed printers in a dispute, Murdoch agreed with a transport company, TNT, to have the papers delivered nationwide by lorry. The railways, a crucial factor in the historic expansion of the national press and the original and only way for bulk amounts of newspapers to reach their readers around the country overnight were, at a stroke, out of the loop. If negotiations failed, Murdoch planned to bypass the printers altogether. Only a few of Murdoch's senior staff, editors and a handful of editorial executives were aware of the audacious contingency plan.

Events were moving fast; the old order was changing. On Boxing Day 1985, as talks with the unions over redundancy and new working arrangements dragged on, the *Financial Times* revealed that another new, serious, upmarket broadsheet newspaper was being developed, based in London and the brainchild of three senior *Daily Telegraph* journalists. It would be contract printed at satellite sites around the country and launched the coming autumn; the unions were nowhere to be seen in their plans, which had been kept discreet for some time. This was clearly a properly funded and organized pro-ject by serious and experienced national journalists, not simply that of an ambitious provincial entrepreneur and non-journalist such as Shah. The development electrified Fleet Street, where recruitment opportunities for newcomers to the national media, and promotions among those already there but below executive level, were notor-iously slow. CVs were suddenly being updated for the anticipated jobs on both new papers. The future of the industry was opening up. Although the plans for what would become the *Independent* news-paper were then in their infancy, as that year ended, Murdoch would have been keenly aware of the future potential competition to *The Times* posed by a non-unionized broadsheet aimed at a similar audi-ence and advertisers as well as the fact that the unions could simply be bypassed by new ventures with a 'greenfield site' mentality and use of new technologies. Talented *Times* staff might be tempted by the new venture. Other rivals might be prompted to follow suit. The need for change in his own company was suddenly even more pressing. It was time to put his plans into action: this was the old buc-caneering Murdoch again. He decided to make his move before the end of January, breathtaking speed for such a monumental upheaval.

On Friday, 24 January, unions representing the 6,000 print and print-related workers on all Murdoch's papers had rejected the redundancy package offered to them and went on strike. Journalists phoning in their copy from all points of the compass were summarily cut off when the copytakers joined in the action. There would be no papers that night. Murdoch ordered News International immediately to announce the strikers would all be dismissed. In the newsrooms, rumours, which had been swirling around for months, intensified. Late in the day the editors gave their staff the deal: break free of the printers, come and join us at Wapping, enjoy the benefits of new technology and you will get a £2,000 bonus. The alternative was the sack. The vast majority of staff on *The Sun* and the *News of the World*, urged on by MacKenzie and David Montgomery, the former *Sun* news executive who had become *News of the World* editor the previous year, had little hesitation in taking the deal – there wasn't much else they could do. MacKenzie cleverly appealed to the fact that many journalists had sometimes felt not just sidelined but like victims in the wars between managements and printers, mainly when their hard work failed to see the light of day: 'The only people that matter anymore', MacKenzie told them, 'are the journalists. There can't be papers without journalists. And with this in mind we are going to make the momentous step from Bouverie Street to Wapping.'[23] There were far more refuseniks at *The Times* and *Sunday Times*, a number of whom fled to the new *Independent*, ironically helping to bolster that paper's ambitions; they would form a large part of its early success story.

The Sun and the *News of the World* moved their operations into Wapping over the weekend, began work on their Sunday and Monday editions and prepared for a bright new future. *The Times* and *Sunday Times* would follow within days. What they did not know that frantic weekend was that Fortress Wapping, as it would become known, would be under siege from striking printers for more than a year, 'a newspaper factory fenced by twelve foot high spiked steel railings, topped by coils of razor wire and monitored by close circuit television'.[24] Journalists entering or leaving would endure abuse, cries of 'Scab!' and threats from pickets, the level of which ebbed and flowed, but was often at its most intense on Saturday nights in order to disrupt the printing of the *News of the World* and the *Sunday Times*. Massive numbers of police officers were drafted in to protect the plant, and armoured buses were used to ferry workers in and out.

Many journalists were unhappy about being unable to come and go as they pleased and the oppressive conditions, not to mention the distance from their favourite Fleet Street watering holes as well as the rest of the capital; a number would soon drift away into other jobs.

During the dispute, hundreds of police officers and others were injured and there were more than 1,200 arrests. While the printers enjoyed wide support within the Labour and trade union movement and there was widespread criticism of some of the police's heavy-handed riot-control tactics, the call for a boycott of Murdoch papers was largely unsuccessful and not a single full day's production was lost. On the first anniversary of the move, there was a huge picket of more than 13,000 demonstrators and violent clashes with the police, of whom 160 were injured, as were scores of protestors. It was the last hurrah – the picket was called off and the printers took their individual payoffs. 'Although production had been sporadically disrupted, no issues . . . had been completely lost. Brenda Dean, the leader of SOGAT [one of the printing unions], later admitted she had known Murdoch had won the moment the first TNT lorry drove out of the plant.'[25]

For Murdoch, the short-term costs were simply a loss leader: his wage bill was massively reduced, future production was assured and the print unions would never again enjoy the same power. As one *Financial Times* executive later put it:

Sunday, January 26, 1986 was the day on which Fleet Street, as we have known it for all our working lives, ceased to exist. That was the day Rupert Murdoch proved that it was possible to produce two mass circulation newspapers without a single member of his existing print workforce, without using railways and with roughly one-fifth of the numbers he had been employing before.[26]

Within a few years, most of Fleet Street would follow suit in bypassing and restricting union power, mainly by off-site printing. But Wapping was not simply a landmark event in journalism – the breaking of the print unions, coming in the wake of the defeat of the miners the previous year, represented a social and political watershed and would form part of the legend around Margaret Thatcher and the creed of Thatcherism. And among the biggest cheerleaders for Thatcherism and its policies – the restrictions on the unions, the sale of council houses, the privatization of national utilities – would be all the Murdoch papers, but most especially *The Sun*.

Another Red-Top Enters the Fray

The *Today* newspaper, Murdoch's move to Wapping, the planned launch of *The Independent* in 1986 and the short-lived Labour-orientated *News on Sunday* as well as Robert Maxwell's ill-fated and equally brief *London Daily News* – a 24-hour newspaper aimed to rival the *Evening Standard* but which lasted only six months after its launch in 1987 – had demonstrated that after decades of inertia, the newspaper business was expanding on the back of new technologies and curbed union power. Now another paper was being planned, one that was designed to capitalize on the growing tabloid market and to out-*Sun The Sun* and the *Star*: the *Sunday Sport*. While the tabloids were regularly accused of peddling pornography, what they produced was, in legal terms, not pornography. Murdoch, Maxwell and Stevens were not pornographers. But the *Sunday Sport* was the brainchild of David Sullivan, who had made a fortune from pornographic films and magazines, which also advertised a string of sexually explicit premium-rate phone lines. He also owned a string of sex shops. Sullivan, an economics graduate who eventually became one of Britain's richest businessmen, had wanted to be a newspaper publisher since his school days, but had never quite got there. Talks with the unions to launch a sports tabloid in the early 1980s had foundered, but by 1986 the climate had changed.

Sullivan would aim the *Sport* at the 9 million people who did not regularly buy a Sunday newspaper and his assumption was that this was a readership further downmarket than the existing Sunday red-tops. He went into partnership with David and Ralph Gold, who owned the Ann Summers chain of sex shops and published a range of soft-core pornographic magazines, for reasons of finance and shared risk and to access to their large distribution network. They also provided him with offices in Islington, just north of the City, where he installed a small group of former tabloid and red-top journalists. The first editor, Austin Mitchelson, told author Mark Killick that the new paper was originally envisaged as sports only, but then Sullivan decided to broaden the appeal.

Good sport, but with some other elements in it – nipples, basically. It was going to be a newspaper that made you laugh. It was to be fun. It was a bridge between comics and newspapers. It was always going to include things other newspapers were not covering. The most famous example was the 'bomber found on the moon.' Stories that were silly, that were just fancied up. It was never going to sell five million like the *News of the World*, but it should get a good slice of the market. We planned to break even at around 200,000 to 250,000 copies.[27]

Despite a ban on television and radio advertising by the Independent Broadcasting Authority (IBA), which was nervous of the background of its owners and its stated intention to include a high nipple and sleaze story count, the *Sport* in fact exceeded its target in the first few weeks post-launch in September 1986, selling more than 350,000 copies by some measures and eventually settling at around 200,000, even with distribution based only around London and the south of England. Its riotous mix of scarcely believable stories of the 'One in Seven People Are Aliens' and 'Elvis Found in a Cave' variety – its circulation peaked at 600,000 when the front-page headline read 'Bomber Found on the Moon' – were modelled on the American supermarket tabloids such as the *National Enquirer*. It appealed to both traditional red-top working-class readers and also a certain type of, for example, City worker, who bought it for a laugh. Another huge draw was the pages of sexually explicit advertising: sex contact small ads and, eventually, vast amounts of advertising for sexually explicit telephone lines, many of them said to be run by Sullivan himself.

Initially, its production values and design were poor – the staff small and largely inexperienced – but it eventually settled down and prospered. Unlike Murdoch, Maxwell or Beaverbook, Sullivan was a relatively non-interventionist proprietor, leaving the journalists to get on with the job and to watch the money roll in. Design improved with the appointment of the third editor, Drew Robertson, who introduced a more magazine-led design for the key pages, cutting out images to make them more prominent in a way similar to that of the less salacious *Sunday World* in Dublin, which was in itself a stylistic copy of the British tabloids. After a year and the ending of the IBA ban, circulation often reached around 500,000.

The entry of the *Sport* into the field showed that, by the mid-1980s, the market for sex and sleaze in newspapers – and, apparently, the public's appetite for it – seemed to be insatiable. Over the previous decade, the tone and content of newspapers, largely led by *The Sun*, had transformed the popular end of the market.

Even before the launch of the *Sport*, Tom Baistow, commentator on the media for the *New Statesman*, would write:

> Today, the British read more newspapers proportionately than any other Western nation and most of them read some of the trashiest, most politically partisan papers in the world – half a dozen mass circulation tabloid dailies and Sundays which have brought British journalism down to the level of the sex and crime pulp magazine, exploiting the sensational and trivial at the expense of the significant, substituting soft porn for hard news and technical slickness for professional integrity, unashamedly pushing their owners' commercial interests while soft pedalling their more controversial activities, distorting the facts of the political scene by biased selection, suppression and character assassination, desperately trying to inflate their circulation by bigger and bigger bingo prizes, flaunting their contempt for the impotent censure of the Press Council, refusing redress to those they have misreported, misrepresented or maligned.[28]

8

THREE HEADLINES

nside Wapping, once the shock of the initial upheaval had worn
off, journalists just got on with the job, trying to ignore the
pickets and abuse they faced coming in and out of the building. There was much grumbling about the site being dry and a
long way from their favourite watering holes around Fleet Street,
but the daily demands of producing a newspaper did not allow
for much reflection or debate. There was always another deadline
around the corner. And MacKenzie did not slow up: the move and
the siege of Wapping emboldened him to reach new heights. There
were wheezes and stunts invoking wartime tropes – one involved
hiring a tank to drive through the picket line carrying fully clothed
Page 3 model Samantha Fox, wearing a tin helmet and greeted by
members of the newsroom attired in combat gear and more helmets. Among the stunts was a headline that would still be debated
decades later, but would also be one of the earliest examples of what
would eventually be called 'fake news'.

Freddie Starr Ate My Hamster

'The thing about Max Clifford,' recalled one broadsheet journalist,

> was he was always so obliging and friendly. Ring up Max for
> a comment or help on just about anything celebrity-related
> and even if you have never spoken to him before, it's like he's
> known you all his life and you're suddenly his best mate and
> he remembers your first name – and uses it a lot – and noth-
> ing is too much trouble. Quotes, access to his clients, it can

all be done. But there was, always, implicitly, a sense of he will do you a favour this time, but, maybe you might return the favour in the future . . . never much likely to happen with a broadsheet of course, but with the tabloids it was different, it was all wheeling and dealing, playing one off against another, you scratch my back etc.[1]

Clifford, who would play a crucial part in shaping and creating tabloid culture for more than two decades, came from the same south London environment as Kelvin MacKenzie. He entered local newspapers as a teenager and eventually became a music industry press officer, where he briefly represented the Beatles, going on to run his own showbiz and PR agency and acting for a wide variety of artists including Joe Cocker and Marvin Gaye, actor Marlon Brando and boxer Muhammad Ali.

One of Clifford's clients in the 1980s was Freddie Starr, a Liverpudlian comedian and impressionist with roots in the northern club circuit who had made the leap into television. Starr's public persona channelled that of a hyperactive teenager, so when *The Sun* heard in March 1986 that while staying with a friend he had asked for a sandwich and, impatient for food, had put her pet hamster between two slices of buttered bread and pretended to eat it, everyone thought it a hoot and, well, probably true. Whether or not Starr had actually bitten *into* the hamster or even eaten any of the sandwich remained unclear. Anyone rational might think it unlikely. The fact that the incident was said to have happened – if it had happened at all – some five years previously was not relevant. MacKenzie had the old Fleet Street maxim 'news is when you find out about something' hardwired into his soul. And being rational didn't come into it when *The Sun* scented a story.

A *Sun* reporter telephoned Clifford to ask if the story was true: Clifford, as he later disclosed, phoned Starr, who denied it. His manager denied it too, and they both asked Clifford to stop the story. Clifford phoned MacKenzie and said that although Starr denied it, he was more than happy for it to go in, because the comedian was about to go on tour and it would be great publicity for him; he knew Starr's career was in a bit of a lull. 'I was happy to encourage it – I was looking after Freddie's career,' Clifford later told the 2012 Leveson Inquiry into phone hacking.[2] MacKenzie let rip: the headline 'Freddie Starr Ate My Hamster' was a distortion. Although the story said Starr '*ate* it', it also quoted Starr's friend, Lea La Salle, the owner of the hamster (named Sonic), as saying: 'He started eating it.' The story also hedged its bets, adding a carefully judged quote from her boyfriend: 'I don't know how much of the hamster he ate.' Whether most readers noticed such qualifications seems unlikely. No one seriously believed, at the time, that the story was true; it rode on the back of the fact that, given Starr's zany persona, it just *might* have happened. It was, to all, a bit of Fleet Street fun. No one actually denied it and everyone went along with the follow-up stunt of getting Starr – actually an animal-loving vegetarian – to pose with a live hamster. Starr had twelve dates added to his tour and, it was said, an extra £1 million to his fee, so could hardly complain.

The story took its place in tabloid mythology and the front-page facsimile was mounted, alongside the 'GOTCHA' front page, on the wall in MacKenzie's office. It would be brought up pretty much every time tabloid headlines were discussed, or Starr's name was mentioned – including when he was arrested on sexual abuse allegations in 2012, when the case was dropped in 2014 and when he died in 2019. Everyone involved later admitted the story was made up: Starr in his 2001 autobiography, Clifford on a number of occasions, including his evidence to Leveson, and La Salle in an interview after Starr's death, an event which *The Sun* inevitably headlined 'Freddie Goes to Join His Hamster'. La Salle did point out that there was a fragment of truth at its core: Starr, jokingly and probably after a drink or two, had actually taken the hamster out of its cage, put the creature between two slices of bread and pretended to take a bite, but then handed it back to her. She added that she was most annoyed by the fact that Sonic had to lick the butter off his fur.[3]

It might otherwise be seen as a bit of harmless tabloid fun – compared with, say, the Muriel Mackay interview, no one was offended or hurt, not even Sonic – but the story demonstrated to the red-top end of Fleet Street that, with softer or human interest stories where it suited the agendas of all involved, it was fair game to make something up or grossly inflate a single piece of information, give it a 'Hey, Martha . . .' headline and watch the circulation rise. Or, as would later be the case, see the hits, retweets and likes soar online. It was also the making of Clifford, who became a major player in the celebrity story market, brokering deals with the tabloids – in particular the *News of the World* – mainly of the 'kiss and tell' variety whereby women (and sometimes young men) would, in return for money, tell all of their relationship with a showbiz celebrity, sports star or politician. Clifford used such dealings to relentlessly promote the interests of his more regular clients. Much later, *The Sun* would offer to put him on a permanent salaried retainer to persuade him to call off a phone hacking case against it.

The Freddie Starr story – a willingness to distort the facts in pursuit of a reader-grabbing headline – characterized the Wapping operation under MacKenzie in the late 1980s. In 1987, *The Sun* topped the league of complaints dealt with by the Press Council, with fifteen upheld, one partly upheld and six rejected. But with a regular sale of more than 4 million, freedom from the unions and a government unlikely to crack down on supportive newspapers, what was there to worry about? Over the next few years, *The Sun* would test that freedom to its limits – and would twice pay a high price for getting it wrong.

'SORRY ELTON'

Even though homosexuality had long been decriminalized, in the 1980s it was still some way from being universally accepted. In pop and showbiz culture, being gay or bisexual had, since pop and fashion's New Romantic movement of the early 1980s, been nothing unusual, with stars such as Boy George being open about the fact. But the HIV/AIDS epidemic had led to unease in some quarters about so-called gay lifestyles and homosexual sex practices, while many popular newspapers would openly call it the 'gay plague'. There was reluctance among politicians, judges, businesspeople and more orthodox showbusiness stars to publicly admit their sexual preferences. Even some pop figures like Freddie Mercury, who died of AIDS, would never admit their bisexuality. This was still an era when, in 1987, Margaret Thatcher could declare to the Tory Party conference: 'Children who need to be taught to respect traditional moral values are being taught that they have an inalienable right to be gay. All of those children are being cheated of a sound start in life. Yes, cheated.' The following year, the Tories introduced the controversial Clause 28 to the Local Government Act, banning local authorities and schools from doing anything to 'promote' homosexuality.

How much of this prejudicial attitude lay behind *The Sun*'s pursuit of Elton John – who had come out as bisexual many years previously – during 1987, it is difficult to say. Irrespective of Elton's sexuality, any story involving a leading and married pop figure with prostitutes would have been, in tabloid eyes, worth publishing. So the story, based on the paid-for disclosures of a man who claimed to have been financially rewarded by Elton John for certain services, published at the end of February 1987 under the headline 'Elton in Vice Boys Scandal' with a teaser reading: 'Star's lust for bondage – see page 4 and 5' was a guaranteed 'Hey, Martha . . .' read. The headlines 'Elton's Kinky Kinks' and 'Elton's Drug Capers' followed over the next couple of days. The stories eventually resulted in a barrage of writs from John, while their authenticity was seriously challenged in a series of stories in the *Mirror*. Two more followed – in April, 'Elton Porno Photo Shame' featured two photos of a naked John in pre-marriage days, and in September, 'Mystery of Elton's Silent Dogs' suggested that his Rottweiler guard dogs had been operated on to remove their barks. By now, Elton's lawyers had filed seventeen legal actions against *The Sun*. Not long afterwards, the rent boy in the original story confessed to the *Mirror* that he had lied.

But it wasn't just *The Sun* that was after homosexuality-related sleaze. On the Sunday after the original Elton John story, the *News of the World* came up with its own similar front page exclusive about popular television presenter and chat-show host Russell Harty. 'Smack Happy Harty My £60 a Night Lover' again featured the confessions of a male escort, spread over two pages inside. While the story had little effect on the career of a much-loved personality who had never made any secret of his homosexuality, it did provoke the other tabloids, *The Sun* included, into unprecedented scrutiny of his private life, descending on his home village in Yorkshire, parking outside his house, searching through his rubbish, harassing locals and offering cash to anyone who could come up with more dirt. When Harty was admitted to hospital in Leeds in May 1988 with liver failure caused by hepatitis B, the hospital came under siege and the specialist treating him was forced to call a press conference to deny that his patient had AIDS. Harty died in June that year, after which *The Sun*, aware dead men cannot sue, ran a story that claimed Harty had 'sodomised and beaten' the male escort and had contracted hepatitis B through gay sexual practices.[4]

At Harty's memorial service that October, the playwright Alan Bennett, a lifelong friend from their days at Oxford, launched a bitter attack on the tabloids. He spoke of how the *News of the World* had set up Harty and reporters had even tried to bribe the vicar. When Harty went into hospital 'one newspaper took a flat opposite and had a camera with a long lens trained on the window of his ward.' Another, said Bennett, posed as a junior doctor, went into the ward and demanded to see Harty's medical notes. One paper sent a large bunch of flowers, containing money and their news desk telephone number, to another patient in the intensive care unit, although it was intercepted by staff. But Bennett admitted that, had Harty recovered, 'he would have gone on going to Mr Murdoch and Mr [Robert] Maxwell's parties and doing his column for a Murdoch newspaper.' MacKenzie, of course, hit back with a *Sun* leader saying it was 'nauseating' for showbiz stars to cheer Bennett's claim:

> He [Harty] died from a sexually transmitted disease . . . caught through his own choice. By paying young rent boys to satisfy him, he broke the law. Some, like ageing bachelor [*The Sun* here using an old-fashioned but once common phrase to describe a homosexual] Mr Bennett can see no harm in that. He has no family. But what if it had been your son whom Harty bedded?[5]

Two months after Bennett's speech and after more than a year of legal wrangling with John's lawyers, in December 1988, *The Sun* gave in, settled the damages claims out of court and agreed to publish an unprecedented front page apology headlined 'SORRY ELTON', admitting it had paid the star £1 million in damages and quoting a *Sun* spokesman saying: 'We are delighted that the *Sun* and Elton have become friends again and are sorry that we were lied to by a teenager living in a world of fantasy.'[6] So far as *The Sun* was concerned, they had kissed and made up, no damage done. The judge in the case was furious that *The Sun* had revealed the deal ahead of it being announced in court.

Shortly afterwards, MacKenzie began to promote Piers Morgan, last heard of writing the 'Poofs of Pop' columns as a way of repairing some of the links with the pop world (an increasingly important sources of news), in the wake of the Elton John debacle. Morgan was an energetic middle-class twentysomething with a background in the fertile landscape of South London weekly newspapers. Guileless but ebullient, he was happy to be regularly pictured with the stars and celebrities as their apparent new best friend. As writer Hunter Davies later noted in an interview with Morgan, he actually knew very little about pop music, but did understand self-publicity. He told Davies: 'I became the Friend of the Stars, a rampant egomaniac, pictured all the time with famous people – Madonna, David Bowie, Sylvester Stallone – hundreds of them. It was shameless, as they didn't know me from Adam.' He also thought that MacKenzie was the greatest journalist he had ever met.[7]

'The Truth'

The Elton John case was only one of many where *The Sun* would have to defend its actions and make recompense. Just a few weeks prior to this it had paid £100,000 to four charities nominated by the queen to settle an action for breach of copyright after MacKenzie had published an unauthorized picture of that year's Royal Christmas card. And shortly after the Elton case, it was further forced to make 'substantial' payments to a woman who was a witness to the controversial shooting dead by the SAS of three IRA suspects in Gibraltar, whom *The Sun* had accused of fabricating her evidence to put the SAS in a bad light. The following year, there was another story for which the headline would be even more controversial than 'GOTCHA' or 'Freddie Starr Ate My Hamster'. More importantly, it would lose *The Sun* a large number of readers, because 'The Truth' was anything but the truth – and, almost three decades later, it would still be a stain on *The Sun*'s reputation.

Britain's worst sporting disaster took place on 15 April 1989, at the FA Cup semi-final match between Liverpool and Nottingham Forest at the Hillsborough ground in Sheffield, when hundreds of Liverpool fans were wrongly let into standing-only pens in order to ease overcrowding outside the ground. In the crush and its aftermath, 97 people died and 766 were injured, almost all Liverpool supporters. While the cause was later firmly attributed to disastrous police crowd-control decisions, in the immediate aftermath rumours were started – it later emerged, by police trying to distract from their errors – that the Liverpool fans had been drunk and violent, were attempting to get in without tickets, had stolen from dead victims and had attacked police and emergency service workers.

MacKenzie fully bought into this narrative and said in a leader the following Tuesday morning – instinctively reflecting his and the paper's own prejudices – that the police had behaved correctly and drunk Liverpool fans, coming from a city with a reputation for crime and disorder, had been the cause of the disaster. Then he went further. The following day, *The Sun*'s whole front page was devoted to a story that still reverberates today. The massive headline 'The Truth' had three straplines below: 'Some fans picked pockets of victims'; 'Some fans urinated on the brave cops'; 'Some fans beat up PC giving kiss of life'. The story repeated the claims that police and emergency services workers had been attacked by Liverpool fans, some of whom had purportedly stolen from victims; it quoted a senior police officer calling them 'animals'. Lacking any details or attribution to named sources – apart from a Tory MP who made it very clear he was only repeating claims he had heard – the story was a piecing-together of local news agency reports, some of which had appeared in the *Sheffield Star* the previous evening. But typically, MacKenzie, whose mantra was 'If you do it, do it big,' ignored cautions from staff and went overboard in the language and presentation, with the headline an obvious hostage to fortune.

In Liverpool – the city had barely begun to bury its dead – there was already widespread anger over graphic pictures of the tragedy that had been published on the Sunday and Monday mornings, but the Tuesday front page was seen as taking insensitive inaccuracy to another level. Within hours of the paper appearing, copies were being publicly burned and newsagents removed them from display. In a matter of days, *The Sun*'s average sale on Merseyside slumped from 520,000 to around 320,000. The *Star*, which had carried a similar story but had qualified the allegations and attributed them to the police, also lost circulation. But it was *The Sun* that bore the brunt of what became an extensive boycott of the paper by individuals and businesses, made worse by MacKenzie refusing to respond publicly and defend the story.

Behind the bullishness, MacKenzie realized he had made a mistake. Anger over a story was one thing, but losing hundreds of thousands of readers was another. He called Kenny Dalglish, the much-respected Liverpool manager, asking for help to resolve what

MacKenzie termed 'a bit of a problem'. Dalglish later recalled that he responded:

'See that big headline you put in, "The Truth"? Just have another one, as big: "We lied. Sorry" in the same size. Then you might be alright.' When MacKenzie said he couldn't do that, Dalglish replied, 'I can't help you then.' MacKenzie simply didn't realize the offence he had caused to a grieving city.[8]

But the pressure was building. Hillsborough was not the only example of *The Sun*'s 'take no prisoners' approach going wrong during this period: the Elton John and Gibraltar stories had also backfired. Readers' complaints were piling up. So Wapping announced that *The Sun* would be the first paper to create a readers' ombudsman (others would follow suit), and that Kenneth Donlan, a former managing editor, would take on the role. Donlan adjudicated on 'The Truth' front page: he said *The Sun* had a duty to report such stories and was only reporting the same allegations as others had done, but he accepted the headline was wrong, since they were only allegations and not established facts. But there was no apology. When in July that year the Press Council ruled the headline was 'insensitive, provocative and unwarranted', Murdoch finally intervened, releasing a statement accepting that the coverage was 'uncaring and deeply offensive' and that the story was deeply regretted. Murdoch also ordered MacKenzie to make a rare public statement and agree to an interview with BBC Radio 4's *World This Weekend*. While still asserting that *The Sun* had only published claims made by some police officers, a comparatively subdued MacKenzie accepted that he had made a 'rather serious error'.

Murdoch and MacKenzie might have hoped that was the end of the matter but in the years that followed, the 'The Truth' story never quite disappeared. In the subsequent inquiries, inquests and court hearings, it was clear the police were responsible. In 2004, long after MacKenzie's departure and following criticism of Everton footballer Wayne Rooney selling his life story to *The Sun*, the paper responded with a front-page editorial apologizing again for 'the most terrible mistake in its history'. But MacKenzie remained unrepentant, declaring in 2006 that the story was in fact true and that he had only apologized because Murdoch had ordered him to. Unaware he was being recorded, he told a private lunch in Liverpool where he was guest speaker:

> I was not sorry then and I'm not sorry now. All I did wrong there was [to] tell the truth. There was a surge of Liverpool fans who had been drinking and that is what caused the disaster. The only thing different we did was put it under the headline 'The Truth'. I went on the *World at One* the next day [it was actually some time later, in July] and apologised. I only did that because Rupert Murdoch told me to. I wasn't sorry then and I'm not sorry now because we told the truth.[9]

Six years later, after the Hillsborough Independent Panel reported in September 2012 that the fans were innocent and the police had conspired among themselves in a cover-up, MacKenzie offered his 'profuse apologies'. He said: 'It has taken more than two decades, 400,000 documents and a two-year inquiry to discover to my horror that it would have been far more accurate had I written the headline The Lies rather than The Truth. I published in good faith and I am sorry that it was so wrong.' MacKenzie added:

> I too was totally misled. Twenty-three years ago I was handed a piece of copy from a reputable news agency in Sheffield in which a senior police officer and a senior local MP were making serious allegations against fans in the stadium.
>
> I had absolutely no reason to believe that these authority figures would lie and deceive over such a disaster. These allegations were wholly untrue and were part of a concerted plot by police officers to discredit the supporters thereby shifting the blame for the tragedy from themselves.[10]

The following day, there was an emphatic front-page apology from then editor Dominic Mohan:

> *The Sun*'s reporting of the Hillsborough tragedy 23 years ago is without doubt the blackest day in this newspaper's history . . . Today we unreservedly apologise to the Hillsborough victims, their families, Liverpool supporters, the city of

Liverpool and all our readers for that misjudgement . . .
Nothing can excuse *The Sun*'s Page One presentation, under
the headline The Truth. It was inaccurate, grossly insensitive
and offensive. This version of events was NOT the truth.[11]

Three decades after the event, the boycott of *The Sun* on
Merseyside and in other parts of the northwest of England, named
'Total Eclipse of the S*N', remains strong. In 2017 Liverpool FC,
shortly followed by Everton, banned *Sun* journalists from its press
conferences and matches, a ban which at time of writing in 2023
remains. If anything, the boycott has grown, supported by Labour-
controlled local authorities, trade unions and football supporters'
groups. Shops, cafés and other businesses proudly display stickers
saying they are a *Sun*-free zone. The movement has even spread to
Northern Ireland. 'By and large you can't get a copy of *The Sun* in
Skelmersdale,' Ian Murray, a West Lancashire county councillor,
told *Vice* in October 2019. 'I know the Asda sells it, but there's a
fella that goes in and puts a pile of papers on top of them. He buries
them every morning, and at the end of every day they all get sent
back because the people that want to read them can't find them.'[12]

Death on the High Seas

As the rest of Fleet Street absorbed the implications of Wapping,
Maxwell was by now, predictably perhaps, tiring of his new toy,
which was only one part of his growing publishing empire. Maxwell
had embarked on an expansion of his printing and publishing
interests, with the aim of making BPCC one of the biggest global
companies. He was investing in various publishing companies and
television stations, publishing the hagiographies of Eastern Bloc
leaders, using his private companies to boost the public ones and
vice versa, while also using assets to invest in property. He borrowed
at extraordinary levels and managed to disguise the extent of debt
in annual reports, transferring the ultimate ownership of all his
businesses to the Alpine tax haven of Liechtenstein. The constant
round of meetings with world leaders such as U.S. president George
Bush, Margaret Thatcher and France's President Mitterrand continued, as well as his dealings behind the Iron Curtain. He fought
criticism or scrutiny of his interests with legal threats and writs at

the slightest provocation – he did win a libel case again *Private Eye* over suggestions he had been offered a peerage by Labour leader Neil Kinnock. Incensed by *Private Eye*'s constant attacks – as well as 'the Bouncing Czech', the Eye also coined the phrases 'Cap'n Bob' and 'The *Daily Maxwell*' – he commissioned Molloy to design a one-off '*Not Private Eye*' spoof magazine as a rebuttal 'to give them some of their own medicine'.[13]

He would make two more serious interventions in the British newspaper scene. In February 1987, with much fanfare, he launched the *London Daily News*, an ambitious and innovative, 24-hour, four-editions-a-day rival to the *Evening Standard* which had been dominant in the capital since the closure of the *Evening News* in 1980 and which many, Maxwell included, believed had become complacent and stale. He recruited the widely respected former *Sunday Times* and *Observer* journalist Magnus Linklater as editor, along with a roster of experienced journalists. Associated Newspapers, owners of the *Standard*, responded by reviving the *Evening News* title, which they still owned, and selling it for just five pence – a spoiler move to confuse readers. Maxwell's concept of a paper that would compete with both morning national newspapers and the London *Evening Standard* and *News* was massively unrealistic and the *London Daily News* never got close to its target circulation of 200,000. He conceded defeat after just six months; the venture cost about £25 million, plus undisclosed damages he had to pay Associated for accusing it of lying about the circulation of the *Standard*. His second venture was *The European*, a serious colour broadsheet launched in early 1990 in the wake of the downfall of the Eastern European communist bloc to serve the new, much wider pan-European audience. Although it never achieved its target circulation, the paper survived the crumbling of his business empire after his death and was bought by the Barclay brothers, owners of the *Telegraph* newspapers. It continued until 1998, serving a largely business audience.

Stott, who had maintained the *Mirror*'s circulation and status in almost four years of warfare with *The Sun*, endeavouring to maintain its reputation as a serious tabloid with a Labour-supporting readership, was sacked by Maxwell over Christmas 1989. Maxwell changed the editors of his three main titles no fewer than sixteen times in seven years. Stott's crime was attempting to publish pictures of the execution of Nicolae Ceaușescu, just after he was deposed as dictator of Romania during the crumbling of the Warsaw Pact over the Christmas and New Year period. Maxwell, who said the dictator was a personal friend, wanted the front page to carry an appeal for donations to a relief fund for the country. Stott was replaced by Fleet Street veteran and former assistant editor of *The Sun*, Roy Greenslade, then managing editor of the *Sunday Times*. Greenslade sensed a moment for reform – he gained Maxwell's backing to order redundancies, ended the Old Codgers's stewardship of the 'Live Letters' page and dumped the *Jane* comic strip. Greenslade understood the tradition of 'serious tabloid' embodied by the *Mirror* and introduced a new tone, believing the moment right for the *Mirror* to regain ground amid discontent over *The Sun*'s intrusion into private lives and in particular the Hillsborough story. He lasted just a year before being sacked. He later told a parliamentary committee that Maxwell was 'an overt interferer . . . He liked to appear in the newspaper as often as he possibly could and he liked to have an involvement in virtually every story, not just in domestic politics but often in foreign politics.'[14] Maxwell objected to Greenslade giving a television interview in which he forecast that tabloid circulations would decline as a consequence of multi-channel television and they fell out when Greenslade refused to publish a headline suggesting the 1991 Gulf War would end within 24 hours, in order to avert the crash in stock-market prices. Stott was recalled to take charge at the *Mirror* again. But before the year ended, Maxwell, 68, was dead.

The death of Maxwell was as extraordinary as much of his life, involving many of the same elements: a confusion of fact and speculation, few absolute certainties and high drama. As 1991 wore on, Maxwell was under considerable pressure on many fronts: his convoluted business affairs were being investigated by the BBC and the *Financial Times*, while the banks were growing impatient over repayment of loans of almost £2 billion. He was moving money around, attempting to keep everyone happy. No one, except perhaps Maxwell himself, knew that the businesses were a hollow shell, the *Mirror* pension fund in particular plundered to finance other ventures or keep creditors at bay. He was engaged in a massive cover-up of their true state. 'He was staring bankruptcy in the face.'[15] In the early morning of 5 November 1991, hours before the *Financial Times* was about to confront his son, Kevin, with what the paper had found about his business affairs, Maxwell disappeared from his £20 million yacht, the *Lady Ghislaine,* named after his youngest daughter, where it was cruising off Tenerife in the Canary Islands. He had taken to the yacht a few days before and spent the previous day and evening seemingly content – he swam in the sea during the day and dined alone, on a fish dish, in a smart Tenerife restaurant. He had made more or less constant telephone calls to his family and others during the evening and when he returned to the boat showed no sign of distress.[16] His naked body was found at sea twelve hours later.

Despite several post-mortem examinations the precise circumstances of his death were never clarified. Some suggested suicide, aware he was heading for almost certain public disgrace and bankruptcy. Given his combative nature over many years, others preferred a heart attack – he was massively overweight, had a bad cold and suffered from pulmonary oedema – or perhaps, as he often did, he went to urinate off the side of the deck and simply fell off. The fact that his body bore signs indicating he might have hung on to a rail until his weight dragged him away or his heart gave out supported the latter. Suggestions he was murdered by either Mossad or MI6 for their own reasons swirled around; there was never any concrete evidence. His body was taken swiftly to his recently adopted home country of Israel, where he had previously said he wished to be buried. Given something close to a state funeral in Israel's Hall of the Nation, his coffin was surrounded by Israel's great and good, with president Chaim Herzog lavish in his praise: 'He scaled the heights. Kings and barons besieged his doorstep. He was a figure of almost mythological stature. An actor on the world stage, bestriding the globe, as Shakespeare says, like a colossus.'[17]

The precise ways in which Maxwell merited such treatment from the Israeli state always remained unclear. He did have newspaper interests in the country, and there were rumours he had helped secretly fund their nuclear weapons research programme through his companies. There was also a disclosure in a book by American journalist Seymour Hersh, published just a few weeks previously, that in 1986 the *Sunday Mirror* – among other newspapers – had been approached by Mordechai Vanunu with the story of Israel's secret nuclear weapons research. Maxwell, according to Hersh, had given the Israelis information about the story and alleged that Nicholas Davies, the *Mirror* foreign editor, had disclosed the location of Vanunu to Mossad.[18] Vanunu's account eventually appeared in the *Sunday Times*; he was later lured to Italy and kidnapped by the Israelis before being jailed. Maxwell and Davies had begun actions for libel, although Davies dropped out; Maxwell's estate apologized and paid Hersh damages after his death. The truth was never fully established.

The obituaries for Maxwell were predictably mixed. In the *Mirror*, Stott ordered the full works and called him 'the man who saved the *Mirror*'. Amid eleven pages of tributes, Joe Haines, who had by now written a hagiography of his boss, called Maxwell a 'giant with vision' whose death removed 'a colossus from the stage'. At *The Sun*, MacKenzie began a bad-taste advertising campaign with a picture of Maxwell and the slogan 'Don't go overboard to buy the *Mirror*.' Others were more clear-sighted: the *Independent on Sunday* said he was 'a liar, cheat and bully' and *The Times* that he was 'an egoist and monstrously improbable socialist'. In the Westminster office of the *Mirror*, on the night the news broke of his death, Alastair Campbell, later press spokesman for Tony Blair but then political editor of the *Mirror*, who had just written a tribute to Maxwell for the following day's paper, punched Michael White, then political editor of *The Guardian*, for having suggested that Maxwell was something of a crook and for making a tasteless joke about the manner of his death; White fought back and the pair had to be separated by colleagues.[19]

White was right. It took a few weeks before the full truth of Maxwell's mendacity emerged, although shares in Maxwell Communication Corporation began to fall immediately. His sons Kevin and Ian, both in their mid-thirties, who had always lived in the father's considerable shadow, were left to salvage the crumbling empire, Scotland Yard's Fraud Squad were called in and the *Mirror* itself began investigating the intricate finances of their 'colossus'. Within a month it had become clear that, beginning as early as 1985, Maxwell had robbed the *Mirror* pension fund of around £440 million in order to prop up his other businesses; the rest of his empire was an estimated £850 million in debt. 'Millions Missing from the *Mirror*', was the *Mirror* headline on 4 December. Most of the pension fund money was eventually recovered, but some non-*Mirror* pensioners failed to get their pension before death. To his credit, Stott ensured the *Mirror* was at the forefront of reporting Maxwell's disgrace. The whole edifice collapsed and what many people had privately believed for a long time was proven: Maxwell was a liar and a massive crook who had been carrying out one of the biggest frauds in history. Some of those involved with Maxwell now publicly regretted their tolerance: Mike Molloy admitted in the *Independent on Sunday* in 1992 that in trusting Maxwell he made 'the biggest mistake of my career'. Paul Foot said, 'We behaved like wimps.'[20]

Amid the collapse of the Maxwell empire, the *Mirror* was singled out for preservation by the banks: pension fund losses aside, the core finances were broadly in good shape and it had successfully held onto the bulk of its readership in the war with *The Sun*. After the tumult of the Maxwell years and the chaos after his death, *Mirror* executives and staff might have hoped for a relatively quiet time. Into the vacuum in October 1992, as the new chief executive, came another divisive figure: David Montgomery.

The Tap Dancer and the *Mirror*

Loved or hated, the defining characteristics of influential editors and newspaper proprietors have always been a strong personality and an ability to motivate and inspire, whether through intimidation or admiration. Maxwell, whatever his faults, had this, and no one could have accused Northcliffe, Beaverbrook, Bartholomew, Cudlipp or MacKenzie of being colourless or cold. While Murdoch's outward personality was on the austere side, he ruled through sheer force of will and a formidable reputation. Montgomery, in contrast, had the demeanour of a particularly straight-laced accountant. From a strongly Protestant, socially conservative background in Northern Ireland, he had joined the Mirror Group's trainee scheme, where his tutor James Dalrymple afterwards observed that he was 'the only guy I've ever known who can walk into a room and reduce the temperature by 10 degrees'.[21] Like others, he may have believed executive power came via the subbing and production ranks – although his restrained manner was probably simply not suited for a public-facing writing role requiring a more outgoing personality and the ability to extract information from a variety of different people. He rose through the subbing hierarchy, firstly at the *Mirror*, where he became chief sub-editor under Molloy, who shared Dalrymple's unease: 'People always found Monty a bit eerie. It was as if he had come from another planet.'[22] Moving to *The Sun* in 1980, he joined the executive ranks, operating under MacKenzie. Promoted to editor of the *News of the World* in 1985, he masterminded the move to Wapping, telling journalists to ignore their union's instruction not to cooperate. In 1987 Murdoch made him editor of *Today*, which Murdoch had now acquired after Shah was forced to concede defeat in his attempt to create a new, full colour national newspaper. When Murdoch bought the paper – as much to prevent anyone else having it as from a genuine desire to begin a new front in a war being fought by the *Mail* and the *Express* for the middle-market readership – he decided to aim it at a slightly different type of reader and gave the role to Montgomery.

Murdoch and Montgomery aimed at a mainly younger, slightly classless, often female reader, uncomfortable with both *The Sun*'s mix of sex, sleaze and slavish Toryism and the *Mirror*'s aura of traditional Labour politics and social issues, but not attracted to the more suburban, conservative appeal of the *Mail* and *Express*, whose readers tended to be both middle-class and middle-aged. These new readers, Montgomery reasoned, were not overtly political but might be the children of those working-class Conservatives who voted Thatcher into power the previous decade. They would be socially liberal, interested in the world about them and in issues such as environmentalism and health, but aspirational; possibly they worked in the rapidly expanding financial services area and dreamed of a nice flat or semi in the suburbs, rather than the former council houses many of their parents had bought. A few of them might be second- or third-generation from Asian or Afro-Caribbean immigrant descent. It was the kind of broad-brush appeal beloved of marketeers. In one interview, Montgomery described the paper's stance:

> There has to be some alternative to the rather strident Tory tabloids and the tunnel-vision *Daily Mirror*, which grinds on supporting the Labour Party; and you wonder whether the people who work there and the proprietor could cope with the Labour Party actually being in power. There has to be another way. We're trying to have opinions which are challenging to the Tory party as well as impatient with Labour policies.[23]

The more contemporary feel of *Today*, a close copy of the American broadsheet *USA Today*, with its clean, calm, design, colour, pictures and a rather bland overall approach, with none of the urgency and sometimes hysteria of the more traditional tabloids, was pitched at them. Or at least it would aim to confuse the buyer in the newsagent. Although *Today* never quite achieved its aim, it may well have succeeded in trimming the *Mirror*'s sails to protect *The Sun*, and that suited Murdoch for a while.

But after four years in the *Today* editor's seat, the paper was still making losses. Montgomery, who had harboured aspirations to be a proprietor himself, fell out with Murdoch over a plan for a management buyout. When the *Mirror*'s bank-appointed board came looking for someone to steady the ship post-Maxwell, they chose Montgomery. This was despite his obvious unsuitability. Assumed to be a natural Conservative, he had been integral to Murdoch's love affair with Thatcherism; he was known for his quietly spoken, buttoned-up manner and therefore hardly the man to re-energize the *Mirror*, with its still often colourful and experienced staff and illustrious heritage. His politics, historically so important to the *Mirror*, remained opaque. Sir Nicholas Lloyd, then editor of the *Daily Express* – who had made Montgomery his protégé at the Mirror Group's *People* and on the *News of the World* – said: 'I would have thought he was a left-wing Tory. When we were on the People he was probably still a Labour voter. Now I would have thought he was a Tory and a capitalist, but not a very right-wing one.' And a colleague on *Today* added: 'His politics are quixotic. He'd support anything he thought popular and in the readers' interests. He'd look at it issue by issue. He's totally pragmatic about newspapers and wouldn't turn the *Mirror* against Labour, because that would be commercial nonsense.'[24]

Despite assurances to staff, Montgomery embarked on immediate cost-cutting, reducing staff and replacing the much-respected Stott with David Banks, another long-standing tabloid veteran. He banned all alcohol from the building. Roy Greenslade, briefly *Mirror* editor, in his obituary of Stott in 2007, put his finger on Montgomery's style: 'Though Montgomery assured Stott that his job was safe, he fired him soon afterwards; when Stott challenged him about the lie, Montgomery is said to have replied that his statement was "accurate at that time".'[25] Montgomery became known for such evasions – he would describe it as 'tap-dancing'. Expediency was all. Banks was a former *Mirror* sub-editor who had spent many years in senior roles at *The Sun* under MacKenzie. Although he claimed to be on the left, he was seen as far less committed to the *Mirror*'s traditional political position than his immediate predecessors. Haines resigned and wrote that it was the end of the *Mirror* as a political force: 'Almost overnight, the *Daily Mirror*, which Hugh Cudlipp built as a political institution in Britain, has been destroyed. The paper that survived, however narrowly, the depredations of Captain Maxwell, has fallen to the artillery of the banks, led by Corporal Montgomery.'[26]

Alastair Campbell and Paul Foot would also leave. Ironically, shortly after his departure from the *Mirror*, Stott was hired by Murdoch as Montgomery's replacement to edit *Today*, recruiting Campbell and another ex-*Mirror* columnist Anne Robinson (later a well-known television presenter), among others. Stott was named Editor of the Year at the 1993 What the Papers Say Awards for his careful reinvention of *Today* as a sober, middle-market paper, but it was eventually closed by Murdoch in 1995; it had never made a profit or carved out its own distinctive voice and audience in a market now dominated by the *Daily Mail*.

Another key Murdoch figure now became part of the *Mirror* management. Two years previously, Maxwell had employed the distinctive figure of Charlie Wilson, an ex-editor of *The Times* who had masterminded that paper's move to Wapping and the former husband of Robinson, as editorial director. Wilson, an unlikely but successful editor of *The Times*, was a former boxer from the East End of Glasgow. He had been shrewd enough to maintain a lowish profile and not be associated with the Maxwell debacle. Small, wiry and naturally aggressive, both respected and feared by those he worked with, he was now promoted by Montgomery to be his number two, as managing director of the group. They made a contrasting pairing: the icy-mannered, tap-dancing, always besuited Montgomery in the boardroom and the close-cropped, sweary, shirt-sleeved Wilson stalking the newsroom, reducing hardened tabloid hacks to tears and inspiring others. The fate of the left-of-centre *Mirror*, the proud creation of Swaffer and Bartholomew, of Cudlipp and King, left almost destitute by Maxwell, had now passed into the hands of two former senior Murdoch executives.

9

THE DARK AGES

I
n 1988, Lord Cudlipp used an address at the funeral of former colleague Sydney Jacobson, once deputy chairman of IPC, to reflect ruefully on the long-term implications of his sale of *The Sun* to Rupert Murdoch almost two decades previously: 'It was', he said,

> the dawn of the Dark Ages of tabloid journalism, when the proprietors and editors – not all but most – decided that playing a continuing role in public enlightenment was no longer the business of the popular press. Information about foreign affairs was relegated to a three-inch yapping editorial insulting foreigners. It was the age when investigative journalism in the public interest shed its integrity and became intrusive journalism for the prurient, when nothing, however personal, was any longer secret or sacred and the basic human right to privacy was banished in the interest of publishing profit.[1]

And that was long before 'The Truth' headline.

The 1980s and '90s were not just the years of major structural and geographical changes in newspapers, but also marked the peak of intense competition between the tabloids, one not seen since the New York yellow journalism wars or the giveaway battles of the 1930s. The fight was between the MacKenzie *Sun* and the Molloy/ Maxwell *Mirror*, who in turn had to combat the even more down-market *Daily Star* and *Daily Sport*. The battle was replicated on Sundays between the *News of the World*, the *Sunday Mirror* and the *Sunday Sport*. At the more sober end of the market, the *Daily Mail* was dominating its rival, the *Daily Express*, but also served as a potential draw to disaffected red-top readers.

This intense competition resulted in intrusions of privacy of both public and private individuals, an erosion of standards when it came to sex and sleaze stories and a widespread obsession with the breasts of young women. It was the era of 'bonk journalism', when money was happily shelled out by *The Sun* and the *News of the World* – edited from 1987 by Wendy 'Gotcha' Henry – to anyone who claimed to have had sex with a celebrity:

> An endless stream of bimbos, street prostitutes, call girls, masseuses, rent-boys, spurned lovers, axe-grinders, black-mailers and even hairdressers poured into the offices of professional kiss and tell merchants. The stories were priced on the rough and ready scale determined by the quantity and quality of the bonks . . . the resulting stories were invariably explicit, detailed and devastating for those involved.[2]

And only a portion of them would involve Max Clifford.

Some of Henry's *News of the World* 'bonk' stories were so over the top that even Murdoch took exception to them, reportedly telling her, 'Sales aren't everything.' In 1988 she was poached by Maxwell and given the editorship of the *Sunday People* – a decision he later regretted. For many years, the *Sunday People*, while enjoying its fair share of stories of the suburban wife-swapping/celebrity misdeeds variety, had languished in the shadow of the *News of the World* and the *Sunday Mirror*. And while Maxwell would turn out to be a massive fraudster, he craved public respectability. So Henry's diet of picture-led sex, showbiz and sensationalism – pictures of plane-crash victims, Hollywood star Sammy Davis Jr's cancer treatment scars and seven-year-old Prince William urinating in public – led to her being sacked after less than two years. She moved to the USA and became editor of *The Globe*, part of another wave of British tabloid journalists taking their tactics across the pond.

In the wake of the Hillsborough, Elton John and Russell Harty controversies, there were growing calls from the public, politicians and other sections of the media to restrain tabloid excesses. *The Sun* was regularly topping the list of complaints to the Press Council, whose director, Ken Morgan, told tabloid editors their tactics would only prompt restrictive legislation, despite it having rejected a written code of conduct in 1977. The council was seen as ineffective and reluctant to take on the might of the tabloids. In the House of Commons, MPs from all sides called for tighter regulation. Mark Fisher, Labour MP for Stoke-on-Trent, was damning: 'There is a cancer gnawing at the heart of the British press,' he said.

> At the lower end of the tabloid market, journalism has been replaced by voyeurism. The reporters' profession has been infiltrated by a seedy stream of rent boys, pimps, bimbos, spurned lovers, smear artists bearing grudges, prostitutes and perjurers. That is the force that makes constituents say to members of Parliament: 'Get on and do something about it.'[3]

More than three hundred MPs backed a plan for a private members' Right to Privacy Bill. But the attempt was deflected when Home Office minister Timothy Renton announced an inquiry by David Calcutt QC, master of Magdalen College, Oxford, into press standards.

By the early 1990s Fleet Street had changed forever. Murdoch's move to Wapping, aided by Thatcherite legislation that curbed the powers of the print, was a landmark moment. The rest of Fleet Street – unable to adapt to new technologies with its cramped sites and restrictive union practices – watched the violent picketing with concern, followed by envy when union resistance collapsed. Within a few years most major newspaper groups had moved to new sites within easy distance of the centres of power, with printing contracted to out-of-town sites, and had adopted new technologies allowing electronic transmission of pages between journalists and print works. In 1987 the Telegraph Group moved to Westferry on the Isle of Dogs, an area being renovated with government money. Here it shared printing facilities with the *Daily Express* group, which the following year exited the famed 'Black Lubyanka' in the centre of Fleet Street, once home to Beaverbrook and Christiansen, in favour of a new building at Blackfriars bridge. The following year, the *Daily Mail* moved to Kensington High Street, to a glamorous new Northcliffe House. Journalists moaned at the separation from their pubs, the loss of the atmosphere and camaraderie of shared spaces and streets.

The Mirror Group, in its purpose-built headquarters in High Holborn where it had been since 1961, was always a geographical outlier and had some of the most restrictive agreements with the unions. The new regime, under Montgomery and Wilson, both veterans of Wapping, was determined to change that and in 1994 moved the *Mirror* to the One Canada Square office tower in the middle of the glossy new Canary Wharf development, where the *Telegraph* newspapers were already ensconced. This, together with a major redundancy programme, brought the *Mirror* into profit. Montgomery, ambitious to become a serious player, began to expand the empire, taking a one-third stake (alongside Irish businessman Tony O'Reilly) in the now financially struggling *Independent*, which, with its sister Sunday title, moved into two floors in the same building, with an agreement to share back-office services. Much of the new Fleet Street became a vertical street, in a tower block.

'Drinking at the Last Chance Saloon'

David Calcutt's 1990 report qualified its criticisms, saying that freedom of expression could trump protection of privacy, but noting that some tabloid editors had been 'let off the leash' in a competitive environment. It recommended replacing the Press Council with a new Press Complaints Commission governed by an editors' code of practice, which was established the following year. The PCC's remit was to adjudicate on complaints alleging breaches of the code to be drawn up by a committee of editors and, on Calcutt's recommendation, it was to be given eighteen months 'to demonstrate that non-statutory self-regulation could be made to work effectively'. If that did not happen, a statutory tribunal would be established.[4] The next year, David Mellor, then chief secretary to the Treasury but who had briefly succeeded Renton as arts and culture minister, would, in a phrase which would resonate for some time, use a television interview to warn the tabloids they were 'drinking at the last chance saloon' and called for more restrictions on the press.[5]

The Sun and others took scant notice. The PCC, under its chair, Lord McGregor, had only limited success, despite compelling the *News of the World* to devote a full page to the commission's 36-point ruling against a story about Labour MP Clare Short's former boyfriend. Two subsequent stories orchestrated by Max Clifford showed there was little intention to restrain themselves. In 1992 Mellor's extramarital affair with actress Antonia de Sancha was revealed in the *Sunday People*, now edited by showbusiness writer Bill Hagerty, and Mellor was forced to resign. De Sancha engaged Clifford to sell her side of the story to *The Sun*, which gleefully reported that the minister liked making love in his Chelsea FC shirt and had penchants for spanking and toe sucking. De Sancha later admitted this had been made up.[6] Did the *People* deliberately target 'last chance' Mellor? Probably not, but it was never going to be a story they were shy of running.

At the *Daily Mirror*, still with its Andy Capp cartoon and mix of traditional Labour values with a dollop of celebrity and showbiz, Montgomery charged new editor David Banks with pursuing, like *Today*, a new, younger, classless reader. So in late 1993, when Clifford brokered a deal for the *Mirror* to pay £100,000 for secretly taken pictures of the Princess of Wales exercising in a London health club, there was no thought this might be an infringement of her privacy or breach of the new PCC rules. The *Mirror* faced criticism from all directions and some advertisers withdrew. Its justification that it was exposing a security risk fell flat; it was censured by the PCC and paid £250,000 compensation to the health club owner, who was sued by the princess. Despite the momentary boost, sales continued to ebb away, dropping to just under 2.5 million; *The Sun*, meanwhile, was back up to 4 million.

Earlier in 1993, Calcutt reported that the PCC had not turned out to be

> an effective regulator of the press . . . It has not been set up in
> a way, and is not operating a code of practice, which enables
> it to command not only press but also public confidence . . .
> it is, in essence, a body set up by the industry, financed by the
> industry, dominated by the industry, and operating a code of
> practice devised by the industry and which is over-favourable
> to the industry.[7]

Later the same year, a report by MPs on the Heritage Committee on the issue of privacy and media intrusion rejected the idea of statutory controls in favour of more 'self restraint' by the media.[8] There was no political will for reform, so the 1990s, perhaps even more than the 1980s, became an era of unrestrained tabloid excess. While the plotlines of the nation's favourite television soap operas – The drama! The arguments! The sex! – attracted parasitical tabloid coverage, there were three real-life soap operas also being enacted for their benefit: the removal of Thatcher, and the sleaze and divisions that followed among the Tory government, mirrored by the rise of New Labour; the arrival of the Premier League, transforming football into spectacle and creating a cohort of young players enjoying rich lifestyles beyond their wildest dreams; and the break-up of the marriage of the Prince and Princess of Wales, a fairytale that ended in grim tragedy. All were set against a growing celebrity culture wherein anyone could be famous for fifteen minutes, fuelled by easy-access cable and satellite news channels that followed the same agenda. At the same time, throughout this era and beyond into the 2000s, some of the so-called serious broadsheet newspapers would often be compelled to follow up tabloid stories because of overwhelming public interest or where it was expedient to do so. While *The Guardian* and *The Independent* would mostly look the other way, *The Telegraph* titles and Murdoch's *Times* and *Sunday Times* newspapers by now had began to regularly reflect the same right-wing agenda as *The Sun*, *Mail* and *Express* while not being averse to the occasional but carefully reported sex or sleaze story involving public figures. Such stories from *The Sun* and the *News of the World* would also often be reported enthusiastically by Sky News, in which Murdoch had a major stake, influencing other television news programmes and in turn creating more pressures on the serious media to follow their news priorities. Such circularity and cross promotion and the impotence of official regularity mechanisms began to cause widespread public concern. This was Planet Tabloid in action.

After the demise of Margaret Thatcher in 1991, the Conservative government had enough problems to handle without alienating its friends in the popular media, so it shied away from any kind of legal restraint. This was in blatant self-interest, reflecting the symbiotic relationship that existed once newspapers had gone from being fringe agitators to big business. When Thatcher's successor, John Major, sought to solidify his mandate the following year, the Tory-supporting end of Fleet Street stayed onside. While Major did not attract the same affection as Thatcher, *The Sun* nevertheless relentlessly attacked Labour leader Neil Kinnock, dubbed the 'Welsh windbag'. MacKenzie's front page on election day in April 1992 carried the headline, 'If Kinnock Wins Today Will the Last Person to Leave Britain Please Turn Out the Lights', with Kinnock's head superimposed onto a lightbulb. This was followed the next day by the brutally triumphant 'It's *The Sun* Wot Won It'. As with other MacKenzie specials, it was a front page that would resonate for its sheer naked audacity and self-promotion. In this kind of relationship, the Tories were never going to offend their friends. Ironically, however, it marked the beginning of the end of *The Sun*'s love affair with Conservatives, at least for a few years. Major's majority was slim and cracks began to show. The government's economic strategy was shattered by the withdrawal from the Exchange Rate Mechanism in September 1992, while a series of sex and sleaze scandals involving Tory ministers and MPs undermined their authority. All were happily reported by the tabloids. A weak government with a narrow majority might lead to an early election, meaning the Tories would not want to jeopardize their Fleet Street support. Result: business as usual.

The Rise of Dacre

While the red-tops revelled in the travails of the Tories, the government could always be sure of support from one loyal sector. Throughout the tabloid wars of the previous two decades, the *Daily Mail* pursued its own solid, unflashy middle way under the steady hand of David English, unwavering in its support for Thatcher and then Major. It remained a very different beast to either the red-tops on one side or the broadsheets on the other. Confident of itself and sure of its audience in middle England, it had no need for gimmicks or dubious stories. The only dividing line was that English did not share the wariness towards Europe articulated by Thatcher and growing among Conservatives. English's successor, Paul Dacre, had a different vision which would have a significant impact on public debate up to and after the 2016 referendum.

Brought up in suburban north London, the son of a reporter on the deeply conservative *Sunday Express*, Dacre joined the *Daily Express* as a graduate trainee in 1970. After a stint in New York, he returned to the *Mail* newsdesk in London, under English's watchful eye. Through hard work and long hours, he became news editor. In the competitive, macho environment of the newsroom, where reporters worked casual shifts and survival of the fittest was the rule – two reporters were sometimes assigned to the same story to see who fared best – Dacre, hitherto relatively low profile, had transformed into a hard-nosed newsroom driver, a middle-market Kelvin MacKenzie: 'The polite and mild mannered boy from the suburbs began to morph into an expletive-spouting monster; his favourite word became "cunt".'[9] Dacre became editor of the *Evening Standard* in early 1991, where, by virtue of being 'vigorous and brutally hard working', he was deemed a success.[10] Within eighteen months he had increased circulation by 26 per cent. He was so good, Murdoch offered him *The Times*.

One of Fleet Street's periodic games of musical chairs was now set in motion: Simon Jenkins, then editor of *The Times*, wanted to return to writing; MacKenzie suggested Dacre, who out of courtesy, and ambition, told English. English, uneasy at a major talent leaving and taking readers to a more middle-market *Times*, offered to step aside to allow Dacre his job. He had always assumed Dacre, whose career he had nurtured, would eventually succeed him. 'He'll be five years at the *Standard* and that's just in time for me to go at the next election,' he said.[11] Stewart Steven, whose relationship with English had cooled in proportion to the rise in circulation of the *Mail on Sunday*, moved to edit the *Evening Standard* replaced by English's long-serving deputy, Jonathan Holborow. English became editor-in-chief and chair of Associated Newspapers. When the music stopped, Dacre was *Mail* editor, a seat he would occupy for the next 26 years, during which time his influence on the whole newspaper world – tabloid and broadsheet – and on the broader political and even cultural landscape would be profound.

Dacre didn't change the *Mail* overnight – it was a big beast and the culture and practices that English had introduced were embedded in the soul of the paper. But while English was a traditional Conservative, Dacre, like Murdoch a Labour supporter at university, was a convert to Thatcherism but had become disenchanted with Major's government. 'You could smell the decadence and weakness . . . John Major was a weak chap,' he declared.[12] He was determined to end the 'slavish mindless appeasement of everything Conservative' that the newspaper had espoused, although over the years the paper would remain steadfastly Conservative, even when being courted by Tony Blair.[13] The following year, some felt Dacre showed poor judgement in backing right-wing Eurosceptic rebels in a vote of no confidence against Major, which he survived. Dacre was also seen internally as wary of any residual influence of English, while some outsiders felt the latter was still pulling the strings. Again, ironically, given *Mail* attitudes in the latter half of his reign, Dacre was clear at the outset that he sought a more diverse, younger readership, with a strong Asian and Black element from the aspiring middle classes to counter a paper often seen as 'boring, slightly racist'.[14] He would demonstrate that with a story a few years later with which he would become indelibly associated. Dacre, working eighteen-hour days and making intense demands on his staff, grew steadily in confidence. He brightened the news pages with a livelier approach, more celebrity coverage and more up-to-date cultural references; he instituted a circulation-boosting Saturday supplement, *Weekend*, which carried television listings, and more newsy, bigger and sharper internal features sections, such as 'Femail', 'Health' and 'Money *Mail*', which became central to the paper's appeal. Readers loved it: the paper was voted Newspaper of the Year at the British Press Awards in 1995 and 1996, with circulation topping 2 million that year, boosted by the closure in November of Murdoch's *Today* newspaper, which the *Mail* saw off with, in Dacre's words, 'a war machine' approach in which it recalibrated itself 'slightly downmarket' for several weeks to 'cream off' their readers.[15] It was a dominance of the middle market that would continue under Dacre's stewardship for more than two decades. The *Mail* won Newspaper of the Year again in 1998 and 2001. And as one demanding, workaholic, sweary editor grew in power and influence, another decided it was time to quit the stage.

New Regimes

In January 1994, after thirteen years in charge, Kelvin MacKenzie finally left *The Sun*. What prompted this always remained unclear, but he may simply have felt it was time and Murdoch had offered him a new challenge. In doing so, perhaps Murdoch sensed a change in the political weather – the strident Thatcher years, suitable to MacKenzie's style, had passed; the less combative figure of Major ran a crumbling Tory administration, while the Labour Party was gaining ground under the leadership of the centrist John Smith and looked almost certain to win the next general election. Perhaps it was time for a less aggressive figure at *The Sun*. MacKenzie also remained tainted by the Hillsborough headline and it might not have been considered politic to have him in view if either party aimed for more press regulation. He was given a highly paid role at Murdoch's new venture, the growing BSkyB television empire, and his deputy, Stuart Higgins, moved into his chair. While *The Sun* would continue in its rumbustious way under successive editors, it would never again display the mixture of wit, chutzpah and sheer recklessness it did under MacKenzie.

Moving into the editor's chair at the *News of the World* in 1994, with its weekly readership of more than 4.7 million, came the slightly unlikely figure of Piers Morgan, last heard of as the publicity-seeking showbusiness reporter for *The Sun* who eagerly exposed the sex preferences of the stars. The former editor of the paper's 'Bizarre' column had been appointed by Murdoch on MacKenzie's advice: 'I owe it all to Kelvin,' he said. At 29, he was the youngest editor of a national newspaper for more than fifty years, since the 25-year-old Hugh Cudlipp had become editor of the *Sunday Pictorial*. Morgan spent a year steering the paper through a series of fairly routine royal exclusives such as the Princess of Wales making amorous telephone calls to an aide, along with political sex scandals, some aided by the intervention of Max Clifford. Morgan upgraded the paper's pop and showbusiness content; there were more celebrities, fewer suburban sex scandals. In 1995 he overreached himself by publishing unauthorized photographs of the then wife of Charles, Earl Spencer, the brother of the Princess of Wales, leaving a private addiction clinic. The result was a PCC censure. Murdoch publicly criticized Morgan – 'the boy went too far' – but, in true Murdoch style, is said to have apologized to him in private for the rebuke.

Back at Canary Wharf, David Banks had been moved upstairs after the Diana gym fiasco; his successor, Colin Myler, lasted a few months. Montgomery, whose empire was slowly growing, approached Morgan, who, less than two years into the *News of the World* job, gladly accepted. Montgomery soon also recruited MacKenzie – frustrated by what turned out to be a non-job at BSkyB – to run a new television station. With Montgomery, Wilson and now Morgan and MacKenzie, the Mirror offices in One Canada Square in Canary Wharf started to feel like an extension of the Murdoch empire – and would soon take on some of its values. Watched benignly by MacKenzie, Morgan began turning the paper into a *Sun* lookalike: headlines were bigger and louder and stories sexier and sleazier, while the celebrity picture count soared. And the word 'Daily' was dropped from the title, on the grounds that '*The Mirror*' was an easy way of expressing similarity with and rivalry to *The Sun*. Molloy, now retired, was not impressed: 'The mantra of Kelvin MacKenzie's *Sun* has become the *Mirror*'s creed. Respect for the truth is regarded simply as the posturing of pompous prats . . . each day reality yields to the triumphs and excesses of a sub-world inhabited by Stringfellow celebrities.' (Stringfellows was the name of a popular Soho lap-dancing club.) The paper was 'mired in sexual trivia', full of soundbites rather than proper stories, and the design was terrible, concluded Molloy.[16] But MacKenzie and Morgan probably didn't care any more; they were happily at war with their previous employer and in a war, all was fair game.

Football's Coming Home

Sport, and football in particular, had long been a tabloid fixture. During the late 1960s and early '70s, stories about the hedonistic lifestyle and glamorous girlfriends of George Best, the Manchester United and Northern Ireland star, had regularly entertained tabloid readers (as they would continue to do right up until his death from alcoholism in 2005). In the late 1980s football was in decline. Attendances were low; the game had been sullied by hooliganism and events like the Bradford Fire of 1985 and the Hillsborough tragedy of 1989. And then along came Paul Gascoigne, a talented young footballer signed to Newcastle United as a schoolboy, who came from a dysfunctional and poverty-stricken background and was described as the 'best footballer in the world' by legendary former Newcastle player Jackie Milburn, speaking on the BBC in 1988, and 'George Best without the brains' by Newcastle chairman Stan Seymour.[17] He was frequently overweight, enjoyed beer and junk food, had suffered from depression as a child and developed an addiction to gambling machines.[18] The exploits of the country's most expensive footballer when he joined Tottenham Hotspur for £2 million in 1989 provided a crucial career boost for an ambitious young feature writer called Rebekah Wade.

Gascoigne became a star of both front and back pages, displaying a reckless naivety in dealing with the media, once calling up the *News of the World* to give his reaction to a story. 'The idea of a footballer ringing up a newspapers to give their side of the story was unheard of. He was like a schoolboy,' said Greg Miskiw, the *News of the World* reporter who later became notorious for his role in the hacking scandal.[19] Gascoigne was part of the England team at the 1990 World Cup in Italy, which exceeded expectations and kick-started the revival of the national game; his tears when the referee booked him during the semi-final, which would have ruled him out of the final had England made it (they lost on penalties to West Germany), endeared him to the nation. Millions who had never previously heard of him were now addicted to the Gazza soap opera; it was tabloid box office. And it was manna from heaven when the somewhat rough-hewn Gascoigne began an often turbulent relationship with Sheryl Failes, a single mother of two, four years his elder, who, while undoubtedly fond of him, clearly also enjoyed the limelight. Somewhat unwisely, they agreed to be interviewed by the *News of the World*'s soft-focus Sunday magazine, with Wade assigned to interview them. This would be the making of Wade's career. A close relationship developed between her and the couple and at every twist and turn of their relationship, as Gascoigne's multiple injuries and personal problems – drinking, bulimia – mounted, Wade was there to record them. She prospered while they were set on a different, more desperate trajectory.

Grammar-school educated, from northwest England, Wade had studied at the Sorbonne and worked as a secretary for Eddy Shah's *Messenger* group at Warrington but was focused on becoming a journalist. She joined the *News of the World*'s Sunday magazine as a secretary in 1989, but by the early 1990s had become a feature writer. Journalist Tim Minogue, then a colleague, recalled later that she was 'very bright, very intelligent, quite good fun. But instead of taking memos, she was always bombarding the features editor with ideas for stories. I've never met anyone so burningly ambitious.'[20] Everyone who encountered Wade testified to her ability to charm those potentially helpful to her career. The flattering Sunday magazine cover story celebrating Gascoigne and Failes's relationship in March 1993 – 'They're a perfect love match' was the headline – was the beginning of a long relationship between Failes and Wade, who sensed tabloid gold. Exclusive followed exclusive and when another tabloid published something critical, Wade would be there to offer consolation and the soft-focus angle. Greg Miskiw said 'Rebekah and Sheryl would go onto talk a lot, have lunch etc. She realized you had this nutter of a footballer who's in love with a woman like Sheryl. They didn't realise how dangerous it was.'[21]

At its advent in 1992, the Premier League changed the landscape of football forever. Murdoch had recognized the unlimited potential of pay-to-view sport on television, a medium league football had largely avoided in order to protect ground attendances. Within a decade, funded by growing television rights payments led by Sky television channel, which was largely owned by Murdoch, the league had become the biggest and highest-valued football competition in the world, ultimately outshining what had been the glamorous leagues of France, Spain and Italy. Its young footballers and some of its managers would become wealthy celebrities, meaning more rich fodder for the tabloids to feast on. In June 1996, when the European Football Championships were held in the UK, England had another successful run and came up against old rivals Germany in the semi-final at Wembley, where thirty years previously they had faced each other in the World Cup Final. To the tabloids, and Morgan in particular, this match and the resonances from it were irresistible and tropes that had not surfaced in an era when memories of the war were still fresh now came to the fore. 'Achtung! Surrender: For You Fritz, Ze Euro 96 Championship Is Over' was the huge *Sun*-like headline on the front page, accompanied by a mocked-up picture of two players – one, inevitably, Gascoigne – wearing wartime tin helmets. Inside, the headline was 'The *Mirror* Declares Football War on Germany.' Morgan also sent a 'tank' – actually an armoured car – to the German team's hotel, although it was stopped by police on the way. Ironically, *The Sun* took a slightly more restrained approach. England, of course, lost on penalties.

Tabloid culture was now no longer confined to the red-tops. The late 1990s would see the spreading of their values and obsessions into the middle-market titles, including Dacre's *Daily Mail*. These values infected broadsheet newspapers and television in their turn, both in the UK and elsewhere. One of the harbingers of this was LIVE TV! Still regarding himself as a media tycoon and long envious of Murdoch's by now growing and profitable Sky empire, Montgomery launched this cable television station in June 1995.

LIVE TV! took advantage of the new cable services being wired into people's homes alongside satellite Sky services and would be run jointly by two stalwarts of popular media, Janet Street-Porter and Kelvin MacKenzie. Street-Porter, a former magazine and television journalist, was said to understand 'yoof' audiences and she would be supervised by MacKenzie, his sure grip on populism coupled with his drive and supposed understanding of what the ordinary viewer might want. With a staff of mostly young television hopefuls shepherded by just a few experienced hands, it launched with heavily youth-orientated programming, chirpy young newsreaders sitting on desks in garishly painted offices and features about fashion, music, lifestyle and popular culture. It was a bold experiment doomed to failure, mainly because it lacked the investment and sufficient creative minds needed to run a television station – a problem Murdoch never had.

Street-Porter, who had never stayed anywhere long, left after four months, complaining that the project had been underfunded from the start. She was also unhappy when MacKenzie signed a deal to screen Rugby League matches. MacKenzie took over, ditched the soft-focus celebrity, lifestyle and rolling news content drawn up by Street-Porter, and brought the tabloid ethos into television: naked and partially naked girls with a hefty side order of novelty and gimmicks. He introduced elements of *Sun*-style titillation, with topless models playing darts and a financial reporter who stripped off during bulletins; for a while, strippers performed in the Canary Wharf offices for late-night viewers. There was also the 'News Bunny' – a man dressed in a rabbit costume who appeared behind the newsreader – a blonde model who read the weather forecast in a bikini and a dwarf who bounced on a trampoline. Despite the publicity this engendered, it was widely derided as being tawdry and sleazy, but for many it was seen as the beginning of what became known as tabloid television (MacKenzie would describe it as 'Carry On' television). Viewing figures never took off and plans for a nationwide series of local stations faltered. To the surprise of many, it managed to struggle on until November 1999, when the plug was finally pulled. But LIVE TV! nevertheless heralded a new era of television, dominated by reality and celebrity-centred programmes, which would intersect with the rise of the online world and eventually the phenomenon of social media.

'Murderers'

Morgan's Euro 96 front pages contradicted an old Fleet Street maxim: 'Never start a campaign that you cannot be certain of winning.' A more experienced editor might have paused before embarking on something where the possibility of success was only 50–50. Such editors confined themselves to generalized campaigns without obvious fixed endpoints: 'better pay for the nurses', 'end these silly EU rules' and so on. Under Dacre, the *Daily Mail* became a strong campaigning newspaper. It would run a series of stories about, say, a particular government policy Dacre took objection to, strongly articulating the arguments against it. If change came, the resulting headline would claim it was due to the *Mail*'s pressure: 'Finally, the Government acts to . . .' or 'At last the rules are changed . . .' It reinforced the *Mail*'s sense of self-confidence and assured the reader that their paper was unafraid to fight for a cause – and, crucially, on the right side.

There was one campaign the *Mail* embarked on which was wholly different and, initially, had no obvious conclusion. The basic facts of the Stephen Lawrence case are now so well known in the UK that they hardly need repeating: in April 1993 the eighteen-year-old black aspiring architect was brutally stabbed to death at a bus stop in southeast London by a group of local racist white thugs. The murder was followed by a bungled police investigation that was tainted by allegations of links to the criminal underworld. The police case against some of those involved and a private prosecution by Stephen's parents, Doreen and Neville Lawrence, faltered through lack of evidence. In February 1997 an inquest jury returned a verdict of unlawful killing by five young men.

There it might have come to a legal dead end but for a serendipitous twist: Dacre had met both the young Stephen and his father when the latter had done some decorating work on Dacre's north London home years previously. Dacre had not made the connection until a furious Neville Lawrence had telephoned him directly to complain about a poorly worded *Mail* story that had wrongly linked a minor riot in the area with the murder investigation; Dacre realized that, contrary to some reflexive opinions about young Black men in south London, Stephen had not been involved in any gang and came from a respectable, hard-working family, the kind with

Jonathan Cainer: How you can find your Valentine

SEE PAGES 50-52

MURDERERS

The Mail accuses these men of killing. If we are wrong, let them sue us

Gary Dobson   Neil Acourt   Jamie Acourt   Luke Knight   David Norris

THE Daily Mail today takes the unprecedented step of naming five young men as murderers.

They may not have been convicted in a court of law, but police are sure that David Norris, Neil Acourt, Jamie Acourt, Gary Dobson and Luke Knight are the white youths who killed black teenager Stephen Lawrence.

We are naming them because, despite

COMMENT: Page 8

a criminal case, a private prosecution and an inquest, there has still been no justice for Stephen, who was stabbed to death in a racist attack almost four years ago.

One or more of the five may have a valid defence to the charge which has been repeatedly levelled against them. So far they have steadfastly refused every opportunity to offer such a defence.

Four have refused to give any alibi for

that night in April 1993. One initially offered an alibi, but it did not stand up when police checked it out.

This week the five refused to answer any questions at the inquest on Stephen, citing their legal right of privilege not to say anything which might incriminate them.

The Lawrence case threatens to damage race relations and the reputation of British justice.

If these men are innocent they now have every opportunity to clear their names in a legal action against the Daily Mail. They would have to give evidence

and a jury in possession of all the facts would finally be able to decide.

Yesterday the jury at Southwark Coroner's Court had little doubt of one thing. It took only 30 minutes to decide unanimously that the 16-year-old A-level student was unlawfully killed, the victim of 'a completely unprovoked racist attack by five white youths'.

The criminal cases against Norris, 20, Neil Acourt, 21, Jamie Acourt, 19, Dobson, 21, and Knight, 20, failed because of a lack of evidence. But if they thought they had got away with the killing they

Turn to Page 6, Col. 2

INSIDE: Andrew Alexander 12, Femail 19, Diary 39, Friday First 42-48, Letters 53, TV 54-56, Coffee Break 67-69, City 70-72, Sport 73-80

'MURDERERS', *Daily Mail*, 14 February 1997.

which *Daily Mail* readers might identify. Dacre subsequently took a strong interest in the case, although the *Mail*'s reporting had been constrained by libel and contempt laws, which covered any references to the guilt of those accused. In the wake of the inquest verdict, Dacre no longer felt any restraint: the next day, 14 February 1997, the front page of the *Mail* was dominated by photographs of the five men suspected of the crime above the headline 'MURDERERS' with the strapline underneath: 'The *Mail* accuses these men of killing. If we are wrong, let them sue us'. It was an unprecedented and direct challenge to the men to sue for libel, since contempt of court applied only when prosecutions were active, as he was reassured by the Attorney General. The reaction from the rest of the media and the public was widespread astonishment: while some applauded the *Mail*'s bravery, others accused Dacre of ignoring the law and saw a cynical way of establishing a defence against any later accusations of racial bias. One former Master of the Rolls, Lord Donaldson, accused Dacre of contempt of court, but his predecessor, Lord Denning, congratulated him.

Dacre had calculated, correctly, that the men would not wish to appear in court to be challenged by the *Mail*'s lawyers on their innocence. Even so, he was, he later confessed, far from confident: 'I was desperately aware of the enormousness of what was being proposed. It's not up to newspapers to accuse people of murder or act as judge and jury,' he said in a video statement on the *MailOnline* website, adding that after signing off the front page, he went home and took a sleeping pill, only to wake up in the middle of the night 'drenched in sweat and convinced my career was over'. And he made another crucial point: 'It was proof the *Daily Mail* had changed. It was the first time that many people in the country realised that black readers were as important to the *Mail* as white ones.'[22] What became a long-running *Mail* campaign led to the ground-breaking Macpherson Inquiry, which defined institutionalized racism (as it had been demonstrated by the Metropolitan Police) and urged a review of the 'double jeopardy' rule that someone could not be tried twice for the same crime. So it was that in 2012, after a change in that law and a fresh police inquiry, two of the men pictured on that front page, David Norris and Gary Dobson, were jailed for life for the murder. The entire episode cemented Dacre's power and self-belief – not always for the best – but, after years of tabloid misbehaviour, it did allow him to correctly claim that: 'Newspapers come in for enormous criticism. Here was a case where they could be an enormous power for good. I'd like to think that we made a little bit of history that day.'[23]

Blair's New Best Friends

Would a New Labour government now take a stronger line on media regulation? In mid-1994, after the death of John Smith from a heart attack, Tony Blair had become Labour leader. Blair was determined to avoid the derision heaped on his predecessors, Michael Foot and Neil Kinnock, by the right-wing side of Fleet Street. The animosity had been largely mutual: the Labour Party and the wider movement had boycotted all Murdoch publications during the Wapping dispute. But Blair now began a strategy of courting proprietors, particularly Rothermere and Murdoch; his guide was Alastair Campbell, former *Mirror* political editor, now his media advisor and spokesman. A few years earlier, Blair, then shadow home secretary, had met Murdoch at a dining club where the latter was said to have been impressed by the young MP's 'puppy-dog, youthful, company-lawyer image'. But like the Tories, Blair faced a delicate balancing act: in addition to widespread concerns at both the grassroots level and about anti-Labour bias in the media, among other things there was also the issue of Murdoch's expansionist plans; alongside his wide range of newspapers his Sky TV empire was rapidly growing, giving him ever more power over public opinion. While many – not just those in the Labour movement – wanted to see legislation designed to prevent extensive cross-media ownership Blair, not an instinctive state-control-type socialist, was reluctant to do anything to alienate the tycoon. In July 1995 he raised eyebrows within his own party when he flew to the other side of the world to speak at Murdoch's conference of his senior executives at a remote Australian holiday resort, Hayman Island. Murdoch jokily introduced him with the words: 'If the British press is to be believed, today is all part of a Blair–Murdoch flirtation. If that flirtation is ever consummated, Tony, I suspect we will end up making love like two porcupines – very carefully.'[24]

Blair and Campbell had taken the advice of the Australian prime minister, Paul Keating, on Murdoch:

He's a big bad bastard, and the only way you can deal with
him is to make sure he thinks you can be a big bad bastard
too. You can do deals with him, without ever saying a deal is
done. But the only thing he cares about is his business and
the only language he respects is strength.[25]

While Blair was anxious to secure his support, Murdoch always liked
to back a winner and could see Labour were almost certain to soon
be in government. But could Murdoch abandon his papers' lifelong support for the Tories? There was another complicating factor:
Europe. Murdoch had opposed further integration with the EU, now
expanding with plans for a common currency, the euro. Antipathy
towards the EU was growing among the Conservative party and
Major, struggling with a small majority, was facing increasing
opposition from a small group of Eurosceptic Tories, whom he was
famously overheard calling 'the bastards' in an off-camera moment
after an interview.

Major, knowing he would have to call an election soon, also
wanted Murdoch's support and invited Murdoch and his daughter, Elizabeth, then running parts of his empire, to a private dinner
at Downing Street in February 1997. What occurred at the dinner
was not disclosed by Major until his evidence to the 2012 Leveson
Inquiry, when he revealed that Murdoch asked – or told – him
to change the government's European policies in favour of withdrawal; if they did not, his papers would no longer support the
Conservatives. The unspoken implication, said Major, by now Sir
John, was that Murdoch wanted to see a referendum on Europe
which might result in a British withdrawal or distancing from further
integration. He told the inquiry: 'It is not very often that someone
sits in front of a prime minister and says: "I would like you to change
your policy or my organisation cannot support you." People often
may think that, but it is not often that a point is put to a prime minister in that fashion.' He would never, he said, have changed his policy,
adding that he was not as close to Murdoch as Margaret Thatcher
had been because he 'did not admire much that was in his newspapers, nor his methods or his political philosophy', and that *The
Sun* had 'lowered the tone' of discourse in public life.[26]

With Labour clearly heading for victory, by the time the election was announced on 17 March, Murdoch had decided. On the

first full day of campaigning, *The Sun* told its 10 million readers in large black font: '*The Sun* Backs Blair'. Its leader said Blair was a 'breath of fresh air' and the Tories were 'divided and rudderless'. Stuart Higgins would later tell broadcasters: 'This is not a decision we have taken lightly. We consider Mr Blair has all the qualities of leadership required to take this great country forward. The Tories are tired, divided and need a good rest to regroup.' Higgins told *Channel 4 News* that the paper would remain critical of New Labour, especially on Europe. During the campaign, Blair was persuaded to write a piece for *The Sun* committing to a referendum before the UK would join the euro. 'Britain would have no truck with the European superstate,' wrote Blair (or, more likely, Campbell on his behalf). Murdoch had got what he wanted and *The Sun*, the *News of the World* and *The Times* all told their readers to vote Labour. Campbell still faced strong criticism from senior party figures such as former leader Kinnock, who said that he had engineered 'a deal with the devil'. Campbell later said of the relationship with Murdoch: 'It's like a wild dog in the corner of the room. And you are aware of it. And you just want to keep it quiet.'[27] In such circumstances, a battle with Murdoch and other proprietors over regulation was never going to happen.

At the *Mail*, a similar courtship had ensued. Before becoming party leader, Blair had lunched with Rothermere and his editors at Northcliffe House, an invitation Kinnock had declined. Blair won over Rothermere, English and former *Daily Telegraph* editor Max Hastings, who had replaced Stewart Steven as editor of the *Standard*. Sir David declared: 'Blair – whether he was alone or with his minders – radiated frankness and honesty.'[28] Dacre was also impressed, but did not share Murdoch's belief that he would triumph at the next election. When it did come, he launched an anti-Europe 'Battle for Britain' campaign, warning that Labour could take Britain further into an integrated Europe and swap the pound for the euro. On election night itself, when the scale of Blair's victory became clear, Dacre is said to have shouted across the newsroom: 'What the fuck is going on? These are fucking *Daily Mail* readers.'[29] Dacre would never be completely reconciled to Blair or New Labour.

Rothermere, in a remarkable move not long after Blair's victory, announced that, when he attended the Lords, he would be moving from the crossbenches to join the Labour benches. In a series of statements and interviews he stressed that while he believed Dacre a 'great editor . . . we do not always share exactly the same views on politics' and later told the BBC's *World at One* that '[Dacre] is entitled to his views and to express them,' but went on, significantly: 'If they start to affect the circulation that will be different.'[30] Entirely predictably, *The Mirror*, despite Morgan's Conservative instincts, stuck with its traditional base and told its readers to vote Labour, while the *Express* stable remained faithful to the Tories.

On 2 May 1997, the morning after Tony Blair's historic landslide election victory, he arrived at a prearranged celebration near the National Theatre on the South Bank in London. To the upbeat strains of D:Ream's 'Things Can Only Get Better', as the sun rose, the triumphant leader mounted a podium and addressed his audience: party members and workers, his soon-to-be Cabinet members and Campbell, guru of dealing with the tabloid media, who were all sharing the historic moment. The television news cameras would also capture another very well-known face in the crowd, Labour-supporting actor Ross Kemp, one of the stars of the massively popular BBC soap *EastEnders*. At his side was his then girlfriend, later wife, who was not then in the public eye: the distinctive red-headed figure of Rebekah Wade, now a rising star as deputy editor of the *News of the World*. Later, her name would become synonymous with the scandal of journalistic bad behaviour that would almost, but not quite, bring down the Murdoch empire. For now, this coming force, who knew a growing story when she saw one and how to associate herself with it, as she had done with Paul and Sheryl Gascoigne, was about to become one of Blair's new best friends.

The Most Hunted Person of the Modern Age

Blair's first few months in office were the honeymoon period many leaders enjoy when first elected. But one event would bring renewed focus on the activities of the tabloid newspapers and, once again, more calls for reform. Reform that never happened.

Ever since the *Daily Mirror* had published, with the approval of his widow, the extraordinary image of Edward VII's dead body obtained by Hannen Swaffer, selling 2 million copies on the day of his funeral in 1910 (the kind of image that would never see the light of day today), the power of royal stories to increase popular newspaper sales had been glaringly obvious. Until the advent of newspaper illustrations, the vast majority of the public had never seen what any royal person actually looked like. The drama of the abdication of King Edward VIII in 1936 saw the private lives of the royal family being examined in hitherto unthinkable ways in the popular media, breaking boundaries that had always existed. Although newspapers everywhere else, particularly in the United States and Canada, had reported the relationship between the Prince of Wales (subsequently the king) and the twice-divorced American Mrs Wallis Simpson, including their holiday together in the Mediterranean in August 1936, British newspapers, by common agreement, did not report the affair, or the king's determination to marry her. That persisted until the Bishop of Bradford appeared to allude to the issue in a speech, although he later claimed he had never heard of Mrs Simpson. The story was run by the *Yorkshire Post* before being picked up by the *Daily Mirror*, which broke the consensus and named Simpson publicly for the first time in its issue of 3 December 1936 under the headline 'The King Wants to Marry Mrs Simpson: Cabinet advises "No"'. The decision to go ahead was taken by Bartholomew and Cudlipp and the story was held back until the last edition, long after chairman John Cowley and his son, who also worked for the paper, had left the building and too late for other papers to follow suit.[31] The political, constitutional and religious row over the issue, leading to Edward's abdication on 11 December, would be front-page news for weeks.

During the Second World War, newspaper and cinema newsreel images of Edward's brother and successor, George VI, and his wife, Elizabeth, staying in Buckingham Palace and going about in London during the Blitz boosted the popularity of the royals, now real people rather then distant figureheads. In the post-war years, the king's daughters, Elizabeth and Margaret, appeared regularly in all the papers, although almost always in officially sanctioned photographs. There was still a strong aura of propriety and restraint around reporting royal affairs. In 1946 the *Sunday Pictorial* broke new ground in asking readers to vote on 'Should Our Future Queen Wed Philip?' – a clear majority were in favour – prompting many, including Arthur Christiansen, then still editor of the *Express*, to wonder whether the question was in good taste.[32]

When the king died in 1952 there was further disquiet at some papers publishing images of the royals appearing grief-stricken. The subsequent first televised coronation, of the young Queen Elizabeth, only increased the pulling power of the monarchy. In the years that followed, speculation about Princess Margaret's relationship with Group Captain Peter Townsend led to the *Daily Mirror*'s famous headline of 19 August 1955, two days before her 25th birthday when she would be free to marry: 'Come on Margaret! Please Make Up Your Mind!' On her birthday, three hundred journalists waited outside Balmoral for an announcement that never came. The headline resulted in a Press Council censure for 'coarse impertinence . . . an offence against the decencies of British public life'. It had little effect. When Townsend returned to Britain after working abroad, the popular press ignored requests from the Palace for restraint and he was mobbed by the media, which chartered an aircraft to fly over the country house where the couple were meeting.

In 1957 the Daily *Mirror* published a story referring to 'malicious rumours' about the marriage of the queen and Prince Philip, then away in the United States, with the headline 'Fly Home Philip'. It was the continuation of what commentator Malcolm Muggeridge had argued, in a remarkably prescient essay in the *New Statesman* in 1955, would become a royal soap opera. Muggeridge shuddered at the 'tedious adulation' of the royal family that the increased media coverage had created, suggesting the royals had developed a taste for 'the publicity which, in theory, they find so repugnant'. They needed proper advice from their courtiers, he said, adding:

The royal family and their advisers have really got to make up their minds – do they want to be part of the mystique of the century of the common man or to be an institutional monarchy; to ride, as it were, in a glass coach or on bicycles; to provide the tabloids with a running serial or to live simply and unaffectedly among their subjects like the Dutch and Scandinavian royal families. What they cannot do is to have it both ways.[33]

This paradox continues up to the present day, leading to a series of extraordinary court battles involving the queen's grandson, his wife and the popular press.

What concerned Muggeridge was just the start. Throughout the succeeding years, the royal soap opera gathered strength, expanded its cast and continued to entertain: Margaret's eventual marriage to society photographer Antony Armstrong-Jones, later Lord Snowdon, the early years of the young royals Charles, Anne, Andrew and Edward, their schooldays, their holidays and first relationships were all gleefully documented in the tabloids. In 1973, after news of the relationship between Princess Anne and Captain Mark Phillips emerged, *The Sun* offered readers the chance to take home a souvenir poster of 'Princess Anne's handsome young escort' for just twenty pence. 'For the Sun, Phillips was an object of fantasy to be commodified and displayed on bedroom walls.'[34] In 1976 the *News of the World* broke the story of the romance between Princess Margaret and society gardener Roddy Llewellyn, with pictures of them on the Caribbean island of Mustique; her divorce from Snowdon followed, as did a raft of headlines on the theme of 'Will the Princess Marry Roddy?', echoing those of twenty years previously. She did not, but Llewellyn would remain a tabloid obsession for a time, the serialization of his 'Own Story' helping to launch the *Daily Star* in 1979, where, ironically, he complained about the 'nightmare of being in the tabloid spotlight'.[35]

As the 1970s wore on, speculation about Prince Charles's future bride mounted, with successive girlfriends being outed, photographed, analysed, dissected and cast aside by the media. A few days after *The Sun* disclosed in 1980 that Charles was seeing the young Lady Diana Spencer – 'Lady Di Is the New Girl for Charles' – *The Sun*'s recently appointed royal photographer Arthur Edwards tracked her down to the west London nursery school where she was teaching and persuaded her to pose with a child in each arm. Conveniently and, according to Edwards, entirely accidentally, the autumnal sun shone from behind through the thin dress she was wearing, showing the outline of her legs all the way up to the thighs. *The Sun* chose not to crop the photograph at her waist: the image, on one hand an appealing portrait of a young woman with two cute children, and, on the other, a prurient male gaze on a guileless young girl in her first dealings with the media, was a sensation. She was said to be horrified, but there was never any turning back from that moment. The woman who would be known as 'The Princess of Sales' for the next sixteen years and beyond had been found. That image was only one of many that defined her, the camera lens documenting her life and eventually, according to many, contributing to her death. In the two months before the 'fairytale' royal wedding in July the following year, her image was on the front page of *The Sun* on average every other day. The wedding, watched by 750 million people worldwide, was a respite from the economic recession and urban riots that had dogged the country. It invoked memories of the Silver Jubilee celebrations of just a few years before, creating a tide of Union Flag-waving jingoism that would also imbue the Falklands War campaign, where Prince Andrew would serve as a fighter pilot, celebrated for simply being there.

Attention on the princess would never let up. In February 1982, she was photographed in secret, pregnant and on a private holiday on a Caribbean beach, with both *The Sun* and the *Star* printing the long-lens images; the Palace issued a public condemnation. Harry Arnold, *The Sun*'s royal correspondent, and Edwards and MacKenzie, were unrepentant – Arnold would later claim the royal couple had been less bothered than the Palace made out. 'She's not as fuddy-duddy as the Palace would have you believe.'[36] The royal press pack had a new focus from the mid-1980s: Sarah Ferguson, who married Prince Andrew in 1986. She was a much more worldly creature and their marriage foundered six years later, though she was gleefully photographed having her toes sucked by her financial advisor by an American poolside. She never quite attracted the same attention, some would say obsession, as Diana, whose every move would be closely monitored; to the tabloids 'Fergie' was great fun, while Diana was global box office.

Princess Diana, as Arnold saw, would turn out to be a careful media manipulator, using friends and favoured journalists to get her side across as her marriage began to deteriorate in the late 1980s and early '90s. Arnold said: 'She felt like a second wife to me, I could look at her face and know she was in a mood. I don't think there is a man who reported her, or, especially took photographs of her, who wasn't a little bit in love with her. And I was, a little.'[37] Some became friends and confidants, particularly Richard Kay of the *Daily Mail*, whom she nicknamed 'Ricardo' and who was the recipient of many late-night calls; he was the last person she called on the night of her death in 1997. In 1991 she cooperated with former *Daily Star* and *Daily Mail* royal reporter Andrew Morton, whose book *Diana: Her True Story*, published the following year, containing details of her bulimia and breakdowns, caused a sensation. Morton was unable

– until after her death – to state emphatically that Charles had been having an affair with his old flame, Camilla Parker Bowles, without giving away that Diana was his source. By now, all restraint over royal reporting had vanished and the soap opera of Muggeridge's warning was in full flow.

In August 1992, *The Sun* published the so-called 'Squidgygate' tapes of the princess in an intimate conversation, recorded several years earlier, with a man presumed to have been her lover, James Gilbey. In December that year, the royal couple separated. Just a few weeks later, the *Mirror* published details of the so-called 'Camillagate' tapes, in which Prince Charles had a highly sexual conversation with Parker Bowles. In 1994, in a televised interview with Jonathan Dimbleby, the prince confessed to adultery, but stressed it had happened only once the marriage had broken down; the following year, the princess gave an interview to the BBC's *Panorama* programme confessing to bulimia and an affair with Guards officer James Hewitt. She stated, in reference to Camilla: 'There were three of us in this marriage.' The phrase would resonate for years. The confession to the affair with red-haired Hewitt fuelled speculation, occasionally referred to in the tabloids, that he was Prince Harry's real father. The affairs on both sides added to the drama and circulation, creating even more tabloid interest. This was peak Diana. Her image was everywhere, not just tabloids around the world, but also women's magazines and the celebrity magazines *Hello!* and Richard Desmond's *OK!*

She became adept at playing the media to her advantage – during a pre-break-up trip to India in 1992 posing on a bench in front of the Taj Mahal for an evocative 'this is me all alone' photograph. On the night of the Dimbleby interview in June 1994, she appeared impeccably groomed and styled in a glamorous, short, off-the-shoulder dress at a fundraising event at the Serpentine Gallery, which she knew would be surrounded by photographers; it was all about making her the focus of interest for the broadcast and the front pages the next day. (Privately the media dubbed it 'her fuck-you dress'; *The Sun*'s headline the next day was 'The Thrilla He Left to Woo Camilla'.) There was also a suggestion the gym photographs, which caused so much trouble for the *Mirror* and prompted a threat to sue by the princess herself, were actually not entirely accidental; why, asked the gym owner, would she be in a public gym and in full makeup? Tina Brown, former editor of *The Tatler* and *Vanity Fair*, a friend of the princess and one of her many biographers, told Canadian TV in 2007 that she would often tip off newspapers about her whereabouts: '[Diana] did want some privacy, but at the same time she couldn't resist giving them the images they wanted.' At the same time, she sought coverage for her own interests and campaigns – to remove landmines from war zones and win better acceptance for AIDS sufferers.

After her divorce, the prospect of the liberated Diana seeking relationships was irresistible: she was no longer within the protective field of the royal machine. She was free to travel as she wished, but could not exert the same control over who followed her around. The paparazzi – the motorcycle-riding freelance photographers selling their pictures to the highest bidders – now had her firmly in their lenses. Stake-outs of the princess would result in photographs such as those sold to the *News of the World* in March 1994 showing her driving a married millionaire art dealer into her rooms in Kensington Palace late at night.

The coverage that followed her post-divorce relationships intensified when it became clear that Dodi Fayed, the son of publicity-loving Mohammed Al-Fayed, the owner of Harrods, the Ritz in Paris and Fulham Football Club, was a serious love interest. Images of the couple together and Diana sitting alone on a diving board on a yacht in the Mediterranean featured heavily in all the tabloids, the *Mirror* at one point paying £100,000 for pictures of the couple embracing. Jason Fraser, one of the freelancers who followed the princess around, later claimed that photographers were there to capture many of these images because she had tipped them off, possibly to make another lover jealous. Fraser estimated that he made around £1 million from sales of the images, although much of that would be to European and American magazines, now imbued with tabloid values, which were able to run extensive glossy photospreads. Up to 2,000 photographers would descend on an area to make their own fortunes.

When the couple arrived in Paris on 30 August 1997, scores of photographers were camped outside the Ritz Hotel. The paparazzi were behind the car when their chauffeur crashed into the wall of an underpass that night, killing himself and Dodi Fayed instantly and fatally injuring the princess, and crowded around the wrecked vehicle. As Prince Harry would say in an interview in 2021: 'The same people who chased her into the tunnel photographed her dying in the backseat of that car.'[38] Her death, its aftermath – the oceans of flowers outside Kensington Palace and much talk of the traditionally tightly buttoned-up British nation discovering its emotional articulacy – and the extraordinary funeral would occupy vast amounts of space in all the newspapers, although none of the tunnel images would ever be seen publicly.

At her funeral, her brother Earl Spencer, whose own wife had been secretly photographed going into an addiction clinic, attacked the media, saying his sister 'talked endlessly' about getting away from England:

> Mainly because of the treatment that she received at the hands of the newspapers. I don't think she ever understood why her genuinely good intentions were sneered at by the media, why there appeared to be a permanent quest on their behalf to bring her down. It is baffling. My own and only explanation is that genuine goodness is threatening to those at the opposite end of the moral spectrum. It is a point to remember that of all the ironies about Diana, perhaps the greatest was this – a girl given the name of the ancient goddess of hunting was, in the end, the most hunted person of the modern age.[39]

His words caused a break in the relationship between the news media and the royals. Sales figures for *The Sun* and the *Mirror* plummeted, due to a wave of public revulsion at the tactics of the photographers, and sympathy for someone whom Blair, using Campbell's words, dubbed 'the People's Princess'. A Gallup poll found that 43 per cent of the public believed the photographers 'extremely' responsible for the crash, compared with 33 per cent who found the chauffeur equally to blame. An official royal photographer taking pictures of the bouquets outside Buckingham Palace was abused by some members of the public in the apparent mistaken belief he worked for the press. The Press Complaints Commission strengthened the editors' code of practice to create what it called the toughest set of press regulations anywhere in Europe, effectively banning the use of long-lens photography to take unauthorized pictures.

It redefined the meaning of 'private places' and held that an editor was responsible for any material obtained through 'persistent pursuit'. Although there had been a gentleman's agreement between the royals and the media concerning the privacy of royal children – this included Diana's sons William and Harry as well as the daughters of Prince Andrew and Sarah Ferguson – the code was beefed up to extend to all their time in education, and to require justification for any content other than the fame, notoriety or position of the child in question's parents or guardian.

Would the tabloids actually respect these rules? In an extraordinary front-page statement worthy of the grand declarations of Northcliffe himself, the *Daily Mail* said its chairman, Viscount Rothermere, had pledged to ban paparazzi pictures. Although the subsequent quote from Rothermere rather qualified the idea of a ban, it was widely interpreted as endorsing one: 'In view of Earl Spencer's strong words and my own sense of outrage, I have instructed my editors no "paparazzi" pictures are to be purchased without my knowledge and consent.'[40] In the longer run, it was a pledge more honoured in the breach than the observance.

'You never see a nipple in the *Daily Express*'

As the century neared its end, Express Newspapers, the company built by Beaverbrook and Christiansen into, at one point, the biggest-selling daily newspaper, which, for decades, had represented the authentic voice of prim, suburban, middle England – so much so that in the 1970s 'punk' poet John Cooper Clarke wrote a work attacking its hypocrisy entitled 'You Never See a Nipple in the *Daily Express*' – was sold to a man whom many called a pornographer and someone with no experience of newspapers. Born in 1951, Richard Desmond, like Robert Maxwell, was from a central European Jewish background, but he had a comfortable upbringing in north London. Leaving school at fifteen, within three years he was advertising manager for musicians' magazine *Beat Instrumental*. He founded two music magazines and created a number of international editions. In 1983 his company, Northern & Shell, launched the UK version of the American top-shelf glamour magazine and *Playboy* rival *Penthouse*. Other so-called adult titles followed, including *Asian Babes*, *Readers Wives*, *Barely Legal* and *Forum*, for which

Richard Desmond
after buying Express
Newspapers,
November 2000.

Richard Desmond after buying Express Newspapers, November 2000.

Alastair Campbell, formerly *Mirror* political editor, wrote under the byline Riviera Gigolo, together with about forty other specialist publications on subjects including cycling, cars, caravanning and cooking. Desmond also ran a premium rate phone-sex company until 1988, sold after British Telecom raised concerns about content. Northern & Shell had also launched the pornographic TV channel The Fantasy Channel in 1995, later rebranded as Television X and expanded to seven channels, bringing in annual profits of around £17 million. In 1993 Northern & Shell launched *OK!* magazine, initially as a monthly, although it became a weekly three years later. The original idea was to ape the success of the Spanish celebrity-obsessed *Hello!* magazine, but it outsold it, with a staple diet of soft-focus coverage of celebrities, particularly their parties, homes and, especially, their weddings. It became one of the largest magazines in the world, with 23 different international editions and a readership of more than 31 million. By the end of the decade, awash with cash and self-confidence, Desmond launched his bid to take over the *Express* newspapers.

The late 1980s and 1990s had been a long period of slow decline for the *Daily* and *Sunday Express*, caught between the red-top wars of the *Mirror* and *Sun* and the resurgence of the *Daily Mail*. Both papers retained a loyal core of ageing readers with their conservative layouts and trenchant, traditional Conservative views. The venerable William Hickey gossip column, with its diet of ageing celebrities and the comings and goings of the minor aristocracy, was an attraction for readers, as were the stable of what Cooper Clarke's poem described as 'angry columns [that] scream in pain'. These were headed by editor Sir John Junor in the *Sunday Express*, with his undying devotion to Margaret Thatcher and antipathy to any kind of social liberalism, and Peter Hitchens, the right-wing polemicist brother of leftish writer and commentator Christopher Hitchens.

The *Express* titles had been kept afloat by the successful launch of the *Daily Star* in 1978, but in 1985 they were eventually bought from Trafalgar House by United Newspapers, which had interests in television and regional newspapers. In 1989 they abandoned the glamorous but cramped 'Black Lubyanka' of Fleet Street and moved to a purpose-built new building in Blackfriars. Two of the *Express*'s editors had been tabloid grandees, and were closer to the ends of their careers than the beginning: after his exit from *The Sun*, Sir Larry Lamb had edited the *Express* from 1983 to 1986, followed by a decade of Sir Nicholas Lloyd (who had worked in senior executive roles at *The Sun*, *News of the World* and the Mirror Group papers), who in turn was succeeded by the lower-profile Richard Addis, a former *Sunday Telegraph* and *Mail* executive.

By 1998 United Newspapers had merged with companies – also with television interests – owned by businessman Lord Clive Hollick, a strong supporter of Tony Blair's New Labour, who became its chairman. Hollick, neither a journalist nor a publisher, believed he saw a gap in the market and decided to revamp the *Express* into a Labour-backing middle-market tabloid closer to the style of the *Mirror*, but avoiding tabloid excess and sleaze. Addis was replaced in May 1998 by Rosie Boycott, then editor of *The Independent*.

Boycott, one of the founders of the radical *Spare Rib* magazine and Virago publishing, was considered a feminist pioneer and, as one of her senior executives described her, 'a bit of a card' – a child of the 1960s, a self-confessed former alcoholic and cannabis smoker who, when much younger, had spent time in a Thai jail on drugs charges. Boycott had revived her career as editor of the British edition of *Esquire*, winning Editor of the Year in 1993 and 1994, and in 1996 had become editor of the *Independent on Sunday* and later also of the daily *Independent*, the first woman editor of a national daily title since Mary Howarth briefly edited the *Daily Mirror* in 1903. Boycott had no experience of newspapers and her interests were strictly in the more relaxed approach of monthly magazines and cultural and literary journalism; for the rigid demands of Sunday and daily journalism, with unbreakable deadlines, news-driven imperatives and broad agendas – editors need to know something about everything – she later admitted, she was wholly unprepared: 'I knew absolutely sweet fuck-all when I left *Esquire*. I'd never been in a newspaper conference. I'd only seen one on telly. I was so scared I was almost unable to breathe.'[41] She grew into the role, was energetic, a natural networker and mostly well liked by colleagues. To move to the *Express* was a remarkable transition – a left-of-centre broadsheet editor had never before edited a tabloid that embodied the very essence of Conservative middle England. It was probably best that the vast majority of *Express* readers had no knowledge of *Spare Rib*, her drug addictions or the fact she once kept a cannabis plant in her office at *The Independent*.

Even though she surrounded herself with a small core of experienced colleagues from *The Independent*, the experiment failed. Circulation continued to fall: younger readers were not tempted, older ones shifted to the buoyant *Mail*. The even more determinedly old-fashioned image of the *Sunday Express* remained a stumbling block; to change it radically enough to attract new readers in an overcrowded and competitive Sunday market would have been a huge gamble. In late 2000 Hollick bailed out and sold the *Express* papers to Desmond's Northern & Shell for £125 million; this was, said advertising industry magazine *Campaign*, greeted with 'abject horror by the majority of the media world'.[42] The magnate with a pornography portfolio now had one of the founding figures of the feminist movement as his editor. It was not destined to last. Boycott left in January 2001 and was followed by a large number of both junior and senior staff, including political editor Anthony Bevins (who had followed Boycott from *The Independent*) and star columnists Peter Hitchens and Mary Kenny, who said she could not work for someone who 'coarsened culture'.[43] Sales continued to slump at both *Express* titles – although Desmond continued support for Labour, to which he had recently donated £100,000. The new editor was Chris Williams, a veteran of the *Express* and *Mail* executive ranks, who perhaps had a surer grasp of what his new proprietor might want. This was an obsessive focus on small mix of stories: mainly conspiracy theories over the death of the Princess of Wales, the vagaries of the British climate and whether there was a cure for dementia; and, later, the disappearance of a young girl in Portugal called Madeleine McCann.

Meanwhile, other tabloids became more focused on covering a celebrity-driven agenda and had something else on their minds: how to hack mobile telephones.

10

THE DARK ARTS

When the extent of unlawful, unethical and unsavoury activities by newspapers exploded into the public consciousness in 2009 and 2010 (largely due to the work of veteran journalist Nick Davies of *The Guardian*), for many it was a revelation that tabloid newspapers, although their transgressions had been known and documented, employed a variety of illegal means to obtain information on ordinary people as well as the more powerful.

The signs had been there: the falsified stories, the taking of a fragment of information and distorting it – Freddie Starr and his hamster – and the numerous kiss-and-tell exclusives. There were other isolated incidents which hinted at something deeper and darker: stories based on phone interceptions of royalty, such as the 'Squidgygate' tapes of the Princess of Wales in intimate conversation with a man presumed to be her lover. In January 1993 an Australian women's magazine, owned by Rupert Murdoch, published the 'Tampongate' or 'Camillagate' tape – a recording of Prince Charles in an even more intimate conversation with Camilla Parker Bowles, the woman he married in 2005, who is now queen. Although *The Sun* and others reported the outline of the story, it was the *Sunday Mirror* and the *Sunday People* that eventually published the full transcript. In both cases, the precise source of the tapes was never established but many believed they were originally made by the British intelligence services and laundered to disguise their origin. Overseas publication allowed British tabloids to claim they were merely reporting material in the public domain. Murdoch denied any suggestion of 'collusion or conspiracy'.

There were other attempts at illegal interception. In his book, *Hack Attack*, Davies revealed how private investigators working for Alex Marunchak of the *News of the World* used radio scanners in 1995 to listen to the telephone calls of the Princess of Wales when she was allegedly having an affair with rugby player Will Carling;[1] in 2000 Neville Thurlbeck, the *News of the World*'s long-standing chief reporter, was tried on corruption charges involving a detective constable at the National Criminal Intelligence Service, which gathered intelligence for police forces, who had allowed him to see criminal records in return for tip-offs about criminals. Thurlbeck allegedly wrote 36 stories on the basis of the information; both men were acquitted for lack of evidence.

A further more significant and tangled affair involving private detectives, the police and the *News of the World* bubbled away for many years. More than three decades later, the circumstances surrounding the death of Daniel Morgan and the failure of subsequent investigations has still to be fully explained. Morgan, 37, was a private detective who was murdered in the car park of a south London pub in 1987; an axe was driven into his head. Morgan was the business partner of another private detective, Jonathan Rees, and they ran a company called Southern Investigations. Morgan had become alarmed at the activities of Rees, who allegedly had links to corrupt police officers who sold information to journalists. Charges against Rees and two others were eventually dropped by the CPS because other offences had emerged, and in 2000 Rees was jailed over his part in a plot to plant cocaine on someone involved in a custody case. During investigations into Rees, police planted a bug in the Southern Investigations office and recorded journalists, including Alex Marunchak from the *News of the World* and others from the *Mirror* and the *Sunday Mirror*, paying Rees for information obtained from corrupt police officers. Nothing ever came of the information because none of them were proved to have committed offences themselves or to have known about the corrupt sources of the information. Morgan's family, meanwhile, continued to press for a public inquiry.

Over the next few years, there were further examples, but no one quite joined the dots – at least publicly – to work out just how extensively newspapers had used what became known as 'the dark arts' in pursuit of their agendas. Southern Investigations, it later became clear, was only one of a number of private investigation agencies being used by the tabloids to get information from corrupt officers, or from official sources by illegal methods such as impersonation or 'blagging'. The story of how the dots were eventually joined began with a fairly routine inquiry by a provincial police force.

In the autumn of 2002, the Information Commissioner's Office began helping a Devon and Cornwall police investigation into leaks, allegedly by serving and retired police officers, from the Police National Computer (PNC) to a private investigations company, Data Research Ltd, run by a man called John Boyall. The inquiry, codenamed Reproof, led to another private investigator, based in Newcastle upon Tyne, who had been instructed by newspapers to search police records on three Labour MPs, including then Chancellor of the Exchequer Gordon Brown. It also led to a civilian worker at Tooting police station who had been supplying PNC information to a Hampshire-based private detective, Steve Whittamore, who was linked to Boyall. The resulting police investigation, Operation Motorman, should have been the catalyst that first exposed the tabloids' devious practices. For a variety of reasons, it did not.

In two raids on Whittamore's office, the Information Commissioner's Office (ICO) and police discovered he had been paid thousands of pounds over several years by national newspapers and magazines for information such as criminal records, vehicle registrations, addresses and, inevitably, ex-directory telephone numbers, mobile numbers and itemized call details, including 'friends and family' call lists. There were many hundreds of requests from more than three hundred journalists relating to thousands of people. While some were legitimate – searching electoral rolls or company records – most were illegal and did not have a public interest justification. Whittamore had kept scrupulous records, 'listing more than 17,000 transactions in separate files known as the Blue Book (mostly News International), the Red Book (*Mirror* Group) and the Yellow and Green books (including the *Mail* and the *Mail on Sunday*), the Express Group, the Observer and a number of magazines'. 'There were almost four hundred named journalists in the files, from investigative reporters and newsdesk executives to showbiz and diary writers. For some, Whittamore's services were not just a useful tool but almost an addiction. One reporter used him 422 times,' *The*

Independent later reported.[2] In his 2012 report on the practices of the press, Lord Justice Leveson would later write: 'It appeared that the ICO had come upon an organised and systematic disregard for the data protection regime of a scale, duration and seriousness going beyond poor practice, beyond breach of the rights and principles of the regime, and into the realms of criminality in its own right.'[3]

Requests for information about murder victims were common. Despite the *News of the World* launching a campaign for 'Sarah's Law', which allows the public to ask the police whether someone in contact with a child has ever been convicted or suspected of child sexual abuse, News International had paid around £300 to Whittamore to investigate the family of Sarah Payne, shortly after the eight-year-old girl was murdered in 2000. The *People* also paid Whittamore for the family's ex-directory numbers. The *News of the World* would also pay more than £200 for details of the parents and other relatives of Milly Dowler, the schoolgirl murdered in Surrey in 2002. The *Sunday Express* used private investigators to obtain the private telephone number of the parents of Holly Wells, shortly after she was murdered in Soham by Ian Huntley in 2002. Whittamore's records went back as far as the late 1990s when the *People* commissioned him to find information about the families of two victims of the 1996 Dunblane massacre of sixteen schoolchildren and one teacher.

Celebrities and other public figures targeted included actress Elizabeth Hurley and her former boyfriend Hugh Grant, MP George Galloway, *Private Eye* editor Ian Hislop, comedians Lenny Henry and Steve Coogan, singer Charlotte Church and former Tony Blair aide Anji Hunter. Some requests were general, some highly specific, relating, for instance, to telephone calls from a number during a specific time period on a given date. Many of the individuals targeted were not themselves well known, but were connected to people in the public eye, such as members of their families, their drivers and assistants and, in one case, a decorator employed by a lottery winner. The information was obtained by Whittamore in a variety of ways, often using 'blagging techniques' – impersonating someone with a legitimate interest in obtaining the information – and often via a network of associates, such as the Tooting police employee being paid for information, or, in another case, an associate of Whittamore who posed as a telephone engineer and used a code word, issued to BT employees, to fraudulently obtain call details.

Even as Whittamore was being investigated, *The Sun* admitted 'listening' to taped phone calls between Cherie Blair, wife of then prime minister Tony Blair, and convicted fraudster Peter Foster over the purchase of a property in Bristol. The PCC censured *The Sun* for the taping, but there was no police investigation. And none of this was to became public knowledge for nine years. The names of the journalists requesting the information were never disclosed, and none were ever prosecuted. Alex Owens, former senior investigating officer for the ICO, told the Leveson Inquiry in 2011 this was despite the fact that investigators had assembled 25–30 potential cases for prosecution 'with all the relevant paperwork showing what information had been requested by the press, how Whittamore used his associates to unlawfully obtain the information and how Whittamore then passed the information obtained back to the journalist for payment'.[4]

In January 2003 Rebekah Wade was made editor of *The Sun*, replacing the slightly off-message figure of David Yelland. She was succeeded by Andy Coulson at the *News of the World*. Two months later, she made a surprise public admission. Giving evidence alongside colleague and, as was later revealed, occasional lover, Coulson, to the House of Commons Select Committee on Culture, Media and Sport, she said: 'We have paid the police for information in the past,' apparently unaware that this was tantamount to an admission of a criminal act. When the committee chair and Labour MP Chris Bryant asked: 'And will you do it in the future?', Wade began to reply: 'It depends,' before being interrupted by Coulson, who swiftly intervened to say: 'We have always operated within the code and within the law.'[5] News International later issued a statement denying it was company practice to pay police for information; Wade later said she had been speaking 'in general terms' about past practice.

Wade and Coulson were joined by Piers Morgan and all spoke in favour of the then existing system of self-regulation. Morgan told the hearing that the PCC had led to improvements in standards of journalism from the 'pretty lawless' state that had previously existed: 'I have worked in Fleet Street for 15 years. I have never known standards to be higher than they are today, particularly in relation to how we deal with ordinary people.'[6] It was around this time that reporters at the *Daily Mirror* were routinely hacking the telephones of both ordinary people and those in the public eye.

That same year, Morgan was filmed admitting to knowing about phone hacking, telling singer Charlotte Church, by then a campaigner for media regulation:

There was a spate of stories that came out because of mobile phones. Journalists found out that if a celebrity hadn't changed their pin code, you could access their voicemails just by tapping a number. Are you really going to tell me that journalists aren't going to do that if they can ring up Charlotte Church's mobile phone and listen to all her messages? All you have to do is actually change the security number.

The footage would not emerge until some years later in a 2012 Channel 4 documentary.[7] Morgan made a number of statements over the next decade admitting such knowledge, but denying that he knew how to do it or that he had ever instructed journalists to do it. He also later denied listening to mobile phone messages, despite admitting in an article in the *Daily Mail* in 2006 that he had been played a tape of a message Paul McCartney had left on the mobile phone of his then wife Heather Mills.[8]

Wade refused three times to return to the committee to be further questioned about police payments. Committee chair Conservative MP John Whittingdale was said to have warned members pressing for a warrant to force her to attend that their private lives might be investigated by the tabloids if they went ahead.[9] Whittingdale later denied the report. Bryant was later ridiculed in a number of stories in *The Sun*, one of which included a picture of him in his underpants which he had posted on a gay dating website; he claimed his telephone had been hacked. The committee's report called on the Home Office and police to 'take note' of the evidence of Wade and Coulson and review measures designed to prevent such payments. It also made recommendations for strengthening the powers of the PCC.[10]

Eventually, seven unnamed journalists from the Mirror Group, News International and the *Daily Mail* were interviewed voluntarily in January 2004. All admitted using Whittamore and all denied they knew the information was obtained illegally, suggesting they believed the CRO initials on the records they were sent stood for Court Records Office, not Criminal Records Office. In early 2005 Whittamore, Boyall, Paul Marshall, a former civilian police worker, and Alan King, a retired police officer, were charged with conspiracy to commit misconduct in public office. Whittamore and Boyall pleaded guilty to a lesser charge of breaching the Data Protection Act. During the hearing, the judge, John Samuels QC, queried why no journalists were on trial, but the prosecution offered no public explanation. To the disappointment of the investigators, who felt the severity of the offences had been underplayed, and following technical and legal constraining factors on the judge's ability to impose more severe penalties – this related to Marshall being given a conditional discharge in an unrelated but more serious theft offence case – all four were given conditional discharges. Further charges against Whittamore and five other private investigators were withdrawn as a result.

In the tabloid newsrooms, life went on. The ICO and police inquiries had not attracted much attention elsewhere in the media – who would want to draw attention to the grubby side of their business? – and there was no widespread political move for reform. In Fortress Wapping, they were sheltered. Coulson, as editor of the *News of the World*, then the biggest-selling newspaper in the country, was different to other tabloid creatures like Morgan and MacKenzie, both larger-than-life personalities. Coulson was more buttoned up, a neatly suited Essex boy, whose outward appearance was deceptive.

> Those who liked Coulson used to say he was calm at the core . . . in spite of his youth, he seemed to have landed fully formed. Others said that he was cold, that no matter what was going on Andy would always survive; behind that mask of mild-mannered competence, he was ruthless.[11]

The news and features departments, presided over by hard-bitten tabloid veterans such as deputy editor Neil 'Wolfman' Wallis, existed in a climate of fear, with executives, reporters and departments competing with each other, even outbidding each other, to buy stories. As with all intensely competitive tabloid newsrooms, 'getting the story' was the sole reason for existence and reporters were under intense pressure to do so by whatever means necessary – with ready funds available. Corners were cut, facts distorted and stories given what was known in the trade as 'top spin'. Sharon

Marshall, who worked as a reporter for the *People* between 1998 and 2002 and at the *News of the World* between 2002 and 2004, later wrote that fabrication of interviews was commonplace: 'Sometimes the quotes were written before we ever left the office. Before we know who we were interviewing.'[12] The *News of the World*, argued Davies, was guilty of 'eye-watering hypocrisy' and had created an editorial distortion which pretended the nation lived by an antique moral code and that anyone who did not abide by it was a legitimate subject for exposure. 'There was no room for doubt or conscience. Human feelings did not come into it.'[13]

In 2005 the paper was on a roll, having been awarded Newspaper of the Year, largely due to three very typical exposés of affairs among the famous: footballer David Beckham with a personal assistant, the English football manager Sven-Göran Eriksson with a secretary at the Football Association and David Blunkett, then Home Secretary, with a magazine publisher. The paper had moved on from its earlier mix of suburban sex parties, randy vicars and gangland crime stories, with a light sprinkling of showbusiness. Now, celebrities – that is, almost anyone in the public eye – were the driving force. And all those award-winning stories had been obtained by hacking into mobile phone voicemails.[14]

Greg Miskiw, then northern editor of the *News of the World*, was another tabloid veteran of the hard-drinking, hard-living tendency. He had, since around 2000, been using the services of Glenn Mulcaire, whom he had poached from John Boyall. Mulcaire, like others in the network, was a 'blagger' who obtained information by deception. He taught Miskiw about phone hacking – that is, intercepting voicemails on mobile phones by guessing or knowing their PIN codes – which most people had left at the factory default of 1234. By the early 2000s Mulcaire, based in an office in south London, was working full time for the *News of the World*. He was paid around £100,000 a year, firstly by Miskiw – who would hire him for his own stories and for those of other reporters – and then after he left, by a news executive, Ian Anderson. While Miskiw tried to keep the technique secret, it spread around the newsroom and many reporters did it routinely. And by now, Jonathan Rees, having served time for drugs offences, had returned to work for the paper as a private investigator. So while its reporters would be breaking the law on a daily basis, outwardly the paper considered itself a beacon of moral standing. The same 'eye-watering hypocrisy' described by Davies allowed it to employ senior politicians such as former Tory leader William Hague as a columnist while its close links with Scotland Yard were manifold: former Metropolitan Police Commissioner Sir John Stevens was also a columnist and Neil Wallis became a paid media advisor to Scotland Yard. The links were at many levels – none more so than with reporter Mazher Mahmood, the so-called 'fake Sheikh'.

Mahmood, from a British Asian background, had been a key figure at the *News of the World* since the early 1990s, delivering a series of spectacular scoops engineered while disguised as a wealthy Arab sheikh. Highly secretive, he never allowed his real image to be published and rarely visited the offices. Sometimes these scoops involved real criminals being convicted as a result of his under-cover work, leading to close links with Scotland Yard. Mahmood later claimed his work had led to the convictions of more than 250 people, although this figure was later revised down to 94. Mahmood had won Reporter of the Year in 1999 for a scoop exposing inappro-priate behaviour by executives of Newcastle United football club. But despite his successes, lawyers suggested that entrapment and borderline illegality on his part was not always supported by a public interest defence. In 2003 the trial of a number of men for an alleged plot to kidnap Victoria Beckham, the former Spice Girls pop star-turned-fashion designer and wife of footballer David, collapsed after it emerged that Mahmood's main informant had been paid £10,000; the judge reported the issue to the Attorney General. The follow-ing year, another scoop involving three men accused of planning a dirty bomb, for which Mahmood worked with Scotland Yard's Anti-Terrorist Branch, led to a trial that ultimately collapsed. Again, the warning signs of a corrupt environment were there, hiding in plain sight. By now, around twenty private investigators were said to be supplying information to newspapers – broadsheets included – which often involved payments to public officials and police officers.

In November 2005 Clive Goodman, the long-serving royal editor of the *News of the World*, was under pressure from Coulson to get more stories about the two young princes William and Harry. Goodman already routinely paid police officers on royal duties for information and had occasionally hacked phones himself, but Coulson wanted more.[15] So Goodman set up a special operation, codenamed Bumblebee, with Mulcaire, who would be paid extra to obtain the phone numbers of fourteen members of the royal household. As a result of the information Mulcaire obtained, Goodman wrote a small item in his diary column about Prince William receiving medical treatment for a knee injury. A week later, there was another story about Tom Bradby, then political editor of ITN and a friend of the princes, loaning William a portable editing suite. Both stories contained details that, it transpired, could only have been obtained from voicemail messages on mobile phones. Bradby realized some of this related to messages he had left and alerted Prince William, setting off a chain of events that, even as this book was being completed in 2023, was continuing. The Metropolitan Police Anti-Terrorist Squad launched Operation Caryatid and arrested Mulcaire and Goodman in August 2006. Police discovered, as with Whittamore, that the hacking extended beyond the royal family. An internal report noted:

> Hundreds of handwritten sheets showed research into many people in the public eye. These included those linked to the Royal Household, Members of Parliament, military staff, sports stars, celebrities and journalists. There was also a quantity of electronic media recovered including recordings of some apparent voicemail conversations. It is clear from these documents that Mulcaire had been engaged in a sustained (years) period of research work in various levels of completion.[16]

More than four hundred people were named, including then deputy prime minister John Prescott and Metropolitan Police Commissioner Sir Ian Blair.[17] Police would also tell Wade that her own phone had been hacked. But it would be some years before any of this saw the light of day.

These unprecedented investigations were taking place against a background of extraordinary closeness between Wade and the government of the day. Ever since Tony Blair and Alastair Campbell made their trip around the world to speak to Murdoch and his senior executives and Murdoch's *Sun* had endorsed Blair ahead of the 1997 election, there had been many connections – these were, of course, in everyone's interests. But with Blair, it had moved beyond the business and into the personal: Wade and her then partner Ross

Kemp had attended the May 1997 Labour victory celebration, Wade had visited Downing Street regularly, reportedly incurring the ire of Blair's wife, Cherie,[18] and there were many lunches, dinners and other social occasions. Blair had also become close to Murdoch, who had married his third wife, Wendi Deng (a former executive of his Asian region Star TV network), in 1999, and Blair became godfather to their first daughter, Grace, born in 2001. When Blair stood down in 2007, *The Sun*, without missing a beat, transferred its affections to his successor, Gordon Brown, and Wade became close to Brown's wife, Sarah, attending an all-female party and overnight stay at Chequers to mark her fortieth birthday.

As police launched their investigation into Goodman and Mulcaire, the IOC finally made public some of the findings of the Motorman investigation. Their report, 'What Price Privacy?', set out how newspapers had used private investigators to obtain confidential information in breach of the Data Protection Act – whether from utility companies, the NHS, government departments or the Police National Computer. The report was damning:

> At a time when senior members of the press were publicly congratulating themselves for having raised journalistic standards across the industry, many newspapers were continuing to subscribe to an undercover economy devoted to obtaining a wealth of personal information forbidden to them by law.

There was frustration at the outcome of the prosecutions of Whittamore and others and it recommended tougher legislation to allow custodial sentences for DPA breaches.

The report noted the scale of Whittamore's work:

> In just one week in 2001, for instance, a named journalist on the news desk of a Sunday newspaper was billed for 13 occupant searches, two vehicle checks, one area search and two company searches, making a total bill of £707.50 plus £123.81 VAT. The following January, the Hampshire detective paid one of his company associates £1,540.00 for 22 vehicle checks at £70 a time. These would have netted him a profit of £1,760.

It added: 'This mass of evidence documented literally thousands of Section 55 offences [of the DPA] and added many more identifiable reporters supplied with information, bringing the total to some 305 named journalists.'[19]

It emerged only later why no journalists were ever prosecuted and only seven interviewed. The 2012 Leveson Report noted: 'DCI Gilmour [the investigating officer from Operation Motorman] said that it was specifically put to them that, by their very nature, details of convictions must have been obtained unlawfully. The journalists simply pleaded ignorance.'[20] The Crown Prosecution Service (CPS) declined to prosecute any of them because of the difficulty of proving the case, about which the inquiry noted that 'some may argue [this] appears overcautious,'[21] adding as a crucial footnote: 'It seems remarkable that notwithstanding all that has been written about criminal records over the years, the journalists all misunderstood the meaning of the acronym "CRO" or believed that a search of court records could have been accomplished within the time of the response.'[22]

In his evidence to Leveson, Alec Owens claimed the idea that the IOC was deterred by the relative failure of the Whittamore prosecutions and the lack of evidence that journalists knew the information was obtained illegally was 'inaccurate and misleading' and that he had been instructed by Richard Thomas, his boss, not to pursue any inquiries into individual journalists and newspapers.[23] One investigator later told *The Independent*: 'It was fear – they were frightened.' And John Whittingdale, chairman of the Culture, Media and Sport committee, said:

There was an absolute lack of any wish on the part of the police or the ICO or those looking into it to start delving into the prosecution of newspapers and journalists. [The ICO] took a list of hundreds and hundreds of journalists' names. Yes, there's a public interest defence but they didn't even bother to go and ask whether that was what they employed Whittamore for.[24]

There was a similar pattern to the investigations into Mulcaire and Goodman. The prosecution was limited to eight cases: the calls involving three members of the royal household plus a handful of other easily provable cases where there was clear evidence of a message being left and it being intercepted before it was accessed by the recipient. Dozens of other potential cases were not pursued and not made public. Only those who fell into the 'national security' category – the royal household, police, MPs and so on – were told they had been hacked. In all other cases, it was left to the telephone companies to contact individuals. Many didn't know their phones had been hacked until much later. Goodman and Mulcaire were charged with a joint offence of conspiracy to intercept communications and then a further sample selection of 21 individual counts showing the unlawful conduct of the two defendants against specific victims, in total involving more than six hundred messages. These were the Prince of Wales's aide Helen Asprey, Jamie Lowther-Pinkerton, private secretary to princes William and Harry, and Charles's communications secretary Paddy Harverson. Mulcaire admitted intercepting messages for Max Clifford, football agent Skylet Andrew, Lib Dem MP Simon Hughes and model Elle Macpherson. They both pleaded guilty and in January 2007 were sentenced to four and six months in prison respectively. And that seemed to be that.

While only the tip of the iceberg had been revealed, at Wapping it was clear that Coulson needed to fall on his sword:

> I have decided that the time has come for me to take ultimate responsibility for the events around the Clive Goodman case. As I've said before, his actions were entirely wrong and I deeply regret that they happened on my watch. I also feel strongly that when the *News of the World* calls those in public life to account on behalf of its readers, it must have its own house in order.

He was replaced by Colin Myler, editor of the *Daily* and *Sunday Mirror* during the 1990s. (A second spell by Myler at the *Sunday Mirror* had ended when he was forced to resign after publishing a story which prejudiced the high-profile assault trial of two Leeds United footballers, leading to the collapse of the case at a cost of £8 million.) Rupert Murdoch subsequently made him editor of the *New York Post*. Les Hinton, the chief executive of News International, told the House of Commons Select Committee on Culture, Media and Sport that he believed Goodman was the only person on the paper who knew about hacking. Myler would tell the Press Complaints Commission that he had established that Goodman was a 'rogue exception' and the PCC, after a very limited inquiry, expressed confidence that the practice had not extended beyond Goodman and Mulcaire. The line had been drawn – it was, all agreed, down to 'one rogue reporter'.

It was clearly hoped that Coulson's resignation and the continued depiction of Goodman as a rogue reporter would be enough to keep a lid on the affair. But it could never last when so many questions remained: how could the police restrict the prosecutions to Goodman when there were dozens of other inquiries relating to non-royal stories, such as those to which Mulcaire had admitted? Could Mulcaire have operated without anyone at Wapping authorizing the expenditure or realizing what was taking place? He had been paid substantial amounts – who signed off the accounts? In December 2006, just as the Goodman/Mulcaire case was nearing court, the ICO, clearly frustrated at its own failure to bring sufficient attention to the issue, published a second report, 'What Price Privacy Now?', aimed at documenting responses to its earlier report, but also adding more information and adding that there was a 'pressing need' for prison sentences for the most serious infringements of the Data Protection Act because other deterrents 'have not worked'. For the first time it made public a list of Whittamore's customers: the *Daily Mail* was the newspaper making most use of Whittamore, with 58 different journalists making a total of 952 transactions; next came the *Sunday People*, with 802 transactions by 50 journalists, the *Daily Mirror* with 681 transactions by 45 journalists, the *Mail on Sunday* with 266 from 33 journalists and the *News of the World* with 228 by 23 journalists. Of the broadsheet newspapers, *The Observer* was top of the list with 103 transactions by four journalists; there were four transactions by one journalist at the *Sunday Times* and two by one journalist at *The Times*.[25] Richard Thomas, the Information Commissioner, would later tell the Leveson Inquiry there were no obvious examples of cases where a public interest defence might be invoked to explain deception techniques: 'I haven't seen a whiff of public interest. It was tittle-tattle. It was fishing.'[26]

The report also said that the media had objected to the idea that all the transactions were fishing expeditions and had argued for an extension to public interest. The IOC also noted, with some irony:

With some journalists implicated as 'buyers' in the report, the Information Commissioner wondered whether some media groups might avoid reporting the story. To a certain extent this proved to be the case as coverage even in the broadsheets at the time of publication was limited. However, all broadsheets featured details of the report on their websites.[27]

None of the tabloids did, which was not unusual. The convictions of Mulcaire and Goodman and the resignation of Coulson the following month were reported in the broadsheets, with some brief mentions in the tabloids, but it was not front-page material and the public, by and large, were left uninformed,

The IOC report had hit on something. It was certainly true that the broadsheets would be more likely to report, usually in a carefully balanced way, on the misbehaviour of the tabloids, while the tabloids would only very occasionally publicly spar with each other, as *The Sun* and *The Mirror* had done over coverage of the Falklands. Underlying this reluctance to criticize each other openly and strongly were a number of overlapping factors. First, there was the instinctive solidarity of participants in a relatively small world – journalists knew each other and had worked with or knew those under fire, even if they did not approve of their methods or the papers for which they worked. Second, there was reluctance to shine a bad light on their profession since the public would always lump all journalists together in one basket. And at the back of their minds was the famous injunction from St John's Gospel: 'He that is without sin among you, let him first cast a stone' (John 8:7). And as Nick Davies wrote in the first line of the introduction to his 2008 book *Flat Earth News*: 'Dog doesn't eat dog. That's always been the rule in Fleet Street. We dig into the world of politics and finance and sport and entertainment. We dig wherever we like – but not in our own back garden.'[28] And who had never jazzed up a quote, put a firm foot in a doorway or bought a police officer a few drinks in return for a little information? But although Davies was determined to be the dog that *did* eat the other dogs, he was not at that point able to report fully on the wider aspects of the 'dark arts'. Neither was he yet aware of the full extent of what was going on.

Then another case where the tabloids got it horribly wrong ended up in court. In early May 2007 a British girl, Madeleine McCann, aged three, had disappeared from her bedroom one evening while on holiday with her parents in Portugal. The British media descended in droves; images of her face dominated the papers for months. The lack of developments allowed speculation to run wild; it went into overdrive when the Portuguese police wrongly named her parents as suspects based on inaccurate DNA results. The tabloids indulged in speculation, fuelled by rumours circulating on then nascent social media platform Twitter. The *Express*, in particular, driven by its editor, Peter Hills, led the way in insinuating the guilt of the parents. Its headlines included speculation that Madeleine had been 'killed by sleeping pills' (supposedly given to allow the parents to eat dinner close by with their friends): 'Find Body or McCanns Will Escape' and 'McCanns or a Friend Must Be to Blame'. A headline in the *Daily Star* read: 'Maddie "Sold" By Hard-Up McCanns'.

The McCanns were not the kind of people to ignore the stories. In March 2008 they accepted £550,000 in damages plus costs and an apology in the High Court from Express Newspapers for 'utterly false and defamatory' stories. Their lawyer said that between summer 2007 and February 2008, the *Express* and *Star* titles had published more than a hundred articles that were defamatory, including ones which suggested they had been responsible for their daughter's death and/or that she had been sold for money, and that the couple were engaged in wife swapping and swinging.[29] In July that year, Robert Murat, a Portuguese property consultant, and two associates received an estimated total of £800,000 from Express Newspapers, the *Daily Mail*, the London *Evening Standard*, the *Daily Mirror*, the *Sunday Mirror*, the *Daily Record*, *The Sun* and the *News of the World* for false stories linking them to the disappearance. Sky News later paid a similar sum.[30]

But the payments did not deter the *News of the World*. In September 2008 the paper apologized a week after publishing extracts from Kate McCann's diaries and said: 'We published the extracts in the belief held in good faith that we had Kate's permission to do so. It is now clear that our belief was misplaced, and that in fact Kate neither approved of nor knew that the extracts were to be published.'[31] The following month, the friends who had been with the McCanns on holiday received £350,000 from Express Newspapers over suggestions they had lied over the circumstances of the disappearance.[32]

Brian Cathcart, then professor of journalism at Kingston University, wrote in the *New Statesman*:

> [The] McCann case was the greatest scandal in our news media in at least a decade . . . Error on this scale, involving hundreds of completely untrue news reports, published on front pages month after month in the teeth of desperate denials, can only be systemic. Judging by what appeared in print, it involved a reckless neglect of ethical standards, a persistent failure to apply even the most basic journalistic rigour, and plenty of plain cruelty.[33]

But even Cathcart did not fully realize at the time that an even bigger scandal was brewing.

Amid the mounting scrutiny of the tabloids, politicians were still happy to maintain close relations with Murdoch. Despite his ignominious exit from Wapping, Coulson had become communications chief to David Cameron, the new young leader of the Conservative Party, who was seen as a serious challenger to the rather stolid Gordon Brown. Labour seemed stale after so many years in office. Matthew Freud, the public relations executive then married to Murdoch's daughter, Elizabeth, arranged with Coulson for Cameron to be flown by private jet to lunch with Murdoch on his yacht, and to subject himself to scrutiny as Blair had once done. By now, Wade had parted from Kemp and was in a relationship with Charlie Brooks, a wealthy racehorse trainer. They lived near Chipping Norton in the Cotswolds, and were part of a fashionable set that included Cameron, Freud and other media and political figures. In June 2009 the wedding of Wade and Brooks was attended by both the bride's current political best friends, Cameron and Brown, as well as Murdoch. It was as though all was well, in all their worlds.

The Dam Breaks

The dam finally broke on 8 July 2009. After some diligent research, Nick Davies was able to reveal in *The Guardian* that News International had paid out more than £1 million to settle three legal actions over phone hacking by private investigators, suggesting that the extent of the activity was much wider than the 'one rogue reporter' stance, with potentially hundreds of victims. The story posted on *The Guardian*'s website that afternoon, head-lined 'Murdoch Papers Paid £1m to Gag Phone-Hacking Victims', would set off a chain of events that would lead directly to the clos-ure of the *News of the World* and the Leveson Inquiry – and is still reverberating even as this book goes to print.

The story said that one of the actions involved Gordon Taylor, chief executive of the Professional Footballers Association, who was paid around £400,000 to settle his damages claim; money was also paid to two associates of his. The payments, said the report by Davies, secured secrecy over out-of-court settlements in the three cases that had threatened to expose evidence of Murdoch jour-nalists using private investigators to illegally hack into the mobile phones of numerous public figures as well as to gain unlawful access to confidential data, such as bank statements. Cabinet ministers, MPs, actors and sports stars were all targets, said the story. Davies quoted police sources saying that there were potentially thousands of victims. He added that Andy Coulson, now director of commu-nications for David Cameron, 'was deputy editor and then editor of the *News of the World* when, the suppressed evidence shows, jour-nalists for whom he was responsible were engaging in hundreds of apparently illegal acts'. The story claimed that, albeit in good faith, the Murdoch executives had misled a parliamentary committee, the Press Complaints Commission and the public. It also said that there were now questions to ask about why the Metropolitan Police had not alerted all those who they believed had had their phones tar-geted and why the CPS had not pursued all possible charges against News Group personnel. Further stories that day gave more details of the activities of Mulcaire and Whittamore and claimed that those targeted included deputy Labour Party leader John Prescott, rock star George Michael and actor Gwyneth Paltrow. Prior to publica-tion, the News International press office had assured Davies, who had asked generally about payments, that there was no truth in the suggestions; after publication, there was no comment. In New York, Murdoch told a TV reporter that it was unlikely to have happened, because he would have known about it if it had occurred. To show his own faith in Wade, now known as Brooks after her marriage, a few weeks later Murdoch promoted her to chief executive of News

International. She was replaced as editor of *The Sun* by Dominic Mohan, another former showbusiness reporter.

In the wake of the Davies story, Scotland Yard ordered a review of the original case, carried out by the highly respected Assistant Commissioner John Yates. To some astonishment, Yates swiftly declared that the number of people hacked was 'a handful' and there was no reason to reopen the inquiry. He later told the House of Commons Culture, Media and Sport Committee that the review had focused only on the eight cases brought to court in 2006 and did not examine the rest of the evidence seized from Mulcaire. In its report the committee criticized him for not pursuing evidence that suggested a wider inquiry was needed.[34] During this period, Neil Wallis, who had left the *News of the World*, was a paid advisor to Yates and Sir Paul Stephenson, the Metropolitan Police Commissioner. The committee added that it was 'inconceivable' that no one other than Goodman knew about the extent of phone hacking at the paper, and that the committee had 'repeatedly encountered an unwillingness to provide the detailed information that we sought, claims of ignorance or lack of recall and deliberate obfuscation'.[35]

Pressure was building. There was concern among MPs and those who believed they had been affected by hacking and that the full

Max Clifford reading from a statement outside Belgravia police station after he was arrested for sexual offences, 6 December 2012.

extent of Mulcaire's activities had not been investigated thoroughly enough by police and the CPS. There was puzzlement over why the CPS had advised police that phone hacking was only illegal in cases where a message was intercepted before its intended recipient had heard it. Davies spoke to former reporters who told him it was inconceivable Coulson had not known what was going on.[36] He spoke to politicians who he knew had been hacked – leading Labour figures such as Charles Clarke, Tessa Jowell and David Blunkett – none of whom wanted to pursue legal actions against News International (by that time Blunkett had a regular column in *The Sun*). Further investigations by Davies and *The Guardian* disclosed in February 2010 that there were potentially more than a hundred victims – not all of whom had been notified by either police or phone companies. Shortly afterwards, Davies also revealed that News International, which continued to deny the wider extent of hacking, had paid Max Clifford, with whom they had been close but had fallen out, around £1 million to settle his hacking damages case against them.[37] The deal was personally negotiated by Rebekah Brooks, she admitted later, to prevent any further public disclosures and to ensure his continued provision of stories.[38] (The deal did not last long. In 2012, Clifford was arrested over sexual offences against young women dating back to the 1970s and in April 2014 he was convicted of eight counts of indecent assault and sentenced to eight years in prison. He died from a heart attack in 2017 while still serving his sentence.)

While the rest of UK media had been slow to follow, in September 2010 the *New York Times*, briefed by Davies, reported on the hacking issue, quoting former *News of the World* reporters who admitted hacking involvement, including former showbusiness reporter Sean Hoare, who said Coulson had 'actively encouraged' him to do it. Sharon Marshall, author of *Tabloid Girl*, repeated a claim that 'It was an industry wide thing,' although no one would acknowledge it publicly.[39]

At the same time, a series of legal actions, mainly by celebrities and others in the public eye who believed they were victims of hacking, were making their way through the courts, all of which involved potentially difficult disclosure requests to News International and the Metropolitan Police. In December 2010 it emerged in these court hearings that Ian Edmondson, *News of the World* news editor under Coulson, had commissioned the hacking of the voicemails of

Sky Andrews – one of the original victims named in the Goodman case – and those of actors Sienna Miller and Jude Law and that Greg Miskiw, news editor when Coulson was deputy editor, was linked to Mulcaire's hacking of former footballer and television commentator Andy Gray. Early in January, Coulson, by now the prime minister's communications chief at Downing Street, resigned again. Edmondson was suspended and the CPS announced a review of its evidence. At the end of the month, the Metropolitan Police gave in: a whole new investigation would begin, codenamed Operation Weeting. Officers would start examining the Mulcaire files: 11,000 pages, around 3,800 names. All previous investigations would be reviewed. The dam had burst and the waters would engulf many figures on Planet Tabloid. Some would drown while others would survive, clinging desperately to the wreckage. Many would escape as though not much had happened.

11

LEVESON

The activities of British tabloid journalists and the lawless landscape they had inhabited over the previous decades would now be subjected to the full rigour of the law and unprecedented public scrutiny. And what the public saw was not pretty or edifying. More and more celebrities and others in the public eye lodged claims against News International, which admitted liability in eight cases, including those of Sienna Miller, designer Kelly Hoppen (Miller's stepmother), former footballer turned commentator Andy Gray and Labour politician Tessa Jowell, offering apologies and compensation. Many such victims now backed a new pressure group, Hacked Off, fronted by actor Hugh Grant, which was formed in alliance with campaigners for greater oversight of the media and ownership. In April 2010 Ian Edmondson, Neville Thurlbeck and James Weatherup, an assistant news editor of the *News of the World*, were all questioned by police.

In July Davies reported in *The Guardian* that Mulcaire had hacked into voicemails left on the phone of missing schoolgirl Milly Dowler, who had disappeared in 2002 (and was later found to have been murdered by serial killer Levi Bellfield). There was an immediate furore and further demands for more inquiries into the newspaper. A few days later, it was reported that Mulcaire might have hacked the voicemails of relatives of British soldiers killed in Iraq and Afghanistan,[1] as well as relatives of the victims of the 7/7 terrorist attacks of 2005.[2] The Royal British Legion announced it was severing all ties with the *News of the World*, while many advertisers withdrew their custom, which directly affected Murdoch's income.

The Dowler story was the last straw. Public and political pressure on News International became immense. Prime minister David Cameron announced that he would finally bow to widespread demands for a public inquiry; it would be chaired by a leading judge, Lord Justice Leveson, and would examine the culture and practices of the British press, the most significant ever such inquiry into newspapers. And then, on 7 July, News International announced that, after 168 years of publication and a long reign as Britain's most-read newspaper, immortalized by George Orwell, the *News of the World* would close after the following weekend's edition. No advertising would be sold and all sales donated to charity. Murdoch knew when to cut his losses. It was a brutally decisive, commercially driven decision. When a limb is gangrenous, sever it. But, in Murdoch's case, you can replace it with something similar, so as not to lose that market and to minimize some of the redundancy payments – he announced a new edition of his biggest-selling newspaper, which predictably would be called *The Sun on Sunday*.

The hacking controversy also put paid to his attempt to buy full control of the money-making BSkyB empire, in which he had only ever had a partial stake. After Cameron, backed by all the News International titles (which had always criticized the BBC at every opportunity), succeeded Brown in spring 2010 (albeit in a coalition with the Lib Dems) Murdoch had put in a bid for full control of BSkyB. Culture secretary Jeremy Hunt – who had allowed a special advisor to open up a back channel to Murdoch while he considered whether the bid infringed monopolies legislation – was about to approve the deal. In the aftermath of the *News of the World* closure, Murdoch withdrew the bid.

The walls came tumbling down. Over the following days, Coulson, Goodman and Wallis were arrested; Brooks, Tom Crone, the *News of the World*'s legal manager, and Les Hinton, former chief executive of News International, all resigned; Brooks was arrested two days later. Sir Paul Stephenson, the Metropolitan Police Commissioner, and Assistant Commissioner Yates both resigned. On 10 July the last edition of the *News of the World* was published with the front page headline: 'Thank You and Goodbye'.

Summoned by the Culture, Media and Sport committee, Rupert Murdoch and his son James appeared before MPs nine days later. Murdoch described it as 'the most humble day of my life' but denied responsibility for the *News of the World*'s illegal activities and said he had not considered resigning. His son also denied knowledge of phone hacking and other activities and said the company was determined to 'put things right'. Towards the end of the hearing, a protestor from the public gallery threw a shaving-foam pie into Murdoch Sr's face.[3] Later, it emerged that when the committee had begun inquiries into hacking in 2009, the *News of the World* had assembled a task force to investigate its members. Thurlbeck later told Labour's Tom Watson, a member of the committee:

> There was an edict came down from the editor and it was find out every single thing you can about every single member: who was gay, who had affairs, anything we can use. Each reporter was given two members and there were six reporters that went on for around 10 days. I don't know who looked at you. It fell by the wayside; I think even Ian Edmondson [the news editor] realised there was something quite horrible about doing this.[4]

Other investigations were now launched by bodies that should have been the first to investigate the hacking but for various reasons had not done so. The Metropolitan Police began Operation Tuleta into computer hacking and Operation Elveden into potential bribery and corruption within the force itself. There were fresh inquiries launched by the Home Affairs Select Committee, the Press Complaints Commission and the Independent Police Complaints Commission (IPCC). Baroness Buscombe, chair of the PCC, stated bluntly that the body had been deliberately misled by the *News of the World* when it had launched an inquiry in the wake of Davies's original 2009 story and that its own statement at the time was incorrect.[5]

The shockwaves were spreading far and wide, with inquiries threatening not just Murdoch's empire and its journalists but the highest echelons of the Metropolitan Police and government, revealing a series of cross-connections and relationships that many felt too close for democratic accountability. One media company had, it seemed, managed to insinuate itself into the most senior levels of the police and the political establishment, entirely for its own commercial ends.

The IPCC launched a series of inquiries into the Met, looking at the relationship between its high command and the *News of the World*. This included the role of former Assistant Commissioner Andy Hayman, who had been in charge of the first, limited hacking inquiries but had resigned in 2007 over dubious expenses claims and a relationship with a member of the IPCC; shortly after his resignation, he began writing a column for *The Times*. Hayman had enjoyed lunches and dinners with Coulson and Neil Wallis at the height of the inquiry. The Home Affairs Select Committee concluded his conduct was 'both unprofessional and inappropriate'. The committee's report said: 'Andy Hayman's cavalier attitude towards his contacts with those in News International who were under investigation . . . even if entirely above board, risked seriously undermining confidence in the impartiality of the police,' and accused him of deliberate prevarication in order to mislead the committee.[6]

The relationship between Sir Paul Stephenson, John Yates and Neil Wallis was also scrutinized: the Met had employed Wallis's media relations company between 2009 and 2010, and Sir Paul had stayed at a health resort also represented by Wallis. Also under investigation was the employment of Wallis's daughter Amy in a civilian role within the Met, and the role of the director of public affairs for the Met, Dick Fedorcio. Fedorcio was put on extended leave in August 2011 and resigned the following year after being charged with gross misconduct.

The Leveson Inquiry

The Leveson Inquiry into the Culture, Practices and Ethics of the Press began public hearings at the Royal Courts of Justice in November 2011. Streamed online and frequently televised, the inquiry became must-see viewing for journalists, MPs, lawyers and the public. It would hear from more than 330 witnesses and receive a further three hundred statements. It was charged with uncovering the extent of illegal activities within the media, the relationship between the press and politicians, and the effectiveness of media regulation. It took evidence from a wide range of individuals, including journalists, politicians and victims of phone hacking. The judge was assisted by a number of advisors, including Shami Chakrabarti, director the civil rights group Liberty, Elinor Goodman, former political editor of Channel 4 news, and Sir Paul Scott-Lee, former Chief Constable of the West Midlands Police.

Brooks, who did not give evidence until May the following year, had been arrested again on suspicion of conspiracy to pervert the course of justice, so the questions she faced were constrained by potential contempt of court issues. She had, she said, a number of supportive messages from government ministers when she left News International, including one from Cameron along the lines of 'keep your head up', and from Blair – but not from Brown. She denied subterfuge or hacking to obtain the story that Brown's son Fraser suffered from cystic fibrosis and claimed she had express permission from the Browns to run the story.[7] The Browns said this was 'untrue'.[8] She had met Blair, she said, at least thirty times during his period in office between 1998 and 2007 – including three dinners with him alone – and exchanged texts with Cameron regularly, although she denied it was several times a day.

When Cameron later gave evidence, the closeness of the relationship between him and Brooks – and her husband, with whom he had been at Eton – became clear in one particularly embarrassing text she sent him on the eve of his debut speech as leader to the Tory party conference in October 2009. It referred to them enjoying what she termed 'country suppers' together – their Cotswold homes were close – and went on: 'I am so rooting for you tomorrow not just as a proud friend but because professionally we're definitely in this together! Speech of your life? Yes he Cam.' That last phrase was *The Sun*'s headline the day after the speech. The inquiry also heard that Cameron routinely signed his texts to Brooks 'Lol', which he believed to mean 'Lots of love' rather than the more well-known version as 'Laugh out loud'. Cameron admitted he had met Rupert Murdoch at least ten times, James Murdoch fifteen times and Brooks nineteen times, estimating that they met every six weeks during their weekends in the country. The prime minister admitted that hiring Coulson had been a 'controversial appointment' that had 'come back to haunt both him and me' but said he had been assured Coulson had no knowledge of phone hacking.[9]

Not since the intimate friendship David Lloyd George cultivated with George Riddell, chairman of the *News of the World*, at the beginning of the last century, had there been such closeness between politicians and what was now the biggest media concern in the UK and, indeed, in the world. Some were both shocked and amused: 'The [country suppers] phrase is delicious,' wrote commentator Jonathan Freedland in *The Guardian*,

> concisely capturing the entire culture and chumminess of the Chipping Norton set, its elite habits and its remoteness from the way most people are living in austerity Britain . . . it shows just how close Cameron and the Murdoch chief executive were – and what a rarefied, monied bubble they both inhabited . . . it shows Cameron as exceptionally close to the top echelon of a corporate empire, permanently mindful of its concerns. No wonder he squirmed as it was read out.[10]

Blair described his relationship with Murdoch as a 'working one' but not, he stressed, personal, and conceded that they had met many times, although he maintained he had never changed a policy to specifically benefit Murdoch or his business interests. In his statement, he said: 'Rupert Murdoch never lobbied me for special favours. What he did do was argue strongly with me about politics. He has decided views. On some issues, I agreed and on some I disagreed.'[11]

But to portray the relationship as purely a business one was disingenuous. Shortly after her Leveson appearance, Brooks, her husband and others were charged with conspiring to pervert the course of justice; at her trial in 2014 it emerged that, just before her first arrest in July 2011, she had an hour-long conversation with Blair, now long out of daily politics, who had offered to act as an unofficial advisor to her, Murdoch and his son James on how to deal with the scandal.[12] And Blair was, of course, godfather to Murdoch's daughter Grace.

And there was another intriguing twist. Just before the Brooks trial disclosure, the magazine *Vanity Fair* had reported that Murdoch had divorced his wife of fourteen years, Wendi Deng, because of rumours of her infidelity and her close relationship to Blair, who had become a frequent visitor to Murdoch properties in the USA and had, it was said, stayed overnight when her husband was absent. The story quoted messages from Deng eulogizing Blair's 'good legs, good body . . . and piercing blue eyes'. The implication was that they had been having an affair, a claim strongly denied by both sides. But it was, as *Vanity Fair* noted, a story that could have come right out of one of Murdoch's tabloids, full of sex, lies, power and money.[13]

But the closeness of the politicians to the Murdoch hierarchy only mirrored the devastation that hacking and other activities visited on lesser mortals. The accounts and evidence of those who had been the victims of hacking or other intrusive practices and breaches of privacy were fundamental to the inquiry. Sally and Bob Dowler, the parents of murdered schoolgirl Milly, described how deleted voicemails had given them hope by suggesting she was still alive.[14] However, contrary to Davies's original story, police had by now established that while the phone had been hacked, the messages had not been deleted by journalists.

Actor Hugh Grant accused the *Mail on Sunday* of using information from phone hacking for stories about his relationship with Jemima Khan; in his evidence, Paul Dacre accused Grant of 'mendacious smears' and rejected Grant's claim that Mulcaire had spent 30 per cent of his time working for Associated Newspapers, saying that there were no records to support this.[15] Grant refused to back down, and the issue was never resolved.[16]

Kate and Gerry McCann told how they felt newspapers had declared 'open season' on them when Madeleine vanished. Gerry McCann said:

> The press can write whatever they like about you without punishment. There are standards but there are no penalties for not sticking to them. I see front page headlines every day ... and I think information is being written and lives are being harmed by these stories and something has to change. The commercial imperative is not acceptable.

His wife said she felt 'totally violated' when the *News of the World* published parts of her personal diaries, which appeared to have been leaked by the Portuguese police.[17] One author of some of the *Daily Express* stories, reporter Nick Fagge, by then working for the *Daily Mail*, later gave evidence that *Daily Express* editor Peter Hill had been 'obsessed' with the McCann story, with stories being placed on the front page regardless of their merit. Lord Justice Leveson observed that stories such as those claiming Madeleine's body had been hidden in the spare-tyre well of a car or that Kate McCann had made a confession to a priest were 'piffle' and 'tittle-tattle'.[18]

The actor Sienna Miller, who had already won damages of £100,000 plus costs from News International, told the inquiry that notes from Glenn Mulcaire included all the mobile numbers she had changed over three months, PINs for her voicemail access and the password for her email, which was later used to hack her computer in 2008. There were also 'about 10 numbers' of friends and family. 'There was one particular very private piece of information that only four people knew about. A journalist phoned up saying they knew about it so I accused my family . . . of selling the story,' Miller said. 'It made me really angry and I felt terrible that I would even accuse people of betraying me like that . . . but it seemed so intensely paranoid [to think] that your house is being bugged. It's really upsetting for them and myself that I accused them.'[19]

The actor and comedian Steve Coogan, who had become a campaigner for press regulation, spoke at length. He described one alleged incident as 'a dispassionate sociopathic act by those who operate in an amoral universe where they are never accountable'. As the victim of several kiss and tell stories he claimed the women in question had been fooled and bribed into giving stories to newspapers. He gave detailed evidence of intrusive stalking and photographing by the *Daily Mirror* and the *Sunday Times* and claimed he had witnessed journalists searching through his rubbish bins. He said victims were deterred from pursuing claims of redress out of fear of renewed exposure and costs.[20]

The Press Complaints Commission was criticized by many witnesses for its ineffectiveness in holding the media accountable and its lack of independence – Dacre had been a member between 1999 and 2008 and currently chaired the Editors' Code Committee, which laid out the code of conduct for journalism over respecting privacy and intrusion, which critics argued was routinely breached. Dacre was among a number of editors and proprietors who gave evidence, all of whom denied knowledge of hacking or intrusive practices, which they condemned, while maintaining the right to hold public figures – pop stars, royalty, politicians – to account. Dacre argued that the press was already in danger of being 'over regulated'.[21]

Piers Morgan, now with his own talk show on CNN in the USA, summed up the approach: 'I have very little sympathy with celebrities who sell their weddings for a million pounds – one of the most private days of their lives – and then expect to have privacy if they get caught having affairs.' So far as hacking was concerned, he had heard rumours that it was rife – everyone had, he said – but said he had never done it or ordered it himself during his periods as editor of the *News of the World* or the *Mirror*. He did repeat his admission that he listened to a tape of a voicemail message left by Sir Paul McCartney for his estranged wife Heather Mills. But he could not disclose any further details as it would compromise a source.[22]

In one of the most eagerly awaited testimonies, Murdoch told the inquiry that he had never asked a prime minister for any favours, and meetings, particularly with Cameron, had often been social occasions. He could not recall the meeting on his yacht. Hacking or using private detectives was just reporters being lazy and he always expected his staff to behave in an ethical fashion. He distanced himself from the *News of the World*, a newspaper he had owned for forty years: 'I never much interfered with it.' If anyone wanted to know what he was thinking, 'look at *The Sun*.' He also upheld the principle that anyone in the public eye was fair game: 'I think it is fair when people have themselves held up as iconic figures or great actors that they be looked at.' Public figures were not entitled to the same privacy 'as the man in the street'.[23] And so it went on.

The inquiry's conclusions, when the full report was published in November 2012, were scathing. Hacking, Lord Justice Leveson decided, was widespread: 'The evidence drives me to conclude that this was far more than a covert, secret activity, known to nobody save one or two practitioners of the "dark arts".' But it was not just about illegal hacking; the overall 'recklessness' in pursuing stories had been 'devastating' to those such as the Dowlers and the McCanns. In the latter case the reporting had been 'outrageous' and some newspapers were guilty of 'gross libels'. And he did not accept that those in the public eye must expect to have their private lives scrutinized; the approach to privacy was 'too casual' and in some cases their families had been pursued and their personal moments 'destroyed'. The report was damning for the Metropolitan Police, who were guilty of 'poor decisions, poorly executed' – particularly those taken during the crucial period between 2006 and 2010, including the decision not to reopen the hacking inquiry after Davies's first stories in 2009, which was 'insufficiently thought through . . . wrong and unduly defensive'. The force's reputation had been damaged by the lavish hospitality its senior officers had enjoyed at the hands of News International. Yates, in particular, should have recused himself from the hacking inquiries because of his friendship with Neil Wallis. But Leveson found no evidence that decisions to limit the hacking inquiry were due to 'undue influence or corruption'.

A second part of the inquiry was due to examine in closer detail the relationship between the media and the police; it had been put on hold because of the need not to prejudice any upcoming trials of journalists on hacking or related charges, including bribing public officials. It never happened.

Demands by newspapers to be trusted with self-regulation were rejected by Leveson, who said they smacked of self-interest. He had heard much evidence to confirm that the Press Complaints Commission was a toothless beast. He recommended the creation of a strong, new, independent body, free from influence from the media or government, that would have the power to investigate serious breaches of the editors' code of conduct and fine newspapers up to £1 million. Legislation should allow for an independent regulator to be organized by the industry, but it 'should also place an explicit [legal] duty on the government to uphold and protect the freedom of the press', backed by a Royal Charter. There should also be a system of arbitration for civil legal claims against published stories.[24] Again, this never happened.

While the Leveson Inquiry was a cathartic, historic moment, allowing the victims of unlawful and unethical press behaviour an opportunity to express their hurt and anger and watch as journalists and proprietors were forced to defend themselves in the full public glare, in hindsight it failed in two of its key objectives: it was not followed by a system of effective oversight and it was prevented from conducting a more in-depth inquiry into press–police relations. Both of these outcomes were the responsibility of the government.

The newspaper industry as a whole rejected Leveson's recommendation for statutory regulation, arguing that it would threaten the independence of the media, potentially leading to government interference and curbing investigative journalism. Victims and campaign groups such as Hacked Off and the Campaign for Media Reform contended that statutory underpinning was necessary to prevent future abuses and protect individuals' privacy. There was a stalemate. The Royal Charter, created by the Privy Council, was condemned as 'deeply illiberal' by the industry, but the High Court rejected the industry's alternative proposals, drawn up by an alliance led by News International, Associated Newspapers, the Telegraph group and others. These groups then established a new, independent regulator to succeed the PCC, which had been disbanded. Even before the Independent Press Standards Organisation (IPSO), not backed by the Royal Charter or the government, came into existence, the Media Standards Trust said that its plans 'fell far short' of Leveson's recommendations, particularly in relation to speedy resolution of complaints, fair redress and the ability to impose sanctions on publishers.[25]

While those behind IPSO stressed it was established to maintain a tighter and more effective way of dealing with complaints and many of its board members were experienced professionals from outside the industry, there were also a number of former senior journalists, including those who had worked on tabloids. At time of writing, the bulk of the industry – national and local newspapers and magazines – are members of IPSO. Some, such as *The Guardian* and the *Financial Times*, stayed outside and established their own internal mechanisms for dealing with complaints.[26]

The Trials

While the industry argued among itself – the liberal newspapers such as *The Guardian* on one side and most of the rest of the industry on the other – and with the government over the future of press regulation, the police continued investigating journalists for the sins of the past. Many journalists and others were arrested, charged and tried. The biggest trial, a seven-month-long marathon starting in October 2013, was that of Brooks, Coulson and other key figures. In the dock alongside them stood Brooks's husband, Charlie, Cheryl Carter, his wife's former personal assistant, and Mark Hanna, the former head of security at News International, all charged with conspiracy to pervert the course of justice – involving allegations they had sought to dispose of potentially incriminating computers and documents. Also charged were Ian Edmundson (his case was later postponed because he was ill), Clive Goodman and Stuart Kuttner. At the start, Glenn Mulcaire, Neville Thurlbeck,

James Weatherup and Greg Miskiw all pleaded guilty to various phone-hacking-related offences.

Brooks and Coulson, who the jury were told at the outset had been on/off lovers for some of the time under consideration, were both charged with phone-hacking-related offences; their considerable defence costs were funded by Murdoch.

The evidence against Brooks was circumstantial. There was no direct evidence to link her to hacking: paperwork had been lost in the passage of time since 2003, as had the hard drive from her computer. Millions of emails had been deleted from the News International system. And the prosecution was unable to link her to the hacking of the voicemails of Milly Dowler, largely because she had been out of the country at the time. Brooks, her husband, Carter and Hanna were cleared while Stuart Kuttner, former *News of the World* managing editor, was found not guilty of conspiracy to hack voicemails. Brooks was also cleared of paying a Ministry of Defence official for stories, a charge stemming from the Operation Elveden inquiry.

Nevertheless, there was a measure of vindication. Sitting together in the dock were four former *News of the World* journalists and one private investigator: Coulson was convicted of hacking conspiracy offences and jailed for eighteen months, former chief reporter Thurlbeck and Miskiw were both given six months, while former reporter Weatherup was given a four-month suspended sentence and Mulcaire six months suspended. Mulcaire and Weatherup were also each ordered to do two hundred hours of community service. After the jury failed to reach a verdict, a retrial was ordered of Coulson and Goodman on charges of conspiracy to commit misconduct in public office relating to the purchase of royal telephone directories from police officers, stemming from Operation Elveden. The cases were eventually dropped.

The conviction of Coulson followed evidence suggesting his closeness to the hacking operation, such as Mulcaire's copious notes during his editorship from 2003 to 2007, Coulson admitting that Thurlbeck had played some voice messages to him, relating to Home Secretary David Blunkett's affair with *Spectator* publisher Kimberly Quinn (police had found tapes of Blunkett's messages in Thurlbeck's safe), and the evidence of two former colleagues, showbusiness writer Dan Evans and Clive Goodman, who both claimed he knew about the hacking. Sentencing Coulson, Mr Justice

Saunders said Coulson's claims of ignorance of phone hacking were not mitigation and 'there was a very great deal of phone hacking' while he was editor. Coulson, who had been under 'considerable pressure' to deliver results as editor, had to take the 'major share of the blame' for hacking at the paper. The sentences, said Hacked Off, destroyed the idea that 'one rogue reporter' was responsible for phone hacking. 'We now know this was a lie. Far from being an isolated incident involving a few "bad apples", the trial has shown that the entire orchard was rotten. "The trial also shone a light on the appalling, systemic newsroom culture of bullying, lies, intimidation and intrusion that has devastated the lives of many people. From royalty and Cabinet ministers to victims of crime and bereaved families, nobody was safe."'[27]

Writing in *The Guardian*, Davies said Brooks and Coulson 'ruined lives'.

They did it to sell newspapers, to please Murdoch, to advance their own careers. One flick of their editorial pen was enough to break the boundaries of privacy and of compassion. The singer's mother suffering from depression; the actor stricken by the collapse of her marriage; the DJ in agony over his wife's affair: none of their pain was anything more than human raw material to be processed and packaged and sold for profit. Especially, obsessively if it involved their sexual activity.

With all the intellectual focus of a masturbatory adolescent, their papers spied in the bedrooms of their targets, dragging out and humiliating anybody who dared to be gay or to have an affair or to engage in any kind of sexual activity beyond that approved by a Victorian missionary. They did it to friends – like Blunkett, for example, sharing drinks and private chats with him and then ripping the heart out of his private life, sprinkling their story with fiction as they did so. And to Sarah Payne: befriended by Brooks in her campaign to change the law about publication of the home addresses of sex offenders; investigated by her paper on the false suspicion that she was having an affair with a detective.

Above all, wrote Davies, they did it to their enemies. 'Among the politicians who they exposed for being gay or for having affairs, the left-wingers easily outnumbered the occasional stray right-winger. In among them were the special enemies who dared to challenge News International.' They had targeted politicians who criticized Murdoch newspapers, such as Chris Huhne, the former home affairs spokesman for the Lib Dems, and Labour's Tom Watson, and they backed Cameron over Brown in the hope it would help Murdoch's bid for full control of BSkyB.

Davies noted the disparity between prosecution and defence: one funded by the public purse, with the bare minimum of lawyers, the other funded by Murdoch, with an army of the best-paid briefs in the land. He cited a 'striking example' of the impact of Murdoch's money:

> The evidence . . . at the core of the hacking scandal is the col-
> lection of notes found by detectives when they first arrested
> Mulcaire in August 2006: 11,000 pages of his barely legible
> scribble and scrawl and doodle. The original police inquiry
> took one look at it and decided it simply did not have the
> resources to go through it all. When Operation Weeting in
> 2011 finally did the job properly, it took it the best part of a
> year. Brooks's Rolls-Royce team did it in three months and
> then had the resources to produce a brilliant analysis.

Parts of that information were used to disprove some of the claims against Brooks.[28]

But the Brooks/Coulson trial was not the end of it. More than a hundred journalists, serving and retired police officers and other public officials and private investigators were questioned as a result of the Weeting, Tuleta and Elveden operations. More than thirty were charged with or pleaded guilty to offences including hacking and payments to public officials. Dan Evans, who had given evidence against Coulson, pleaded guilty to phone-hacking conspiracy, misconduct in public office and unauthorized access to computer material, for which he eventually received a ten-month suspended sentence. Although Neil Wallis had been arrested in July 2011, he was not charged with conspiracy to hack phones until 2014 and was cleared at his trial the following year. Wallis has since become a regular media commentator.

In November 2014 Ian Edmundson, former *News of the World* news editor and assistant editor, who had pleaded not guilty at

Rebekah Brooks giving evidence to the House of Commons Culture, Media and Sport Committee, July 2011.

the start of the Brooks trial but whose case was delayed by illness, changed his plea to guilty and was sentenced to eight months in prison for hacking offences committed over a six-year period; victims included Tessa Jowell and Labour deputy leader John Prescott. The Brooks trial heard that he was one of four news editors for whom Mulcaire had worked and Edmundson's name had been found on 334 pages of his notes.[29]

In July the following year, Jules Stenson, former features editor of the *News of the World*, was given a four-month suspended sentence and fined £5,000 plus £18,000 costs after pleading guilty to the same offences as Wallis; both charges were based on evidence given by Dan Evans. The court heard that Evans was ordered by Stenson to hack phones when he arrived from the *Sunday Mirror*, using both mobiles and the company landlines; records showed that in just one seven-month period in 2006, Evans had used company phones for hacking on 120 occasions. While Evans said Stenson had encouraged him, Stenson made it clear Coulson had been the driving force. Outside court, Stenson repeated earlier apologies to hacking victims, and apologized to the *News of the World* staff who had had their lives 'severely affected by the action that we, but primarily Andy Coulson, took'.[30]

Mr Justice Saunders was clear when he sentenced Stenson:

> Stenson's case, accepted by the prosecution, is that Mr Coulson was the driving force behind the recruitment of Dan Evans, who by his own admission, had been phone hacking at the *Sunday Mirror* before he went to the *News of the World*. Mr Stenson's case is that he allowed himself to be drawn into phone hacking because he was put under pressure to produce stories by Mr Coulson and he was driven to use illegal means in order to avoid the sack.[31]

While News International had admitted hacking took place at the *News of the World*, it had always rejected suggestions hacking had been practised at *The Sun*. But what was clear from Operation Elveden was that the *Sun* newsroom was happy to pay large amounts for stories to public officials, an illegal act. After a series of trials involving almost thirty journalists, mainly from *The Sun* but also from the *News of the World* and Mirror Group Newspapers, charges against several were dropped while others were cleared at trials or had their convictions overturned on appeal. They included *The Sun*'s head of news Chris Pharo, chief reporter John Kay and chief foreign correspondent Nick Parker, although the last was convicted of handling the stolen phone of an MP, a charge that related to the separate Operation Tuleta. All had claimed their actions were in the public interest and that it had always been the case that journalists bribed public officers, a fact supported by a number of media commentators. According to an Open Democracy analysis of the trials, these led to stories such as that Jamie Bulger murderer Jon Venables had a 36-inch TV in his cell, which could only really have come from those with inside knowledge:

> One Surrey police officer sold [*Sun*] reporter Jamie Pyatt three witness statements from a rape inquiry. A Broadmoor orderly, Robert Neave, sold the medical records of the

Yorkshire Ripper Peter Sutcliffe. A senior press officer in Her Majesty's Revenue and Customs, Jonathan Hall (paid a total of £17,000), sold details of the next day's budget to Whitehall correspondent Clodagh Hartley. A medium-ranking Ministry of Defence official, Bettina Jordan Barber, received £100,000 between 2004 and 2011 for stories about kit failures, the identity of soldiers killed in action and sexual misconduct cases …A Sandhurst instructor, Sergeant John Hardy, sold information on Princes William and Harry to [*Sun*] royal editor Duncan Larcombe.[32]

Pyatt, Hartley and Larcombe were all among those cleared by juries. Some, such as Pharo, said they did not know exactly who was being paid and that reporters routinely exaggerated the status of their sources; reporters claimed their work was accurate and within the editors' code of conduct. Paradoxically, more than thirty police and prison officers and other public officials were convicted at separate trials for the same offences, having been paid thousands of pounds for information and tip-offs. Some questioned whether the estimated £13 million spent on the inquiry had been justified.

The cases also shed light on the prevailing culture in the *Sun* newsroom, which had changed little from the days of Kelvin MacKenzie and demonstrated the pressures under which executives and reporters worked, where twelve-hour days and bullying were common: Clodagh Hartley claimed she was 'frightened' of *The Sun*'s political editor Tom Newton Dunn. She told the Old Bailey: 'Pretty much after I started, he was bullying.' When Pharo turned down a chance to be *The Sun*'s New York correspondent because his partner had fallen pregnant, he received a phone call from *The Sun*'s then deputy editor, Neil Wallis, who was 'incandescent with rage'. 'He said I was a fucking idiot, that I had fucked my life up. It was a job for a single man. He was furious because he had put my name forward for the job and basically I had embarrassed him.' Pharo said Brooks, then his editor, could 'occasionally be fine' – but more often than not 'she was nothing short of a nightmare.' He would receive up to twenty abusive emails a day from her, from 7.30 a.m., when the papers were delivered to her home. One day he presented a 'terrible' news list to the paper's morning conference. 'She got all of the pieces of paper, screwed them into a ball and threw them at my face,' then shouted: 'If you can't put together a fucking news list in the next hour you can fuck off.' Brooks later emailed all staff, asking: 'Have any of you got a story because my idiot news editor can't find any.' Pharo recalled on another occasion, when the *News of the World* had a scoop about David Blunkett, Brooks texted him and picture editor John Edwards: 'If you fucking cunts aren't capable of matching them, I'll sack the lot of you and replace you with them.'[33]

Such was the workplace conduct of the former best friend of Tony Blair and David Cameron. When the dust had settled a bit in later 2015, she was welcomed back into the fold by Murdoch as the senior and powerful Chief Executive Officer of News UK, the new name of his UK holding company. It was as though nothing had happened.

The exact number of victims of phone hacking and other intrusive activities will never be known, but runs into many thousands. Whittamore registered more than 13,000 requests for information; Mulcaire had 4,000 names on his list. Scotland Yard said at least 4,700 victims had been hacked by the *News of the World* alone. While many of these names were public figures, there were many others who had come to the attention of the tabloids – personal assistants, drivers, neighbours, agents and relatives of those public figures – and also the families and relatives of those who had died in tragic circumstances. These included not just the families of Milly Dowler and Madeleine McCann, but the relatives of victims of the 9/11 and 7/7 terrorism attacks in New York and London, the families of servicemen and women killed in Iraq and Afghanistan, the families of the two young girls murdered in Soham in 2002, and the family of Jean Charles de Menezes, the Brazilian man killed in error by police after the 7/7 attacks. Many of these sought redress through the courts. Most claims were settled privately and the actual sums never disclosed, but the cost would eventually reach many millions. And that was just the Murdoch papers.

Hacking at the Mirror Group

Throughout the Leveson Inquiry, the other tabloid groups – Associated Newspapers, Express Newspapers and Mirror Group – had all maintained that hacking and other illegal or unethical practices had never taken place at their newspapers. For the *Mirror* titles, former editor Piers Morgan and then current editors Richard Wallace of *The Mirror* and Tina Weaver at the *Sunday Mirror* all denied knowledge of any hacking, although they conceded it might have happened. Wallace specifically denied knowledge of hacking within the showbusiness team, which had been alleged by another reporter, James Hipwell, also in evidence to Leveson.[34] But police inquiries now turned to the Mirror Group. Not long after Leveson concluded, Weaver and Wallace, who had been in a long-term relationship, were both made redundant when the titles were merged. In March 2013 Weaver, a member of the Press Complaints Commission, now heavily pregnant, was arrested, together with other executives: *Sunday People* editor James Scott, his deputy Nick Buckley and former *Sunday Mirror* deputy editor Mark Thomas. Wallace was also questioned. The *Mirror* share price dropped by a fifth in one day after the arrests. All were released on bail pending charges.

As with the News International group, many civil claims had been and would be lodged against Mirror Group Newspapers, which, in September 2014, ultimately conceded a number of claims and offered compensation to victims including the former England football manager Sven-Göran Eriksson and actor Christopher Eccleston. This was the first admission that its papers had been involved in hacking and related activities. In February 2015, it published an extensive apology to 'all its victims of phone hacking', which it said was an 'unacceptable intrusion' into private lives.[35] Its fund earmarked for compensation claims was now £12 million, it said.

In a number of cases, compensation could not be agreed and it fell to the High Court to determine the level of damages. In one critical and revealing case in May 2015, evidence from Dan Evans about his time at the *Sunday Mirror* working alongside Weaver and Wallace convinced Mr Justice Mann to award a record total of more than £1 million in damages to eight claimants, the highest amounts going to three people: £260,250 to actor Sadie Frost, and the next highest, £188,250, to footballer Paul Gascoigne. Alan Yentob, the former BBC executive, was awarded £85,000 and was the only claimant who was not himself the subject of stories resulting from hacking; instead, the hearing heard, he was hacked in order to find out information about the people who might be leaving messages on his phones, such as the celebrities on *Strictly Come Dancing* or the stars of *EastEnders*, as well as his many social contacts, including architect

Lord Richard Rogers and his wife, restaurateur Lady Rogers. In his ruling the judge, Mr Justice Mann, said Yentob's phone was probably hacked at least twice a day and sometimes more over a period of seven years in the early 2000s.

Mr Justice Mann's two-hundred-page ruling, which was not released in unredacted form until 2018 because of the need to avoid prejudicing any future trials, gave a clear and detailed account of how phone hacking was conducted at *Mirror* newspapers – Hipwell's evidence was that it had begun around 1999 – and included this passage relating to the *Sunday Mirror*:

> In April 2003 the deputy editor, Mr Mark Thomas, left the paper to become the editor of *The People*. Mr Evans was called into an office by Mr Buckley and told that Mr Thomas had taken with him a valuable source of information, which turned out to be information about telephone numbers which could be hacked. Mr Buckley then showed Mr Evans how to access a voicemail message, using Mr Yentob's voicemail as an example. It seems that he was bold enough to dial straight through to the number and get the voicemail without using double-tapping - he explained to Mr Evans that Mr Yentob never picked up his phone (so it would always go to voicemail). He showed him how to press certain keys once the voicemail system intervened in order to access the voicemail menu and then to listen to the calls, having entered the PIN. Later on at the meeting Mr Buckley produced two mobile phones and told Mr Evans about the double tap method. During this meeting Ms Weaver popped in and out on more than one occasion. Mr Evans' evidence was also that she made it clear that Mr Evans' job for the foreseeable future was to rebuild Mark Thomas's database. For this purpose Mr Evans was given hundreds of mobile phone numbers and other details, such as dates of birth. This information came from Ms Weaver and Mr Thomas.

Other details emerged: Evans would sometimes use pay-as-you-go burner phones and dump them in the Thames near the paper's offices in Canary Wharf; incoming voicemails were used to identify the numbers of callers, so their phones could be hacked and other numbers logged, a process known as harvesting. Evans would spend several hours a day on hacking. 'If he got useful or interesting information from listening to a message he would pass it "up the chain of command" (which meant to Mr Buckley and Ms Weaver, and Mr Richard Wallace after his appointment as deputy editor, and Mr James Scott) for consideration of what action to take about it.' There was also extensive use of private investigators. The judge made it clear he was unhappy at how Mirror Group Newspapers (MGN) had repeatedly denied the existence of hacking until forced to by the action. He also criticized MGN for the 'aggressive' cross-examination of the claimants, 'plainly inconsistent with the contrition expressed in the apologies', and made it clear this was a factor in the level of damages.

The ruling was damning for the management and journalists at MGN. The judge singled out Sly Bailey, then MGN Chief Executive, for telling the Leveson Inquiry she had no evidence of hacking and that therefore there had been no need for an investigation – despite the statement of one former journalist, David Brown, to an unfair dismissal case he had brought in 2007 that he had been aware of hacking of celebrities while working at the *Sunday People*. The judge said of Weaver and Wallace:

> In evidence given to the Leveson Inquiry Mr Wallace (by then editor of the Daily *Mirror*) denied knowledge of phone hacking amongst the showbusiness team. I have already accepted Mr Evans' evidence that he sat across the table from Mr Wallace doing it, so it follows that the inaccuracy of this statement has been established for the purposes of this trial. In evidence given to the Leveson Inquiry Ms Tina Weaver, then still editor of the *Sunday Mirror*, denied knowledge of phone hacking or even of gossip of it. I have already found that she was involved in it, and she clearly had knowledge of it in the evidence I have referred to, and in the light of those findings this evidence was wrong.

For good measure, he added: 'I also find it likely that some of the witnesses were aware of Mr Brown's allegations by the time of the Leveson Inquiry if not before – it is inconceivable that in the face of that inquiry, with senior journalists and executives giving evidence, that some of them did not know about it.' On Weaver he also said: 'Ms Weaver's involvement in Mr Evans' initial instruction about hacking, and her subsequent involvement in stories knowing their source, means that knowledge of and participation in phone hacking existed at the highest level on the actual journalism (as opposed to the Board or administrative) side of the business.' The judge concluded that phone hacking was 'widespread, institutionalised and long-standing' at MGN.[36]

A number of *Mirror* journalists were also interviewed under caution, including Piers Morgan, who had already been interviewed two years previously. In July 2015 Lee Harpin, agenda editor of all three *Mirror* titles, was arrested and questioned.

But in December 2015 came the final word from the Crown Prosecution Service – operations Weeting and Golding (the specific investigation into MGN) would be ended and no charges brought against any of those arrested or questioned from MGN or from News Corp, including members of the company management. 'After a thorough analysis, we have decided there is insufficient evidence to provide a realistic prospect of a conviction and therefore no further action will be taken in any of these cases,' said Alison Saunders, director of public prosecutions at the CPS. 'Potential charges for phone hacking and perverting the course of justice were considered,' the CPS said. 'After thorough analysis of the evidence, it has been decided that no further action will be taken for either charge.' Morgan would tweet: 'I'm now going to get spectacularly drunk.' *The Guardian* reported: 'A civil lawyer who acted for one of the victims in that trial (which resulted in the judgement by Mr Justice Mann) said the CPS decision was "quite unbelievable" given Mirror Group's admissions during the case.'[37]

While the CPS decision provoked anger among victims and campaign groups, it was, in the jargon of the trade, not exactly front-page news anymore. The trials had been and gone and had resulted in relatively few convictions of journalists, compared to the broader sweep of allegations. Even some more ethically minded journalists were inclined to agree with Rupert Murdoch when he was recorded telling his staff in 2013: 'We're talking about payments for news tips from cops: that's going on a hundred years.'[38] It was an echo of earlier times and tabloid wars in the United States and Australia, not to mention the *News of the World*'s regular bottle of Scotch to the duty sergeant at Scotland Yard. And there was, of course, a public interest defence.

Another related case now emerged that sullied the reputation of the *News of the World* even further. The methods of Mazher Mahmood, the so-called 'fake sheikh', had long been the subject of speculation around Fleet Street and concern among lawyers, mainly that he used entrapment methods. Despite that, there was no doubt that while some of his stories targeted royals – Sophie, Countess of Wessex, and Sarah, Duchess of York, among others – MPs, sports stars and other celebrities, others had led to the jailing of criminals. But his actions in the case of the alleged plot to kidnap Victoria Beckham in 2003 had led to a collapsed trial and referral by the judge to the Attorney General of the conduct of the *News of the World*. Another case, in 2004, involving an alleged 'dirty bomb' also collapsed. After the *News of the World* was closed, Mahmood simply transferred his activities to the *Sunday Times*, where he had worked much earlier in his career. Giving evidence to the Leveson Inquiry, where he insisted on appearing with the online feed on audio only, Mahmood claimed that he had helped prosecute more than 260 criminals.[39] He was forced to make a fresh statement after an investigation conducted by the law firm Linklaters for his employer News International at the request of *Sunday Times* editor John Witherow found evidence of only 94 individual convictions.[40]

Nick Davies, 2014.

He later went to work for the *Sun on Sunday*. In July 2014, a prosecution on drugs charges of singer Tulisa Contostavlos, formerly of the group N-Dubz, which had followed a *Sun on Sunday* story, collapsed after the judge suggested Mahmood might have perjured himself over the evidence of a witness. The Crown Prosecution Service immediately began an inquiry into dozens of cases involving Mahmood; a BBC *Panorama* programme in December that year also questioned his methods. In September 2015, he was charged with conspiracy to pervert the course of justice in the Contostavlos case. In October 2016, he was convicted and jailed for fifteen months.[41]

When, a year later, the government decided against pursuing Part Two of the Leveson Inquiry, the Mazher Mahmood case, suggesting other illegal activities at the *News of the World* not fully considered during the hearings, would be cited, with some vigour, by Lord Justice Leveson as a vital reason why the second half should go ahead, whether it was under him or another judge. While the investigations and criminal and civil trials into allegations of hacking and corruption had continued, Part Two, which was due mainly to examine the relationship between the media and the police, had been put on hold. So it was not until December 2017 that the government told Lord Justice Leveson it was minded not to go ahead with it following a public consultation that was 'broadly in favour' of cancellation. A joint letter to the judge from Culture, Media, Digital and Sport secretary Karen Bradley and Home Secretary Amber Rudd said most of the terms of reference of the Leveson Inquiry had been met, including those relating to the role and conduct of the police, and any further misbehaviour by journalists would be mitigated by the reforms already put in. There was also the fact that the inquiry had focused on the traditional press but government now recognized the landscape had changed with the proliferation of digital and social media. 'Newspapers are now in a very different position than when hacking took place,' they said. Work on regulating the digital sphere was under way.

In an incendiary and excoriating response in January 2018 the judge said he 'fundamentally disagreed' with the decision and made it clear he believed there was much still to be examined to meet the terms of reference set out by David Cameron in 2011, particularly the issue of corrupt relationships between the police and the press. He accused the government of breaking promises: 'I have no doubt that there is still a legitimate expectation on behalf of the public and, in particular, the alleged victims of phone hacking and other unlawful conduct, that there will be a full public examination of the circumstances that allowed that behaviour to develop,' he wrote. 'That is what they were promised.'

The judge said he was not convinced by assurances that the media landscape was now different and that the press was now sufficiently well regulated, pointing to the review of IPSO by the Media Standards Trust in 2013 which suggested that it failed to meet twenty of his recommendations as to the proper form of regulation, including those that would guarantee independence and the handling of complaints. This, he said, could be examined in Part Two.

Most significantly and crucially, Lord Justice Leveson also stressed that the inquiry had only examined a small portion of the wrongdoing and much had emerged since that required further investigation: the trials had included 'conflicting and irreconcilable' accounts by different people working within the same organization while the conviction of Mahzer Mahmood 'also raises issues of an entirely different species of unlawful or improper conduct'. Lord Justice Leveson said that it might have been thought that the civil litigation would expose 'where the truth lies' but in fact no trial involving News International had been contested to judgement and 'it has not been challenged that the extent of wrongdoing within News International has been far greater than the Inquiry was informed.' Recent substantial payments in civil cases, he said, had related to *The Sun*, which the inquiry had been told had not been implicated in unlawful or improper conduct, and to Trinity Mirror (owners of the *Daily* and *Sunday Mirror*), where, again, none of the litigation had been contested to liability. 'It must be in the public interest that the extent of the wrongdoing is publicly exposed not least because the press itself would have been the very first to do just that if it were to have occurred in any other organisation.' He added: 'In short, in neither Part One nor the trials have there been answers to "who did what to whom".'[42]

The judge was brushed aside by the Government, who confirmed its decision in the House of Commons a few weeks later. Aside from media reform campaigners, no one took his side. The Government was right on one thing – the media landscape had changed. By the second decade of the twenty-first century, the world – and journalism – had moved on in unquantifiable leaps and bounds. The dark arts now seemed to belong to the dark ages. Out there was a brave new digital world created by a unique combination of advancing technologies and brash, all-pervasive new platforms that gave a public voice to all. This was churnalism 2.0 and it transformed tabloid journalism.

12

CHURNALISM 2.0

Even at his most pessimistic, Nick Davies could not perhaps have forecast where journalism was heading when *Flat Earth News* was published in 2008. In the book, Davies took aim at journalists who simply recycle press releases from public relations companies or rely entirely on news agencies for copy, perhaps adding a little bit here and there, but essentially not doing much original reporting, let alone leaving their office. It was particularly acute for young, early career journalists, pressured into producing multiple stories every day.

'This is churnalism. This is journalists who are no longer out gathering news but are reduced instead to passive processors of whatever material comes their way, churning out stories whether real event or PR artifice, important or trivial, true or false.'[1] While others claimed credit for inventing the word, there is no doubt that 'churnalism' was a sign the industry as whole was changing dramatically, largely for the worse. Even a small survey of quality newspapers, commissioned by Davies, found that 80 per cent of stories were not original and only 12 per cent were generated by their own reporters.[2] Much of this was due to smaller staffing levels, cost cutting and the multiple improvements in communications and the onset of the digital world which simply made it less necessary for journalists to actually leave their desks. In the fiercely competitive world of the tabloids and the popular newspapers, it would be more tempting to cut corners and, for some, take advantage of the modern technologies to hack phones and make other digital intrusions. And we know now where that ended. But now, in the post-Leveson era, the pace of change was accelerating. Who needed to hack phones or leave their offices or even rely on PR handouts, when it was all being brought to them, on their digital screens . . .

Going Digital

In 2011, in the middle the hacking drama, *The Guardian* had taken the first serious leap into the digital future for British newspapers. Until then, despite the rapid growth of newspaper websites, the broad policy of most papers remained that the print edition would be the first point of publication of the bulk of content which would only go online afterwards, sometimes hours later. *The Guardian* now decreed that no longer would stories be held back until the following morning; instead, they would be published as soon as they were ready, whatever time of the day or night. In this respect, *The Guardian* was only following the practice of the BBC website and online-only organizations, such as HuffPost and Buzzfeed, but these were creations of the digital world itself. It was a historic step: the time-honoured, orderly rhythms of daily and weekly production with rigid deadlines would no longer reign supreme in the journalistic mind. Print editions would continue but the emphasis had switched, and newspaper publishing would now finally follow the 24-hour news channels. Nothing would ever be the same again.

Most other publications would soon follow suit. A variety of different approaches were taken. Some publications had or would create an online replica, a mobile or desktop app that followed the numbered page formulation of the printed paper and could be accessed for a subscription as an alternative to the larger, messier, website. For the tabloids, there was recognition that cost and availability still restricted their online audiences, which only built up gradually as online technologies expanded and became cheaper and more ubiquitous; by 2009 more than half British homes had access to broadband, but coverage and prices were still limiting factors for the homes of less well off and working-class families. Advances in mobile and wi-fi technology, the increasing sophistication of smartphones and tablets would follow and prices eventually dropped – for ordinary people mobile phones and Internet access were no longer a luxury, they became an everyday necessity. Greater access would fuel demand and websites, without the limitations of the physical page and the sheer technical demands of the production cycle – the need to get those copies on the lorry, the train or the plane to the furthest points of the compass – would become insatiable beasts, sucking up every kind of content, drawn from any available source.

By now the definition of what a tabloid was had changed dramatically. In 2003, in a bid to diversify its readership, *The Independent* began publishing a tabloid-sized version, but decreed as the *Daily Mail* had once done that it be known as a 'compact' to distinguish it from the traditional tabloid market; within a year, the broadsheet edition was dropped. *The Times* would follow shortly and in 2005 *The Guardian* introduced a smaller size, somewhere between a compact and a broadsheet, before going fully tabloid along with *The Observer* in 2018. By now, the term 'compact' had largely disappeared from use. In 2010, again aiming to diversify the market, *The Independent* also launched a much cheaper and more cheerful tabloid version, *The i*. The tone was bright and breezy but still serious, the stories short and sharp, the pictures plentiful and the masthead in red, but it had no trace of traditional tabloid material: there was no sleaze and gossip, no pictures of scantily clad women and the celebrity coverage was restrained. It dealt with serious issues – politics, social policy, the environment – in a smart and accessible way, its political stance broadly following that of its parent paper: it didn't, unlike other tabloids, tell its readers what to think or how to vote and its approach was mostly slightly left of centre, spotlighting social issues and reflecting public concerns. It became a great success and in 2015 was named British Newspaper of the Year; here, many believed, was the modern model tabloid.

Three Tweets and a 'Like'

On top of all the usual sources for news now came the big beasts of social media, which, as they gained users, increased their importance to the news-gathering industry. Facebook, started in 2004, Twitter, started in 2006, and – ultimately probably the most important of all for the tabloid agenda – Instagram, launched in 2010, would collectively, as the second decade of the twenty-first century wore on, become probably the single most significant source of stories for tabloid and popular newspapers. Each would serve slightly different functions for newspapers: Facebook, particularly in America, became an alternative source of news for many, particularly after criticism of the mainstream media from politicians and the emergence of the 'Fake News' slur promulgated by Donald Trump in his 2016 campaign for the U.S. presidency and after. Twitter, as its universality became engrained in Western society, became a primary means of communication for journalists and news organizations to promote their work, but also an increasingly vital source of stories and information, both serious and trivial. Twitter would eventually be used by every type of organization, government and public-sector body to get their message across and act as a point of contact with the public – for many, bypassing the media in the process. But it was also used by journalists as an information source and to hoover up exchanges and posts on the site that might have been too utterly trivial even for tabloid newspaper or local newspaper down-page space filler, such as the story on the *MailOnline* in September 2019 that recounted how a Glaswegian woman had complained of crippling pain after spending the night wearing her shoes on the wrong feet. The rest of the world became aware of this because she had told a friend, who had then tweeted a picture the woman had herself proudly posted on Instagram of her wearing the shoes, with a comment 'And [she] only just realised this morning she was wearing them on the wrong feet. This lassie man.'[3]

A new rule soon emerged: any social media post about anything, anywhere, by anyone that attracted either disparaging or enthusiastic comments or both was probably worthy of a story. While Instagram was crucial for celebrity-picture-led stories, Twitter would provide material for endless, if slight, stories based on a few tweets: for instance, a story about a television presenter mispronouncing a word, or perhaps wearing a new hairstyle or tie, might result in a spate of tweets from random members of the public criticizing said presenter, to be followed by a few in their defence. These might only represent a minute fraction of the viewing public, but would within minutes be turned into a news story: 'Angry fans took to social media to slate [insert name of presenter] for wearing a garishly patterned tie . . .'. Equally, an aspiring actress showing off a revealing new dress or flamboyant hairstyle might prompt a few tweets about how 'gorgeous' or 'sexy' she looked, which would then result in a 'Fans raved about . . .' headline. Celebrity postings were particularly closely watched: the boyfriend of a minor female pop star had failed to like some of her Instagram pictures? A celebrity couple rumoured to have split now unfollow each other on social media? All easy fodder. These stories would appear quickly, be overtaken just as rapidly and mostly would not appear in the print editions.

The growth of these platforms and the Internet itself in the decade from 2011 was exponential: in that year, about 2 billion people around the world were regularly using the Internet, around 30 per cent of the global population. Ten years later, the figure had become 4.9 billion, or about 60 per cent of the population. Social media use followed a similar trajectory, with 1.4 billion users in 2011, rising to 4.5 billion in 2021. The average time a person globally would spend on social media was almost 2.5 hours each day, using an average of 6.7 different platforms – the top four being Facebook, YouTube, WhatsApp and Instagram.[4] The latter's rise in users was equally steep – from around 90 million users in 2013, not long after it had been bought up by Facebook, to 2 billion by the end of 2021.[5]

Instagram, which began as a simple portal for displaying the photographs taken on your new smartphone but then expanded to include photo stories and videos, quickly became the platform of choice for younger people. By the end of 2021 more than half those 2 billion users were under 34, with 62 per cent in the 18–34 bracket. As a primarily visual medium, Instagram had become the favourite platform for the creatives of the world, especially in the fashion and photography worlds and among actors, artists and musicians of all kinds. More so than the other platforms, Instagram would become a platform of commerce. This younger audience of consumers was the dream of advertisers and marketeers the world over. Instagram would soon spawn what became known as 'influencers' – usually young and photogenic people, often women, who would photograph themselves in exotic locations or eating in expensive restaurants. It was embraced by celebrities and public figures as diverse as the Premier League's young rich footballers and the stars of the latest generation of reality shows – whether it was the amazingly successful *Love Island*, a dating (or 'coupling', as it became known) competition among photogenic, swimsuit-clad young people who were purposely isolated, *Big Brother*-style, on the Mediterranean island of Majorca, which began in 2015, the BBC stalwart *Strictly Come Dancing* or programmes featuring cookery and baking competitions. All of these programmes and others would have, as part of their marketing strategies, a big presence on all social media platforms, providing endless and easily available content for journalists.

The unlimited content online, coupled with the explosion of social media, would have a transformative effect on tabloid news-rooms. Journalists were still reliant on public relations companies or individuals to deliver a portion of their stories but increasingly did not need to leave their offices or even pick up a telephone because of the vast number of stories from around the globe that could easily be scooped up and, with minimal effort, channelled onto their web-sites. All that content from social media postings by reality TV shows, as well as the individual postings of the minor celebrities the pro-grammes created and the interactions between them, were rich seams of stories for the tabloids to mine. Since space was more or less infinite, the restrictions on images – so crucial to tabloid content – were now a thing of the past. Where a news story about a celebrity arriving, say, at a film premiere or the red carpet of an awards cere-mony, even going shopping, to the gym or filling their car with petrol (an increasingly popular sub-genre, largely reliant on paparazzi fol-lowing celebrities in America), might once have been only afforded one or two images on a tightly designed tabloid page, it might now contain six or eight or more images, no matter how similar they might be. Some would also be accompanied by short video clips drawn from any number of sources: agencies; taken by passers by, since everyone now has a smartphone; television production companies; or the social media posts of celebrities themselves. The ubiquity of high-quality phone cameras among the general public created a whole new and unimaginably large cadre of amateur photographers and reporters who were happy to post their work on social media, and sometimes even happy for media organizations to either steal it or – sometimes – pay. The global village had truly arrived.

When 24-hour rolling news channels first appeared in homes, public spaces and newsrooms, there was genuine eagerness for their content, the thrill of always being up to date with what was happen-ing. Once the novelty had worn off, they began to be seen by many as just aural wallpaper with moving images: news was always 'break-ing' somewhere, a reporter was always excitedly talking to camera, usually at some length, because there were, after all, 24 hours to fill. So it was with the websites of many tabloid newspapers. While domestic politics or other news would always get due prominence, their websites would be filled with an endless scroll of content aggregated from everywhere around the world, regardless of any domestic interest. On top of this, outside agencies supplied content to create further links, which to some consumers would be indistinguishable from the host site, offering anything from 'Best Undertakers in [wherever in the UK the reader happened to be based]' to 'Twenty Actors You Never Knew Were Gay' to '[Insert name of celebrity] Without Make-Up Has Left Us All Shocked', all of which garnered clicks for advertisers. These appeared alongside picture links to stories from the newspaper itself, either current or from the recent archive, leaving readers to roam free in this wilderness. The concept of reading, in the self-contained environment of your newspaper, a summary of the day's news for your county, according to whatever factors determined their selection by journalists, no longer existed online.

When it came to pure news, locality was no longer quite the key factor in coverage decisions for websites aiming for hits from anywhere on the globe. So a story on a particularly gruesome murder in, say, Moscow or Manhattan might get as much coverage as its equivalent in Manchester: a grabby, buzzword-heavy headline that failed to mention a location and could have occurred almost anywhere in the world – such as 'Model Beaten to Death by Billionaire Sugar Daddy After Drink and Drug Fuelled Sex Romp' – would simply generate the required clicks. There being no relative limit on story size, all manner of sundry information, images and screengrabs from social media or elsewhere could be incorporated. While this could be commended for giving the reader greater access to information, it is deeply unlikely that many readers would make it to the end. Content, and loads of it, was now king: never mind the quality, feel the width.

In an earlier era, newspapers that followed up stories they did not have from their rivals would always be one edition behind on the night or by the next day's paper. And hitherto there had always been a desire to ensure that stories taken from rivals had some extra content, a new angle or extra information: journalistic pride expected it and editors would simply have demanded it. Now, such old customs were happily thrown aside. Stories could easily and swiftly be copied and pasted across from rivals almost in their entirety and with only the briefest acknowledgement of the source buried in the text, as in 'xxx told *The Sun*' or 'as reported in the *Mirror*'. Most of the time this blatant theft was shrugged off; in the online world, where everything has to be online immediately, there is no time to carry out extra research, put in calls or even send emails. Sometimes, stories would carry a get-out clause at the end – '*MailOnline/The Mirror/The Sun* (delete accordingly) has contacted representatives of xxxx (insert name of celebrity or showbusiness figure or so on) for comment.' Mostly, there was little attempt to update stories. Everyone, including the readers, moved on, clicked through, scrolled down. Everyone benefited, everyone felt the width.

And so, alongside cover sales and readers, a new metric measured the effectiveness and impact of an individual piece of journalism: clicks. The more hits or clicks a story had on a website, the better its overall totals would be, all the better to charge advertisers for their banner ads that intruded into the interface with the reader. As print sales plummeted in the years after Leveson, clicks became the new readers and so stories were now defined as clickbait. This term came to mean anything that might, however briefly, attract the attention of a reader. So now the measurement of success for eager young reporters in tabloid newsrooms was not whether they were able to turn a story tip into an exclusive or get a great interview or quote that provided a headline: instead, it was how many stories could they turn over each day, to feed a 24-hour news cycle in which everything and everyone was always online. In most newsrooms, in addition to the television screens showing the news channels, there were now large monitors showing clicks on stories in real time, so stories with rising numbers would get promoted to more prominent positions on the site. In the past, gauging individual contributions to newspapers was often arbitrary: while the impact of some stories could be measured broadly by public reaction, leaps in sales figures, readers' letters or even angry phone calls, these only represented a fraction of the total readership. Much of newspaper content had been a mixture of intelligent guesswork and an instinctive under-standing of the nature of the reader – proprietors and editors like Murdoch, Northcliffe, Cudlipp and MacKenzie had that in their blood. But the figures measuring your clicks were fixed, unchallengeable and up there for all the newsroom to see. So it became all about productivity: writing the stories with the most clicks became almost the only measure of success, particularly for younger, more aspirant journalists. Such was churnalism 2.0.

MailOnline

Just over a decade after its creation, *MailOnline* had become the market leader, role model and uber-dominant force in this new online tabloid world. Having been among the leading sceptics among what would now be called legacy, that is, long-standing and printed media, Associated realized it would have to embrace the inevitable and launched its own website in 2003. The first years were low-key; it did not enjoy the resources devoted to Associated's other publications, and fear over detracting from the vital circulation figures was very real. The rise of *MailOnline* began in 2008 when career Associated executive and former *Scotsman* editor Martin Clarke was given the helm. Clarke, like Kelvin MacKenzie a grammar-school boy from the north Kent/outer London fringes, and a protégé of Dacre, was very much in the old-school mode of tabloid editor, as writer Jane Thynne outlined in a profile for the *Independent on Sunday* in 2006, when he had taken over the editorship of *London Lite*: 'Clarke's editorial demeanour has attracted a range of tributes from former colleagues – "vile", "offensive", "appalling", "obsessive", "childlike" and "foul-mouthed" being among the less flattering.' Thynne went on: 'Another journalist, who refused to be named, said: "The stories were always 'mince' or 'shit' and a typical conference might end, 'you are all fucking cretins and this is all crap.' He once said to me: 'You've got to go and shout at the bastards or they won't respect you.'"'[6]

Once under Clarke and unlike most other popular or tabloid newspaper websites, *MailOnline* was given licence by Associated to become not simply a digital version of the publication, but to develop a distinct branding and a brighter, more appealing look that were markedly different from the rather carefully conservatively designed parent paper, although it retained the *Mail* name in old-fashioned Gothic font at the top of the page. In retrospect, it was a stroke of commercial and journalistic genius, although it was perhaps more by accident than design. Elsewhere, *The Guardian* had been the only other newspaper to differentiate the branding of its online presence, as *Guardian Unlimited*, although it dropped the name in 2008 as part of its move to a 'digital first' newsroom. Associated persisted with *MailOnline*: the separate brand would diversify its audience from a very domestic one to an international appeal. Again like

The Guardian, it would eventually have separate home pages for the UK, the United States and Australia. It would also, Dacre and Harmsworth realized, be necessary to establish a separate team to avoid a drain on – and dilution of – the already overworked *Mail* staff. And, crucially, it avoided the high moral tone while retaining many of the other elements of the printed *Daily Mail*, the prime contents of which would always be found on the site. Clarke would marshal a team of eager young social-media-savvy journalists who were happy to sit in front of a screen all day and to harvest stories from whatever source. This was their world, anyway. Its headlines – whether on the latest domestic political story, the doings of the royal family, celebrities of all shapes, sizes and backgrounds, or a gory murder case or court story from anywhere in the world – would be long and detailed, designed to attract the reader, but also assist in its prominence on search engine Google. While Clarke insisted *MailOnline* was not a red-top tabloid – 'We are a middle market newspaper. Our copy is not sensationalist or the kind of stuff you'd see in the *The Sun* or the *Mirror*'[7] – the reality was different: 'Thirty seconds or so spent perusing the site itself would suggest otherwise.'[8] Its audience was also markedly different to that for the printed *Mail*: younger, better educated, even more female in composition and more international, urban and metropolitan.

Much *MailOnline* content, as with other tabloid websites, was now also derived from television series, particularly highly popular reality shows like *Strictly Come Dancing*, *Love Island*, *Made in Chelsea* and *The Only Way Is Essex*. In the United States, programmes, such as *The Real Housewives of Beverly Hills* or *Selling Sunset*, about glamorous estate agents in California, would also be featured. All such programmes now had extensive PR operations linked to social media channels and expected their multimedia content – stories, pictures, video clips – to be swept up by the tabloid websites, who duly obliged. And of course one of the primary sources of content for all would be the activities of the Kardashians, whose rise to fame almost exactly mirrored that of *MailOnline*. The Kardashian clan were a California-based family whose presence ran through the celebrity world like arteries through the human body. By the second decade of the century, they epitomized the phrase 'famous for being famous', although the sheer commercial success and riches they had generated indicated supreme business and public-relations acumen. The matriarch was Kris Jenner, who had been married to Robert Kardashian, famous as lawyer to O. J. Simpson, the former football star and actor who was tried and acquitted of the murder of his ex-wife and her male friend. Having had three daughters and one son, the couple parted in 1991 and Jenner then married former athlete and Olympic medallist Bruce (now Caitlyn) Jenner and they had two daughters. The oldest of the three daughters from the first marriage, Kim Kardashian, emerged into celebrity land as stylist to Paris Hilton, heir to the Hilton hotel empire and herself a constant tabloid presence on both sides of the Atlantic. Her fame was amplified after a tape of her having sex was leaked online. The Kardashians would soon come to dominate the celebrity media landscape, fuelled by a reality television show, *Keeping Up With the Kardashians*, started in 2007, which documented their lives and their relationships. Clothing, perfume, cosmetics, endorsements and other branding followed. They documented their glamorous, sexy lives on social media – mainly Instagram – in considerable but carefully curated and glossily sexualized detail. Their every offline move was followed by paparazzi photographers. By 2015 Kim Kardashian, by then married to rapper Kanye West, was named on *Time* magazine's list of 100 Influential People and, according to *Forbes* magazine, was worth around $53 million. In 2019 the youngest of the Kardashian daughters, Kylie Jenner, a model and socialite, was said to be worth £1 billion owing to the growth of her heavily Instagram-marketed cosmetics business, and in summer 2022 became the most followed woman and the second most followed person on Instagram, with more than 360 million followers. Three of her siblings also featured in the top twelve. Such activities provided massive amounts of tabloid content for both news websites like *MailOnline* and the numerous tabloid-orientated celebrity gossip websites that had sprung up around the world during the 2000s and for which the Kardashian clan provided huge amounts of copy and pictures.

In what would be called colloquially the 'sidebar of shame', the *MailOnline* home page carried a column of clickable and celebrity-led teaser stories on the right-hand side, each with a picture and twenty or so words of soundbite to entice the reader to click through. It became a guilty pleasure for many who might otherwise have shunned the Dacre *Mail*. These new readers came via other links, such as shared stories on social media: 'Who then see some content down the right rail and get sucked in, and sucked in and sucked in – and the next thing you know you're bookmarked and they are coming to you despite themselves,' boasted Clarke.[9] It was rare for there not to be a Kardashian story in this mix. In the hours after their appearance at, say, a film premiere, awards ceremony or shop opening or perhaps at some carefully curated family event – a holiday, a restaurant visit, a baby shower, the launch of a new clothing line – the sidebar of shame might carry two or more separate pieces, each adorned with multiple photographs and links to other Kardashian stories. As the *Financial Times* noted, paraphrasing Samuel Johnson's famous dictum about London: 'If you are tired of *MailOnline*, you are tired of Kim Kardashian's life – and most readers are not.'[10]

The commercial success of the Kardashians spawned a legion of copyists across social media – mostly young women and would-be celebrities and the *Love Island* wannabes, aping the new sexualized, voluptuous, lip-filler, botoxed style of glamour. Those celebrities who felt their image needed a boost would know that a series of Instagram shots of their 'beach body' photographed in some scenic location would be seized upon with relish. And to match this, a whole new lexicon emerged out of *MailOnline*. Celebrities who wanted to announce a new relationship would do so on Instagram with some carefully staged images and were thereby said to have gone 'Instagram official'. But some of the language felt at times unduly prurient and salacious; the kind of language that, even in the heyday of *The Sun*'s Page 3 era, would probably never have made it into print. So, for instance, a story based around a series of images of a minor Hollywood actress might refer to her 'gorgeous curves', 'curvy figure' or 'golden tresses', while rears were usually either 'pert' or 'peachy'. Bikinis or shorts were almost invariably described as 'TINY', often in capitals for emphasis, and the person wearing them put on a 'leggy display'. Instragram influencers and models were said to 'flaunt their curves' or 'tease their followers', or were said have 'posed up a storm' or to be 'putting on a busty display'. There would be lines such as, *The model, 27, slipped into a skimpy thong swimsuit that she teamed with a pair of thigh-high silver boots for the sultry Instagram post. She flicked her wet brunette locks over one shoulder as she looked back at the camera for the social media update.* Or: *She commanded attention as her low cut outfit put her lithe legs and ample cleavage on full display.* Why would newspapers pay the paparazzi for shots when this content was being served up for free by its very subjects? A typical story about British socialite Lady Victoria Hervey – a tabloid and *Daily Mail* regular for at least two decades – visiting a beach in California lingered on the fact that she 'flaunted her very flat tummy and slim waist'. There were 34 pictures, many very similar, including one with a surfboard and two of her red-carpet appearances at unrelated events. There was, of course, mention of the new swimwear line she was promoting, which may have had something to do with the number of pictures. The story was nothing more than the fact of her visit to the beach, padded out with details and some quotes lifted from an interview with the *Daily Mail* the previous year.[11]

There was regular and exhaustive, detailed emphasis on make-up, hair and accessories, presumably in the expectation that women readers would be interested in that kind of information. Such stories began to have boxed inserts with headlines such as 'Get the look' – advice to readers on where to buy said bikini or dress or similar versions – with links to websites that earned the papers a small sum for each link clicked.

Strangely, despite the lubricious prose elsewhere, the language in some stories occasionally resembled something out of the lushly worded romantic fiction of writers like Barbara Cartland, with carefully coy words and phrases. A celebrity couple – perhaps a pair who had been long married – seen embracing or sharing a kiss on the cheek were deemed to be 'packing on the PDA', an acronym for 'public display of affection'. If said couple were perhaps photographed going to a restaurant or to the theatre, they were often described as on a 'date night'. And partners or boyfriends of female celebrities were often called 'beaus' in text and headlines, a phrase probably not used elsewhere in journalism since the early part of the century. Some of this reflected the language of Middle America and was clearly influenced by the U.S. market *MailOnline* was heavily targeting – stories about very minor American celebrities filling up at a petrol station or carrying a takeaway coffee in a Hollywood street would often find their way into UK pages, despite being largely unknown to domestic readers.

Men on their own did not escape the lingering coverage of their looks and clothing. A story about actor Damian Lewis visiting a music festival in London contained the following:

The actor, 51, looked smart in black jeans and a dark patterned shirt as he and his friend grabbed a bite to eat at the
festival in Victoria Park. He completed his ensemble with a
pair of white trainers while he fixed a pair of sunglasses in
his shirt's neckline. He styled his rouge tresses in a middle
parting and accessorised with a silver pendant necklace and
a watch.[12]

Again, the story was padded out with background details about
Lewis, the recent death of his wife, actor Helen McCrory, and his
new relationship; there were fourteen pictures, five of which were
of him at the festival, all remarkably similar. And since when was a
man's hair described as 'rouge tresses'?

The formula worked. By 2015 *MailOnline* was the biggest
English-language news website in the world, attracting 11 million
users a day. It was only behind three Chinese publications in terms
of numbers but was more global in its reach. Such dominance
continues. It had established the template of selling advertising
online and was turning into a money-making machine. Banner
advertising permeated the pages, and there were sponsored links
to buy versions of all the celebrity clothes described in such detail
as well as short TV-commercial-style advertising videos ahead of
those video shorts.

MailOnline's relentless hoovering up of content from other publications, together with a determination to publish its content as soon
as possible and a ruthlessly driven but often relatively inexperienced
staff, easily led to errors. According to former U.S.-based reporter
James King, 'the Mail's editorial model depends on little more
than dishonesty, theft of copyrighted material, and sensationalism so absurd that it crosses into fabrication.' Acknowledging that
newspapers had always repurposed the work of others and sought
the most attention-grabbing headlines, he argued that *MailOnline*
simply went further: 'I saw basic journalism standards and ethics
casually and routinely ignored. I saw other publications' work lifted
wholesale. I watched editors at the most highly trafficked English-
language online newspaper in the world publish information they
knew to be inaccurate.'[13] *MailOnline* rejected the criticisms totally.
In 2014 it admitted publishing an entirely inaccurate story about
the actor George Clooney.[14] In 2017 *The Sun* accused it of copyright

infringement,[15] the same year that the online encyclopedia Wikipedia said *MailOnline* was an 'unreliable source'.[16]

The End of Page 3

While it was unlikely there were ever any completely naked breasts on *MailOnline*, there was plenty of exposed female flesh there and even more on Instagram. Both fed off each other as celebrities, showbiz personalities and glamour models competed to show as much as possible without actually infringing its 'no nipples or pubic hair' policies. At the same time, the ubiquity of the Internet meant that both actual nipples and all kinds of pornography were just a few clicks away, if anyone wanted to find them. But also, there was, of course, a growing recognition across society that, to put it in its simplest terms, what had become known as the male gaze had in many ways led to the exploitation of women, which, in a climate of genuine equality, should not continue. So, did *The Sun* need to continue with Page 3, for so long part of its brand?

Larry Lamb had, as long ago as 1989, admitted his regret at making Page 3 part of the language.[17] Although feminists and others had always criticized it, the first serious opposition came from Labour MP Clare Short, who campaigned to get it banned. She failed to garner enough support in the House of Commons for her private members' bill in 1986, and *The Sun*, under MacKenzie, treated her with derision, labelling her 'killjoy Clare'.[18] The end finally came in the wake of a 'No More Page 3 Campaign', launched in 2012 by writer Lucy-Anne Holmes, who declared that Page 3 was there 'for no other reason than the sexual gratification of men'.[19] Her petition attracted 240,000 signatures and support from MPs and across civil society. *The Sun* could see the writing on the wall and, to the relief of most staff, Page 3 was dropped from its Irish edition in 2013, from UK editions in 2015 and from the website in 2017. The *Daily Star* continued with its 'Starbirds' until 2019.

But for the tabloids, it was a small concession: who needed Page 3 when in late 2023 *The Sun* could still satisfy the male gaze by running photospreads and a video culled from Instagram with headlines and text such as 'Who is the festive queen when it comes to saucy posts in their pants? These gorgeous celebs spent a lot of 2023 stripping down to their lingerie on Instagram.'[20]

Desmond Bows Out

In 2018, after eighteen years of ownership, Richard Desmond decided it was time to shed himself of the *Express* and *Star* titles, together with the *OK!* celebrity magazine, in a £125 million sale to Trinity Mirror, which would largely end his involvement in publishing to concentrate on property deals (although he would retain a nominal stake in Trinity). He had also owned the TV station Channel Five between 2010 and 2014. His ownership was not a success. One media commentator noted that Desmond had not invested in quality journalism or television but had made a small fortune through the deals, getting out at a time when the *Express* was no longer viable:

> When Desmond bought the *Daily Express* it was still selling more than 1 million copies a day, almost half that of its rival the *Daily Mail*. During his ownership its sale has fallen to 364,933, and the once mass-market paper has been overhauled by high-end titles, the *Daily Telegraph* and *The Times*. The *Mail* now outsells the hollowed-out *Express* by four to one.[21]

Desmond had also never taken a clear political line with the *Express* – initially supporting and donating to Labour, taking it back to its natural home with the Conservatives and then endorsing and funding Nigel Farage's UKIP party until that too faded. Desmond was also renowned for once goose-stepping, Nazi-style, in the middle of a business meeting involving German investors in the printing works the *Express* jointly owned with *Telegraph* newspapers.[22]

Trinity Mirror now rebranded itself as Reach plc and became the biggest concern in British tabloid publishing; the new company had a huge number of local daily and weekly newspapers as well as the national titles. In many ways, these main national titles were an unlikely match: the *Mirror* had continued its dogged support of the Labour Party and a determinedly less sleazy approach to tabloid journalism while the *Express* remained defiant in its appeal to a middle-market, suburban Tory readership. Its obsessions, as reflected on its front pages, had for some years been what it believed to be unanswered questions over the death of the Princess of Wales, the variations of the weather and the likelihood of a cure or treatment for Alzheimer's disease, perhaps reflecting the age of its readership. And then there had been the McCann story, for which the *Express* had been punished in the courts and criticized by the Leveson Inquiry.

While the print versions of the Reach national titles and also *The Sun* were by now much reduced in pagination, they retained a certain amount of individual style and identity, with named writers. Their websites, however, began to look strikingly similar – a garish jumble of *MailOnline*-style celebrity content drawn from social media and paparazzi images, together with stories based on a few tweets. These were punctuated by banner advertising and endless links both to more of the website's own content and invariably, at the bottom of the page, by now ubiquitous advertising-heavy online aggregated content sites that specialized in photography-based click-bait such as 'Twenty Hollywood Stars Who You Didn't Know Were Gay', which readers would be expected to confuse with the website's own original content.

Crucially, all the tabloid websites remained free to access and therefore needed to rely on heavy banner advertising and various affiliate links – and clickbait sites – for revenue despite the annoyance of many readers. Of the tabloids, only *The Sun* ever experimented with a £2-a-week subscription paywall, introduced by Murdoch, a lover of pay per view in the sporting world, in 2013 and which saw its average 30 million a month readers drop to around 250,000 in a year. In mid-2015 the paywall was largely relaxed and by November, shortly after Rebekah Brooks rejoined, it was scrapped entirely. The only other exception is the *Mail*, which under the Mail Plus brand offers subscription access to an online version of the *Daily Mail*, shorn of the *MailOnline* content (which is now charging for access) and appearing in a page-style format as well as some of the content of the *Mail on Sunday* and its glossy magazines. In the second decade of the century, while this digital battleground was being created and the post-Leveson court cases and inquiries continued, on another front the battle lines of a new political war were drawn up that would galvanize the popular end of Fleet Street in a manner not seen since Thatcherism. Another neologism would define the conflict: Brexit.

13

THREE EXITS, THREE COURT CASES

Long before the word 'Brexit' first appeared, ahead of the referendum of 2016, the British tabloid newspapers – with the exception of the Labour-supporting *Mirror* – had shown ever-increasing negativity towards what was originally called the European Common Market, which the UK joined in 1973. This opposition rose incrementally as what became known as the European Union expanded in size and ambition over the following decades. The tabloid media – and the right-of-centre broadsheets, largely the *Telegraph* and Murdoch-owned *Times* newspapers and their Sunday editions – both reflected and encouraged the loud voices of anti-European politicians, including a growing number of Conservative MPs, who were themselves giving voice to grassroots supporters. When the 2016 referendum took place, the dominant strident tone of the right-leaning tabloids influenced the vote with historic consequences, polarizing much of Britain and leading to years of domestic political and economic upheaval. The rest of Europe and much of the world looked on in horror. The full consequences of the decision were still being played out in the post-Brexit years as the British economy continued to struggle, inflation soared and there was a cost-of-living crisis made worse by the economy absorbing the impact of Brexit while also struggling with the costs of the pandemic and the war in Ukraine. It is not an exaggeration to say that, with hindsight, the tabloids were instrumental in changing British history when it came to the Brexit issue. Many voices would argue, for the worse.

The Brexit Bombardment

The often visceral opposition to the European Union vented by the right-wing tabloids before and after the 2016 referendum was not a new phenomenon. It had its roots deep in the national character as well as reflecting more recent social changes. Initially this opposition – or antipathy – stemmed from a variety of factors, echoing the baser nationalistic and jingoistic prejudices of a large number of working-class and lower middle-class people, who formed the vast bulk of tabloid readers, many of whom had grown up in the aftermath of the Second World War or had parents or family who had. An appeal to these traits and cultural memories had been part of *The Sun*'s journalism during the Falklands conflict. But Europe was different again – this was more personal. There was a historical (if hard to justify or critically understand) cultural prejudice towards the French, exemplified by Kelvin MacKenzie's headlines like 'Hop Off You Frogs' (following a complaint by French farmers about imports of cheap British meat) – condemned as 'tasteless and puerile' by the Press Council – and the notorious 'Up Yours Delors' in response to French-inspired Euro expansion. For older readers and perhaps some of those MacKenzie grew up with in the lower-middle-class fringes of London, a collective memory of two world wars fought against Germany, now the standard-bearer for European expansion alongside France, was an underlying factor. And although the *Mirror* broadly supported the EU, Piers Morgan's tasteless 'Achtung Surrender' headline during the Euro 96 football tournament perhaps mirrored some of these instinctive embedded attitudes and might not have been seen as offensive by some readers. For the *Mail* and the *Express* it was also simply a matter of reflecting these same long-standing, nationalistic instincts of their readers in the suburbs, small towns and shires. No matter how many times their readers took a holiday in Europe or celebrated the arrival of different foods in their high street and local restaurants, the same attitudes were sufficiently widespread to require that they be reflected and reinforced by those papers. Or perhaps those who ran those papers felt that way and assumed the majority of readers did as well. It was chicken and egg, but which came first could never be easily defined or explained.

In the 1980s the popular papers, led by *The Sun* and the *Mail*, were happy to give unwavering support to Margaret Thatcher in her resistance to European expansion (while following her in never quite advocating British withdrawal), particularly in the negotiations leading to the 1992 Maastricht Treaty, which created the European Union and set the path towards common defence and security policies as well as a single currency. The *Mail* under David English had supported the UK staying in Europe in the 1975 referendum, but when Paul Dacre, whose time as U.S. correspondent had given him a much more Atlantic-centred approach, took over in 1992, the expansionist policies of the union soon became a target.

By the 1990s, in the run-up to Maastricht and afterwards, much of the anti-Europe tone, soon to be dubbed 'Euroscepticism' among rightward-leaning British tabloids and anti-Europe politicians, was in part due to the work of one particular journalist, Boris Johnson, who was the *Daily Telegraph*'s Brussels correspondent between 1989 and 1994. Johnson – previously sacked by *The Times* for fabricating quotes – would set the agenda with a series of over-egged and sometimes largely made-up stories about 'meddling' or 'bungling' Brussels bureaucrats – regulating condoms or straightening cucumbers, for instance – or Franco-German plots against British interests, with, again, a sense of earlier conflicts running through the language referencing old battles and prejudices. Editors and reporters would feel compelled to follow up these stories, irrespective of their veracity. Peter Guilford, a former *Times* correspondent, told *The Guardian*: 'We are under pressure to follow it up. So there was this sort of Eurosceptic-generating machine that we were all part of, and Boris was driving harder than anyone else . . . he was always playing on Second World War themes.'[1] The anti-EU Referendum Party and then the United Kingdom Independence Party (UKIP), led by Nigel Farage, as well as Eurosceptic Conservative MPs in the Bruges Group and latterly the European Research Group, would always be on hand to support any anti-Europe stories while the right-wing newspapers themselves would eagerly devote space to them both in news coverage and the comment pages. This rising tide of Euroscepticism in the *Mail* and the *Express* was defined by a 1999 study as the idea of a mythical 'British way of life' under threat from a European superstate, which advocated socialism and a single currency and entailed 'surrendering British economic independence and sovereignty to Europe and to Germany in particular'.[2]

With Rupert Murdoch, the approach was less viscerally xeno-phobic, more practical. This reflected his belief that he had more influence on British politicians and policies than he could ever hope for in Europe; it was Murdoch who sought guarantees on further Europe involvement as a condition for his support for Tony Blair in the mid-1990s. A 2012 study stated: 'The newspaper mogul's commercial interests in promoting deregulated media markets have kept him closely watchful of European affairs in Britain, and he has proved particularly willing to back leaders and parties he believes will be most conducive to the furtherance of these interests.'[3] Another study noted that between 1996 and 2016, 92 per cent of *The Sun*'s editorials displayed a negative tone towards European integration and 80 per cent were classified as Eurosceptic.[4] Readers were being groomed.

In office from 1997, Tony Blair and chancellor Gordon Brown were reluctant for many reasons to join the euro and presage greater economic unity with Europe; Brown's famous 'five tests' for joining did not include support from Murdoch, but there was not a single politician or journalist who doubted Murdoch's support was the sixth and Dacre's probably the seventh. Murdoch was later quoted as saying: 'When I go into Downing Street they do what I say; when I go to Brussels they take no notice.'[5] He subsequently wrote to *The Guardian* to deny the statement: 'I have made it a principle all my life never to ask for anything from any prime minister.' 'I have never asked for anything from any prime minister.'[6] He really didn't need to ask, since his views were well known. And Sir John Major, as his evidence to Leveson showed, would have disagreed.

Following the expansion of the EU to admit a raft of Eastern European nations – including Hungary and Poland in 2004 and Bulgaria and Romania in 2007 – many citizens of these countries made to their way to the UK under Freedom of Movement legislation. Even before this came into effect, *The Sun* was calling to 'Halt the Asylum Tide Now' and carried a YouGov poll showing that 77 per cent of people thought 'some parts of our cities are no longer truly British.'[7] On the same day, the *Daily Express* front page reported that the UK was 'set for a new influx of 200,000 immigrants from former Soviet bloc countries'.[8] Following the rule changes and the large numbers of arrivals from the former Eastern Bloc countries, there were genuine concerns in some parts of Britain – particularly in some of the less well-off areas whose readers were schooled by *The Sun*, *Mirror* and *Star*, such as declining coastal towns and the post-industrial parts of the north of England – that public services, such as local GP practices and schools, were struggling to cope. Others celebrated the new diversity this brought to Britain: new shops selling Eastern European foodstuffs sprang up on high streets, while whole areas of the economy – service, catering and leisure industries, trades like plumbing and building and, crucially, a large slice of the social care sector – came to depend on the new arrivals. At the same time, refugees and asylum seekers from conflict zones across the world were making their way to Western Europe, on boats and rafts to Mediterranean islands and under Freedom of Movement within the EU. Many journeyed to Calais, where they slept rough in tents and tried to get to the UK, hiding in lorries or paying people smugglers to take them across the Channel in small boats.

Tabloid focus on these stories over many years, sometimes confusing economic and illegal migrants with genuine asylum seekers and still giving voice to Eurosceptic politicians, fuelled debate and, for many, anger. The *Express*, under the formerly Labour-supporting now-turned Eurosceptic Richard Desmond, launched a 'Britain out of Europe' campaign in 2013, utilizing the English crusader logo on the masthead of its front page to support 'the struggle to repatriate British sovereignty'. A typical headline read: 'Britain Is Full and Fed Up. Today join your *Daily Express* Crusade to stop new flood of Romanian and Bulgarian migrants.'[9] These were, of course, people legally entitled to come to the UK under EU Freedom of Movement rules. The following year, a petition organized by the paper led to a parliamentary vote over whether Britain should have a referendum on EU membership. The paper would also give a regular platform to by-then former UKIP leader Nigel Farage; in 2015 Desmond donated £1 million to UKIP's 2015 general election campaign.

In April 2015 *Sun* columnist and deliberate controversialist Katie Hopkins wrote that migrants were 'cockroaches', adding that she did not care for their wellbeing: 'No, I don't care. Show me pictures of coffins, show me bodies floating in the water, play violins and show me skinny people looking sad. I still don't care.'[10] The column was strongly criticized from all sides but the strongest condemnation came from Zeid Ra'ad Al Hussein, the UN Commissioner on Human Rights, who urged the UK authorities to take action on such 'hate speech'. The statement added:

To give just one glimpse of the scale of the problem, back in 2003 the *Daily Express* ran 22 negative front-page stories about asylum seekers and refugees in a single 31-day period. Asylum seekers and migrants have, day after day, for years on end, been linked to rape, murder, diseases such as HIV and TB, theft, and almost every conceivable crime and misdemeanour imaginable in front-page articles and two-page spreads, in cartoons, editorials, even on the sports pages of almost all the UK's national tabloid newspapers . . . Many of these stories have been grossly distorted and some have been outright fabrications. Elsewhere in Europe, as well as in other countries, there has been a similar process of demonization taking place, but usually led by extremist political parties or demagogues rather than extremist media.[11]

The new press watchdog, IPSO, set up after Leveson, rejected complaints that the column was 'inaccurate' and accepted *The Sun*'s defence that it was an opinion piece.[12]

Such was the background when David Cameron secured a Conservative majority at the general election in May 2015. The new prime minister continued to face *Mail* headlines such as 'The Swarm on our Streets' in July 2015 and 'How many more can we take? Number of migrants entering Britain breaks all records in humiliating blow to Cameron' the following month. He eventually gave way to demands among the growing number of Conservative Eurosceptic MPs – being also aware that the UKIP vote was seriously eroding his party's support in many parts of the country – and granted a referendum in May 2016. By now the debate over leaving had acquired its own pithy shorthand label: Brexit. And Boris Johnson, author of all those anti-EU stories, who became a Conservative MP, then Mayor of London, by now back in the House of Commons, emerged as the leader of the Leave Campaign. In what became a close and often divisive campaign, resulting in a 52–48 vote to leave, the *Mail*, the *Express* and *The Sun* (the *Daily Star*'s reporting tended to be either jokey or dismissive of Europe and never influential in the same way) adopted what was later dubbed a 'bombardment approach' in support of the Vote Leave campaign. Noting that more tabloid readers made up their minds in the final stages of the campaign than non-tabloid readers, a study said: 'The "bombardment approach"

. . . with its fixation on immigration was so pronounced in the final stages . . . that it tipped the balance in terms of influencing the outcome of the result.' It went on to say, 'It is clear that *The Daily Mail* and *The Daily Express*, along with *The Sun*, have collectively developed into an influential, agenda-setting . . . Eurosceptic triumvirate' in the final 25 days before the vote, concluding that front-page headlines overwhelmingly promoted anti-immigration themes. Nine of the *Express*'s nineteen headlines referred to migrants, as did six of the *Mail*'s, but, 'more subtly than *The Daily Express*, a further seven front pages are directly linked to the theme of immigration although not explicitly mentioning the words migration, migrant or immigration in the titles. These headlines clearly serve to undermine the positive case for the freedom of movement in the EU.' Such headlines included the *Express*'s 'Proof 'We Can't Stop Migrants'', the *Mail*'s 'Fury over Plot to let 1.5m Turks into Britain' and *The Sun*'s 'Calais Migrant Riot Let Us in Before You Vote Out'. Other headlines included: 'Outrage At Bid to "Rig" EU Vote', 'Huge Boost to EU Exit Hopes', 'We Will Thrive Outside the EU', 'Your Country Needs You: Vote Leave Today' (*Express*); 'Why staying in Europe Could Harm Your Pension', 'If You Believe in Britain, Vote Leave', 'Nailed: Four Big EU Lies' (*Mail*); 'BeLEAVE in Britain', 'What Queen Asked Dinner Guests: Give Me 3 Good Reasons to Stay in Europe – Sorry Ma'am We Can't Think of One', 'You Can Free UK from Clutches of EU Today – Independence Day: Britain's Resurgence' (*Sun*).[13]

Dacre ignored a private plea from a genuinely alarmed Cameron to tone down some of the *Mail*'s anti-Europe rhetoric, telling Cameron he and his readers had been committed Brexiteers for 25 years. According to the BBC's *Newsnight* programme, Cameron then approached *Mail* chairman Lord Rothermere to ask him to sack Dacre. None of those involved would ever confirm the details, but they were never comprehensively denied.[14]

This was Planet Tabloid at its most strident and political. And here again, the stridency of the tabloids would set the agenda for coverage of the debate in the two influential serious newspapers – *The Times* and *Sunday Times* – because they reflected both *The Sun* and Murdoch's own agenda, and *The Telegraph* because the anti-immigration tone aligned with the views of many of their predominately right-wing readership and because their former journalist and now occasional columnist Boris Johnson had in part driven the anti-EU debate. The Ethical Journalism Network condemned it as 'an abdication of basic journalist ethics'.[15] A new campaign, Stop Funding Hate, was established with the aim to persuade advertisers not to use newspapers – mainly the *Mail*, *The Sun* and the *Express* – that used 'fear and division' to fuel sales and demonized refugees and migrants. The campaign, said its founder Richard Wilson, an NGO worker, would 'call out' advertisers who preached values of honesty and decency while funding newspapers that traded in 'hate, prejudice and lies'.[16]

Former *Sun* editor David Yelland said later:

> If you go back and look at the front pages day after day of *The Sun* and the *Mail* and the *Express* during the referendum, they told lies on a daily basis about what would happen – how simple it would be to leave the EU, what the problem with the EU would be and so on . . . If you talk to anyone in Europe about the tabloid press, they say that it is the fundamental thing which swept the vote.[17]

In April 2018, after Desmond had sold the paper, the new *Daily Express* editor Gary Jones, who had taken over the previous month, told Parliament's Home Affairs Select Committee investigating the treatment of minority groups in print media that he wanted to change the tone of the paper and that some stories in the past had been 'downright offensive', had made him feel 'very uncomfortable' and had contributed to 'Islamophobic sentiment' in the media.[18]

The vote to leave did not settle the argument and heralded an unprecedented period of national upheaval and argument. David Cameron, who had campaigned for Remain, resigned and when Johnson, his expected successor, pulled out, former Home Secretary Theresa May emerged as Prime Minister but struggled to both negotiate an exit agreement with the EU and keep a lid on the factions within her party. In the years of domestic political turbulence that followed, the *Mail* in particular kept up in its aggressive tone. On 11 November 2016, a front page condemning High Court judges who had ruled that Parliament must approve any legislation to put the Brexit vote into law carried a provocative headline dubbing them 'Enemies of the People' who were out of touch and 'defied' 17.4 million Brexit voters. It resulted in widespread condemnation and more than 1,000 complaints to IPSO. The story was written by the political editor, James Slack, who shortly afterwards went to Downing Street as press officer for May. The following April, when May called a snap election to try to reinforce her shaky position, the *Mail* carried a particularly tightly cropped image of her grim and determined face under a 'Crush the Saboteurs' headline, with a strap headline defining the 'Saboteurs' as 'game-playing Remoaners' and unelected lords. The dark and angry tone of both front pages reflected the mood of the times, and joined the canon of Dacre's most significant headlines before his slightly unexpected resignation in 2018. But they were not his last.

Catch and Kill

Alongside Brexit, another new phrase entered the journalistic lexicon in the middle of the decade, as millionaire and former reality television star Donald Trump campaigned to be president of the United States: 'catch and kill'. This is what it is called when someone signs a legal agreement with a publication to tell their story exclusively to that publication (usually for a fee), in the belief that their story will be published. That is the 'catch'; the 'kill' is when the story is never published. British and indeed U.S. tabloids had, of course, sometimes used this tactic, usually to undermine rivals or perhaps as a favour to one PR person or celebrity as part of the intricate web of dealings between such parties. (The reverse process of accepting money to bury stories had in fact been legal in the riotous days of publishing in Regency London until the 1843 Libel Act.) But never before had it been used so nakedly and for such politically partisan ends as in the *National Enquirer*'s actions on behalf of Trump.

By 2016 the *Enquirer* had achieved a number of serious scoops among its diet of crime and celebrity news but it was now languishing. In the 1990s, while still under the control of Scot Iain Calder, it was praised for its coverage of the O. J. Simpson murder trial, which led to several exclusives; it had published pictures of the semen-stained dress of White House intern Monica Lewinsky, who had an affair with President Bill Clinton. Calder, its controlling figure for so long, stepped back in 1995 and by the early 2000s its circulation had suffered under competition from the raft of more soft-focus celebrity magazines and the increasing celebrity content in all other publications, soon to be followed by Internet gossip sites like TMZ. By 2005 its circulation had dropped to just over 1.1 million. Aiming to replicate the Calder era, its owners, American Media Inc., now run by U.S. publishing executive David Pecker, employed rising star Paul Field, then associate editor of *The Sun* and formerly of the *Mail* and *Mail on Sunday*, to head up a team of twenty British tabloid journalists to revitalize the *Enquirer*'s newsroom. The experiment lasted just over eighteen months before Field and his team were sacked, all with payoffs. Field returned to the *Mail on Sunday* and other executive roles within Associated. The *Enquirer*, it was said, was suffering from a lack of resources, both staff and budgets – which had been diverted to *Star* magazine – and was penalized for being outside the Hollywood PR machine with which their more compliant rivals were happy to align.[19] However, it did revive its reputation in 2008 with a series of stories about presidential candidate John Edwards having an extramarital affair, which led to it being eligible to be considered for the Pulitzer Prize.[20] It did not win.

In the run-up to Trump's success in the 2016 presidential election, the *Wall Street Journal* revealed that Karen McDougal, a former Playboy Playmate, had been paid $150,000 by AMI for the story of her affair with the businessman a decade previously, but it did not publish the story. This was classic 'catch and kill'. The *Wall Street Journal* quoted Pecker as saying that Trump was 'a personal friend'.[21] In 2018 it also emerged that the *Enquirer* had paid a former porn star, Stormy Daniels, $130,000 to remain quiet about her affair with Trump. In June 2018 the *Washington Post* revealed that the *Enquirer* had sent stories about Trump and his opponents to his lawyer, Michael Cohen, for approval prior to publication. The story quoted one *Enquirer* source as saying:

> Since Trump become president and even before, [Pecker] openly just has been willing to turn the magazine and the cover over to the Trump machine . . . if it was a story specifically about Trump, then it was sent over to Michael, and as long as there were no objections from him, the story could be published.[22]

In December 2018 Cohen was sentenced to three years in prison for what a judge described as a 'veritable smorgasbord' of offences, including the hush-money offences.[23] At the same time, Pecker admitted making the payments as part of a deal in order to avoid prosecution.[24] In 2021 the Federal Election Commission fined the *Enquirer* $187,000 because the payment to McDougal had effectively been an undeclared electoral contribution.

The Last Silverback in Fleet Street

When Dacre announced his retirement as editor in June 2018, there were many raised eyebrows around Fleet Street and politics. During the previous decade, he had remained while the big beasts around him – MacKenzie, Morgan, Coulson and so on – had left the stage, leaving much paler shadows in their wakes. Of the great tabloid era of the 1980s and '90s, and early 2000s, only Rebekah Brooks survived, running Murdoch's UK newspapers. While Dacre would never, ever concede that the *Mail* was a 'red-top', his newspaper – and it was 'his' from front to back – dominated the popular end of the market and influenced the agendas of all other newspapers, popular and serious, wherever they were on the political spectrum. It had become, as former employee Helen Lewis wrote, 'the most influential newspaper in Britain and its editor has the purest power of any person in Britain'. He was, she wrote, 'Fleet Street's last silverback gorilla'.[25]

No popular editor other than MacKenzie had imposed their identity so completely on their publication as Dacre. Under Dacre the paper was, as John Lloyd, director of journalism at the Reuters Institute at Oxford University, wrote in the *Financial Times*, 'a daily and brilliantly disciplined savaging of government follies, progressive fads and flouters of the time-honoured verities of British and family life'.[26] Writing in the *London Review of Books* in 2017 in the aftermath of Brexit, Andrew O'Hagan said Dacre's 'worst effect' on the *Mail* 'has been to let it seem mired in the things it hates, as if society's worst excesses were mostly an outgrowth of its own paranoid imagination'. He added: 'A quiet news day at the *Mail* nowadays is taken up with the search for people to punish, or "name and shame", as if that alone could lift the spirits, but it wasn't always like that.' The paper, he wrote, was a 'bubbling quagmire of prejudice posing as news, of opinion dressed as fact, and contempt posing as contempt for that portion of the world's population that doesn't live in Cheam'. He went on to define the *Mail*'s character: 'its relentless outrage, its stifling sense of mission, its much diminished interest in human daftness and its poker-faced determination to see everything as a non-laughing matter'.[27]

Dacre himself had reigned largely by terror and by repeated use of the c-word to denigrate his senior executives. His own prejudices and feelings ran through the paper like sap through a tree. A workaholic, he was driven to his office in Kensington High Street from either his London house or his Sussex farmhouse by his chauffeur, would spend twelve or fourteen hours in the office and then would be driven home again. While such hours were normal among editors, Dacre, unlike MacKenzie or Morgan, was never clubbable, never one to share a drink with even his senior colleagues. In his worldview, wrote Lewis, 'the decent people of Britain are silenced and denigrated by an elite that includes, but is not limited to, judges, the House of Lords, "fat cat bankers", jobsworth council employees, the European Union and the BBC.' Liberals, she said, defined the paper by its excesses: the appalling front page describing judges as 'enemies of the people'; the description of Mick Philpott, who killed six of his seventeen children, as a 'vile product of Welfare UK'; the attack on then Labour Party leader Ed Miliband's late father Ralph, a Jewish refugee who volunteered in the Navy, as a man who 'hated Britain'. And they could not understand how 'someone who earns almost £2.5m a year, spends a month at a time on the British Virgin Islands, owns a fishing estate in the Scottish Highlands and a house in West Sussex, and edits the loudest and angriest of Britain's newspapers, can see himself as an underdog. But Dacre does.'[28] Unlike late-period MacKenzie, Dacre was rarely given to public statements and was naturally a relatively shy man outside the environment of his office; one of his few public interviews was on BBC's *Desert Island Discs* where, after a selection of Bing Crosby, Handel, Verdi and Aaron Copland's *Fanfare for the Common Man*, he chose a subscription to *The Guardian* as his luxury because 'its patronising, right-on, sanctimonious political correctness gets me so angry it would give me the energy and the willpower to get off that island.'[29] There was no ambiguity about his worldview.

Dacre was given a non-job as editor-in-chief of both the *Mail* and *Mail on Sunday* and a seat on the Associated board, meaning he was still in the building – although this was a technicality, since he was rarely seen. Whether he retained the support of Lord Rothermere remained unknown but an indication came when his replacement was named as Geordie Greig, a very different beast indeed. Perhaps this was a sign of a feeling that it was time to move on from the Dacre era. Greig had been editor of the *Mail on Sunday* since 2012. Under his editorship, it had often taken a different, more liberal line on stories than the *Daily Mail*, in particular by supporting Remain in the 2016 Referendum. Greig, educated at Eton and Oxford, could not have been more different to Dacre: a former *Sunday Times* literary editor and editor of both society bible *The Tatler* and the *Evening Standard*, a socially liberal, metropolitan sophisticate, not the conservative voice of the suburbs and shires. He was almost certainly a Tory voter by habit and background – but one of the old-fashioned, so-called 'One Nation' Tories, by now horrified at what the party had become. He was well connected among both the upper classes and cultural elites, a regular at London's literary events and society gatherings, but also a natural journalist – when editor of the *Standard* he had interviewed the notoriously reticent artist Lucian Freud, a scoop he had been chasing for fifteen years, and would go on to write a book about Freud. His last weekend editing the *Mail on Sunday* in August 2018 was disrupted by a dash to the deathbed of writer V. S. Naipaul, where he read poetry to the ailing author. Furthermore, he was slight of build, always courteous in manner and softly spoken in comparison to the tall, stooped and permanently angry Dacre, a definite disadvantage among the other would-be 'silverbacks' of the Fleet Street zoo. Many believed it would not last. Greig had declared in 2017 that Brexit was 'a dangerous illusion'. And so, in a valedictory piece for *The Spectator* in June 2018, Dacre declared: 'Support for Brexit is in the DNA of both the *Daily Mail* and, more pertinently, its readers.' (He was correct, in the sense that he had largely put it there.) He continued: 'Any move to reverse this would be editorial and commercial suicide.'[30] The rest of Fleet Street watched eagerly.

Greig calmed down the tone of the *Mail*, although he was not about to alienate readers by suddenly opposing Brexit; he backed May's attempts to get a deal and then Johnson when he eventually succeeded May in July 2019. In turn, Dacre's former deputy, Ted Verity, now editing the *Mail on Sunday*, turned that paper from Remain to Brexit. But Greig was said to have angered Dacre when he began a campaign supporting the MMR vaccine for children, apologizing for the newspaper's role in giving prominence to the vaccine's discredited links to autism during Dacre's editorship.

The next row was conducted not in the plushly carpeted corridors of *Mail* headquarters but on the pages of the *Financial Times*, where Greig told an interviewer in October 2019 that advertisers were flocking to the *Mail* – a seeming rebuttal of the Dacre era when many had stepped back from the paper after pressure from campaigning groups such as Stop Funding Hate and a feeling the *Mail* was too toxic to be associated with.[31] Dacre, furious, then wrote a letter to the *Financial Times*, saying: 'He claims 265 advertisers came back to the *Daily Mail* in his year as editor. In fact, far more than that number left during the same period.' Dacre said that under his editorship the newspaper had 'won an unprecedented number of awards for the quality of its journalism and its countless great campaigns' – he mentioned the Stephen Lawrence campaign and one launched against plastic bags – and ended with a final barb, damning with faint praise: 'As for Mr Greig, I congratulate him for making a solid start as editor and continuing so many of those campaigns but I'm sure he'll forgive me for suggesting that he (or his PR) defers his next lunch with the FT until he has notched up a small fraction of those journalists' achievements.'[32] Greig wisely resisted further comment, although the parent company, DMG Media, did point out that income from the new advertisers 'more than offset' the loss of others.

In the 2019 general election the *Mail* supported Johnson – or, rather, as Greig had put it to the *Financial Times*, 'anyone but Corbyn', referring to then left-wing Labour leader Jeremy Corbyn – and, like the other tabloids, vociferously backed him through the final push to get the UK's withdrawal from the EU completed in January 2020.

The new Johnson government had a secure eighty-seat majority, but Johnson remained obsessed with staying on the right side of the right-wing media, as former Conservative Chancellor Kenneth, now Lord, Clarke, later told the BBC: 'Boris wasn't interested in Parliament. The main people he was accountable to were the *Daily Mail* and the *Daily Express* and the *Daily Telegraph*. In taking a political decision, tomorrow morning's headline in the *Daily Mail* mattered far more than tonight's vote in the House of Commons.'[33]

Johnson now moved to appoint a number of Conservative allies to key cultural roles. Dacre was publicly backed by Johnson to become the new head of Ofcom, the body that regulates broadcasting, mobile phone networks and the Royal Mail, as well as some aspects of social media. Dacre, as a lifelong newspaper man and, until it became inevitable, an online sceptic, who had long avoided even using a computer in the *Mail* newsroom, was not an obvious choice. But he was an outspoken critic of the BBC and a government supporter. However, the interview panel rejected him as 'not appointable'. The government then decided to rerun the whole process, which to many, even some Tory MPs, seemed like a blatant fix; there were problems finding enough people willing to sit on the interview panel. Julian Knight, the Conservative chair of the culture Select Committee, told *The Guardian* Dacre should not be allowed to stand again. 'The recruitment process is being re-run despite the absence of any adequate explanation being provided by government on the need to do so,' he said.

> Where a previous candidate has been deemed to be un-appointable for a post, they should be ruled out of re-applying. However, this crucial line is missing from the campaign information to recruit Ofcom's next chair. It would be extremely alarming if this was a deliberate omission rather than an oversight and we are seeking clarification.[34]

Shortly afterwards, without any fanfare, it was announced that Dacre had left the *Mail*, bringing to an end 42 years with the newspaper. Or did it?

What followed was a typically brutal Fleet Street executive merry-go-round, forced by a combination of political and commercial pressures. In November, Greig, who had overseen highly critical *Mail* coverage of the various crises and controversies surrounding Boris Johnson's premiership, was suddenly ousted and replaced by Ted Verity, who would have oversight of both titles, although company lifer David Dillion soon became *Mail on Sunday* editor – a move which was aimed at bringing both operations closer together to conserve resources at a point where Rothermere was moving DMG away from being a publicly listed company and back into private ownership. At the same time, New York-based Richard Caccappolo, who was an ally of Martin Clarke and had assisted him in turning *MailOnline* into a global brand, was made head of the media business side of DMG, seen by some as securing Clarke own's power base; since 2018 he had also had the role of DMG Publisher, overseeing all the *Mail* titles, which now also included *The i*, the former tabloid version of *The Independent*, which it had bought from the *Standard* and was developing into its own brand. Shortly after that, Dacre withdrew his second application for the Ofcom job and, in a letter to *The Times*, attacked the civil service for obstructing such appointments – 'if you are possessed of an independent mind and are un-associated with the liberal/left, you will have more chance of winning the lottery than getting the job.'[35] Within days he was back at Derry Street, in his old job as editor-in-chief, welcomed by both Verity and Clarke. Dacre's new position, it was made clear, was not to conduct day-to-day editing, but to be there in an 'advisory' role. Within a few more days, Clarke resigned to 'pursue new challenges', which Rothermere 'reluctantly accepted'. Who was the winner here? If anyone, not Dacre or Verity, or Clarke. But perhaps it was Jonathan Rothermere, the 4th Viscount, great-grandson of Harold Harmsworth, who made the company founded by his brother, Alfred, into a global media brand. What either man would have made of *MailOnline*'s obsession with the Kardashians can only be speculated.

Under the new regime, the *Mail* was back on track, supporting Johnson throughout his travails and ultimate resignation the following year. It transferred that uncritical support to enthusiastic backing of his successor, Liz Truss. When she was forced to resign in late 2022 after a disastrous budget led to a slump in the economy, the *Mail*'s support went to the third prime minister of the year, Rishi Sunak. And then, of course, it gave a weekly column to Boris Johnson.

The Megxit Massacre

Princes William and Harry had grown up in the tabloid spotlight. At a very young age they had endured widespread coverage in all media of the supposed affairs of both their parents – with intimate details of their extramarital relationships splashed across front pages and news bulletins – and their eventual very public separation and divorce. These are events that would have been deeply embarrassing and distressing to any young boys. It left both of them with a very personal deep distrust of the media. Despite this, they had also been part of the informal contract the royal family had with the media which allowed occasional access to the princes – formal royal visits and photo opportunities for events such as birthdays and first days at school in return for privacy at other times. Once Prince Harry passed the age of eighteen and the contract ended, the tabloids gave plenty of space to covering his private life, including his girlfriends. Rumours of youthful drug taking and his ill-advised wearing of a swastika-adorned Nazi uniform at a 2005 party predictably caused widespread criticism. It was about then that private investigators working for the *News of the World* began hacking into the voicemails of royal aides, the disclosure of which had led to the convictions of Glenn Mulcaire and Clive Goodman and was part of the chain of events that led eventually to the Leveson Inquiry.

By the time Prince Harry met American actress Meghan Markle on a blind date in 2016, he was seen as having matured from a somewhat rebellious youth, the 'spare' to his older brother's 'heir', into a serious-minded former Army officer who had gained respect for his military service in Afghanistan and his work on behalf of injured ex-service personnel. In the post-Leveson years, the tabloids had, it was believed, largely avoided intrusive activities involving the royals. But right from the start it was obvious that Markle was no Diana or Kate Middleton, by then Duchess of Cambridge and the wife of Prince William, who were both easily classified as white, 'safe' English roses with no family secrets or previous boyfriends to come out of the woodwork. At the same relationship stage, the worst thing the tabloids could do with Diana was photograph her in an inadvertently see-through dress and with Kate the only evidence of debauchery was a slightly revealing costume during a student fashion show. With Markle there was plenty for the tabloids to go on. Here was a woman with a history: three years older than the prince, divorced, mixed race, from an 'ordinary' background – rather than the resolutely middle-class one of the Middleton family or the aristocratic one of Diana – and who had become a leading actress in a major U.S. television drama series, *Suits*, which had occasionally featured her in romantic, though not overly sexual, situations.

It didn't start well. Sexist and racist tropes were employed right from the off once the relationship became public. At the beginning of November 2016, a piece published in the *MailOnline* attempted to portray Markle as growing up surrounded by crime and violence and was headlined: 'Harry's Girl Is (Almost) Straight Outta Compton', in a reference to the notoriously crime- and drug-affected Compton neighbourhood of Los Angeles, which was in fact more than 20 kilometres (14 mi.) away from where Markle's mother lived in Crenshaw, a much less troubled and more suburban area.[36] A few days later, 'Harry's Girl on Pornhub' said the front-page headline on *The Sun*, contrasting with a large image of a glamorous Kate Middleton dressed entirely in white and showing a small amount of demure leg: the titillating reference to the pornography website alluded to what *The Sun* called 'steamy sex scenes', which were in fact clips from *Suits* rather than pornographic content.[37] After it was pointed out that the story was over-egged and that Buckingham Palace were angry *The Sun* dropped the Pornhub story from its website and was more complimentary in a leader the next day, saying Markle had more in common with a modern British family than those in the 'fusty royal corridors': 'Meghan, with her divorce, her ethnic background and fake-it-til-you-make-it work ethic is much more the 21st-century woman, something the future of the royal family may depend on.'[38] (It was not until February the following year that, after some further representations from the palace, it published a one-paragraph apology.[39]) In the following days in the *Mail on Sunday*, Rachel Johnson, sister of Boris Johnson, weighed in again when she wrote: 'Miss Markle's mother is a dread-locked African-American lady from the wrong side of the tracks.' She said that if the couple had children, 'the Windsors will thicken their watery, thin blue blood and Spencer pale skin and ginger hair with some rich and exotic DNA.'[40] The prince and the Palace strongly and publicly objected to these stories, issuing a statement condemning the 'wave of abuse and harassment' and the 'racist undertones' of comment pieces.[41]

At about the same time, Prince Harry's later court action would claim, *The Sun* had hired a private detective to investigate his girlfriend's background in California. And the entitled insistence of the tabloids that the prince must bow to their will was made abundantly clear by Katie Nicholl, royal correspondent for the *Mail on Sunday*, who told LBC radio:

If he really wants this to go away, there [are] one or two things he could do. You give the press what they want. You make a statement, or you give an interview or you issue a picture. There has not been one picture of them together. Fleet Street will not rest until they have got their picture of them together and they have got some words either from Prince Harry or Meghan about the relationship.[42]

In the run-up to their eventual wedding, there was continued coverage of the rift between Markle and her estranged father, Thomas, who was happy to be paid money by both British and U.S. newspapers for his views on his daughter and his disappointment at not being invited. But by the time they married in May 2018, there was some true love and much hypocrisy on display. The event resonated well with the country and even the tabloids applauded its diversity: the gospel choir, the American preacher and an audience that included Hollywood and Bollywood royalty as well as British. The *Sun on Sunday* was effusive: the front-page headline over a picture of the couple kissing said 'KISSTORY', and inside, a leading article said, 'We couldn't be more thrilled for them. It was a day that will live long in the memory – and was a wonderful symbol of the country we have become.'[43] The *Sunday Express* dubbed them the 'House of Windsor's new golden couple',[44] and the *Mail on Sunday*, with 47 pages devoted to the event, said: 'We rejoice in their happiness and wish them a long and blessed marriage.'[45] The honeymoon did not last.

Over the next year, the tabloids continued to milk Thomas Markle for stories about his relationship with his daughter and repeated suggestions of a rift between Markle, now Duchess of Sussex, and pregnant, and the Duchess of Cambridge. As *The Guardian* noted,

Other critical coverage of the couple has ranged from their use of private jets to their refusal to allow media coverage of the christening of their baby son Archie or name his godparents. They have also been criticised for the £2.4m cost to the public purse for renovations at their Windsor home, Frogmore Cottage.[46]

Now the duke launched an unprecedented attack on the media: while he stressed the couple believed in media freedom, there had been a 'ruthless' campaign against his wife that had escalated over the past year throughout her pregnancy, which had continued after the birth of their son. His statement, placed on the couple's website in October 2019, added:

> There is a human cost to this relentless propaganda, specifically when it is knowingly false and malicious, and though we have continued to put on a brave face – as so many of you can relate to – I cannot begin to describe how painful it has been . . . Because in today's digital age, press fabrications are repurposed as truth across the globe. One day's coverage is no longer tomorrow's chip-paper. I have been a silent witness to her private suffering for too long. To stand back and do nothing would be contrary to everything we believe in.[47]

True to their word, the duchess launched a legal action for copyright infringement against Associated Newspapers over publication in the *Mail on Sunday*, then under Ted Verity, of parts of a letter she had sent to her father, which he had given to the paper.

The website Buzzfeed would later publish a list of twenty cases where critical coverage of the Duchess of Sussex contrasted with a more favourable approach to the Duchess of Cambridge. For instance, one *Daily Mail* story supporting a picture of the pregnant Duchess of Cambridge had the headline: 'Not Long to Go! Kate Tenderly Cradles Her Baby Bump',[48] while a year later a similar picture of the Duchess of Sussex carried a comment from Liz Jones, a *Mail on Sunday* feature writer, saying 'Personally, I find the cradling a bit like those signs in the back of cars: Baby on Board. Virtue signalling, as though the rest of us barren harridans deserve to burn alive in our cars.' The headline was: 'Why Can't Meghan Keep Her Hands Off Her Bump?'[49] One story in the *Daily Express* on Markle's love for avocados during pregnancy carried the headline 'Meghan Markle's Beloved Avocado Linked to Human Rights Abuse and Drought, Millennial Shame',[50] which contrasted with an earlier, favourable story about Prince William giving his wife an avocado to help with morning sickness. There were similar contrasts in other stories regarding where the couples would spend Christmas, their decisions to establish personal brands and the choice of flowers and air fresheners for their respective weddings – in each case the actions of the Duchess of Sussex were presented in a much more critical way than those of her sister-in-law.[51] In the United States, where the weekly celebrity gossip magazines' and websites' obsession with British royals had intensified when it was established that a U.S. actress was in a relationship with the son of the Princess of Wales, some of the headlines from the outset had been even more brutal and fact-free: 'Monster Meghan Breaks Queen's Heart',[52] 'Harry Trapped in Marriage from Hell!',[53] 'Harry and Meghan Shotgun Wedding! HUMILIATED QUEEN Orders Red-Haired Rogue to Marry Pregnant TV Star'.[54] And, even as this book was being completed, there has been no easing-off on the couple: 'Their Ultimate Revenge, William and Kate Destroy Meghan' is the headline in U.S celebrity and gossip magazine *The Globe*.[55]

Three Cases

The fightback had begun. One Monday morning in late March 2023, a cluster of photographers and camera crews were waiting outside the Royal Courts of Justice in the Strand hoping to catch a few shots of some of the celebrities who might or might not be there for a long-anticipated court case. They might have included Sir Elton John and actresses Elizabeth Hurley and Sadie Frost as well as Baroness Doreen Lawrence, mother of victim of racist murder Stephen Lawrence. All were taking legal action against Associated Newspapers, publishers of the *Daily Mail*, *MailOnline* and the *Mail on Sunday*, over phone hacking and other illegal activities. It was a preliminary hearing to deal with an attempt by Associated to have the case thrown out on timing grounds, so not all those taking action were expected to attend. To everyone's surprise, a black taxi pulled up and the most interesting name on the legal action stepped out, accompanied by two burly security guards: Prince Harry, the Duke of Sussex, had flown in unexpectedly from his new home in California, although there was no specific reason for him to be there. The fact that the prince – who, like his brother William, grew up believing his mother had been hounded by the tabloids and had died at least partially as a result of their actions – had crossed the Atlantic simply to sit in the courtroom to see his case being fought indicated only one thing: after years of tabloid torment, he was out for justice.

While coverage of the various hacking-related trials had petered out, particularly after the announcement by the CPS in 2015 that there would be no further criminal prosecutions, some civil cases had continued but attracted little publicity. The release of Mr Justice Saunders's unredacted summing-up in the Gulati case in 2018 only really attracted attention among press reform campaigners, despite some of its damning conclusions. But for the Duke of Sussex, the pain was still being inflicted in the continuing coverage of himself and his wife, despite their retirement from royal duties and move to California. It was clearly time to get serious. Twelve years after Leveson, the whole spectre of phone hacking and illegal activities by British newspapers would once again come under scrutiny.

In 2018, at a party at the French home of Elton John – no stranger to tabloid attention himself – the duke had met barrister David Sherborne, who had acted as lead counsel to the Leveson Inquiry, interrogating Murdoch, Morgan, Brookes, Weaver and others.[56] By now, the duke believed the royal family had agreed a discreet and unpublished deal with Murdoch's News Group Newspapers that the family would refrain from any legal actions until all other investigations had been concluded and in return for a public apology. However, despite correspondence between Robert Thomson, the chief executive of News Corp (Murdoch's UK holding company), Rebekah Brooks and the queen's director of communications Sally Osman and private secretary Sir Christopher Geidt, as well as the private secretaries for the two princes, no agreement on an apology was ever reached, due to what the duke would later claim was 'filibustering' by MGN. By the time the duke met Sherborne he was frustrated and angry at the lack of progress. Sherborne advised the duke that he had a clear claim of phone hacking and intrusion. He advised the duke to find his own lawyers, but, of course, would be delighted to act for him.[57] The following year, lawyers for the duke lodged actions: the first against News Corp, but also against Associated Newspapers and Mirror Group Newspapers, all making a series of allegations of illegal activities and breaches of privacy. Prince Harry's various actions would not reach court until that day in March 2023.

While the cases were making their slow progress through the legal system, the Sussexes had decided to stand back from being regular 'working' members of the royal family – with the ceremonial duties that involved – and move to California, Markle's home state and closer to her mother, the only grandmother of their child, which they did in March 2020. The tabloids immediately dubbed this move 'Megxit'. They were accused of abandoning their responsibilities to Crown and country and there was a raft of speculative stories that stemmed from the decision: would they continue to receive royal funding, would Harry continue with his various royal titles and honorary positions, would they return for future royal occasions, such as the queen's Platinum Jubilee in 2022? Rather than remove themselves from tabloid coverage and speculation, as they might have hoped, they had only intensified it. It would continue to plague them.

In December 2021 the duchess was awarded undisclosed but 'substantial' damages – estimated to be at least six figures – and a portion of her equally substantial costs for breach of copyright over the publication of the letter to her father by Associated Newspapers. Tellingly, the headlines in the *Mail*, by then edited by Verity, and other tabloids – as well as the BBC and *The Guardian* – focused on the fact that she had been awarded only a token £1 in damages for the other element of her claim, the breach of privacy, a legal route she had chosen not to argue in order to focus on the copyright aspect. It was typical of the way the couple were misrepresented in the popular media. As Brian Cathcart, formerly of Hacked Off and professor of journalism at Kingston University, put it:

> Those who chose the 'just £1' angle not only misled their readers and viewers and they not only went with the herd in a way journalists are not supposed to do; they also played along with the *Mail*'s systematic misrepresentation of a case it was always doomed to lose and which in the end it lost very badly indeed.[58]

After that first day of the hearings in March 2023, Prince Harry spent almost a week in the courtroom, sometimes alongside celebrities like Sir Elton, hearing lawyers for Associated Newspapers attempt to have the case thrown out on the basis that the claims had been lodged out of time. The claims themselves alleged that nineteen private investigators placed phone taps on landlines, taped microphones to windows, bugged cars, intercepted voicemail, blagged information ranging from bank statements to flight details, and put their celebrity targets under surveillance. They are said to have worked for around eighty journalists at the *Daily Mail* and *Mail on Sunday*, which had always denied, in the strongest possible terms, that its staff ever used illegal or intrusive methods. Associated lawyers described the claims as a 'pre-planned and orchestrated attempt' to drag the *Mail* titles into the phone-hacking scandal by a coalition of journalists and anti-press campaigners. The claims were 'unsubstantiated', 'highly defamatory' and a 'fishing expedition', said Associated in its response to the claim.[59] Judgement was reserved.

The following month, a similar hearing, not attended by the duke, took place when News Group Newspapers also tried to argue that the action was out of time; the duke's claim revealed publicly for the first time that the Duke of Cambridge had agreed a 'massive' compensation payment with the Murdoch papers sometime in 2020.[60] This was after a 'hands off' agreement between the royals and Murdoch dating from around 2012 – that is, just after Leveson – involved them delaying any civil action until all other claims had been exhausted.[61] Prince Harry also claimed that his father, then Prince of Wales, together with his assistants, had tried to stop him in October 2019. 'I was summoned to Buckingham Palace and specifically told to drop the legal actions because they have an "effect on all the family"'.[62] At this hearing, lawyers for Prince Harry claimed News UK had engaged in 'years of deliberate concealment, destruction of evidence, cover-up at the highest level and false denials even given under oath', adding, 'The invasion of his personal conversations and relationships caused distress, as his privacy was constantly violated and his safety jeopardised. [Prince Harry] is appalled by the tactics used by journalists to interfere with and ruin his relationships, and feels sick knowing that these actions were conducted unlawfully.'[63]

The claim alleged that journalists were involved in illegally intercepting voicemail messages, obtaining private information (such as itemized phone bills or medical records) by deception or 'blagging', and using private investigators to commit these unlawful information-gathering acts on their behalf. It was also alleged that unlawful activity was used to obtain highly sensitive information about the state of mind of Prince Harry's late mother, Diana, Princess of Wales, his welfare at the age of ten and their relationship. The claim alleged that an American private investigator was instructed as recently as 2016 to obtain information about his emerging relationship with Meghan, including her (confidential) social security number and other personal information about her family, which was used as the basis for two articles in *The Sun*. In this case, the other claimant was actor Hugh Grant, who by now had joined the board of Hacked Off and had become a leading campaigner against media intrusion and for more a more accountable press.

In July 2023 Mr Justice Fancourt ruled that the trial for unlawful gathering of information could go ahead the following year in conjunction with the claims by Grant and others, but rejected the hacking part of the claims because the duke had not made his claim within the six-year limit after being made aware of the allegations; the judge rejected the idea of a secret agreement as a reason for the delay because there was no evidence to support the existence of such an agreement.[64]

But it was the third case which would give the prince a personal public platform. Here he was one of four people bringing actions against Mirror Group Newspapers. The others were less well known: *Coronation Street* actors Michael Turner and Nikki Sanderson and Fiona Wightman, the former wife of comedy actor Paul Whitehouse. All claimed that hacking had been used to obtain stories about their private lives and that MGN editors and news executives were fully aware of these methods. And the trial was doubly significant – it would be used to arrive at a level of damages and it would be used as a test case for almost a hundred further claims from a wide range of celebrities and others in and out of the public eye. MGN had already paid out more than £100 million to settle about six hundred other claims, which had had been agreed out of court. This trial would centre on more than two hundred stories involving all four claimants, of which around 140 were about the prince; 33 stories were the specific focus of his case.

On Tuesday, 6 June 2023, he made history by becoming the first royal to give evidence in court for more than 130 years, telling the court that he had experienced hostility from the press since the day he was born and that 'cruel' stories about him had damaged his relationships with those around him. Over the course of two days of evidence, the prince repeatedly asserted that stories were obtained by illegal and intrusive methods, but, as most observers noted, he struggled to provide details, relying on broader statements.[65]

Putting the MGN defence, barrister Andrew Green KC, while expressing sympathy for the 'extraordinary' level of intrusion the prince had faced, argued that it did not follow that all of it was unlawful, and that stories had been obtained by legitimate means while others were follow-ups to reporting elsewhere. The prince's claims, he said, were entirely speculative and, unlike the 2015 case where MGN had admitted hacking, there was little evidence that the stories had been obtained by illegal means.

In a separate, 55-page-long witness statement, the prince said the tabloid media had created 'an alternative and distorted version of me'. 'They then start to edge you towards playing the role or roles that suit them best and which sells as many newspapers as possible, especially if you are the "spare" to the "heir",' he said. 'You're then either the "playboy prince", the "failure", the "drop out" or, in my case, the "thicko", the "cheat", the "underage drinker", the "irresponsible drug taker" . . .' Stories suggesting that his real father was former Army officer James Hewitt, with whom his mother had a relationship after he was born, were 'hurtful, mean and cruel', while the thought of Piers Morgan and other journalists listening to his mother's private messages made him 'physically sick'. He recounted how journalists were at an airport arrivals hall when he arrived to meet his then girlfriend Chelsy Davy. 'I recall thinking how on earth did they know I was going to be there, but now it's obvious.' He said: 'I felt I couldn't trust anybody, which was an awful feeling for me, especially at such a young age.'[66]

The rest of the hearing was a rerun of earlier claims and denials. Dan Evans, whose evidence had been crucial in the 2015 case, repeated his claims of what he termed 'corporate grooming' by Tina Weaver when he joined the *Sunday Mirror*, while Brian Basham, a former journalist now running a business research company, gave evidence that he had warned MGN chairman David Grigson in 2012 that his employees had been involved in hacking but nothing was done: 'the company covered up wrongdoing.' In turn, Sly Bailey, the former MGN chief executive who had left in 2012 with a reported £900,000 payoff, took to the witness box to deny she had orchestrated a cover-up and that she gave misleading evidence to the Leveson Inquiry. And while MGN admitted that it had spent around £9 million on private investigators between 1996 and 2011, subcontracted by reporters to research individuals, often targeting bank or NHS records, Green argued that while some of them might have used unlawful methods, the majority of information came from legitimate databases.

The court also heard from Graham Johnson, who had been a senior reporter and investigations editor at the *Sunday Mirror* from 1997 to 2005 and who in 2013 had become the only journalist to voluntarily confess to police to phone hacking, for which he had received a suspended sentence. He claimed he had been instructed to do it in 2001 by then deputy editor Mark Thomas, with the knowledge of Tina Weaver, then editor, and that he had commissioned private investigators to find records on celebrities and buy police intelligence reports. He told the court:

> The *Mirror* is no different to an organised crime group. This is a true crime story which is constantly evolving. By any definition it can be defined as an organised crime group because it was involved in systemic crime over many years, involving hundreds of people, involving a hierarchy of people.[67]

Lawyers for the claimants also drew attention to a series of incidents linked to Piers Morgan, *Mirror* editor between 1995 and 2004, which suggested he knew about phone hacking and blagging: the lunch where Morgan urged a phone company executive to tell his customers they should change the PIN numbers on their mobiles, because journalists could listen to their voicemail messages; the evidence of a former intern who told the court he overheard a journalist reassuring Morgan that a story about the singer Kylie Minogue was accurate because it had come from her voicemails; and the agent for TV presenter Ulrika Jonsson, who couldn't work out why Morgan seemed to know so much about her client. There were a number of other occasions when he demonstrated knowledge of hacking: in his book *The Insider* and in interviews for the BBC's *Desert Island Discs*, and with Charlotte Church and Naomi Campbell.[68] However, he had told the Leveson Inquiry that he had never, to his knowledge, listened to illegally obtained voicemail messages.[69]

At the end of the hearing, Mr Justice Fancourt made an extraordinary statement. He deliberately listed 29 journalists who he considered should or could have given evidence. Morgan was one of them. Others included Mark Thomas, the former editor of the

People, and Gary Jones, former reporter for the *Mirror* and now editor of the *Daily Express*. Also included was former *News of the World* deputy editor Neil Wallis, who had been cleared of hacking.[70] Wallis had recently criticized the bringing of civil claims, in a BBC documentary: 'You have just about anybody who's ever appeared in a tabloid newspaper saying – give me large wadges [*sic*] of cash please. I think it's actually a legal scandal.'[71]

When the ruling by Mr Justice Fancourt came, on 15 December, it was as damning as it could be for MGN, once the home of Hugh Cudlipp and the Zec brothers, of Cassandra and Keith Waterhouse. At all three MGN newspapers – the Daily and Sunday *Mirror*s and the *Sunday People* – unlawful information gathering was widespread and private investigators were an 'integral part' of the news-gathering operation. Fifteen of the 33 sample articles at the centre of the case utilized phone hacking or unlawful information gathering, said the judge, although the remaining eighteen did not 'stand up to careful analysis'. He said phone hacking at the papers had become 'widespread and habitual' from 1998 and continued as an 'important tool' until 2011, even, to some extent, during the Leveson Inquiry. There

Piers Morgan, 1998.

was 'no doubt', ruled the judge, that Piers Morgan and two directors were fully aware of the practices: Bailey, the former chief executive, and Paul Vickers, group legal director (although the judge said other directors were not aware). These two executives 'knew about the illegal activity that was going on at their newspapers and could and should have put a stop to it. Instead of doing so, they turned a blind eye to what was going on, and positively concealed it,' he said. Others aware or likely to have been aware of phone hacking were Richard Wallace, now at Murdoch's new TalkTV, where Morgan now had his own show, and Gary Jones, *Daily Express* editor.

The judge effectively accused the company of a cover-up, saying it had emerged relatively unscathed from Leveson, where it had failed to give 'full disclosure' to the inquiry, adding that a decision had been taken 'at a high level' that the publisher's interests 'were best served by keeping a lid on as much as possible of what had happened'. Claims by MGN that it did not have the ability to investigate allegations of unlawful activity were untrue. He added: 'Even today, MGN is not being open about the extent to which voicemail interception and unlawful information gathering went on at its newspapers.' The duke was awarded £140,600 in damages. Of the three others who were part of the claim, Turner was awarded £31,650 with the judge ruling that phone hacking or other illegal activities had been involved in four of the 27 articles submitted in his claim. The claims of Sanderson and Wightman were dismissed as being out of time although in both cases the judge found evidence of hacking or other illegal activities in some of the articles and invoices they submitted.[72]

In a statement read out on his behalf by Sherborne, the duke said the Metropolitan Police and the Crown Prosecution Service should now investigate. 'Today', the duke said, 'is a great day for truth, as well as accountability.' He added, 'This case is not just about hacking – it is about a systemic practice of unlawful and appalling behaviour, followed by cover-ups and destruction of evidence, the shocking scale of which can only be revealed through these proceedings.' Other reactions were equally predictable. The Metropolitan Police said they would examine the judgement carefully. MGN said the judgement allowed it to 'move forward. Where historical wrongdoing took place, we apologise unreservedly, have taken full responsibility and paid appropriate compensation.' Moving forward in this case will mean responding to up to one hundred further civil claims for which the hearing acted as a test case to assess the level of damages. And Piers Morgan said in a statement read to the media outside his house that the duke 'wouldn't know truth if it slapped him in his California-tanned face', and claimed the Duke and the Duchess of Sussex, were trying to 'destroy the British monarchy'. He said the hearing had been full of 'false allegations' about him by 'old foes' and he repeated his denials of ever hacking a phone or asking anyone else to: 'Nobody has provided any actual evidence to prove that I did.'[73]

CONCLUSION
The Current Condition
of Planet Tabloid

Brian Cathcart, journalist, academic and one of the founders of Hacked Off, wrote in *Byline Times* in May 2023:

> Why is the United Kingdom in a mess? Our problem is the press. That's not to say they made the mess on their own – they obviously had help – but fundamentally, indeed overwhelmingly, it's down to them. It is the corporate national press, whose messages pervade and poison all other media, that has normalized the abnormal in the UK, that has made what is wrong appear right, that has stoked contempt and hatred for the weak and the poor, that has facilitated and concealed corruption, that has engineered applause for the brutal and the stupid and that has corroded what was honest and decent. And in making that mess the press has also made itself more powerful than it has ever been before – so powerful, indeed, that it will take an act of great courage by the whole country to call it to account.

Dr Robert Saunders, reader in modern British history at Queen Mary University of London, wrote on X, formerly known as Twitter, in September 2023: 'The media are the vascular system of a democracy: like arteries, they carry the nutrients on which the health of our democratic debate depends. Yet too many outlets just pump sewage into the political bloodstream. That poisons the entire body politic.'

THE POST-PRINT FUTURE BECKONS

In the years after Leveson, as tabloid websites grew ever larger, fed on a diet of churnalism, print circulations continued to shrink in inverse proportion. Since the growth of the online world, the industry had long wondered which newspaper would be the first to go completely online. As it happens, it was *The Independent*, which dropped its print versions and scrapped the *Independent on Sunday* in spring 2016, becoming digital only.

By early 2020 the overall physical circulation figure of UK national newspapers had dropped over the previous twenty years by more than 55 per cent to 7.4 million. *The Sun* had shrunk from 3.5 million average daily sales in 2000 to 1.25 million (a decrease of 58 per cent), the *Express* from 1 million to a little over 250,000, the *Mirror* from 2.27 million to 451,000 (a 63 per cent drop) and the *Mail* from 2.35 million to 1.1 million (a 45 per cent drop). The Sunday titles showed the same pattern, with the *Sunday People* selling under 140,000 copies a day, losing 74 per cent of its circulation over the previous ten years. The former broadsheets, such as *The Guardian* and *The Times*, catering for different markets, were as bad.[1]

It was hardly surprising that this was the point when many major newspapers then withdrew from the ABC, formerly the Audit Bureau of Circulations, which had registered and published newspaper circulation figures for decades: all the Murdoch titles left in March 2020, the *Telegraph* papers and *The Guardian* and *Observer* in September 2021. It was now only clicks that counted, not circulation, so new metrics were needed to measure the reach of news websites, which can be available across different platforms and apps.

As the century wore on, only the giveaway London tabloids – Associated's *Metro* in the morning and the *Evening Standard* in the afternoon – kept their pagination and their advertising up, with a regular, still buoyant captive readership. But then both would suffer disproportionally from the lack of travel – particularly commuter journeys – during the COVID-19 pandemic of 2020–21. Even when normal life resumed, all the national print circulations suffered as the nation either worked from home or used its smartphones to obtain the information – whether news, games, music, books or social media – it needed on the daily commute. By November 2023, discounting the free *Metro*, which claims a circulation of 951,000, the biggest recorded circulation was that of the *Daily Mail*, with 720,000, followed closely by the *Mail on Sunday* with 615,000 and the *Daily Mirror* with 245,829. A fraction of their previous highs.[2]

Online, it is a very different story. The biggest news website in the UK remains the *MailOnline*, which in November 2023 had a growing total of 24.9 million visits per month to its website and apps, the second biggest number in the UK after the BBC, which had 38.3 million, although that includes its entertainment and sports channels. *The Sun* and the *Mirror* were not far behind, with 23.6 million and 22.8 million respectively; the *Express* had 12.6 million and the *Star*, 8.3 million. Globally, *MailOnline* or the *Daily Mail*'s website was the fifth-biggest news website in the world, with 409 million visits in June 2023 – the BBC came top, at 1.1 billion. The next highest British-based news British website was *The Guardian*, with 349 million hits per month; *The Sun* was further down, with 164 million. Against these figures, a few hundred thousand or so in print circulation seemed insignificant.[3] The future was always going to be online. As the third decade continued, the question remained: who would be next to succumb to the digital world?

MEANWHILE, AT MURDOCH'S *SUN* . . .

On 15 February 2020 television presenter Caroline Flack, who had risen to fame as a result of presenting the tabloid-friendly *Love Island* reality show on ITV, whose personal life had been the subject of intense media scrutiny, who had suffered from depression and was on remand accused of attacking her then boyfriend, committed suicide. It was not known whether she had seen an article in *The Sun* the previous day about what it termed a 'brutal' Valentine's card mocking her. After her death, the article was taken down. An analysis of media coverage by *The Guardian* showed that there were 387 stories about her in the national media before her death; 99 of those were in *The Sun*. A quarter of all stories were negative in tone, with about 18 per cent positive.[4] Within two days of her death a petition had been signed by more than 200,000 people. 'The headlines, harassment and trial by media has to end and they must be held accountable,' it said, calling on the government to investigate the maltreatment of those in the public eye, including Caroline Flack, Prince Harry and Meghan Markle. Many felt that was precisely what the Leveson Inquiry had set out to do.[5]

THE POWER AND INFLUENCE OF MURDOCH CONTINUES

Nigel Farage, former leader of UKIP and then the Brexit party, who did so much to bring about the 2016 referendum, told a BBC documentary on Murdoch in 2020 that the price of the tycoon's support for Tony Blair in 1997 was the promise of a referendum on the euro. 'If Rupert Murdoch had not done that, we would have joined the Euro in 1999 and I doubt Brexit would have happened. It was a decisive intervention from Rupert Murdoch.' After the interview, but before the cameras stopped rolling, Farage told the interviewer that he had checked with Murdoch if it was okay to say that. Murdoch had said yes, he added. Murdoch has always denied asking politicians for favours.[6]

Despite predictions that the hacking legal and compensation costs would ultimately cost Murdoch's businesss more than £1 billion, even before the Prince Harry cases, the mogul was not short of money. In April 2022, following the sale of Sky News after a ruling by the Competition and Markets Authority that the broadcaster be separated from the remainder of Murdoch's UK assets, Murdoch launched TalkTV, a digital news channel dominated by opinionated comment from presenters. It was feared that it would replicate Murdoch's Fox TV in the United States, whose support for Donald Trump helped him win the presidency and continued when he challenged the result of the 2020 election. TalkTV's head of news was, at time of writing, former *Daily Mirror* editor Richard Wallace, and its first major initial signing was Piers Morgan. Rebekah Brooks, as chief executive of News UK, is in overall control. All featured in the hacking controversy.

In summer 2023, as Prince Harry's court action against Murdoch's newspapers continued, the 92-year-old magnate, whose media empire spans the world and who had divorced his fourth wife, Jerry Hall (the former wife of Rolling Stone Mick Jagger), the previous August, held a summer party at Spencer House in central London. The house is owned by Earl Spencer, brother of the late Princess of Wales, who had criticized the media at his sister's funeral. As well as prime minister Rishi Sunak, several members of the Cabinet and former prime minister Liz Truss, others attending included the Labour leader Sir Keir Starmer, who, according to opinion polls, was looking likely to succeed Sunak when the next election came in 2024 or early 2025, and Sadiq Khan, the Mayor of London. At least Sir Keir did not have to travel to the other side of the world to court Murdoch, as his predecessor, Tony Blair, once did.[7]

IN THE NEW, CELEBRITY SATURATED ONLINE WORLD, THE LEGACY OF *THE SUN*'S HILLSBOROUGH COVERAGE CONTINUES

In a court case that threw light on the new interrelationships between social media, celebrities and the tabloids – specifically *The Sun* – as well as entertained the nation, a High Court judge ruled in July 2022 against Rebekah Vardy, wife of Leicester City and England footballer Jamie Vardy, who had sued for libel Coleen Rooney, wife of Wayne Rooney, the former England captain. Coleen Rooney had used Twitter to publicly accuse Rebekah Vardy, a former friend, of leaking stories from her private Instagram account – one for friends and family only – to *The Sun*. She established this by planting false information on the account, to which only Rebekah Vardy retained access, only to see that information appear as stories in *The Sun*. Rebekah Vardy denied leaking the Instagram information, despite her admitted long history of giving tips and stories to *The Sun*, including staging images of her leaving hospital after giving birth. Ruling in favour of Coleen Rooney, Mrs Justice Steyn said Rebekah Vardy and her agent had lost vital evidence in the form of WhatsApp messages between them, some of which disappeared when the agent accidentally dropped her phone overboard during a boat trip. During the case, Coleen Rooney, from Liverpool, referred to *The Sun* as 'the scum'.[8]

THE CASE OF DANIEL MORGAN

After five inquiries failed to get to the root of why Daniel Morgan was murdered and to untangle the web of corruption surrounding the case, the Government established an independent but non-statutory inquiry that eventually reported in June 2021 that the

Metropolitan Police was institutionally corrupt and had consistently obstructed investigations into the case. Morgan had been a partner in a firm of private investigators, Southern Investigations, which had earned hundreds of thousands of pounds for investigating celebrities and others. The panel criticized the former commissioner, Lord Stevens, for writing a column for the *News of the World*, and added: 'It is appropriate for the panel to state that the demonstrated links between personnel at the highest levels of the Metropolitan Police and people working for a news organisation linked to criminality associated with the murder of Daniel Morgan, are of serious and legitimate public concern.'[9] In July 2023, the Met admitted errors of liability and corruption and paid an undisclosed sum in damages to the Morgan family.

SUDDENLY, MURDOCH WAS GONE
FROM THE STAGE, ALMOST

In September 2023 Rupert Murdoch announced that he would be retiring as head of his global media empire, becoming 'chairman emeritus' and leaving his son Lachlan in charge. Speculation about which of his children – Lachlan, James, Elizabeth or the more retiring Prudence – would succeed him had been rife for years, if not decades. It had inspired the successful television series *Succession*, about the warring group of children of a powerful global media baron, Logan Roy, which, for many, was simply a mirror on the Murdoch dynasty. Kelvin MacKenzie predicted that staff at two of his less successful broadcasting ventures – Times Radio and TalkTV (the challenger to the more strident GB News) – would soon be out of work, but that Rebekah Brooks would be fine. 'As Rupert said to me: "Rebekah certainly knows how to game my family".' As for Lachlan, who had rarely visited Britain and spent most of his life working for Murdoch's interests elsewhere in the world: 'He doesn't give a fuck about the UK.'[10] Most also believed Rupert was retiring in name only – since he retained control of the family trust, he retained control of the company. Tributes from his employees, like Morgan, were fulsome; others, less so: Adrian Wooldridge, columnist for *Bloomberg*, wrote: 'Murdoch is the only contemporary figure who can be spoken of in the same breath as the great press barons of yesteryear' – Alfred Harmsworth, the Napoleon of

Fleet Street who invented the tabloid; William Randolph Hearst, who perfected the arts of sensationalism, salaciousness and war-mongering; and Lord Beaverbrook, who competed with Hearst in his enthusiasm for blurring the line between reporting the news and making it. If Hearst gave the world Orson Welles's *Citizen Kane*, and Beaverbrook Evelyn Waugh's Lord Copper, Murdoch gave it Logan Roy, the foul-mouthed master of family dysfunction.'[11]

There had been one earlier tribute worth noting. It came in 1994 when Dennis Potter the playwright, then suffering from terminal cancer, was interviewed by Melvyn Bragg for Channel 4:

> I call my cancer, the main one, the pancreas one, I call it Rupert, so I can get close to it, because the man Murdoch is the one who, if I had the time – in fact I've got too much writing to do and I haven't got the energy – but I would shoot the bugger if I could. There is no one person more responsible for the pollution of what was already a fairly polluted press, and the pollution of the British press is an important part of the pollution of British political life.[12]

THE COMPETITOR TO *THE SUN*, THE *DAILY STAR*, LINGERS ON, ITS WEBSITE BOASTING THAT IT IS THE 'HOME OF FUN STUFF'

The *Star*'s website has many stories about and pictures of semi-naked female celebrities – the usual roster of *Love Island* competitors and Instagram models – together with a generous helping of crime- and sex-related stories. Its printed edition has made a point of creating irreverent and humorous front pages with a narrow choice of stories, frequently relating to the weather, where a heatwave forecast would invariably provoke such stereotypical images as a donkey in a straw hat and sunglasses. Other favourite subjects are stories in the 'Strange Newes' tradition about aliens or invasive animals, and there are very occasional interventions into politics, such as the headline in June 2021 when then health secretary Matt Hancock was criticized by Dominic Cummings, former aide to Boris Johnson: 'Hopeless bloke said hopeless bloke is hopeless, says hopeless bloke.' It was accompanied by headshots of the three, all mocked up as red-nosed clowns. All good fun stuff.[13]

AFTER THE DEATH OF PRINCESS DIANA, VISCOUNT HARMSWORTH
PLEDGED TO RESTRICT THE USE OF PAPARAZZI PHOTOGRAPHS

In 2022 the Independent Press Standards Organisation upheld complaints of harassment and breach of privacy against *MailOnline* by actress Lily James, who was the subject of 51 articles over a five-month period in late 2020 and early 2021, including eighteen published in one week alone. The actress argued that *MailOnline* had created a market for photographs of her and that she had been photographed while moving home, sitting in a restaurant where she had deliberately positioned herself out of public view and in the grounds of a hotel. Before her formal complaint, the actress had notified the regulator three times about *MailOnline*'s 'persistent and intrusive' behaviour, resulting in privacy notices being circulated, but to no effect.[14]

DISTRUST IN THE INDUSTRY'S OWN SYSTEM
OF REGULATION REMAINS

In 2022 Hacked Off published an analysis of IPSO rulings during 2020, arguing that it had failed to establish itself as a regulator. It took too long to determine rulings – six months on average – and upheld only a fraction of complaints; 98 per cent of complaints were never investigated. Since its inception in 2014, it had never fined any newspaper. On average, any corrections were seven times shorter than the offending article. Hacked Off said the organization was 'a sham' and lacked full independence.[15] IPSO rejected the criticisms as 'ill informed'.

DESPITE THE PLEAS FOR PRIVACY FROM THE DUKE AND DUCHESS
OF SUSSEX, THE TABLOIDS HAVE CONTINUED TO WRITE ABOUT THEM
EXTENSIVELY

In June 2023, as the Duke of Sussex was continuing with his legal claims again the Murdoch newpapers and just a few days after leading politicians paid court to the tycoon at his summer party, IPSO ruled on a column in *The Sun* the previous December by television presenter Jeremy Clarkson. He wrote that he 'hated' the Duchess of Sussex and, in a reference to a scene in the TV series *Game of*

Thrones, was 'dreaming of the day when she is made to parade naked through the streets of every town in Britain while the crowds chant, "Shame!" and throw lumps of excrement at her'.[16] 'IPSO said the column discriminated against the Duchess.'[17] *The Sun*, which took down the column online but had claimed it was fair comment, was ordered to carry a summary of the ruling on its front page and online. The column had prompted 25,000 protests to IPSO – the most it had ever had about one piece – and sixty MPs complained to *Sun* editor Victoria Newton about 'violent misogynist language'. Clarkson responded: 'Oh dear. I've rather put my foot in it . . . I made a clumsy reference to a scene in *Game of Thrones* and this has gone down badly with a great many people. I'm horrified to have caused so much hurt and I shall be more careful in future.'[18] Some saw it as a non-apology.

THE RELENTLESS COVERAGE OF THE MARRIAGE OF
THE DUKE AND DUCHESS CONTINUES

In September 2023 *Private Eye* magazine noted that during the summer the *Daily Mirror,* the subject of just one of the duke's actions, had sometimes published up to seventeen articles a day about the relationship between the couple, adding that 'not one of the hundreds of pieces appeared to be based on evidence.' Most were ripped off from other sites with anonymously sourced quotes saying the couple had marriage and financial problems, with the various articles referencing each other as sources. 'Welcome to the hall of, er, *Mirrors* . . .,' said the *Eye*.[19]

AFTER ALL THIS, WOULD KEIR STARMER REVIVE LEVESON PART TWO?

Against this backdrop and in the wake of the December 2023 ruling by Mr Justice Fancourt, which accused Mirror Group Newspapers of widespread hacking, other illegal activities and what amounted to a cover-up during the Leveson Inquiry, would Keir Starmer, the Labour leader and quite possibly the next prime minister, instigate Part Two, which Lord Leveson had argued was critical to fully understand the nature of the illegal and unethical practices.

Steve Coogan, the actor, hacking victim and now campaigner in support of Hacked Off said:

We must give up on the Tories, who are wholly owned by the Rothermeres, Barclays and Murdochs, but it is clearly unsustainable, if the rule of law counts for anything in this country, that a new prime minister, who is rightly proud of being a former chief prosecutor, fails to reinstate the second half of the Leveson inquiry so it can correct the false evidence it was given in the first part. Keir Starmer, are you listening?[20]

Starmer may still be forced to listen. As this book went to the printers in spring 2024, the other two actions by the duke against Associated and News Group continue with the dozens of claims in the *Mirror* case still needing to be resolved. So, one thing is clear: in 2024 the newsmongers of Planet Tabloid are likely to be on trial, in every sense of the word, once again.

IN THE DUKE'S WITNESS STATEMENT IN HIS ACTION AGAINST MIRROR GROUP NEWSPAPERS, HE SAID:

Our country is judged globally by the state of our press and our government – both of which I believe are at rock bottom. Democracy fails when your press fails to scrutinise and hold the government accountable, and instead choose to get into bed with them so they can ensure the status quo. The fact that it was not just the journalists who were carrying out the unlawful activity, but also those in power who were turning a blind eye to it so as to ensure that it would continue unabated – and who then tried to cover it up when the game was up – is appalling.

The fact they're all ganging up to protect each other is the most disturbing part of all, especially as they're the mothership of online trolling. Trolls react and mobilise to stories they create. People have died as a result and people will continue to kill themselves by suicide when they can't see any other way out.

How much more blood will stain their typing fingers before someone can put a stop to this madness?[21]

References

1 'STRANGE NEWES'

1 S. J. Taylor, *The Great Outsiders: Northcliffe, Harmsworth and the Daily Mail* (London, 1996), p. 73.
2 Ibid.
3 Ibid., p. 74.
4 Quoted in Paula E. Morton, *Tabloid Valley: Supermarket News and American Culture* (Gainesville, FL, 2009), ebook.
5 James Grant, *The Newspaper Press: Its Origin, Progress, and Present Position* (London, 1871), p. 33.
6 Mitchell Stephens, *A History of News* (London and New York, 1988), p. 112.
7 *A Fresh Whip to all Scandalous Lyers; or A True Description of the Two Eminent Pamphiteers, or Squibtellers of This Kingdom*, 1647, quoted in Bob Clarke, *From Grub Street to Fleet Street: An Illustrated History of English Newspapers to 1899* (London, 2004), p. 25.
8 Jason McElligott, 'John Crouch, A Royalist Journalist in Cromwellian England', *Media History*, X/3 (2004), pp. 139–55 (p. 143).
9 Thomas Macaulay, *The History of England from the Accession of James the Second* (London, 1848), vol. I, p. 293.
10 Lindsay O'Neill, 'Dealing with Newsmongers: News, Trust and Letters in the British World, *c.* 1670–1730', *Huntingdon Library Quarterly*, LXXVI/2 (2013), pp. 215–33.
11 Roger Wilkes, *Scandal: A Scurrilous History of Gossip* (London, 2002), p. 21.
12 Ibid., p. 27.
13 Andrew Marr, *My Trade* (London, 2004), pp. 8–9.
14 Wilkes, *Scandal*, pp. 31–3.
15 Clarke, *From Grub Street*, pp. 69–70.
16 Iain Stewart, 'Montesquieu in England: His "Notes on England", with Commentary and Translation', Oxford University Comparative Law Forum, www.ouclf.law.ox.ac.uk, 2002, text after n. 82.
17 Wilkes, *Scandal*, p. 36.
18 Ibid., p. 40.
19 Clarke, *From Grub Street*, p. 183.
20 Wilkes, *Scandal*, p. 40.
21 James Grant, *The Great Metropolis* (London, 1837), vol. II, chap. 5.
22 G. A. Cranfield, 'The *London Evening-Post* and the Jew Bill of 1753', *Historical Journal*, VIII/1 (1965), pp. 16–30.
23 Clarke, *From Grub Street*, p. 273.
24 Ibid., p. 271.
25 Richard Altick, *The English Common Reader: A Social History of the Mass Reading Public, 1800–1900* (Columbus, OH, 1967), p. 168.

2 THE RISE OF THE MOGULS

1 Bob Clarke, *From Grub Street to Fleet Street* (London, 2004), p. 305.
2 Roger Wilkes, *Scandal: A Scurrilous History of Gossip* (London, 2002), p. 56.
3 Cyril Bainbridge and Roy Stockdill, *The News of the World Story* (London, 1993), p. 19.
4 Linda Stratmann, *The Illustrated Police News* (London, 2019), p. 8.
5 Ibid., p. 135.
6 Bainbridge and Stockdill, *The News*, p. 34.
7 Stratmann, *The Illustrated Police News*, p. 138.
8 Frederic Hudson, *Journalism in the United States, 1690–1872* (New York, 1873), pp. 417–18.

9   Daniel Cohen, *Yellow Journalism:*
    Scandal, Sensationalism and Gossip in the
    Media (New York, 2000), pp. 12–14.
10 David Anthony, 'The Helen Jewett
    Panic: Tabloids, Men, and the
    Sensational Public Sphere in Antebellum
    New York', *American Literature*, LXIX/3
    (1997), pp. 487–514 (p. 493).
11 Don C. Seitz, *The James Gordon Bennetts:*
    Father and Son, Proprietors of the New York
    (Indianapolis, IN, 1928), p. 55.
12 Cohen, *Yellow Journalism*, pp. 10–11.
13 *New York Sun*, 6 April 1836.
14 Robert C. Bannister, 'Bennett, James
    Gordon', in *Encyclopedia of American*
    Biography, ed. John A. Garraty (New
    York, 1975), pp. 80–81.
15 Cohen, *Yellow Journalism*, pp. 18–19.
16 Brett Griffin, *Yellow Journalism:*
    Sensationalism and Circulation Wars
    (New York, 2019), p. 30.
17 'Joseph Pulitzer', https://spartacus-
    educational.com, accessed 17 October
    2023.
18 Harold Evans, *The American Century*
    (New York, 2000), p. 94.
19 'The Press: 50 Years of Hearst', *Time*,
    https://content.time.com, 15 March
    1937.
20 Ben Procter, *William Randolph Hearst:*
    The Early Years, 1863–1910 (New York,
    1998), ebook.
21 Ibid.
22 Cohen, *Yellow Journalism*, pp. 23–4.
23 Brooke Kroeger, *Nellie Bly: Daredevil,*
    Reporter, Feminist (New York, 1994),
    ebook.
24 Cohen, *Yellow Journalism*, p. 28.
25 Griffin, *Yellow Journalism*, p. 48.
26 Ibid., p. 57.
27 Ibid., p. 58.
28 Ibid., p. 43.
29 Ibid., p. 66.
30 W. A. Swanberg, *Citizen Hearst: A*
    Biography of William Randolph Hearst
    (New York, 1996).
31 S. J. Taylor, *The Great Outsiders:*
    Northcliffe, Harmsworth and the Daily Mail
    (London, 1996), p. 9.

32 Clarke, *From Grub Street*, p. 305.
33 Ibid., p. 301.
34 T. P. O'Connor, 'The New Journalism',
    New Review (October 1889), pp. 423–34.
35 Clarke, *From Grub Street*, p. 309.
36 Taylor, *The Great Outsiders*, p. 35.
37 *Daily Mail*, 4 May 1896, p. 7.
38 Taylor, *The Great Outsiders*, p. 35.
39 Tom Clarke, diary entry for 1 January
    1912, in *My Northcliffe Diary* (London,
    1931), p. 49.
40 T. Jeffrey and K. McClelland, 'A World
    Fit to Live In: The *Daily Mail* and the
    Middle Classes, 1918–39', in *Impacts*
    and Influences: Media Power in the
    Twentieth Century, ed. J. Curran,
    A. Smith and P. Wingate (London,
    1987), chap. 2.
41 Kevin Williams, *Read All About It: A*
    History of British Newspapers (London,
    2010), p. 130.
42 Paul Ferris, *The House of Northcliffe: The*
    Harmsworths of Fleet Street (Worthing,
    1971), p. 20.
43 Taylor, *The Great Outsiders*, p. 35.
44 Derek Griffiths, *Fleet Street: Five Hundred*
    Years of the Press (London, 2006), p. 121.

**3 'SEE THAT YOU SECURE A COPY FOR
MADAM'**

1   Paul Ferris, *The House of Northcliffe: The*
    Harmsworths of Fleet Street (London,
    1971), p. 120.
2   S. J. Taylor, *The Great Outsiders:*
    Northcliffe, Harmsworth and the Daily Mail
    (London, 1996), p. 82.
3   Hugh Cudlipp, *Publish and Be Damned!*
    The Astonishing Story of the 'Daily Mirror'
    (London, 1953), p. 10.
4   Ferris, *The House*, p. 121.
5   Henry Hamilton Fyfe, *My Seven*
    Selves: An Autobiography with Portraits
    (London, 1935), available at https://
    spartacus-educational.com.
6   Quoted in Tom Driberg, *'Swaff':*
    The Life and Times of Hannen Swaffer
    (London, 1974), p. 33.
7   Chris Horrie, *Tabloid Nation* (London,
    2003), p. 24.

8 Hamilton Fyfe, *My Seven Selves*.
9 Horrie, *Tabloid*, p. 26.
10 Ibid., p. 31.
11 Ibid., p. 26.
12 Cyril Bainbridge and Roy Stockdill, *The News of the World Story* (London, 1993), p. 52.
13 Ibid., p. 57.
14 R. D. Blumenfeld, *The Press in My Time* (New York, 1933), p. 161.
15 Hamilton Fyfe, *Sixty Years of Fleet Street* (London, 1949), pp. 107–8.
16 Bainbridge and Stockdill, *The News*, p. 63.
17 Ibid., pp. 62–3.
18 F. Williams, *Dangerous Estate: The Anatomy of Newspapers* (London, 1957), p. 235.
19 A.J.A. Morris, 'Riddell, George Allardice, Baron Riddell', *Oxford Dictionary of National Biography*, www.oxforddnb.com, 6 January 2011.
20 George Orwell, 'The Decline of the English Murder', *Tribune*, 15 February 1946.
21 Taylor, *The Great Outsiders*, p. 82.
22 Ibid., p. 159.
23 Tom Clarke, *My Northcliffe Diary* (London, 1931), p. 90.
24 Ibid., p. 107.
25 *New York Sun*, 12 June 1917.
26 Irene Cooper Willis, *England's Holy War: A Study of English Liberal Idealism during the Great War* (London, 1928), p. 245.
27 Hansard 5C, 16 April 1919.
28 Clarke, *My Northcliffe*, p. 246.
29 Taylor, *The Great Outsiders*, p. 205.
30 Ibid., pp. 204–5.
31 Ibid., p. 206.
32 Clarke, *My Northcliffe*, pp. 293–4.
33 Taylor, *The Great Outsiders*, p. 210.
34 Clarke, *My Northcliffe*, pp. 293–4.
35 Taylor, *The Great Outsiders*, p. 219.
36 Clarke, *My Northcliffe*, p. 302.
37 Anonymous, *The History of The Times, 1912–1948* (London, 1952), pp. 699–701.
38 Cecil King, 'The Evil Adventurer', in *The Beaverbrook I Knew*, ed. L. Gourley (London, 1984), p. 41.

39 Matthew Engel, *Tickle the Public: One Hundred Years of the Popular Press* (London, 1996), pp. 114–15.
40 York Membery, 'Horoscopes: Tales of the Expected', www.express.co.uk, 29 August 2010.
41 D. George Boyce, 'Aitken, William Maxwell [Max], first Baron Beaverbrook', *Oxford Dictionary of National Biography*, www.oxforddnb.com, 23 September 2004.
42 Martin Conboy, *The Press and Popular Culture* (London, 2001), p. 108.
43 Engel, *Tickle*, pp. 104–15.
44 A.J.P. Taylor, *English History, 1914–1945* (London, 1979), p. 310.
45 B. A. Chisholm and M. Davie, *Beaverbrook: A Life* (London, 1992), p. 503.
46 Kevin Williams, *Read All About It: A History of the British Newspapers* (London, 2010), p. 131.
47 Henry Wickham Steed, *The Press* (London, 1938), pp. 28–30.
48 Adrian Bingham and Martin Conboy, *Tabloid Century: The Popular Press in Britain, 1896 to the Present* (Oxford, 2015), p. 11.

4 THE PREROGATIVE OF THE HARLOT

1 George Ward Price, *Sunday Dispatch*, 5 January 1930.
2 William D. Rubinstein, *Twentieth-Century Britain: A Political History* (London, 2003), p. 176.
3 Martin Pugh, *Hurrah for the Blackshirts! Fascists and Fascism in Britain between the Wars* (New York, 2013), p. 41.
4 Ibid., pp. 40–41.
5 Ibid., p. 47.
6 Harold Rothermere, leading article, *Daily Mail*, 24 September 1930.
7 Chris Horrie, *Tabloid Nation* (London, 2003), pp. 39–40.
8 Richard Norton-Taylor, 'Months before War, Rothermere Said Hitler's Work Was Superhuman', *The Guardian*, 1 April 2005.
9. Bill Hagerty, *Read All About It! 100 Sensational Years of the Daily Mirror* (Lydney, 2003), p. 36.

10 Daniel Cohen, *Yellow Journalism: Scandal, Sensationalism and Gossip in the Media* (New York, 2000), p. 75.

11 Matthew Engel, *Tickle the Public: One Hundred Years of the Popular Press* (London, 1996), p. 157.

12 Dennis Griffith, *Fleet Street: Five Hundred Years of the Press* (London, 2006), p. 246.

13 Tom Baistow, *Fourth-Rate Estate: Anatomy of Fleet Street* (London, 1995), p. 42.

14 Griffith, *Fleet Street*, p. 246.

15 Horrie, *Tabloid*, p. 54.

16 Hugh Cudlipp, *Walking on the Water* (London, 1976), p. 49.

17 Hugh Cudlipp, *Publish and Be Damned! The Astonishing Story of the 'Daily Mirror'* (London, 1953), p. 81.

18 Horrie, *Tabloid*, p. 54.

19 Donald Zec, *Put the Knife in Gently! Memoirs of a Life with Legends* (London, 2003), p. 30.

20 Cudlipp, *Walking*, p. 59.

21 Cudlipp, *Publish*, p. 133.

22 Donald Zec, 'Fiddling My Way to Fleet Street', *British Journalism Review*, 11/1 (March 2000), pp. 12–20.

23 Cudlipp, *Publish*, p. 82.

24 Horrie, *Tabloid*, p. 66.

25 Ibid., p. 41.

26 Ibid., p. 67.

27 Cudlipp, *Publish*, p. 177.

28 Ruth Dudley Edwards, *Newspapermen: Hugh Cudlipp, Cecil Harmsworth King and the Glory Days of Fleet Street* (London, 2004), p. 155.

29 Hagerty, *Read All About It!*, p. 55.

30 Cecil Harmsworth King, entry for 24 September 1942, in *With Malice Towards None: A War Diary* (New York, 1970).

31 Horrie, *Tabloid*, p. 66.

32 Royal Commission on the Press, 1947–9, pub. June 1949.

33 Horrie, *Tabloid*, p. 7.

34 Martin Conboy, '*Language in the Mirror: An Idiom for the Masses*', *Mirror Historical Archive 1903–2000*, Cengage Learning (EMEA) Ltd, 2019.

35 Cudlipp, *Walking*, p. 193.

36 Ibid., p. 187.

37 Dudley Edwards, *Newspapermen*, pp. 198–9.

38 Horrie, *Tabloid*, pp. 78–9.

39 Cudlipp, *Walking*, p. 259.

40 Horrie, *Tabloid*, p. 80.

41 A.J.P. Taylor, *English History, 1914–1945* (London, 1965), pp. 665–6.

42 Maurice Edelman, *The Mirror, A Political History* (London, 1966).

43 Horrie, *Tabloid*, p. 90.

44 Dudley Edwards, *Newspapermen*, p. 237.

45 Ruth King's diary entry for 15 June 1964, quoted in Dudley Edwards, *Newspapermen*, p. 341.

46 Richard Crossman, 10 May 1968, in *Diaries of a Cabinet Minister* (London, 1975), vol. III.

47 Quoted in Dudley Edwards, *Newspapermen*, p. 183.

48 Cudlipp, *Walking*, p. 351.

49 Michael Dove in *Sunday Express*, 2 June 1968.

50 Dudley Edwards, *Newspapermen*, p. 397.

51 Hugh Cudlipp Archive, Cardiff University, at https://archiveshub.jisc.ac.uk/data/gb1239-432/432/2/5 and https://archiveshub.jisc.ac.uk/data/gb1239-432/432/2/8, accessed 11 October 2023.

52 Cudlipp, *Walking*, p. 393.

53 Dudley Edwards, *Newspapermen*, p. 393.

54 Cudlipp, *Walking*, p. 378.

5 *THE SUN* RISES

1 Chris Horrie and Peter Chippendale, *Stick It Up Your Punter! The Uncut Story of the Sun Newspaper* (London, 1990), p. 21.

2 Larry Lamb, *Sunrise: The Remarkable Rise and Rise of the Best-Selling Soaraway Sun* (London, 1989), p. 3.

3 Harold Evans, *Good Times, Bad Times* (London, 1983), p. 159.

4 Michael Leapman, *Barefaced Cheek: The Apotheosis of Rupert Murdoch* (London, 1984), p. 55.

5 Michael Wolff, *The Man Who Owns the News: Inside the Secret World of Rupert Murdoch* (New York, 2008), pp. 13, 17.

6 Leapman, *Barefaced*, p. 24.

7 Tom Bower, *Maxwell: The Outsider* (London, 1988), p. 23.

8 Ibid., pp. 26–8.

9 *News of the World*, Editorial, 20 October 1968.

10 Leapman, *Barefaced*, p. 55.

11 Horrie and Chippendale, *Stick It Up*, pp. 11–13.

12 Hugh Cudlipp, *Walking on the Water* (London, 1976), pp. 202–3.

13 Lamb, *Sunrise*, p. 8.

14 Roy Greenslade, 'Night the Sun Came Up', *The Guardian*, www.theguardian. com, 15 November 1999.

15 Lamb, *Sunrise*, p. 14.

16 Ibid., p. 19.

17 Ibid., p. 20.

18 Horrie and Chippendale, *Stick It Up*, p. 19.

19 Lamb, *Sunrise*, p. 110.

20 Ibid., p. 139.

21 Ibid., p. 28.

22 Horrie and Chippendale, *Stick It Up*, p. 22.

23 Germaine Greer quoted ibid., p. 29.

24 Lamb, *Sunrise*, p. 187.

25 Ibid., p. 59.

26 Ibid., p. 78.

27 Ibid., p. 28.

28 Ibid., p. 111.

29 Ibid., pp. 110–11.

30 Horrie and Chippendale, *Stick It Up*, p. 57.

31 Lamb, *Sunrise*, pp. 165–6.

32 Quoted in Horrie and Chippendale, *Stick It Up*, p. 36.

33 Tom Baistow, *Fourth Rate Estate: An Anatomy of Fleet Street* (London, 1985), p. 42.

34 Horrie and Chippendale, *Stick It Up*, p. 146.

35 Mike Molloy, *The Happy Hack* (London, 2016), p. 15.

36 Paula E. Morton, *Tabloid Valley: Supermarket News and American Culture* (Gainesville, FL, 2009).

37 Paul McCann, 'The Man Who Made a Monster', *The Independent*, 22 June 1997.

38 Derek Jameson, *Touched by Angels* (London, 1988), p. 98.

39 Horrie and Chippendale, *Stick It Up*, p. 70.

40 Robert Harris, *Gotcha! The Media, the Government and the Falklands Crisis* (London, 1983), p. 41.

41 Quoted in Dennis Griffith, *Fleet Street: Five Hundred Years of the Press* (London, 2006), p. 350.

6 GOTCHA

1 Chris Horrie and Peter Chippendale, *Stick It Up Your Punter! The Uncut Story of the Sun Newspaper* (London, 1990), p. 75.

2 Quoted in Michael Leapman, *Barefaced Cheek: The Apotheosis of Rupert Murdoch* (London, 1984), p. 143.

3 Comment article, *Columbia Journalism Review*, XVIII/5 (January–February 1980), pp. 22–3.

4 Horrie and Chippendale, *Stick It Up*, p. 86.

5 Andy McSmith, 'Kelvin MacKenzie: Loudmouth', *The Independent*, 14 June 2008.

6 Horrie and Chippendale, *Stick It Up*, pp. 147–8.

7 Mike Molloy, *The Happy Hack* (London, 2016), p. 290.

8 Horrie and Chippendale, *Stick It Up*, p. 105.

9 Robert Harris, *Gotcha! The Media, the Government and the Falklands Crisis* (London, 1983), p. 45.

10 Horrie and Chippendale, *Stick It Up*, p. 117.

11 Harris, *Gotcha*, p. 48.

12 Horrie and Chippendale, *Stick It Up*, pp. 118–19.

13 Editorial, 'Dare Call It Treason', *The Sun*, 7 May 1982.

14 Adrian Bingham and Martin Conboy, *Tabloid Century: The Popular Press in Britain, 1896 to the Present* (Oxford, 2015), p. 153.

15 Piers Morgan, 'No Stereotypes Were Harmed in the Making of this Film', *Daily Telegraph*, 18 September 2005.

16 S. J. Taylor, *An Unlikely Hero: Vere Rothermere and How the Daily Mail Was Saved* (London, 2002), p. 177.
17 Ibid., p. 179.
18 Ibid., pp. 182–3.
19 Ibid., p. 183.

7 THE DAILY MAXWELL

1 Mike Molloy, *The Happy Hack* (London 2016), p. 250.
2 Rondle Owen Charles Stable and Sir Ronald George Leach, *Report on the Affairs of the International Learning Systems Corporation Limited and Interim Report on the Affairs of Pergamon Press Limited*, HM Stationary Office (London, July 1971).
3 Interview with the author, September 2019.
4 Ibid.
5 Molloy, *Happy*.
6 Tom Bower, *Maxwell: The Outsider*, 2nd edn (London, 1991), pp. 359–60.
7 Chris Horrie, *Tabloid Nation* (London, 2003), p. 157.
8 Ibid., p. 156.
9 Bower, *Maxwell*, p. 369.
10 Ibid., p. 378.
11 Molloy, *Happy*, p. 250.
12 Horrie, *Tabloid*, p. 165.
13 Bower, *Maxwell*, p. 382.
14 Ibid., pp. 392–3.
15 Ibid., p. 387.
16 Molloy, *Happy*, p. 293.
17 Horrie, *Tabloid*, p. 168.
18 Ibid., p. 174.
19 Bower, *Maxwell*, p. 406.
20 Quoted in Horrie, *Tabloid*, p. 173.
21 Molloy, *Happy*, p. 293.
22 Richard Stott, *Dogs and Lampposts* (London, 2002), pp. 126, 231.
23 Chris Horrie and Peter Chippendale, *Stick It Up Your Punter! The Uncut Story of the Sun Newspaper* (London, 1990), p. 186.
24 Roy Greenslade, *Press Gang: How Newspapers Make Profits from Propaganda* (London, 2003), p. 475.
25 Horrie and Chippendale, *Stick It Up*, p. 205.
26 Quoted in Jeremy Tunstall, *Newspaper Power: The New National Press in Britain* (New York, 1996), p. 18.
27 Mark Killick, *Sultan of Sleaze: The Story of David Sullivan's Sex and Media Empire* (London, 1994), p. 72.
28 Tom Baistow, *Fourth Rate Estate: An Anatomy of Fleet Street* (London, 1985), p. 2.

8 THREE HEADLINES

1 Interview with the author, October 2020.
2 Max Clifford, evidence to Leveson Inquiry, 9 February 2012.
3 Tom Pegden, 'Freddie Starr: Woman Reveals What REALLY Happened on Day He "Ate Her Hamster"', *The Mirror*, 10 May 2019.
4 Chris Horrie and Peter Chippendale, *Stick It Up Your Punter! The Uncut Story of the Sun Newspaper* (London, 1990), p. 300.
5 Quoted ibid., p. 301.
6 Lead story, 'Sorry Elton', *The Sun*, 19 December 1988.
7 Hunter Davies, 'From City Boy to World Leader', *The Independent*, 13 December 1994.
8 Kenny Dalglish, *My Liverpool Home: Then and Now* (London, 2010), p. 237.
9 'Ex-*Sun* Editor: I Was Right on Hillsborough', *Liverpool Daily Post*, 1 December 2006.
10 'Hillsborough: MacKenzie Offers "Profuse Apologies" for *Sun* Front Page', *The Guardian*, 12 September 2012.
11 'The Real Truth', *The Sun*, 13 September 2012.
12 Davey Brett, 'The Movement to Boycott the *Sun* is Bigger than Ever', *Vice*, 18 October 2019.
13 Mike Molloy, *The Happy Hack* (London 2016), pp. 296–7.
14 House of Lords Select Committee on Communications, First Report, https://publications.parliament.uk, June 2008.
15 Chris Horrie, *Tabloid Nation* (London, 2003), p. 186.

16 Tom Bower, *Maxwell: The Outsider,*
2nd edn (London, 1991), pp. 536–8.

17 'Maxwell, Colossus Even in Death,
Laid to Rest on Mount of Olives', *Jewish
Telegraphic Agency,* 11 November 1991.

18 Seymour Hersh, *The Samson Option:
Israel's Nuclear Arsenal and American
Foreign Policy* (London, 1991),
pp. 312–14.

19 Michael White, 'White vs Campbell',
The Guardian, 5 November 2001.

20 Quoted in Peter Thompson, 'Maxwell,
the Fallout', Association of *Mirror*
Pensioners, www.mirrorpensioners.
co.uk, March 2021.

21 Horrie, *Tabloid,* p. 196.

22 Ibid., p. 196.

23 Quoted in Michael Leapman, 'Unlikely
Face at the "Mirror"', *The Independent,*
28 October 1992.

24 Ibid.

25 Roy Greenslade, 'Richard Stott,
Obituary', *The Guardian,* www.
theguardian.com, 1 August 2007.

26 Horrie, *Tabloid,* pp. 199–200.

9 THE DARK AGES

1 Quoted by Sir Harold Evans, 2013
Hugh Cudlipp lecture, London College
of Communication, 28 January 2013.

2 Chris Horrie and Peter Chippendale,
*Stick It Up Your Punter! The Uncut Story
of the Sun Newspaper* (London, 1990),
p. 240.

3 Hansard, 21 April 1989, col. 615.

4 David Calcutt QC, 'The Committee on
Privacy and Related Matters' (London,
1990).

5 *Hard Talk,* Channel 4, 21 December 1991.

6 Julia Stuart, 'Antonia de Sancha:
I Kissed, I Told, and Then . . .', *The
Independent,* 13 December 2013.

7 Sir David Calcutt QC, 'Review of Press
Self-Regulation', January 1993.

8 National Heritage Committee, 'Privacy
and Media Intrusion', 1993.

9 Adrian Addison, *Mail Men: The
Unauthorised Story of the Daily Mail*
(London, 2017), p. 231.

10 Ibid., p. 255.

11 S. J. Taylor, *An Unlikely Hero: Vere
Rothermere and How the Daily Mail Was
Saved* (London, 2002), p. 257.

12 Ibid., p. 270.

13 Ibid.

14 Ibid.

15 Ibid., p. 273.

16 Chris Horrie, *Tabloid Nation* (London,
2003), p. 209.

17 Paul Gascoigne and Hunter Davies,
Gazza: My Story (London, 2004).

18 Rob Stewart, 'The Life and Times
of Paul Gascoigne', *The Telegraph,*
www.telegraph.co.uk, 14 February
2008.

19 *Gazza,* BBC documentary, www.bbc.
co.uk/iplayer, 13 April 2022.

20 Ian Irvine, 'Rebekah Wade: The Feisty
First Lady of Wapping', *The Independent,*
www.independent.co.uk, 5 November
2005.

21 *Gazza.*

22 'Paul Dacre, Daily Mail Editor, on
the Risks He and the Mail Ran to
Secure Justice for Stephen Lawrence',
MailOnline, www.dailymail.co.uk,
4 January 2012.

23 Taylor, *An Unlikely Hero,* p. 178.

24 Fran Abrams and Anthony Bevins,
'Murdoch's Courtship of Blair Finally
Pays Off', *The Independent,* 11 February
1998.

25 David Folkenflik, *Murdoch's World:
The Last of the Old Media Empires* (2013),
ebook.

26 Sir John Major, evidence given to
Leveson Inquiry, www.discoverleveson.
co.uk, 12 June 2012.

27 *The Rise of the Murdoch Dynasty,*
www.bbc.co.uk/iplayer, 14 July 2020.

28 Sir David English, 'Diary', *The Spectator,*
http://archive.spectator.co.uk, 7 October
1995.

29 Roy Greenslade, '18 Years of
Uncertainty, 16 Days of Doubt',
The Guardian, www.theguardian.com,
17 May 1997.

30 Taylor, *An Unlikely Hero,* p. 305.

31 Bill Hagerty *Read All About It! – 100 Sensational Years of the Daily Mirror* (Lydney, 2003), pp. 45–6.

32 Adrian Bingham and Martin Conboy, *Tabloid Century: The Popular Press in Britain, 1896 to the Present* (Oxford, 2015), p. 111.

33 Malcolm Muggeridge, 'The Royal Soap Opera', *New Statesman*, www.newstatesman.com, 22 October 1955.

34 Bingham and Conboy, *Tabloid Century*, p. 121.

35 Ibid., p. 123.

36 S. J. Taylor, *Shock Horror! The Tabloids in Action* (London, 1991), p. 153.

37 Ibid., p. 152.

38 Prince Harry interview with Oprah Winfrey, CBS, 7 March 2021.

39 Earl Spencer's funeral oration, Westminster Abbey, www.bbc.co.uk, 6 September 1997.

40 '*Mail* Leads the Way in Banning Paparazzi Pictures', *Daily Mail*, 8 September 1997.

41 Simon Hattenstone, 'Rosie Outlook', *The Guardian*, 30 July 2002.

42 Colin Grimshaw, 'Is All OK at Desmond's *Express*?', www.campaignlive.co.uk, 29 October 2001.

43 Matt Wells, 'Columnist Leads *Express* Exodus', www.theguardian.com, 28 November 2000.

10 THE DARK ARTS

1 Nick Davies, *Hack Attack: How the Truth Caught Up with Rupert Murdoch* (London 2015), p. 99.

2 Ian Burrell and Mark Olden, 'Exposed after Eight Years: A Private Eye's Dirty Work for Fleet Street', *The Independent*, www.independent.co.uk, 14 September 2011.

3 *Leveson Inquiry: Report into the Culture Practices and Ethics of the Press*, available at www.gov.uk, vol. III, p. 1004, para. 1.4, November 2012.

4 Alex Owens, evidence given to Leveson Inquiry, www.discoverleveson.com, 30 November 2011.

5 Minutes of Evidence, Select Committee on Culture, Media and Sport, https://publications.parliament.uk, 11 March 2003.

6 Ibid.

7 Hugh Grant, *Taking on the Tabloids*, Channel 4, 28 November 2012.

8 Piers Morgan, 'I'm Sorry, Macca, for Introducing You to This Monster', *Daily Mail*, www.dailymail.co.uk, 19 October 2006.

9 *Channel 4 News*, 10 September 2010.

10 Fifth Report, House of Commons Select Committee on Culture, Media and Sport, https://publications.parliament.uk, May 2003.

11 Davies, *Hack*, p. 29.

12 Sharon Marshall, *Tabloid Girl* (London, 2010), p. 226.

13 Davies, *Hack*, p. 40.

14 Ibid., p. 45.

15 Ibid., p. 49.

16 Internal Metropolitan Police briefing document Operation Caryatid, National Archives, Exhibit JMY3A-14, Leveson Inquiry, www.discoverleveson.com.

17 Tom Watson and Martin Hickman, *Dial M for Murdoch: News Corporation and the Corruption of Britain* (London, 2012), p. 41.

18 Davies, *Hack*, p. 165.

19 'What Price Privacy? The Unlawful Trade in Confidential Personal Information', The Information Commissioner (May 2006).

20 *Leveson Inquiry Report*, vol. 1 (2012), p. 265, para. 2.13.

21 Ibid., para. 2.15.

22 Ibid., footnote to para. 2.15.

23 Statement to Leveson Inquiry, www.discoverleveson.com, 30 November 2011.

24 Burrell and Olden, 'Exposed after Eight Years: A Private Eye's Dirty Work for Fleet Street'.

25 'What Price Privacy Now?', Information Commissioner's Office (February 2007), p. 27.

26 *Leveson Inquiry Report*, vol. 1, p. 272, para. 3.18.

27 'What Price Privacy Now?', p. 10.

28 Nick Davies, *Flat Earth News* (London, 2009), p. 1.

29 Mark Sweeney and Leigh Holmwood, 'McCanns Accept *Express* Damages and High Court Apology', *The Guardian*, www.theguardian.com, 19 March 2008.

30 Oliver Luft and John Plunkett, 'Madeleine McCann: Newspapers Pay Out £600,000 to Robert Murat', *The Guardian*, www.theguardian.com, 17 July 2008.

31 Ben Dowell, 'News of the World Apologises for Publishing Kate McCann's Diary', *The Guardian*, www.theguardian.com, 22 September 2008.

32 Matthew Moore, 'Madeleine McCann: *Daily Express* Publishes Apology to "Tapas Seven"', *Daily Telegraph*, www.telegraph.co.uk, 16 October 2008.

33 Brian Cathcart, 'The Real McCann Scandal', *New Statesman*, www.newstatesman.com, 23 October 2008.

34 'Press Standards, Privacy and Libel', Select Committee on Culture, Media and Sport (February 2010).

35 Ibid.

36 Davies, *Hack*, pp. 199–200.

37 Nick Davies and Rob Evans, 'Max Clifford Drops *News of the World* Phone Hacking Action in £1m Deal', *The Guardian*, www.theguardian.com, 9 March 2010.

38 Fiona Hamilton, 'Brooks Paid Max Clifford £1m for His Silence', *The Times*, www.thetimes.co.uk, 5 March 2014.

39 Don Van Natta Jr, Jo Becker and Graham Bowley, 'Tabloid Hack Attack on Royals, and Beyond', *New York Times*, www.nytimes.com, 1 September 2010.

11 LEVESON

1 Mark Hughes, 'Phone Hacking: Families of War Dead "Targeted" by News of the World', *The Telegraph*, www.telegraph.co.uk, 7 July 2011.

2 'News of the World Hacked 7/7 Family Phones', www.bbc.co.uk, 6 July 2011.

3 Evidence to Culture, Media and Sport Committee, https://publications.parliament.uk, 19 July 2011.

4 Tom Watson and Martin Hickman, *Dial M for Murdoch: News Corporation and the Corruption of Britain* (London, 2012), pp. 86–8.

5 Tara Conlan, 'Phone Hacking: Buscombe Admits News of the World Lied to PC', *The Guardian*, www.theguardian.com, 19 July 2011.

6 'Unauthorised Tapping or Hacking of Mobile Communications', Home Affairs Select Committee, https://publications.parliament.uk, 20 July 2011.

7 Evidence given to Leveson Inquiry, www.discoverleveson.com, 11 May 2012.

8 'Gordon Brown Denies Approving Cystic Fibrosis Story', www.bbc.co.uk/news, 11 May 2012.

9 Evidence given to Leveson Inquiry, www.discoverleveson.com, 14 June 2012.

10 Jonathan Freedland, 'That Rebekah Brooks Text to David Cameron: Decoded', *The Guardian*, www.theguardian.com, 14 June 2012.

11 Evidence given to Leveson Inquiry, www.discoverleveson.com, 28 May 2012.

12 'Phone-Hacking Trial: Blair "Advised Brooks Before Arrest"', www.bbc.co.uk, 19 February 2014.

13 Mark Seal, 'Seduced and Abandoned', *Vanity Fair*, https://archive.vanityfair.com, March 2014.

14 Evidence given to Leveson Inquiry, www.discoverleveson.com, 21 November 2011.

15 Ibid.

16 'Actor Hugh Grant Stands by Phone Hacking Claim', www.bbc.co.uk/news, 11 February 2012.

17 Evidence given to Leveson Inquiry, www.discoverleveson.com, 23 November 2011.

18 Ibid., 21 December 2011.

19 Ibid., 24 November 2011.

20 Ibid., 22 November 2011.

21 Ibid., 6 and 9 February 2012.

22 Ibid., 20 December 2012.

23 Ibid., 25 April 2012.

24 *Leveson Inquiry: Report into the Culture, Practices and Ethics of the Press*, available at www.gov.uk, vol. III, part L, pp. 1801–18, November 2012.

25 Media Standards Trust, 'Analysis of Proposals for Independent Press Standards Organisation', https:/inform. org, 19 July 2013.

26 See https://manage.theguardian.com/ help-centre/article/how-to-make-a-complaint-about-guardian-or-observer and https://help.ft.com/faq/complaints/how-do-i-raise-a-complaint, both accessed 1 March 2024.

27 'Hacked Off Responds to Phone Hacking Trial Verdicts So Far', https://hackinginquiry.org, 24 June 2014.

28 Nick Davies, 'Phone-Hacking Trial Was Officially about Crime; But in Reality, It Was about Power', *The Guardian*, www. theguardian.com, 25 June 2014.

29 Josh Halliday, 'Ian Edmundson Jailed for Eight Months over Phone Hacking', *The Guardian*, www.theguardian.com, 7 November 2014.

30 Lisa O'Carroll, 'Ex-News of the World Features Editor gets Four-Month Suspended Sentence', *The Guardian*, www.theguardian.com, 6 July 2015.

31 Sentencing remarks of Mr Justice Saunders, R -v.- Stenson, www. judiciary.uk, 6 July 2015.

32 Martin Hickman, 'Life and Death in the *Sun* Newsroom', Open Democracy, www.opendemocracy.net, 26 October 2015.

33 Ibid.

34 Evidence given to Leveson Inquiry, www. discoverleveson.com, 21 December 2011.

35 'Phone Hacking: We're Sorry', *Daily Mirror*, 13 February 2015.

36 Ruling by Mr Justice Mann in *Gulati & Others v MGN Limited*, www.bailii.org, 21 May 2015.

37 Mark Sweeney and Josh Halliday, 'No Further Action on UK Media Phone Hacking, Chief Prosecutor Says', *The Guardian*, www.theguardian.com, 11 December 2015.

38 *Channel 4 News*, 'Revealed: The Rupert Murdoch Tape', 3 July 2013.

39 Evidence to Leveson Inquiry, www. discoverleveson.com, 12 December 2011.

40 Ian Burrell, 'Fake Sheikh's Editor Fails to Find Evidence for His Grand Claim to Leveson', *The Independent*, www. independent.co.uk, 21 August 2012.

41 'Mazher Mahmood, "Fake Sheikh" Jailed over Tulisa Case', www.bbc.co.uk/ news, 21 October 2016.

42 Consultation on the Leveson Inquiry and its Implementation, https://gov.uk, 1 March 2018.

12 CHURNALISM 2.0

1 Nick Davies, *Flat Earth News* (London, 2008), p. 59.

2 Ibid., p. 52.

3 Harriet Johnston, 'Woman Complained about Her Shoes Hurting All Night Only to Discover She'd Been Wearing Them on the Wrong FEET', *MailOnline*, www. dailymail.co.uk, 23 September 2019.

4 See Reportal, *A Decade in Digital*, https:// datareportal.com, 29 November 2021.

5 Statista.com, 'Number of Internet and Social Media Users Worldwide', July 2022.

6 Jane Thynne, 'You've Got to Go and Shout at the Bastards or They Won't Respect You', *Independent on Sunday*, 3 September 2006.

7 Interview with Australian media website Mumbrella, 20 February 2013.

8 Adrian Addison, *Mail Men: The Unauthorized Story of the Daily Mail* (London, 2017), p. 338.

9 Ibid., p. 339.

10 Henry Mance, '*MailOnline* and the Next Page for the "Sidebar of Shame"', *Financial Times*, 24 September 2014.

11 Caroline Feraday, 'Lady Victoria Hervey Poses Up a Storm on the Beach in Skimpy Silver and White String Bikini', *MailOnline*, www.dailymail.co.uk, 6 July 2019.

12 Kate Dennett, 'Damian Lewis Cuts a Smart Figure in a Black Shirt and Jeans as He Watches Nick Cave and the

Bad Seeds Perform at All Points East Festival', *MailOnline*, www.dailymail.co.uk, 29 August 2022.

13 James King, 'My Year Ripping Off the Web with the *Daily Mail Online*', www.gawker.com, 4 March 2015.

14 'Correction and Apology', *Daily Mail*, www.dailymail.co.uk, 9 July 2014.

15 Jane Martinson, '*Sun* Threatens Legal Action Over Alleged *MailOnline* Copyright Breach', *The Guardian*, www.theguardian.com, 25 April 2017.

16 Jasper Jackson, 'Wikipedia Bans *Daily Mail* as "Unreliable Source"', *The Guardian*, www.theguardian.com, 9 February 2017.

17 Larry Lamb, *Sunrise: The Remarkable Rise and Rise of the Best-Selling Soaraway Sun* (London, 1989), p. 110.

18 Chris Horrie and Peter Chippendale, *Stick it Up Your Punter! The Uncut Story of the Sun Newspaper* (London, 1990), p. 200.

19 Lucy Anne Holmes, 'Exclusive: We've Seen Enough Breasts – Why I Started the No More Page 3 Campaign', *The Independent*, www.independent.co.uk, 21 September 2012.

20 Georgette Culley, 'Small Wonders: From Abbey Clancy to Helen Flanagan – Who Is the Festive Queen When it Comes to Saucy Posts in Their Pants?', *The Sun*, www.thesun.co.uk, 14 December 2023.

21 Ian Burrell, 'Goodbye Richard Desmond, the Press Baron Who Liked Money More than Papers', https://inews.co.uk, 9 February 2018.

22 Chris Tryhorn, Lisa O'Carroll and Owen Gibson, 'Desmond Taunts *Telegraph* in "Nazi" Tirade', *The Guardian*, www.theguardian.com, 22 April 2004.

13 THREE EXITS, THREE COURT CASES

1 Jennifer Rankin and Jim Waterson, 'How Boris Johnson's Brussels-Bashing Stories Shaped British Politics', *The Guardian*, www.theguardian.com, 14 July 2019.

2 P. Anderson and T. Weymouth, *Insulting the Public? The British Press and the European Union* (London, 1999), ebook.

3 Oliver Daddow, 'The UK Media and "Europe": From Permissive Consensus to Destructive Dissent', *International Affairs*, LXXXVIII/6 (November 2012), pp. 1219–36.

4 S. Vasilopoulou, 'Continuity and Change in the Study of Euroscepticism: Plus ça change?', *Journal of Common Market Studies*, LI/1 (January 2013), pp. 153–68.

5 Anthony Hilton, 'Stay or Go, the Lack of Solid Facts Means It's All a Leap of Faith', *Evening Standard*, www.standard.co.uk, 25 February 2016.

6 Rupert Murdoch, Letters, *The Guardian*, www.theguardian.com, 19 December 2016.

7 *The Sun*, 18 August 2003.

8 *Daily Express*, 18 August 2003.

9 Ibid., 31 October 2013.

10 Katie Hopkins, 'Rescue Boats? I'd Use Gunships to Stop Migrants', *The Sun*, 17 April 2015.

11 'UN Rights Chief Urges UK to Curb Tabloid Hate Speech, End "Decades of Abuse" Targeting Migrants', Statement by UN Human Rights Commissioner, https://news.un.org, 24 April 2015.

12 William Turville, 'IPSO Rejects Accuracy Complaint over Katie Hopkins' *Sun* "Cockroaches" Column', https://pressgazette.co.uk, 13 August 2015.

13 Kathryn Simpson and Nick Startin, 'Tabloid Tales: How the British Tabloid Press Shaped the Brexit Vote', *Journal of Common Market Studies*, LXI/2 (March 2023), pp. 302–22.

14 Emily Maitlis and Jake Morris, 'David Cameron "Tried to Get *Mail* Editor Sacked" over Brexit Stance', www.bbc.co.uk/news, 1 February 2017.

15 Gareth Harding, 'Media Lies and Brexit: A Double Hammer-Blow to Europe and Ethical Journalism', Ethical Journalism Network, https://ethicaljournalismnetwork.org, 2016.

16 Louise Ridley, 'The Sun, Daily Mail and Express Advertisers Targeted in "Stop

Funding Hate" Campaign', *HuffPost*, www.huffingtonpost.co.uk, 16 August 2016.

17 David Yelland, interview with Sky News, December 2018.

18 Jim Waterson, 'Daily Express Editor Calls Its Front Pages "Downright Offensive"', *The Guardian*, www.theguardian.com, 24 April 2018.

19 Edward Helmore, 'Where Did It All Go Wrong?', *The Guardian*, www.theguardian.com, 10 April 2006.

20 Ed Pilkington, 'Shock! Horror! *National Enquirer* Wins a Pulitzer. Not', *The Guardian*, www.theguardian.com, 13 April 2010.

21 Joe Palazzolo, Michael Rothfield and Lukas Alpert, '*National Enquirer* Shielded Donald Trump From Playboy Model's Affair Allegation', *Wall Street Journal*, www.wsj.com, 4 November 2016.

22 Sarah Ellison, '*National Enquirer* Sent Stories about Trump to His Attorney Michael Cohen before Publication, People Familiar with the Practice Say', *Washington Post*, www.washingtonpost.com, 21 June 2018.

23 Tom McCarthy and Erin Durkin, 'Trump's Former Fixer Michael Cohen Sentenced to Three Years in Prison', *The Guardian*, www.theguardian.com, 12 December 2018.

24 Tom Winter and David K. Li, 'Publisher of *National Enquirer* Admits Paying Hush Money to Help Trump Ahead of 2016 Election', www.nbcnews.com, 12 December 2018.

25 Helen Lewis, 'Paul Dacre was Fleet Street's Last Silverback Gorilla', *New Statesman*, www.newstatesman.com, 13 June 2018.

26 John Lloyd, 'Consumed by Scandal', *Financial Times*, 14 April 2012.

27 Andrew O'Hagen, 'Who's the Real Cunt?', *London Review of Books*, XXXIX/11 (1 June 2017).

28 Lewis, 'Paul Dacre Was Fleet Street's Last Silverback Gorilla'.

29 *Desert Island Discs*, www.bbc.co.uk, 25 January 2004.

30 Paul Dacre's Diary, 'The Daily *Mail* Will Commit Editorial Suicide If It Turns against Brexit', *The Spectator*, www.spectator.co.uk, 13 June 2018.

31 Henry Mance, 'Geordie Greig: Provocation Is a Good Thing', *Financial Times*, www.ft.com, 4 October 2019.

32 Paul Dacre, 'A Solid Start, But Greig Has Some Way to Go', Letters, *Financial Times*, www.ft.com, 12 October 2019.

33 Lord (Kenneth) Clarke, speaking on *Reflections*, BBC Radio 4, www.bbc.co.uk, 26 July 2023.

34 Jim Waterson, 'Paul Dacre "Should Be Banned from Re-Applying" as Ofcom Chair, Says Tory MP', *The Guardian*, www.theguardian.com, 15 September 2021.

35 Paul Dacre, 'Ofcom and Me', Letters, *The Times*, 19 November 2021.

36 Ruth Styles, 'Harry's Girl Is (Almost) Straight Outta Compton: Gang-Scarred Home of Her Mother Revealed – So Will He Be Dropping by for Tea?', *MailOnline*, www.dailymail.co.uk, 2 November 2016.

37 Lucy Jones, 'Harry's Girl on Pornhub', www.thesun.co.uk, 4 November 2016.

38 '*The Sun* Says', *The Sun*, www.thesun.co.uk, 5 November 2016.

39 'Miss Meghan Markle – An Apology', *The Sun*, www.thesun.co.uk, 11 February 2017.

40 Rachel Johnson, 'Sorry Harry, but Your Beautiful Bolter Has Failed My Mum Test', *Mail on Sunday*, 6 November 2016.

41 Statement by Communications Secretary to Prince Harry, Kensington Palace, www.royal.uk, 8 November 2016.

42 Quoted in Robert Booth and Lisa O'Carroll, 'Prince Harry Attacks Press over "Wave of Abuse" of Girlfriend Meghan Markle', *The Guardian*, www.theguardian.com, 16 November 2016.

43 'The Sun Says', *Sun on Sunday*, www.thesun.co.uk, 19 May 2018.

44 Leading article, *Sunday Express*, www.express.co.uk, 19 May 2018.

45 Leading article, *Mail on Sunday*, www.dailymail.co.uk, 19 May 2018.

46 Jim Waterson and Caroline Davies, 'Meghan Sues *Mail on Sunday* as Prince Harry Launches Attack on Tabloid Press', www.theguardian.com, 2 October 2019.

47 Statement on https://sussexroyal.com/media, 1 October 2019.

48 Sofia Brennan and Rebecca English, 'Not Long to Go – Pregnant Kate Tenderly Cradles her Baby Bump While Wrapping up her Royal Duties ahead of Maternity Leave – and William Confirms She's Due "Any Minute Now"', *MailOnline*, www.dailymail.co.uk, 22 March 2018.

49 Liz Jones, 'Why Can't Meghan Keep Her Hands Off Her Bump?', *MailOnline*, www.dailymail.co.uk, 26 January 2019.

50 Carly Read, 'Meghan Markle's Beloved Avocado Linked to Human Rights Abuse and Drought, Millennial Shame', www.express.co.uk, 23 January 2019.

51 Ellie Hall, 'Here Are 20 Headlines Comparing Meghan Markle to Kate Middleton that May Show Why She and Prince Harry Left Royal Life', *Buzzfeed*, www.buzzfeednews.com, 13 January 2020.

52 'Monster Meghan Breaks Queen's Heart', *National Enquirer*, available at www.intouchweekly.com, 30 September 2019.

53 'Harry Trapped in Marriage from Hell!', *National Enquirer*, available at www.intouchweekly.com, 27 June 2020.

54 'Harry and Meghan Shotgun Wedding! HUMILIATED QUEEN Orders Red-Haired Rogue to Marry Pregnant TV Star', www.globemagazine.com, 19 December 2016.

55 'Their Ultimate Revenge, William and Kate Destroy Meghan', www.globemagazine.com, 30 October 2023.

56 Laura Elston, 'Harry Launched Legal against MGN after Bumping into Barrister in France', *The Independent*, www.independent.co.uk, 7 June 2023.

57 Ibid.

58 Brian Cathcart, 'The False Tale of Meghan's £1 Damages: A Case Study in Bad Journalism', www.bylineinvestigates.com, 10 January 2022.

59 Tom Symonds, 'Prince Harry Privacy Case: Battle with *Mail* Owner Begins', www.bbc.co.uk, 1 April 2023.

60 Jim Waterson, 'Murdoch Firm "Paid Secret Phone-Hacking Settlement to Prince William"', *The Guardian*, www.theguardian.com, 25 April 2023.

61 Sian Harrison, 'Duke of Sussex Bids to Rely on "Secret Agreement" in Claim against News Group', *The Independent*, www.independent, co.uk, 5 July 2023.

62 Dominic Casciani and Francesca Gillett, 'King Charles Tried to Stop Prince Harry's Hacking Claim, Court Hears', www.bbc.com/news, 25 April 2023.

63 Waterson, 'Murdoch Firm "Paid Secret Phone-Hacking Settlement to Prince William"'.

64 Caroline Davies, 'Prince Harry's Lawsuit against *Sun* Publisher Can Go to Trial, Judge Rules', *The Guardian*, www.theguardian.com, 27 July 2023.

65 Dominic Casciani et al., 'Prince Harry: I Couldn't Trust Anybody Due to Phone Hacking', www.bbc.com/news, 6 June 2023.

66 Statement of Prince Harry, Duke of Sussex, www.documentcloud.org/documents/23835120-bl-2019-001787, accessed 31 October 2023.

67 PA Media, 'Hacking "Whistleblower" Graham Johnson Says *Mirror* Hacking Was "Organised Crime"', *Press Gazette*, https://pressgazette.co.uk, 18 May 2023.

68 Jim Waterson, 'What Piers Morgan Knew about Phone Hacking – in His Own Words', *The Guardian*, www.theguardian. com, 11 May 2023.

69 Evidence given to Leveson Inquiry, www.discoverleveson.com, 20 December 2012.

70 Kevin Rawlinson and agencies, 'Privacy Trial Judge Asks Why Piers Morgan Has Not Given Evidence', *The Guardian*, www.theguardian.com, 23 June 2023.

71 *Scandalous: Phone Hacking on Trial*, www.bbc.co.uk, 15 June 2023.

72 The Duke of Sussex and others -v- MGN Limited, www.judiciary.uk, 15 December 2023.

73 Alexandra Topping, 'Prince Harry Hails Phone-Hacking Case Win as "Great Day for Truth"', *The Guardian*, www.theguardian.com, 15 December 2023.

CONCLUSION: THE CURRENT CONDITION OF PLANET TABLOID

1 Freddie Mayhew, 'UK National Newspaper Sales Slump by Two-Thirds in 20 Years Amid Digital Disruption', *Press Gazette*, https://pressgazette.co.uk, 26 February 2020.

2 Charlotte Tobitt and Aisha Majid, 'National Press ABCs: *The i* and FT Report Steadiest Circulations in November', *Press Gazette*, https://pressgazette.co.uk, 19 December 2023.

3 See Aisha Majid's rolling monthly ranking of the top 50 newsbrands in the UK at https://pressgazette.co.uk. The most recent at the time of writing was published on 8 March 2024.

4 Niamh McIntyre, Laith al-Khalaf, Jessica Murray and Pamela Duncan, 'Caroline Flack: Scale of Negative Media Coverage before Death Revealed', *The Guardian*, www.theguardian.com, 21 February 2020.

5 Manori Ravindran, 'Caroline Flack's Death Prompts UK Petition Demanding Media Inquiry', *Variety*, www.variety.com, 16 February 2020.

6 *The Rise of the Murdoch Dynasty*, episode 1, 'Kingmaker', www.bbc.co.uk, 14 July 2020.

7 Toby Helm and Michael Savage, 'Champagne with Rupert Murdoch . . . Keir Starmer's Labour Is Preparing for Power', *The Observer*, www.theguardian.com, 9 July 2023.

8 'Wagatha Christie: Rebekah Vardy Loses Libel Case against Coleen Rooney', www.bbc.co.uk/news, 29 July 2022.

9 Vikram Dodd and Dan Sabbagh, 'Daniel Morgan Murder: Inquiry Brands Met Police "Institutionally Corrupt"', *The Guardian*, www.theguardian.com, 15 June 2021.

10 Jim Waterson and Mark Sweeney, 'What Does Rupert Murdoch's Resignation Mean for His UK Media Outlets?', *The Guardian*, www.theguardian.com, 21 September 2023.

11 Adrian Wooldridge, 'Rupert Murdoch Was the Last of the Press Barons', *Bloomberg*, www.bloomberg.com, 24 September 2023.

12 Dennis Potter, interviewed by Melvyn Bragg, Channel 4, broadcast 5 April 1994.

13 Front page headline: 'We think we've got this right: Hopeless bloke said hopeless bloke is hopeless, says hopeless bloke', *Daily Star*, www.dailystar.co.uk, 17 June 2021.

14 Bron Mahar, 'Ipso Upholds Harassment Complaints Against *MailOnline*', *Press Gazette*, 30 September 2022.

15 Hacked Off, 'The Facts on IPSO', https://hackinginquiry.org, March 2022.

16 Jeremy Clarkson, 'One Day, Harold The Glove Puppet Will Tell the Truth about a Woman Talking B*****ks', *The Sun*, www.thesun.co.uk, 17 December 2022.

17 'IPSO Ruling: IPSO Upholds Complaint against *The Sun*', www.ipso.co.uk, 30 June 2023.

18 Jessica Elgot, 'Jeremy Clarkson Column on Meghan Breaks Watchdog's Complaints Record', *The Guardian*, www.theguardian.com, 20 December 2022.

19 'Hackwatch: Splitting Heirs?' *Private Eye*, 8 September 2023.

20 Toby Helm and Vanessa Thorpe, 'Labour Backs Away from Press Reforms after Prince Harry's Phone-Hacking Court Victory', *The Guardian*, www.theguardian.com, 16 December 2023.

21 Witness statement of Prince Harry the Duke of Sussex, in HRH the Duke of Sussex and Mirror Group Newspapers Limited, available at www.scribd.com, 4 February 2023.

Further Reading

Addison, Adrian, *Mail Men: The Unauthorised Story of the Daily Mail* (London, 2017)

Bainbridge, Cyril, and Roy Stockdill, *The News of the World Story* (London, 1993)

Bingham, Adrian, and Martin Conboy, *Tabloid Century: The Popular Press in Britain, 1896 to the Present* (Oxford, 2015)

Bower, Tom, *Maxwell: The Outsider* (London, 1988)

Clarke, Bob, *From Grub Street to Fleet Street: An Illustrated History of English Newspapers to 1899* (London, 2004)

Cohen, Daniel, *Yellow Journalism: Scandal, Sensationalism and Gossip in the Media* (New York, 2000)

Cudlipp, Hugh, *Publish and Be Damned: The Astonishing Story of the Daily Mirror* (London, 1953)

——, *Walking on the Water* (London, 1976)

Davies, Nick, *Flat Earth News* (London, 2009)

——, *Hack Attack: How the Truth Caught Up with Rupert Murdoch* (London, 2015)

Edwards, Ruth Dudley, *Newspapermen: Hugh Cudlipp, Cecil Harmsworth King and the Glory Days of Fleet Street* (London, 2004)

Engel, Matthew, *Tickle the Public: One Hundred Years of the Popular Press* (London, 1996)

Griffin, Brett, *Yellow Journalism: Sensationalism and Circulation Wars* (New York, 2019)

Hagerty, Bill, *Read All About It! 100 Sensational Years of the Daily Mirror* (Lydney, 2003)

Horrie, Chris, *Tabloid Nation* (London 2003)

——, and Peter Chippendale, *Stick It Up Your Punter! The Uncut Story of the Sun Newspaper* (London, 1990)

Lamb, Larry, *Sunrise: The Remarkable Rise and Rise of the Best-Selling Soaraway Sun* (London, 1989)

Leapman, Michael, *Barefaced Cheek: Rupert Murdoch* (London, 1988)

Leveson, Rt Hon. Lord Justice, *Inquiry into the Culture, Practices and Ethics of the Press: Report* (London, 2012)

Marr, Andrew, *My Trade* (London, 2004)

Molloy, Mike, *The Happy Hack* (London, 2016)

Stephens, Mitchell, *A History of News* (London and New York, 1988)

Taylor, S. J., *The Great Outsiders: Northcliffe, Harmsworth and the Daily Mail* (London, 1996)

University of Kingston Journalism Department, *Discover Leveson*, www.discoverleveson.com (2014)

Wilkes, Roger, *Scandal: A Scurrilous History of Gossip* (London, 2002)

Acknowledgements

I should like to thank my employers, Goldsmiths, University of London, and in particular my colleagues in the Department of Media Communications and Culture for granting me the research time and resources to enable me to complete a large part of this book. With grateful thanks to my partner Angie and my sons Leo and Max for the time they gave me to complete this book. And also to all the remarkable, diligent and ethical journalists with whom I worked over the years.

At Reaktion Books, I must express my deep gratitude to David Watkins for originally commissioning me to write this opus and to publisher Michael Leaman for allowing me time to finish what had originally been intended to be a sprint, but turned into a marathon and is all the better for it. And my thanks also to my editor at Reaktion, Amy Salter, for her exceptional eye for detail and her patience when another deadline needed an extension.

My huge thanks must also go to my friend Deborah Maby for her brilliant copy-editing on large sections of this work as well as her research assistance for parts of chapters One and Nine. And I am indebted to another friend, Nina Hirsh, for prompting me on the origins of the word 'tabloid'.

The staff of Senate House Library, University of London and of the London Library were invaluable and I would also like to thank Alison Harvey of the Special Collections and Archives of the University of Cardiff for her assistance accessing parts of the Hugh Cudlipp archive. The Discover Leveson website, created by the University of Kingston journalism department, was a remarkably valuable resource.

And finally, of course, my thanks go to those who, for one reason or another, I cannot publicly identify, but who gave me their time, advice, help and information in making this work possible.

Photo Acknowledgements

The author and publishers wish to express their thanks to the sources listed below for illustrative material and/or permission to reproduce it. Some locations of artworks are also given below, in the interest of brevity:

Alamy Stock Photo: pp. 137 (Keystone Press), 152 (PA Images), 292 (PA Images); DMG Media Licensing: p. 239; Flickr: pp. 275 (Andy Thornley, CC BY 2.0), 300 (*Financial Times*, CC BY 2.0); Houghton Library, Harvard University, Cambridge, MA: p. 19; Imperial War Museum, London: p. 108; Library of Congress, Washington, DC: pp. 51, 53, 55, 60, 63, 88; National Maritime Museum, Greenwich, London: p. 26; National Portrait Gallery, Smithsonian Institution, Washington, DC: p. 48; News Licensing: p. 178; Shutterstock: pp. 170, 190 (Bill Cross/*Daily Mail*), 253 (Stuart Clarke), 348 (Peter Macdiarmid).

Index

Page numbers in *italics* indicate illustrations